MARRIAGE REFERENCES

and

FAMILY RELATIONSHIPS

of

Charles City, Prince George, and Dinwiddie Counties, Virginia 1634-1800

F. Edward Wright

Colonial Roots
Millsboro, Delaware
2015

Colonial
Roots

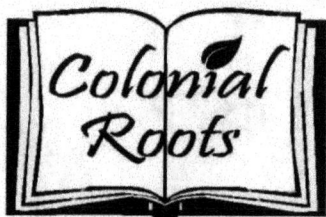

Helping you grow your family tree

ISBN 978-1-68034-029-7

CONTENTS

iii

Introduction

Herein I have attempted to identify marriages of persons who lived in Charles City, Prince George and Dinwiddie counties beginning with the formation of Charles City County in 1634 and continuing with Prince George County which was formed from the southwestern portion of Charles City County in 1703. It logically followed that the records of Dinwiddie County would be included since that county was formed from Prince George County in 1752.[1] Thus I have included marriages and relationships for all three counties ending in 1800. Whenever possible, the children and parents of the bride and groom are identified.

This is one of a series of publications designed to help in the research of one's family history. This work is derived from the previous abstracts and research of others which I consider reliable. When it appeared the earlier work is in error, I have so indicated. All these sources should be consulted, including the primary sources from which these books have been derived.

During the period covered here, second and third marriages were commonplace. Several married four and five times. Widows frequently married a subsequent husband within months of the death of her deceased husband.

One should also consult the three volumes of the fourth edition of John Frederick Dorman's, *Adventurers of Purse and Person Virginia 1607-1624/5*. Dorman covers the major families of this period, drawing from a wide range of sources. Researchers who discover a marriage listed in this book that gives Dorman's work as its source should consult his work for additional information on connected families.

One of the evidences of a marriage is a marriage bond which was frequently dated on the same day as the marriage itself. Dates of the marriage bond are given and, in some cases, dates on which the marriage took place.

When researching early families, a major hurdle is recognizing variations in the spelling of surnames. Many of the variations are obvious such as Allen and Allan; Jenkins and Jinkins; Ligon and Lygon; and Ladd and Lead, etc. Here are some variations found in the records of these counties which are not quite so obvious:

- Alle and Alley
- Batte and Bott

v

- Childers and Childress
- MacGhea, Macgahea and McGee
- Parham and Parram
- Pattison and Patterson
- Pettypoole and Poole
- Rives and Reeves
- Wilkerson and Wilkinson
- And many more

Some assumptions made in deriving marriages were the following:
1. That the couple had married before the arrival of their first known child
2. That the administratrix or executrix of an estate was likely to have been the widow, but not always
3. That existence of a marriage bond or prenuptial agreement strongly suggested that the marriage actually took place

It is helpful to know that a minor was appointed by the court when a significant estate was inherited. When he or she reached the age of 14 they were allowed to choose their own guardian.

Several terms no longer have the same meaning today as they did in the early history of Virginia. Without an understanding of these terms, one may easily make wrong assumptions.

For example:
- Cousin – most often referred to a niece or nephew.

- Son or daughter sometimes referred to a son-in-law or daughter-in-law.

- Son-in-law or daughter-in-law frequently referred to a step-child.

- Guardianship – a guardian was appointed when a minor inherited property of significant value. In some cases the father was appointed guardian of his children when they inherited property. When the father proceeded in death before his wife, the widow was often appointed guardian of her children and in other cases someone else was appointed. When a minor reached the age of 14, he or she could select their guardian. Often a brother or brother-in-law was selected; sometimes a future husband was selected.

- o Minor - A minor or infant during this period referred to a male under the age of 21 and a female under the age of 18 (and sometimes 21). The marriage of a minor was normally approved by a guardian or parent.

I have included marriages of persons even though they are indicated as residents of other counties. In many cases these are persons who once lived in one of the three counties and later resided elsewhere. In the case of deed transactions, they may be selling land in Henrico County which they inherited from persons who once resided in the county.

F. Edward Wright
Lewes, Delaware
2015

1 - Carol McGinnis, *Virginia Genealogy Sources & Resources* (Baltimore, Maryland: Genealogical Publishing Company, 1993)

(N) – name unknown; otherwise the maiden name; e.g., Jane (Smith) Jones indicates the maiden name is Smith and the married name is Jones.

admin. – administrator of the estate

admx. - administratrix

APP1 - John Frederick Dorman, *Adventurers of Purse and Person Virginia 1607-1624/5,* 3 Volume A-F, Genealogical Publishing Co., Baltimore, MD, 2004

APP2 - John Frederick Dorman, *Adventurers of Purse and Person Virginia 1607-1624/5,* Volume G-P, Genealogical Publishing Co., Baltimore, MD, 2005

APP3 - John Frederick Dorman, *Adventurers of Purse and Person Virginia 1607-1624/5,* Volume R-Z, Genealogical Publishing Co., Baltimore, MD, 2007

bapt. - baptized

bef. – before

bet. - between

Bland Papers – *The Bland Papers: Being a Selection from the Manuscripts of Colonel Theodorick Bland, Jr. of Prince George County, Virginia* edited by Charles Campbell. Published in Petersburg, Va., Edmund & Julian C. Ruffin, 1840.

BPR – *The Vestry Book and Register of Bristol Parish, Virginia, 1720-1789,* transcribed and published by Churchill Gibson Chamberlayne, Richmond, VA, 1898. Portions missing: parts of D, E and F. Also a significant number of errors.

CCCR – Benjamin B. Weisiger, III, *Charles City County Virginia Records, 1737-1774,* Iberian Publishing Company, Athens, Ga., 1986

CCLW – Kimberly Curtis Campbell, *Caroline County Virginia "Lost" Wills, 1727-1852 and Related Records from other sources, Volume 1,* published by Iberian Publishing Company, Athens, Ga., 2012

CCMB – "Marriage Bonds in Charles City County," published in *The William and Mary Quarterly*, Vol. 8, No. 3 (Jan., 1900), pp. 193-196

CCOB (1655-58) – Beverley Fleet, *Charles City County Court Orders, 1655-1658*, originally published as Volume 10, *Virginia Colonial Abstracts* (1941), later in "Virginia Colonial Abstracts," which is contained in GVAT - Virginia Genealogies #3, 1600s-1800s (CD 187)

CCOB (1658-61) – Beverley Fleet, *Charles City County Court Orders, 1658-1661*, originally published as Volume 11, *Virginia Colonial Abstracts* (1941), later in "Virginia Colonial Abstracts." which is contained in GVAT - Virginia Genealogies #3, 1600s-1800s (CD 187) .

CCOB (1661-64) – Beverley Fleet, *Charles City County Court Orders, 1661-1664*, originally published as Volume 12, *Virginia Colonial Abstracts* (1941), later in "Virginia Colonial Abstracts," which is contained in GVAT - Virginia Genealogies #3, 1600s-1800s (CD 187)

CCOB (1664-65) – Beverley Fleet, *Charles City County Court Orders, 1664-1665*, originally published as Volume 13, *Virginia Colonial Abstracts* (1942), later in "Virginia Colonial Abstracts," which is contained in GVAT - Virginia Genealogies #3, 1600s-1800s (CD 187)

CCOB (1677-79) – Margaret McNeill Ayres, *Charles City County, Virginia Order Book, 1676-1679*, abstracted and compiled by Margaret McNeill Ayres (1968). It actually covers the period, 1677-1679. Self published, Memphis, Tenn., 1968

CCOB (Fragments, 1685) – Beverley Fleet, *Charles City County Court Orders, 1685*, originally published as Volume 13, *Virginia Colonial Abstracts* (1942), later in "Virginia Colonial Abstracts," which is contained in GVAT - Virginia Genealogies #3, 1600s-1800s (CD 187)

CCOB (1687-95) - Benjamin B. Weisiger III, *Charles City County Virginia Court Orders, 1687-1695*, Iberian Publishing Company, Athens, Ga., 1980

CCOB (Fragments, 1696) – Beverley Fleet, *Charles City County Court Orders, 1696*, originally published in Volume 13, *Virginia Colonial Abstracts* (1942), later in "Virginia Colonial Abstracts," which is contained in GVAT - Virginia Genealogies #3, 1600s-1800s (CD 187)

CCW&D (1725-31) - Benjamin B. Weisiger III, *Charles City County Virginia Colonial Records, 1725-1731*, Iberian Publishing Company,

Athens, Ga., 1984

d. – died

dau. – daughter

DB – Deed Book

dec'd. – deceased

exec. – executor of the last will and testament

extx. – executrix of the last will and testament, usually the widow but sometimes a daughter

GVA – Virginia Genealogies #1, *Genealogies of Virginia Families* (CD162). Genealogies of Virginia Families from *The Virginia Magazine of History and Biography* (Baltimore, Md.: Genealogical Publishing Co., Inc., 1981)

GVAT - Virginia Genealogies #3, 1600s-1800s (CD 187). All four volumes of "Genealogies of Virginia Families" from *Tyler's Quarterly Historical and Genealogical Magazine* and the complete set of *Virginia Colonial Abstracts* originally published by the Genealogical Publishing Company

GVAW - Virginia Genealogies #2, *Genealogies of Virginia Families* (CD186). Genealogies of Virginia Families from *The William and Mary College Quarterly* (Baltimore, Md.: Genealogical Publishing Co., Inc., 1982)

HCDB 1 – cypalcorp, *Henrico County Virginia Deed Book 1 (1 October 1781 – 7 April 1785)*, Iberian Publishing Company, Athens Ga., 2014

HCDB 2 – cypalcorp, *Henrico County Virginia Deed Book 2 (2 May 1785- 1 December 1788)*, Iberian Publishing Company, Athens, Ga., 2014

HCDB 3 – cypalcorp, *Henrico County Virginia Deed Book 3 (5 January 1789 – 11 May 1792)*, Iberian Publishing Company, Athens, Ga., 2014

HCDB 4 – cypalcorp, *Henrico County Virginia Deed Book 4 (11 November 1792 – 3 October 1795)*, Iberian Publishing Company, Athens, Ga., 2014

HCDB 5 – cypalcorp, *Henrico County Virginia Deed Book 5 (4 April 1796 – 8 May 1800)*, Iberian Publishing Company, Athens, Ga., 2014

HCW 1 – Benjamin B. Weisiger III, *Colonial Wills of Henrico County, Virginia 1677-1737*, Iberian Publishing Company, Athens, Ga., 1976

HCW 2 – Benjamin B. Weisiger III, *Colonial Wills of Henrico County Virginia 1737-1781*, Iberian Publishing Company, Athens, Ga., 1977

HCW&D 1 – Benjamin B. Weisiger III, *Henrico County Virginia Colonial Wills & Deeds 1677-1737*, Iberian Publishing Company, Athens, Ga., 1976

HMM – F. Edward Wright, *Quaker Records of Henrico Monthly Meeting – and other Church Records of Henrico, New Kent and Charles City Counties*, Colonial Roots, Lewes, Del., 2002

intestate – without a last will and testament

KGDB3 - *King George County Deed Book No. 3, 1743-1752* (abstracted by Ruth and Sam Sparacio), published by The Antient Press. Page number of abstracts (volume covering 1735-1752) is given.

KGOB1721-1724 – Mary Marshall Brewer, *King George County Order Book,1721-1724*, Lewes, Del., Colonial Roots, 2007

Legislative Petitions – Library of VA website

LWT – last will and testament

m. - married

OP – William F. Boogher, comp., *Overwharton Parish Register, 1720-1760* (By the Author, 1899; reprint Baltimore, Md.: Clearfield Publishing Co., 1994)

PGM – Benjamin B. Weisiger, III, Prince George County Virginia Miscellany 1711-1814, Iberian Press, Athens GA (1992)

PGR – Benjamin B. Weisiger III, *Prince George County Virginia Colonial Records 1733-1792*, Iberian Press, Athens, Ga., 1993

PGW&D (1710-1713) – Benjamin B. Weisiger III, *Prince George*

County, Virginia Colonial Wills & Deeds 1710-1713, Iberian Publishing Company, Athens Ga., 1995

PGW&D (1713-1728) – Benjamin B. Weisiger III, *Prince George County Virginia Colonial Wills & Deeds 1713-1728*, Iberian Publishing Company, Athens, Ga., 1994

res. – resident or resided in

RWP – Revolutionary War Pension Files, digital images, Fold3.com (http://www.fold3.com) [subscription website]

SWBC – William Lindsey Hopkins, *Some Wills from the Burned Counties of Virginia*, Iberian Publishing Company, Athens, Ga., 1995

testate – with a last will and testament

unm. - unmarried

VBR - Jeannette Holland Austin, *Virginia Bible Records,* Westminster, Md.: Heritage Books, Inc., 2008, pp. 246-7.

VG&B – *Virginia Genealogies and Biographies, 1500s-1900s* (CD 550)

W&M – *William and Mary Quarterly*

Marriage References and Family Relationships of
Charles City, Prince George and Dinwiddie Counties

Abbet, William m. Agnis (N). Their son John b. 26 Feb 1740.
{BPR:277}

Abbington, John of Martins Brandon Parish m. bef. 8 Feb 1725, Mary
(N). {PGW&D (1713-1728):140}

Abernathy, (N) m. Christian, dau. of Susannah Tilman. Their children:
Christian (dau.) and Robert. {PGW&D (1713-1728):23}

Abernethy, Charles m. Ellis (N). Their son William b. 4 Apr 1742.
{BPR:278}

Abernothy, David m. Ann (N). Their dau. Lucy b. 14 Feb 1740.
{BPR:277}

Aberneathy, John m. Lucy (N). Their son Frederick b. 2 Sep 1745.
{BPR:278}

Abernethy/Abernathie, Robert m. bef. 14 Apr 1657, Sara, widow and
mother of Sara Cubishe. {CCOB (1655-58):98}

Abernathy, Robert m. Mary (N). Their children: Mary (b. 16 Apr 1721),
John (b. 1723), Elizabeth (b. 20 May 1730) and Amy (b. 30 Jan 1732).
{BPR:275, 276, 277}

Abernethy, Robert m. Sara (N). Their son Robert b. 27 Mar 1742.
{BPR:278}

Acrill, Capt. William (d. by 1738) m. Anne, dau. of Richard and Rebecca
Cocke. Their children: Hannah, Susanna and Rebecca. {CCCR:82, 131;
HCW 2:156; APP1:125-35; GVAW (Genealogies of Virginia Families)
II, Cl-Fi:104-8, 119-20, 132}

Adaman, Thomas m. Mary (N). Their children: William (b. 2 Jul 1722)
and Thomas (b. 6 Oct 1724). {BPR:275}

Addams, James d. by 1692 leaving a widow, Elizabeth. Elizabeth m. 2nd
(N) Heath. {CCOB (1687-95):140}

Adams, James d. by 1722, Rachel Adams, admx. {PGW&D (1713-
1728):82}

Adams, John m. Catherine (N). Their dau. Sarah b. 30 Apr 1726. {BPR:276}

Adams, Judith was presented in March 1745 for having a bastard child. Dismist. {CCCR:109}

Adams, Thomas Sr. (d. 1722) of Martins Brandon Parish m. Elizabeth (N). Children: Thomas, William (had a son Thomas), Benjamin, David, Henry and Mary (m. (N) Phillips). {PGW&D (1713-1728):85}

Adams, Thomas m. Mary (N). Their son Samuel b. 11 Aug 1793.

Adams, William m. by Apr 1762, Lucy, dau. of David Davidson. {CCCR:154}

Addison, Christopher m. Mary (N). Their children: Thomas (b. 12 Sep 1730) and Winifred (b. 8 Oct 1732). {BPR:276, 277}

Addeson, Thomas (d. by 1739) m. Ann (N). Their children: Thomas (b. 1 Apr 1722), Ann (b. 11 Feb 1730) and Christopher. {PGR:45, 67; BPR:275}

Adkins, Howell of Sussex Co. m. Susannah (N). Their son Binns b. 13 Mar 1792. {BPR:278}

Alberry, Emanusl m. bef. 26 Jun 1678, (N), widow of William Traylor. {CCOB (1677-79):61}

Aldridg, Peter m. Elizabeth (N). Their children: Mary (b. 22 Feb 1739), John (b. 14 Jun 1743) and Mille (b. 25 Jan 1744). {BPR:277, 278}

Aldrige, William of Prince George Co., planter, gave his dau. Margery Aldrige 80 acres in 1713, having given his son William an equal amount earlier. {PGW&D (1710-1713):33}

Aldrige, William m. Ellis (N). Their dau. Joanna b. 10 Jan 1741. {BPR:278}

Alexander, John m. Martha (N). Their son Robert b. 2 Jan 1733. {BPR:277}

Alfriend, Benjamin d. by 1746, Susanna Alfriend, admx. {CCCR:111}

Alfriend, Joseph d. by 1758, Sarah Alfriend, admx. Dau. Hannah chose Littlebury Hardyman, Gent., her guardian. In 1762 Jane, orphan of Joseph Alfriend, chose Littlebury Hardyman her guardian. {CCCR:139, 155, 156}

Allan, Charles recorded a deed of gift to Joel Allan in 1747. {CCCR:112}

Allen, Elizabeth had a dau. Martha b. 28 Oct 1742. {BPR:278}

Allen, Elkana m. Sarah (N). Their children: William (b. 3 Sep 1726) and Sarah (b. 28 Dec 1728). {BPR:276}

Allen, John, brother of Tally Allen, m. bef. 8 Aug 1738, Ruth (N). {PGR:13, 46}

Alley/Alle/Allen, Abraham m. Mary (N). Their children: Ann (b. 25 May 1722), Drury (b. 1 Dec 1724), Winefritt (b. 22 Apr 1727) and Mary (b. 13 Jul 1730), Eleonore (b. 27 May 1733), Lucy (b. 12 Sep 1735), Miles (b. 18 May 1741) and Mason (b. 20 Nov 1743). {BPR:275, 276, 277}

Alley, Drury m. Abigail (N). Their dau. Sukey b. 21 28 Aug 1752). {BPR:278}

Alley, Henry m. Mary (N). Their son Tally b. 24 Aug 1721. BPR:275}

Alley, Richard m. bef. 8 Aug 1738, Elizabeth (N). {PGR:13}

Alley, Winifreid had a son Shade, bapt. 12 May 1751. {BPR:278}

Ambrose, Thomas d. by 1802, John Ambrose, admin. {PGM:11}

Ampee, Frances was presented in 1759 for having a bastard child. {CCCR:141}

Anderson, Rev. Charles (b. ca. 1670, d. 7 Apr 1718) of Westover Parish m. Frances (N) (d. by 1739). Their children: Elizabeth (m. John Stith), *Frances (m. Thomas Pinkard), *Jane (m. Ellyson Armistead) and Charlotte (m. Henry Taylor), James and Charles. {CCCR:86, 90; GVAW IV:231; GVAT I:59; PGW&D (1713-1728):44; *W&M Vol. 4, No. 3 (Jan., 1896):143-148 (states that dau. Frances m. Ellyson Armistead)}

Anderson, Henry of Prince George and Henrico cos. m. 1st 1 Sep 1704, Prudence Stratton, dau. of Edward and Mary (Sheppey) Stratton. Their

children: Henry, Ann (m. 1st Benjamin Ward, m. 2nd Capt. Edward
Friend), Judith (m. 1st William Cocke, m. 2nd Francis Redford), Edward,
John (d. testate, 1733, without issue), Frances (m. Thomas Watkins),
Elizabeth and Sarah. Henry m. 2nd Elizabeth (Claiborne) Crawford, dau.
of William Claiborne and probable widow of Ralph Crawford. They had
children: Elizabeth (b. 25 Jun 1728), Claiborne/Clyborn (b. 21 Dec 1732)
and Henry (b. 4 Jan 1734). {APP1:601; APP3:166-7, 171; HCW 1:191,
193; PGW&D (1713-1728):138; BPR:276, 277}

Anderson, James d. by 1711 leaving a son, Matthew Jr. {PGW&D (1710-
1713):5}

Anderson, James of Surry Co. m. bef. 14 Apr 1719, Mary (N). {PGW&D
(1713-1728):45}

Anderson, James m. 1718, Elizabeth Ligon, dau. of Thomas and
Elizabeth (Worsham) Ligon. Their children: Charles (b. ca. 1730) and
John (b. 4 May 1734. {APP2:271, 278-9; BPR:277}

Anderson, James, son of William and Sarah (Pate) Anderson, m. 8 Feb
1766 in Prince George Co., Hannah Tyler (b. 25 Dec 1740, d. 12 Jan
1803). {APP 2:545}

Anderson, Jane, a white woman, had a Mulatto dau., Ruth Anderson (b.
12 Jul 1733) who was ordered to be bound out until age 31. {PGR:35;
BPR:277}

Anderson, John, son of James and Elizabeth (Ligon) Anderson, m. 1st
Elizabeth (N). Their dau. Amey b. 18 Jun 1734. John m. 2nd Martha (N).
{APP2:271, 278-9; BPR:277}

Anderson, Mathew Jr. of Bristol Parish d. ca. 1718. In his LWT he
named brothers, William and James Anderson; and sister Elizabeth
Liggon. {PGW&D (1713-1728):35}

Anderson, Peter of Martins Brandon Parish (d. by 1726) m. Mary (N).
{PGW&D (1713-1728):145}

Anderson, Reynard. In 1662 Rev. William House confessed that he
married Reynard Anderson and Elizabeth Skiffin without lycence or legal
publication of banns. Rineer/Renald Anderson was appointed in 1689
guardian to his four sons: Matthew, William, John and Henry. Rineer d.
by 1690 leaving a widow, Elizabeth who m. 2nd Edward Hughes. {CCOB
(1661-64):373; CCOB (1687-95):75, 104, 130}

Anderson, Thomas (d. ca. 1711) m. Mary (N). Children:James (eldest son), Charles, Mary (m. (N) Rees) and Jane/Jean. Son-in-law: William Sanders. Mary m. 2nd Cornelius Cargill. {PGW&D (1710-1713):7, 21, 23}

Anderson, William d. by 1690 leaving a widow Anne, much in debt. {CCOB (1687-95):78}

Anderson, William m. bef. 10 Jan 1`714/15, Mary (N). {PGW&D (1713-1728):5}

Anderson, William m. Jean (N). Their sons: David (b. 29 Nov 1750) and James (b. 21 Jan 1753). {BPR:278}

Andrews, Ann had an illegitimate dau. Mary b. 18 Oct 1725. {BPR:276}

Andrews, John m. bef. 4 Jun 1688, Susan, widow of John Turbifeild. {CCOB (1687-95):19}

Andrews, Richard m. Mary (N). Their children: Isham (b. 19 Apr 172-), Francis (b. 10 Aug 1725), William (b. 13 May 1726), Henry (b. 3 Feb 1729) and Pheboe (b. 26 Mar 1732). {BPR:275, 276, 277}

Andrews, Thomas m. Jane (N). Their children: Mary (b. 14 Apr 1723), Elizabeth (b. 11 Nov 1726) and Martha (b. 16 Mar 1731). {BPR:275, 276}

Andrews, William m. Amy (N). Their son Ephraim b. 4 Feb1720/1. {BPR:275}

Andrews, William m. Avis/Avice (N). Their children: George (b. 14 Jan 1722/3), Winifred (b. 1 Jun 1724, m. (N) Granger), Avice (b. 7 Dec 1727), John (b. 7 Jul 1729) and Luciana (b. 9 Sep 1731). Other children (by Avis?): Thomas, Epheram, Abraham, Lucy, Richard, and Mark. {BPR:275, 276; SWBC:49}

Anthony, Charles, son of Christopher Anthony of Bedford Co. m. 8th da., 8th mo., 1797, Elizabeth Ladd, dau. of John Ladd of Charles City Co. with consent of parents (at Goose Creek Monthly Meeting). {HMM:81, 87}

Anthony, Christopher (b. 1744) m. 1st Judith Moorman and m. 2nd Jun 5th 1775 Mary, dau. of Samuel and Hannah (Bates) Jordan. {VGA (Genealogies of Virginia Families I, A-Ch:13)}

Anthony, Joseph m. Rhoda (N). Their children: Samuel Parsons (b. 2nd da., 12th mo., 1792), Thomas Clarke (b. 1st da., 6th mo., 1796, Charles (b. 31st da., 3rd mo., 1798) and Judith (b. 29th da., 8th mo., 1800). {HMM:80, 83}

Apperson, Samuel m. Jane (N). Both d. by 1757. Son?: John. {CCCR:11, 138}

Archer, Abraham, age 49 in 1741. {CCCR:93}

Archer, Field m. Elisabeth (N). Their son Field b. 1 Jul 1734. {BPR:277}

Archer, George m. Mary (N). Their children: Frances (b. 8 May 1722), Judith (23 Apr 1724), Sarah (b. 31 Dec 1730) and Jean (b. 12 Jul 1732). {BPR:275, 276, 277}

Archer, George m. Sarah (N). Their dau. Mary b. 25 Jun 1728. {BPR:276}

Archer, Richard m. Tabitha (N). Their children: George (b. 30 Apr 1734), William (b. 20 Sep 1738) and Roger (b. 10 May 1741. {BPR:277}

Archer, Thomas m. Alice (N). Their children: Thomas (b. 3 Oct 1734) and Fredrick (b. 13 Nov 1740). {BPR:277}

Archer, Capt. William of Dinwiddie Co. d. ca. 1694, leaving a widow, Hannah/Susanna Archer. Susanna Archer was also widow of Thomas Jennings of London, merchant. {CCOB (1687-95):201; CCCR:159}

Archer, William m. Anne (N). Their children: George (b. 31 Jul 1721), Martha (b. 7 Dec 1727), Frances (b. 14 Aug 1730 and Phebe (b. 3 Sep 1733). {BPR:275, 276, 277}

Archer, William m. Mary (N). Their children: Sara (b. 28 Jan 1742) and Mary (b. 16 Sep 1745). {BPR:278}

Ardington, Edward d. by 1677, leaving widow, Ann. {CCOB (1677-79):23}

Armistead, Ellyson m. 1st (N)(N). They had a dau. Frances who probably d. young. Ellyson m. 2nd ca. 1741, Jane Anderson, dau. of Rev. Charles Anderson. {CCCR:98; GVAT I:159-60}

Armistead, Thomas m. Margaret (N). Margaret d. 1777-92, predeceasing her husband. In her LWT she named son John Pawn, husband Thomas Armistead, dau. Anna Currie Armistead; and mentioned lands in Halifax Co. {PGR:164}

Armistead, William d. by 1762, Judith Bray Armistead, widow. {CCCR:153}

Ast, John d. by 1658, leaving widow, Mary, and children. Mary d. by 1659, James Crewes, exec. {CCOB (1658-61):195, 230}

Aston, Ferdinando b. ca. 1626. {CCOB (1658-61):236}

Aston, Lt. Col. Walter (d. 6 Apr 1656, age 49) m. Hanna, widow of (N) Batt by whom she had a son, William. Walter and Hanna Aston were parents of Susanna (m. Lt. Col. Edd. Major (d. by 1656))) and Walter (d. 29 Jan 1666, aged 27 years and 7 months). {CCOB (1655-58): 59, 77; W&M Vol. 4, No. 3 (Jan., 1896):144}

Aston, Walter of Charles City Co., probable son of Walter Aston and Hannah Hill, in his will in 1666, named his sisters, Mary Cocke and Elizabeth (2nd wife of Thomas Binns). {GVAW (Genealogies of Virginia Families) IV:547; SWBC: 28}

Atkins, Richard (d. ca. 1718) m. Sarah (N). Dau.: Mary (m. James Fletcher). Grandchildren: Richard and Sarah Fletcher. {PGW&D (1713-1728):34-5}

Atkinson, John m. Elizabeth (N). Their dau. Mary b. 5 Sep 1741. {BPR:277}

Atkinson, John m. by Nov 1745, Jane (N). {CCCR:108}

Atkinson/Atkerson, Roger of Dinwiddie Co. m. Ann, dau. of John and Margaret (Jordan) Pleasants. Children of Roger and Ann Atkinson: Dorothy (6/1/1756, d. 10(?)/-/1767), John (b. 1/2/1759, d. bef. his father), Jane (b. 18/2/1762, m. Gen. Joseph Jones), Roger (b. 28/2/1764), Anne (b. 1/10/1766, m. John Ponsonby), Thomas and Robert (youngest son). Roger gave his son Thomas Atkerson, land in the town of Blandford in 1790 which he immediately sold. Roger was brother of Dorothy Stevenson (d. bef. Roger) and half-brother of Catherine Dennis. {HMM:65; HCW 2:137-41, 141-2; APP2:372, 376, 387; APP3:298, 303; GVAW III:100; PGR:143, 147; SWBC:49}

Avery, (N) m. Mary (N). Mary d. 1766-7 leaving children: Charles and Molly Avery. {PGR:174}

Avery, Billy Haley, son of Edward Avery (d. 1789) m. (N)(N). Children: Betsey Simmons Avery, Lucy H. Avery, Mary Ann Avery, William H. Avery, and Edward Avery. {PGR:118; SWBC:203}

Avery, Edward Sr. (d. 1789) gave his grandson Edward Avery Keeling 300 acres in 1788, adjoining land of Billy Haley Avery. One of the witnesses was Lucy Keeling. In 1789 Edward Avery Sr. gave his son Billy H. Avery, 5 Negroes. Edward was father of Edward, Billy Haley and dau. Mary Ann (m. George Keeling). {PGR:100, 115, 118}

Avery, Edward (d. 1789-90) of Martins Brandon Parish m. Sarah (N). Children: William, Randolph, John, Elizabeth and Polly. {PGR:134}

Avery, William (d. by 1711) m. (N)(N). Children: Richard, Mary (m. George Tillman) and John. {PGW&D (1710-1713): 16}

Aycock, Richard m. Mary (N). Their dau. Elizabeth b. 4 Dec 1742. {BPR:278}

Aylett, Thomas m. Sarah (N). Both d. by 1688. {CCOB (1687-95):18}

Backhurst, Bolling (d. in 1786), m. Susannah (N). His brother, James Backhurst. {SWBC: 28}

Bachurst, James m. bef. 18 Nov 1772, Elizabeth (N). {CCCR:51}

Bachurst, John (d. by 1744), m. Ann, widow of Samson Merredeth. Ann Bachust was presented in 1745 for having a bastard child. Dancy Stanly entered as security for her and case dismist. {CCCR:102, 104, 106}

Backly, Thomas m. Ester (N). Their children: Ann (b. 28 May 1722) and Thomas (b. 24 Jun 1724/5). {BPR:281}

Backnall, Lawrence probably m. Sarah, dau. of Sarah Evans. Sarah's children: William, Lawrence, Elizabeth and Henry Backnall. {PGW&D (1710-1713):12-13}

Bagley, Richard d. by 1663 leaving minor children, Richard, Mary, Jane and Fortune. His widow m. Robert Cobcutt. {CCOB (1661-64):398, 419; CCOB (1664-65):588}

Bailey. See Bayley.

Baird, Ephraim d. by 1787. Benjamin Baird and John Baird Jr., execs. of Ephraim Baird sold 200 acres to Thomas Baird. {PGR:104}

Baird, Hamlin m. bef. 20 Feb 1802, Mary, probable dau. of William Edwards. {PGM:10}

Baird, John m. Polly (N). Their son John Bate b. 8 Feb 1792. {BPR:293}

Baird, Reuben m. by Jan 1745 Mary (N). {CCCR:105}

Baker, (N) m. bef. 6 Jun 1664 Ann, widow of (N) Flouraday by whom she had a son, William Floriday, whom she was able to exempt from the levy. {CCOB (1664-65):554}

Baker, William m. Ann (N). Elizabeth Thompson stipulated in 1769 that following her death, Ann, wife of William Baker, was to receive 50 acres devised to said Elizabeth by the will of Ling Thompson dated 1760. {CCCR:17}

Baldin, William m. Elisabeth (N). Their dau. Phebe b. 16 Dec 1733. {BPR:286}

Balfour, James (d. by Dec 1742) m. Elizabeth (N). William Balfour (brother) and Elizabeth, execs. Elizabeth was pregnant at the time the will was written in Oct 1742. Children: Andrew, Margaret Balfour and James. Elizabeth Balfour d. by 1743, William Winston and Malcolm Stuart, execs. {CCCR:96, 101; SWBC: 28}

Ballard, (N) (d. by 1677) m. Mary (N). {CCOB 1676-79:13}

Ballard, (N) (d. by 1726) m. Elizabeth (N) (d. by 1726), sister of Sarah (m. Henry Soane). Children: Martha Ballard, Thomas Ballard, Francis Ballard (d. by 1728), Rebecca Ballard, Anna/Ann Elizabeth (m. Capt. Henry Talman), John Ballard, Elizabeth (m. William Firth) and William Ballard. {CCW&D (1725-31):16-17, 26; GVAW:IV:774}

Balleston, Thomas d. by 1677. His widow m. 2nd Jonas Luscomb. {CCOB (1677-79):35}

Banister, Rev. John (d. by 1692) m. (N) widow of Abraham Jones. Rev. Banister apparently had a child. {CCOB (1687-95):136, 143, 190, 191, 194}

Banister, John m. Wilmet/Willmuth (N). Their children: Martha (b. 21 Dec 1732) and John (b. 26 Dec 1734, d. 30 Sep 1788). {BPR:285, 287}

Banister, John (d. 30 Sep 1788 near Petersburg), son of John and Willmuth Banister, m. 1st (N)(N) and m. 2nd Elizabeth, dau. of Theodorick Bland. {APP 1:349}

Banister, John of Dinwiddie Co. (d. by Jan 1789) m. Ann (N). Children: John Monroe, Robert, and Theodoric Blair Banister (all underage); Elizabeth Bland Banister; and Maria Ann Banister. {SWBC:50}

Banks, James (d. 1732-3) m. Mary (N). Their children: James, Charles (b. 18 Sep 1716), Mary (b. 21 Nov 1718), Sarah (b. 10 Nov 1721), Prissilla (b. 31 Jan 1722/3) and William (b. 17 Apr 1725). {BPR:279, 280, 281; PGR:178}

Barber, John (d. by 1693) m. Dorothy (N), admx. {CCOB (1687-95):160}

Barber, Richard m. Agnis (N). Their children: Ruth (b. 14 Oct 1720), John (b. 21 Apr 172-), Abigail (b. 27 Oct 1723), Ann (b. 22 Aug 1728), Amy (b. 30 Aug 1730) and Richard (b. 17 Feb 1732). {BPR:279, 280, 282, 283, 285}

Bardin, Patrick m. Rose (N). Their son Randolph b. 12 Mar 1724/5. {BPR:281}

Barefoot, George b. ca. 1624, d. by 1677. His widow m. Henry Preston. Henry Preston d. by 1679. Henry Preston m. the extx. of Thomas Stevenson. {CCOB (1661-64):452; CCOB (1677-79):34, 111}

Barker, Henry m. bef. 3 Dec 1658, Margaret (N). Margaret was age 47 in 1665. {CCOB (1658-61):166; CCOB (1664-65):616}

Barker, John m. bef. 3 Oct 1673, Ann, widow of George Marshall. {CCOB (Fragments):538}

Barker, John m. bef. 1685, Dorothy, dau. of Samuel Eal. {CCOB (Fragments, 1685):2}

Barker, Michael d. by 1659 leaving a widow, Elizabeth. {CCOB (1658-61):174}

Barker, Nathaniel m. Sally (N). Their dau. Mary Chambless Barker, b. 9 Jan 1792. {BPR:294}

Barham, Joseph, a child by a Negro man and white woman (Mary Barham), bound to Charles Christian, Jul 1744. {CCCR:103, 148}

Barker, James m. bef. 20 Aug 1656, Elizabeth, widow of James Warradine. James Barker d. by 1658 leaving a son James. In 1658 Elizabeth gave her son to her "brother" Henry Barker and his wife Margaret. {CCOB (1655-58): 23, 59, 65; CCOB 1658-61:166}

Barker, Jethrow, orphan, complained in 1679 of abuse by his mother-in-law (*step-mother*). He chose William Sanders as his guardian. {CCOB (1677-79):98}

Barker, John (d. by 1673) m. widow Pitt. His tract of land descended to sister Sarah, wife of Richard Taylor who m. 2nd Robert Lucy and to his sister Elizabeth who m. Phillip Limbrey. {CCOB (1655-58): 42; CCOB (1661-64):465; CCOB (1677-79):26}

Barker, John d. by 1690 m. (N). Son: Joel. Admx. of John's estate m. John Good. {CCOB (1687-95):99}

Barker, William (d. by 1655) m. Frances, dau. of James Ward. Children: Sarah (m. 1st Richard Taylor, m. 2nd Robert Lucy, m. 3rd Capt. James Bisse), John (m. widow Pitt) and Elizabeth (m. Phillip Limbrey). Frances m. 2nd Robert Netherland/Letherland and m. 3rd Lt. Col. Thomas Drew. {CCOB (1655-58): 42; CCOB (1661-64):465; VG&B:149}

Barloe, John m. bef. 29 Apr 1692, Ann (N). {CCCR:72}

Barnes, Easter was presented in 1745 for having a bastard child. {CCCR:106}

Barnes, George (d. by Apr 1784) was the brother of Esther Barnes, John Barnes (father of William and Lucy), and Duke [Barnes?]. {SWBC: 28}

Barnes, James m. Elizabeth (N). Their dau. Rebeccah b. 17 Mar 1792. {BPR:293}

Barnes, Marmaduke m. by Jul 1743, Charity (N). Marmaduke Barnes d. by 1761, George Barnes, admin. {CCCR:99, 146}

Barnes, Richard (d. by 1739) m. bef. 28 Feb 1725/6, Sarah (N). {CCW&D (1725-31):9-11; CCCR:86}

Barnes, Susanna, servant to John Baxter, confessed on 15 Oct 1679 that she had a bastard child. {CCOB (1677-79):112}

Barnet, James d. by 1677, Elizabeth, widow. {CCOB 1676-79:8}

Burnet, John d. by 1677, leaving a son, Joseph. {CCOB (1677-79):23}

Barnett, Nathan m. bef. 13 Apr 1770, Rebecca (N). {CCCR:30}

Burnet, Richard m. Joyce (N). Their dau. Debora b. 17 Feb 1740/1. {BPR:287}

Barr, William m. bef. 9 Feb 1801, Jane (N), extx. of Richard Stewart, the younger. {PGM:8}

Barret, David m. Mary (N). Their son David b. 23 Oct 1730. {BPR:283}

Barrat, James m. bef Jun 1737, Sarah (N). {CCCR:78}

Bartlet, Samuel m. Catharine/Cattorn (N). Their children: Elizabeth (b. 25 Jan 1730) and William (b. 6 Jul 1733). {BPR:284, 285}

Barton, William d. by 1711. {PGW&D (1710-1713):5}

Barten, William m. Lettis (N). Their son Robert b. 11 Dec 1733. {BPR:285}

Bartholomew, Charles m. 1st Frances (N) and m. 2nd 2 Feb 1693, Rebecca, sister of Frances and widow of Major Francis Poythress. They were married by Rev. George Robinson of Bristol Parish, Henrico Co. Rebecca and Frances had same mother but different fathers. Charles and Rebecca had a dau. Anne. Rebecca was also mother of Rebecca Poythres). {CCOB (1687-95):181; PGW&D (1710-1713):12, 13}

Bates, Benjamin (d. 7/1/1804) of York Co., son of Fleming Bates, m. 1 May 1760, outside the Society of Friends), Hannah Green. Children of Benjamin and Hannah Bates: Mary (b. 28/1/1761), Edward (b. 9/5/1763), Sarah Jordan (b. 17/3/1765), Susannah Fleming (b. 12/4/1767, m. outside the Society of Friends), Benjamin (b. 10/17(?)/1769), Martha (b. 2/-/1773), Fleming (b. 16/5/1775), Martha (b. 9/5/1778) and Elisha (b. 10/7/1781). Benjamin Bates, father to the above, d. 7/1/1804. Fleming

Bates, grandfather to the above, d. 12/3/1784, in his 72nd year. {HMM:35, 43, 47, 65, 79; APP2:396}

Bates, Edward, son of Benjamin Bates of York Co., m. 9th da., 10th mo., 1787, Elizabeth Harrison, dau. of William Harrison of the co. afsd., with consent of parents at Skimmanse Meeting House in York Co. Children of Edward Bates and Elizabeth: Matilda Jordan (b. 7th da., 7th mo., 1788), Sarah Jordan (b. 17th da., 12th mo., 1791), Edward (b. 12th da., 5th mo., 1794, d. 1st da., 7th mo., 18--), Benjamin (b. 28th da., 9th mo., 1796), Margaret (b. 12th da., 11th mo., 1798), Hannah (b. 7th da., 1st mo., 1801), Fleming (b. 17th da., 4th mo., 1803) and William (b. 20th da., 7th mo., 1805). {HMM:72, 83}

Bates, Elisha. Children of Elisha Bates and his wife Sarah: Anna (b. 5th da., 9th mo., 1804), Mary Morton (b. 11th da, 2nd mo., 1806?), Lucy H. (b. 13th da, 9th mo., 1808), Rebecca (b. 28th da., 2nd mo., 1810), William Jordan (b. 17th da., 2nd mo., 1812) and Deborah H. (b. 7th da., 5th mo., 1815). {HMM:83}

Bates, Fleming (d. 1784), son of John Bates, dec'd., of York Co., m. 5th da., 1st mo., 1737, Sarah Jordan, dau. of Benjamin Jordan, dec'd., of Nansemond Co. Sarah, widow of Fleming Bates, d. 1787. Their children: Benjamin (b. 173-) and Thomas Fleming. {HMM:20, 65, 80, 82; APP2:376}

Bates, George and Elizabeth Crispe/Culpe were cleared by the Society of Friends on 15/9/1707 to marry. {HMM:5; APP1:207}

Bates, George and Grace Fleming were cleared to marry on 8/12/1711. {HMM:6}

Baites, Henry of Wyanoake Parish m. bef. 8 Nov 1715, Elizabeth (N). {PGW&D (1713-1728):11}

Bates, James (d. by 1769), son of James and Sarah (Robinson) Bates, m. 23 Nov 1762, Elizabeth Hunnicutt. Their children: James and Ann. Elizabeth Bates, widow and admx. of James Bates, dec'd., apprehended from the advice she received that she cannot with safety do anything in respect to the settlement of the matter in dispute between her late husband and Benjamin Jordan. Elizabeth m. 2nd Samuel Winston of Caroline Co. {HMM:38, 40-1, 47, 48; APP1:207-9}

Bates, James, son of James and Elizabeth (Hunnicutt) Bates, dec'd., of York Co., m. 4th da., 5th mo., 1790, Ann Ladd, dau. of James Ladd of

Charles City Co., at Waynoak Meeting House. Relations at wedding:
James Ladd, James D. Ladd, Benjamin Bates, Junr., Joseph Ladd,
Benjamin Crew, Exum L. Crew, John Crew, John Ladd. Children of
James and Ann Bates: Joseph Denson (b. 18th da., 5th mo., 1791, d. 17
Nov 1872), James (b. 24th da., 2nd mo., 1793, d. 15th da., 1st mo., 1820),
Henrietta Maria (b. 1st da., 3rd mo., 1795, m. Jonathan Butler), Joshua (b.
2nd da., 8th mo., 1797) and Elizabeth (b. 9th da., 9th mo., 1799). HMM:73,
74, 83; APP 1:210}

Bates, John Jr. (d. 1722-3) of York Co., son of John Fleming, m. 18th da.,
3rd mo., 1710, Sewsanah Fleming Jr., daughter of Charles and Sewsanah
Fleming, at the house of Charles Fleming. Their children: Fleming, John,
Charles, James, Hannah and George (d. young). {HMM:8; APP1:209}

Bates, John (d. by 1720), son of George Bates, m. Hannah (N). Children:
John, Isaac (to whom he left a mill and 2 acres), Hannah (may have m.
Tarleton Fleming) and Ann. {CCW&D (1725-31):33; APP1:208}

Bates, John (d. by 1758) m. ca. 1739 Sarah Adams(?). The orphans of
John Bates were "put to school." The treasurer (of the Society of Friends
(Quakers) was to pay 8 shillings. On 7th da., 1st mo., 1758 it was reported
that the widow of John Bates was about to be married by a priest
(minister) to a person of ill fame "who may prove harmful to the children
and what little estate belongs to them." James Binford and Robert
Pleasants were to apply for administration of the estate and to procure an
order of the court to have them bound out to suitable masters. Sarah,
widow of John Bates, m. (N) Evans ca. 1758. On 4th da., 1771 it was
reported that Sarah Bates [dau. of John Bates of Charles City Co., dec'd.]
late member of Wainoak Meeting was married by a priest to a man not of
the Society and of ill fame and had removed to some distance before the
matter was known [disowned]. In 1773 it was reported that Elizabeth
Bates [dau. of John Bates, dec'd.] was married by a priest to a man not of
the Society [disowned]. {HMM:21, 31-2, 32, 33, 49, 51}

Bates, Richard of Dinwiddie co. m. bef. 5 Jul 1790, Sarah (N).
{PGR:149}

Bates, Thomas m. bef. 1 Jun 1752 Annis (N). Son John owned land
adjoining his father in 1752. {HCDB (1750-1774):25, 67}

Batt, (N), d. by 1655, leaving a widow Hanna and son William. Hanna
m. 2nd Walter Aston. {CCOB (1655-58): 69, 78}

Batte, Henry (d. by 1721), probable son of Henry Batte (who d. by 1703),

m. bef. 3 Dec 1678, Mary Lound. Their children: Henry (d. by 1727 without issue), William, Anne (m. Edward Stratton), Mary (m. John Poythress Sr.), Elizabeth (m. William Liggon), Rachel (m. James Parham) and Sarah (m. Abraham Jones). {CCCR:73; APP 3:166; PGW&D (1713-1728):72-3, 77-8, 96, 170-1}

Batte, Robert, son of William and Mary (Stratton) Batte, m. Martha Peterson, dau. of John and Martha (Thweatt) Peterson. Children: John (b. 17 Jun 1757, d. 19 Sep 1816), Frederick, Mary (m. 1st Francis Burwell Green, m. 2nd William Epes), Martha (m. 1st Charles Erskine, m. 2nd Philip Jones, m. 3rd Nathaniel Colley) and Robert. Robert gave his son Robert Batte, Jr. 150 acres and several slaves in 1790. In 1791 Robert gave his dau. Martha and her husband Nathaniel Colly several slaves. {PGR:136, 164; APP 3:174-5}

Batte/Bott, Thomas m. 1st Mary (N). Thomas was father (probably by Mary) of Thomas (b. ca. 1662, d. 1691), Mary (m. Peter Jones of Charles City Co.), Amy and Sarah (m. in 1696 John Evans Jr.). Thomas m. 2nd ca. 1686, Amy (N), widow of (1) (N) Butler, (2) Essex Bevill and (3) Henry Kent. {GVAW V:759; HCW 1:16; CCOB (1687-95):10}

Bott, Thomas m. Elizabeth (N). Their children: Thomas (b. 14 Dec 1721), Anne (b. Dec 1724) and Miles (b. 21 Feb 1733). {BPR:279, 280, 286}

Batte, Thomas m. Frances (N). Their dau. Mary Anne Jones b. 10 Mar 1792. {BPR:294}

Batt(e), William (probably d. by 1659), son of (N) and Hanna Batt and brother of Thomas and Henry Batte, m. bef. 4 Dec 1656, Susan (N). {CCOB (1655-58): 78, 96, 187}

Batte, William of Prince George Co., son of Capt. Henry Batte, m. May 1704, Mary Stratton, dau. of Edward Jr. and Martha (Sheppey) Stratton. Their children: Henry, Thomas (b. 3 Jul 1721), Robert (b. 16 Oct 1727, d. 1805-7), William, Mary (m. Abraham Cocke), John (d. 8 Oct 1729) and Ann (d. 6 Oct 1729). {APP3:167; HMM:93 (Henrico Co. Court records); BPR:279, 282, 283} [*There were probably other children born between 1704 and 1721.*]

Batte/Batts, William, son of William and Mary (Stratton) Batte, m. Agnes (N). Children: William, John, James (d. unm.), Thomas, Agnes (m. 1st James Baugh, m. 2nd John Aldridge), Martha (m. Judkins Hunt), Mary (b. 16 Apr 1744, d. young) and Henry (b. 17 Feb 1745, d. young).

{APP 3:175-6; BPR:289, 290}

Batty, Christopher was in a dispute with his dau. Elizabeth Frost, widow of John Frost, in 1689. Christopher also had a son James who appeared in court in 1693. {CCOB (1687-95):63}

Batty, James m. bef. 4 Dec 1689, Frances, widow of James Hardeway. Their dau. Mary m. (N) Parsons. {CCOB (1687-95):71; PGR:1, 29}

Baugh, James m. Elizabeth (N). Their son William b. 5 Apr 1723. They gave land to their son John Baugh in 1738. {BPR:280; PGR:28; PGW&D (1713-1728):174}

Baugh, James m. Margrett (N). Their son William b. 7 Oct 1735. {BPR:287}

Baugh, James m. Martha (N). Their children: James (b. 2 Dec 1740) and Adam (b. 1 Feb 1743/4). {BPR:287, 289}

Baugh, John m. Elizabeth (N). Their children: Luis (b. 25 Jun 1724) and Francis (b. 3 Apr 1734). {BPR:281, 286}

Baugh, John m. Anne (N). Their dau. Mary b. 22 Nov 1743. {BPR:289}

Baugh, Peter m. Elizabeth (N). Their dau. Jane b. 15 Nov 1721. {BPR:279}

Baugh, Robert discharged his guardian Peter Williams in 1788. {PGR:107}

Baugh, Robert m. Martha (N). Their dau. Mary Johnson Baugh b. 30 Sep 1793. {BPR:295}

Baugh, Robert d. 1795. {BPR:295}

Baugh, Thomas m. Martha (N). Their children: Mary (b. 20 Mar 1743/4) and Phebe (b. 13 Oct 1745). {BPR:289, 290}

Baugh, William m. Ann (N). Their son James b. 3 Jul 1749. {BPR:291}

Baxter, Edward (d. by 1727) of Charles City Co. m. Elizabeth (N). He was brother of Tabitha (m. Edward Calwell), Sarah (m. William Royall) and Elizabeth (m. 1st Godfrey Ragsdale, m. 2nd John Cocke). {HCW 2:44; APP3:47; CCW&D (1725-31):14; SWBC:28}

Baxter, John m. bef. 3 Apr 1673, Margaret (N), age 25 in 1673. {CCOB (Fragments):516, 539}

Baxter, John m. bef. 14 Feb 1692, Sarah (N). {CCW&D (1725-31):44; CCCR:70}

Baxter, John (d. by Sep 1801) m. Patsey (N). They had a son James b. 4 Nov 1791. Other children: John, Polly, Patsey, Wiley, William, Peterson, and Nancy. Dau. Sally Fitmash died leaving children John and Polly Fitmash [Tidmash/Titmarsh?]. {BPR:293; SWBC:204}

Baxter, William m. Mary (N). Their son James b. 17 Feb 1741/2. {BPR: 288}

Baley, (N) m. Martha (N). Their dau. Ann was bound out in 1739. {PGR:62}

Baly/Baley, Henry m. Ann (N). Their son George b. 2 Jun 1725. {BPR:281}

Balie/Baly, Henry m. Avis (N). Their children: John (b. 23 Oct 1727), William (b. 10 May 1733) and Martha (b. 30 Mar 1735). {BPR:282, 285, 287}

Bayley, Jacob d. by 1689 leaving a widow, Elizabeth who m. 2nd Richard Griffin. Jacob's dau., Elizabeth, m. William Short. {CCOB (1687-95):74, 138; PGW&D (1713-1728):173}

Bailey, Park m. by Apr 1760, Cybella (N). {CCCR:143}

Bayly, William m. bef. 1 Apr 1729, Susannah (N). {CCW&D (1725-31):33}

Beadle, William m. by Sep 1758, Anne (N). {CCCR:141, 153}

Beale, John d. by 1761, Elizabeth Beale, admx. {CCCR:149}

Beavil – See Bevell.

Beck, Andrew gave his son Andrew Jr. 300 acres in Bristol Parish in 1724. {PGW&D (1713-1728):126-7}

Beck, Andrew m. Elizabeth (N). Their children: Elizabeth (b. 26 Oct 1720), Andrew (b. 4 Mar 1724/5), Amy (b. 22 Oct 1727) and John (b. 30 Apr 1732). {BPR:279, 281, 282, 284}

Beck, Joseph m. Mary (N). Their children: Phoebe (b. 16 Apr 1742) and Charles (b. 29 Jan 1743/4). {BPR: 288, 289}

Beck, Moses of NC, brother of Andrew Beck of Bristol Parish, m. Mary (N). Their children: John (b. 4 Nov 1720) and Mary (b. 27 May 1725). {PGR:180; BPR:279, 281}

Beckwith/Bickwith, Henry m. Ann (N). Their children: Nehemiah (b. 6 Nov 1740), Thomas (b. 17 Aug 1742) and Charles (b. 28 Oct 1744). {BPR:287, 288}

Beddingfield/Benningfield/Field, Theophilus (b. ca. 1634, d. by 1678) of Martins Brandon Parish m. Naomy. He was father of Mary (bapt. 6 Feb 1660). Naomy m. 2nd Peter Good. {CCOB (1658-61):270; CCOB (1661-64):452; CCOB (1677-79):9, 57, 80}

Belcher. See Belsher.

Bell, James m. bef. 31 Dec 1716, Martha, widow of Edward Marks and sister of William Santom of Martins Brandon Parish (d. ca. 1717). Martha was mother of Edward Marks and James Bell. {PGW&D (1713-1728):25, 54-5}

Bell, James m. by Aug 1761, Martha (N) and had a son James as of 1767 and son John in 1768. {CCCR:4, 11, 35, 150-1}

Bell, John of Martins Brandon Parish (d. ca. 1723) m. 1st (N)(N) and m. 2nd Alice (N). John gave his son James, 207 acres in 1713. Grandchildren: James Bell and James Smith, son of William Smith. {PGW&D (1710-1713):38-9; PGW&D (1713-1728):95}

Bell, John, grandson of James Bell, m. bef. 16 Aug 1768, Elizabeth (N). {CCCR:8}

Belcher, George m. Elizabeth (N). Their children: Robert (b. 4 Nov 1733) and William (b. 12 Mar 1733). {BPR:285, 286}

Belcher/Belchair, George m. Lucy (N). Their children: Woody (b. 22 Feb 1740/1) and Mary (b. 9 May 1742). {BPR:287, 288}

Belcher/Belsher, William m. Mary (N). Their children: William (b. 4 Jun 1720), Thomas (b. 28 Jun 1722), Edward (b. 10 Mar 1728) and George (b. 18 Jul 1731). {BPR:279, 282, 284}

Bentley, John m. Mary (N). Their children: dau. (b. 19 May 1730), Sarah (b. 1 Jun 1732) and Maryellis (b. 12 Dec 1733). {BPR:283, 284, 286}

Benton. See Burton.

Benwood, Joseph m. Amy (N). Their dau. Mary Anne b. 3 Feb 1793. {BPR:294}

Bernard, William d. by 1691 leaving widow, Anne. {CCOB (1687-95):126}

Berry, Henry m. Anne (N). Their dau. Betty b. 16 Aug 1743. {BPR:289}

Bettis, Edward was father of James who was bound out in 1738. {PGR:25}

Bevell/Beavil, John m. Mary (N). Their children: Lucy (b. 19 Nov 1727), Susanna (b. 4 Jan 1732) and Martha (b. 4 Mar 1734). {BPR:282, 285, 286}

Bevell/Beavil, Robert m. Ann (N). Their children: James (b. 2 Nov 1721), Robert (b. 10 Oct 1723), William (b. 2 Oct 1726), Joseph (b. 11 Dec 1730) and Frances (b. 12 Dec 1732). {BPR:279, 280, 281, 283, 285}

Biggins, John d. by 1803. Heirs: Fanny, Raglin, Patsy and Susan Biggins. {PGM:30}

Biggins, Richard m. Elizabeth (N). Their children: Ann (b. 24 Jun 1741), Lucretia (b. 7 Nov 1743) and Arthur (b. 26 Oct 1745). {BPR: 287, 289, 290}

Bilbro, Thomas (d. ca. 1718) m. Sarah (N). Children: John, Thomas, James, Sarah and Elizabeth. {PGW&D (1713-1728):38}

Bilbro, Thomas d. by 1738, Susanna Bilbro, extx. {PGR:35}

Binford, Ann. On 4/2/1792 it was reported that Ann Binford married a man not of the Society - disowned. {HMM:76}

Binford, Aquila, son of Peter and Rebekah Binford of Prince George Co., m. 7th da., 1st mo., 1758, Mary Ladd, dau. of James and Judeth Ladd of Charles City Co., at the meeting house in Charles City Co. {HMM:33}

Binford, James, son of John and Agnes (Mosby) Binford of Charles City

Co., m. 4th day, 3rd mo., 1751, Martha Chappell, dau. of Thomas Chappell of Prince George Co. They married at the meeting house near White Oak Swamp. Children: James, Martha, Nancy/Ann, Benjamin, Thomas, Sarah Moseby, Samuel and possibly John Mosby Binford. {HMM:27, 70; APP3:751-2; HCWB1:13}

Binford, James, son of Thomas Binford of Prince George Co. m. 5th da., 1st mo., 1777, Hannah Crew, dau. of Andrew Crew of Charles City Co., at their meeting house in Waynoak in Charles City Co. They removed to the limits of Rich Square Monthly Meeting in NC. {HMM:55, 56}

Binford, James d. by 1782. {HCWB1:57}

Binford, James m. (license dated 1 May 1796), Elizabeth G. Carter. {GVAW I:357}

Binford/Benford/Beuford, John (son of James Benford) of Prince George County m. 12th da., 9th mo., 1719, Agness Mosby (daughter of Edward Mosby) of Henrico County. Their children: John, James, Mary and Agnes (m. Benjamn Chappell). {HMM:9; APP 3:721, 752}

Binford John, son of John Binford of Charles City Co. and brother of James Binford, was disowned in 1757 because of several disorders unbecoming the purity of the Society (Quaker) as frequently taking spirituous liquor to excess, keeping bad company, and lately marrying a woman by a priest (minister) not of the Society of Friends (Quakers). He m. bef. 5 Nov 1757 Sarah (N). Children: James, Agnes and Mary. {HMM:31; APP3:751; CCCR:32}

Binford, John, brother of James Binford, m. bef. 1 Aug 1770, Sarah (N). Children: James, Agnes and Mary. {CCCR:32}

Binford, John d. by 1771. Sons: John and James. {CCCR:42-3}

Binford, John, son of Thomas Binford of Henrico Co., dec'd., m. 3rd da., 8th mo., 1754, Susanna Ellyson, dau. of Robert Ellyson of New Kent Co., at Robert Ellyson's. Children of John and Susanna Binford: Robert (b. 30/7/1755), Thomas (b. 11/4/1758), Mary (b. 4/11/1760), John (b. 7/1/1764) and Martha (b. 12/8/1766, m. ca. 1783 outside the Society of Friends (Quakers), disowned). {HMM:29, 31, 65, 68}

Binford, John (son of Thomas Binford) and Elizabeth Crew, announced their intentions of marriage on 3rd da., 12th mo., 1785. {HMM:69}

Binford, Peter m. 7th da., 6th mo., 1731, Rebeckah Chapell, dau. of Thomas Chapell of Prince George Co. {HMM:17, 18}

Binford, Robert. 6/4/1782. Robert Binford condemned his marrying outside the Society and complying with military requisitions. {HMM:67}

Binford, Sherwood, son of Thomas Binford (d. 1815) m. (license dated 7 May 1800), Martha Parker. {GVAW I:357}

Binford, Thomas, brother of Peter Binford, d. 1752, owning land in NC. Thomas m. Elizabeth (N) (d. by 1789). Children: John, James, Priscilla (m. Benjamin Watkins), Thomas, Betty Kinsie/Betty Kinny (m. outside the Society of Friends, ca. 1762), Sarah, William and Mary. In his LWT Thomas also named nephew James Binford. In her will Elizabeth named sons William and Thomas Binford and grandchildren: Patsey Pankey, Thomas (son of son John), Priscilla Ladd and Thomas Pankey. {GVAW I:357; HMM:29, 37; HCW 2:56}

Binford, Thomas m. 1755, Judeth Lead. {HMM:16-17, 30}

Binford, Thomas m. Margaret (N) of Rich Square, NC. Their children: Elizabeth Hill (b. 10/3/1785, d. 7/3/1789), Parmilia (b. 28/10/1787, d. 15/3/1790) and Eli Hill (b. 17/10/1789) and Margaret d. 8/11/1789. {HMM:65}

Binford, Thomas m. (license dated 12 Aug 1790) Betsey Brackett, dau. of John Brackitt. {HCWB1:101; HMM:95; HCDB 1:48; GVAW I:357}

Binford, Thomas, of Burleigh Monthly Meeting, son of Peter Binford of Prince George Co., m. 6th da., 12th mo., 1772, Ruth Crew, dau. of Ellyson Crew of Charles City Co., at the meeting house in Charles City Co. On 4/12/1773 a certificate was requested for Ruth, wife of Thomas Binford, now a resident within the limits of Blackwater Monthly Meeting. {HMM:51}

Binford, Thomas (d. 1815) m. (license dated 30 Dec 1794), Priscilla Warriner. Children: William, Mary Ann/Marian (m. William Pemberton), Thomas, Sherwood, John K., Joseph and Nancy (m. (N) Childress). Grandchildren: Elizabeth K. Binford, Ann H. Binford, Nancy Johnson, James M. Binford, Joseph Binford. {GVAW I:357; HCDB 3:33-4; HCDB 5:66}

Binford, William m. bef. 2nd da., 11th mo., 1777 Martha (N). {HMM:56, 60}

Binford, William m. (license dated 6 Dec 1798), Sarah Binford. {GVAW I:357}

Bingham, William m. Mary (N). Their son John b. 27 Mar 1792). {BPR:294}

Binns, John m. by Jul 1760, Mary, admx. of Robert Clopton. {CCCR:144}

Birchenhead, Randolph (d. 1711) m. Elizabeth (N). Dau. Elizabeth (m. (N) Pool). {PGW&D (1710-1713):12}

Birchett/Burchett, Drury m. Elizabeth (N). Their children: William (b. 12 May 1756), Elizabeth (b. 4 Jan 1760), Drury (b. 23 Jul 1762) and Susanna (bapt. 7 Jul 1771). Drury gave his son Drury 100 acres in 1789. {PGR:114; BPR:292, 293}

Birchett, Edward of Prince George Co. d. ca. 1713, leaving a widow Ann. Children: Robert, Sarah Baptis (m. (N) Curtis), Lundy and possibly Mary Norton. {PGW&D (1710-1713):34, 36}

Birchet/Burchet, Edward m. Margret (N)*. Their children: Agnis (b. 6 Jan 1721/2), Agnis (b. 6 Jan 1720/1), James (b. 19 Nov 1724) and Abraham (b. 15 Jun 1730). {BPR:279, 280, 281, 283} *See note below.

Burchet, Edward m. Mary (N) [Margaret]*. Their children: William (b. 30 Dec 1722) and Drury (b. 1 Jan 1731). {BPR: 280, 298} *Sometimes Marg. is read as Mary which would suggest that this family and the one above are the same.

Birchett, Edward Jr. m. Sarah (N). Their children: David (b. 15 Apr 1749), Peter (b. 6 May 1750), Agness (b. 6 Apr 1753), Edward (b. 6 Jun 1755), Ephraim (b. 5 Mar 1758), Henry (b. 5 Aug 1761), Daniel (b. 1764) and Theoderick (b. 23 Jan 1769). {BPR:291, 292, 293}

Birchet, John m. Frances (N). Their son Drury b. 2 Jul 1749. {BPR:291}

Birchett, Robert (d. 1759-60) m. Jeane (N). Children: Rebecker, Robert (b. 8 Apr 1744), John (b. 17 Oct 1749), James (b. 6 Aug 1755), Mary and Martha (b. 14 Oct 1752). In his LWT Robert named son-in-law (*stepson*?): Thomas Blick and son Robert as execs. {PGR:79; BPR:289, 291, 292}

Birchett, Robert d. 1792. Probable children: William, Elizabeth, James,

Edward (b. 17 Mar 1741/2), Robert and daus. who m. John Lacey and (N) Bingham. {PGM:22; BPR:288, 294}

Birchet, William m. Frances (N). Their son William b. 20 Dec 1744. {BPR:289}

Bird, Elizabeth had a son Richard Bird, b. 7 Jul 1767. {BPR:293}

Bird, Martha had a son Robert Bird, b. 24 Jul 1756. {BPR:293}

Bird, William m. Hannah (N). They had a dau. Elizabeth. Hannah m. 2nd William Duke. {CCOB (Fragments):531}

Bishopp, Capt. John d. by 1662 leaving a son, Edmond (b. ca. 1646). Sylvanus Stokes, was appointed his guardian. {CCOB (1661-64): 367}

Bishop, John, son of John Bishopp, m. bef. 9 Feb 1663/4, Sarah, dau. of Mary Laurence Rose. Their children: Henry, Sarah and Elizabeth Bishop. {CCOB (1664-65):520, 521; CCOB (1677-79):16}

Bishop, John (d. ca. 1716) m. Sarah (N) (d. ca. 1722). Children: John, William, Henry (d. testate without issue, 1718), Mary (m. (N) Potts), Hannah (m. (N) Reves), Harmon (d. by 1714) and James. Grandson: Mason Bishop. {PGW&D (1713-1728):17, 39, 89}

Bisse, Capt. James m. bef. 18 Dec 1688, Sarah, widow of (1) Richard Taylor and (2) Robert Lucy. {CCOB (1687-95):26-7, 38}

Black, John (d. by 1693) of Sherly Hundred Island, m. bef. 3 Jun Mary (N) who survived him. {CCOB (Fragments):527; CCOB (1687-95):149}

Blackborn, John m. bef. 4 Jun 1694, Elizabeth, widow of John Hood. {CCOB (1687-95):179}

Blackman, John m. Suffiah/Sephirah (N). Their children: Lucy (b. 29 Dec 1733), Abraham (b. 14 May 1741) and Wood (b. 22 Mar 1744/5). {BPR:286, 287, 290}

Blackman, Thomas (b. ca. 1656, d. ca. 1715) m. Ann (N). Children: Mary and Thomas. {PGW&D (1713-1728):11}

Blackston(e), John m. Mary (N). Their children: William (b. 27 May 1729) and Mary (b. 8 Nov 1734). {BPR:282, 287}

Blackwell, John m. Martha Vaughan, dau. of Samuel Vaughan. Their dau. Anne b. 15 Feb 1793. {BPR:294}

Blanchet, John m. Elizabeth (N). Their children: Thomas (b. 22 Feb 1729/30) and William (b. 25 Feb 1733). {BPR:283, 286}

Bland, John (d. 8 Jun 1680), merchant of London, m. Sarah Green (d. 4 Mar 1712/13) and owned land in Charles City Co., adjoining land occupied in 1693 by Theodorick Bland and John Bland. Children: John (d. young), Giles and Thomas (d. young). [It would appear that John spent much of his time in London while Sarah resided in Charles City Co.] {CCOB 1676-79):86; CCCR:75; APP1:326-7}

Bland, John, merchant of Prince George Co., son of John and Ann (Buck) Bland, m. 23 Apr 1791, Mary Long. Children: Anna Buck (b. 12 Mar 1792, d. 26 Mar 1832, m. 9 Feb 1809, Henry J. Harrison of Sussex Co.). John Bland d. Dec 1794. {APP1:351; BPR:294, 295}

Bland, Peter m. bef. 4 Feb 1801, Anne (N). {PGM:8}

Bland, Richard (b. 1665, d. ca. 1720), son of Theodorick Bland, m. 1st Mary Swann, dau. of Col. Thomas Swann, and m. 2nd bef. 10 Apr 1711, Elizabeth, dau. of William Randolph of Turkey Island. Children: Richard, Theodorick, Mary (m. Henry Lee), Elizabeth (m. Col. William Beverley) and Anna (m. 1st Capt. Robert Munford, m. 2nd George Currie). {PGW&D (1710-1713):10; PGW&D (1713-1728):60; VG&B (Old Churches, Ministers and Families):446; APP1:330; Bland Papers:149; APP 1:331-5}

Bland, Richard gave his son John 100 acres in 1760, adjoining land he gave to son Peter Bland. {PGR:80}

Bland, Col. Richard (b. 20 Feb 1730/1, d. 25 Jan 1786) m. 8 Oct 1761, Mary Bolling. Children: Richard, Ann Poythress (b. 1765, m. 1st John Morison, m. 2nd Peter Woodlief), John (b. 1767, d. 1777) and Elizabeth Blair (b. 1770, m. William Poythress). {PGR:82, 137; APP1:342}

Bland, Richard, son of Col. Richard and Mary (Bolling) Bland, m. 24 Dec 1787, Susannah, dau. of Col. Peter and Elizabeth (Bland) Poythress. {PGR:150, 169; APP 1:156, 341-2}

Bland, Theodorick* (d. 23 Apr 1672), son of John Bland, m. 1660, Anne Bennett. Anne m. 2nd St. Leger Codd and d. Nov 1688 at Wharton Creek, Kent Co., MD. Sons: Theodorick, Richard and John. {APP1:327-8;

CCOB 1676-79):62 (*shows name as Thomas vice Theodorick)}

Bland, Theodorick, son of Theodorick (d. 1672) and brother of John and Richard Bland (d. 1680) m. Margaret Man. Children: John and Theodorick. {APP1:330}

Bland, Capt. Theodorick m. Frances (N). Their children: Theoderick (b. 21 Mar 1740), Elizabeth (b. 4 Jan 1739/40, m. John Banister), Theoderick (b. 21 Mar 1741/2), Mary (b. 22 Aug 1745), Ann (b. 5 Sep 1747), Jane (b. 30 Sep 1749) and Frances (b. 24 Sep 1752). {BPR: 288, 291, 292}

Bland, Theodorick (d. ca. 1790), son of Theodorick and Frances (Bolling) Bland, m. Martha Daingerfield. In his LWT Theodorick named nephews: Theodorick Bland Randolph, Robert Banister and John Randolph. They had a child who d. young. Martha m. 2nd Nathan Blodget of Dinwiddie Co. and m. 3rd (N) Corran, a sea captain. {PGR:137, 164; Legislative Petitions – Library of VA website; APP1:334, 348-50}

Blanks, James m. by Apr 1761, Catherine/Kitturo (N). {CCCR:47, 148}

Blanks, James (d. by Dec 1793) m. Elizabeth (N). He d. leaving sons Thomas, Henry, and John Blanks; daus. Nancy (m. (N) Manly), Mary Blanks, Jane Blanks, and Betsey Blanks. Granddaus. Nancy and Susan Warberton, daus. of Benjamin Warberton (decd.). {SWBC: 29}

Blanks, Nicholas m. by Feb 1750, Rebecca (N). {CCCR:124}

Blanks, Thomas d. by 1659 leaving a widow who m. 2nd William Smith. {CCOB (1658-61):198}

Blanks, Thomas m. bef. 4 Aug 1679, Mary, widow of Jeffrey Mumford. {CCOB (1677-79):108}

Blasnour, James d. by 1678. Son: James, admin. {CCOB (1677-79):40}

Bleighton, Haley m. by Apr 1762, Hannah, dau. of David Davidson. {CCCR:154}

Blaton, Mary had a dau. Sarah b. 24 Jan 1729, d. 1 Feb 1729. {BPR:282}

Blayton, Thomas m. bef. 16 Jun 1677, (N), widow of Jeramyah Woodhall. {CCOB 1676-79:3}

Blaxton, John m. Mary (N). Their son Rice b. 16 Sep 1732. {BPR:284}

Blick(e), Benjamin m. bef. 14 Jul 1712, Elizabeth, dau. of John Williams. Their children: Benjamin (b. 26 Mar 1721), John (b. 27 Oct 1725), Martha (b. 5 May 1734) and ?Jane (b. 1752). {BPR:280, 281, 287, 292; PGW&D (1710-1713):22}

Blick, John Jr. m. Sarah (N). Their son Patrick b. 10 Oct 1792. {BPR:294}

Blodget, Nathan of Dinwiddie Co. m. (agreement dated 4 Oct 1791) Martha Bland, widow of Theodorick Bland. Martha m. 3rd (N) Corran, a sea captain with whom she want to France. She d. 1804 in France. {PGR:137, 164; Legislative Petitions – Library of VA website; APP 1:350}

Bly, Mary had a dau. Sarah b. 29 Apr 1726. {BPR:281}

Bobbitt, Liewes m. Elizabeth (N). Their son Miles b. 22 Jan 1731. {BPR:284}

Bobbitt, William d. by 1703, son: William. {PGW&D (1713-1728):96}

Bobby, Thomas ("the younger, d. ca. 1721) m. (N) (N). Children: sons Rumball (d. an infant without issue), and Geddes (d. without issue); daus. Elizabeth (m. James Balfour, had son James Balfour) and Rebecca (m. William Winston, left heir-at-law Geddes Winston). {SWBC: 29}

Boilsys, Peter m. Susanna (N). Their son John b. 5 Oct 1745. {BPR:290}

Boisseau, Holmes m. bef. 8 Apr 1740, Rebecca (N). {PGR:66}

Boisseau, Holmes John Alexander (d. by 1794), m. Mary Ann Glover. Probable children: Holmes, Elizabeth and Joseph. {PGM:22, 29; GVAT (Genealogies Of Virginia Families) I:149]

Boisseau, James (d. by 1789) m. Mary (N). Their children: Daniel, Lucy, Patrick, David, Anne, Elizabeth (b. 20 Sep 1733), James (b. 22 May 1736), Sarah (b. 3 Mar 1738), Susanna (b. 17 Oct 1741), John (b. 12 Feb 1747/8), Benjamin (b. 28 Feb 1753) and Molley Holt/Mary (b. 25 Sep 1756, Joseph Watkins). {BPR:287, 291, 292; W&M, Vol. 23, No. 3 (Jan., 1915): 215}

Boisseau, James m. Anner (N). Their children: Daniel (b. 4 Mar 1760) and James (b. 13 Nov 1761). {BPR:292}

Boisseau, John (b. 14 Mar 1764, Dinwiddie Co.), son of James Boisseau and nephew of Benjamin Boisseau. He lived in Lunenburg Co. for about 10 years, then moved back to Dinwiddie Co. In 1806, he and his family moved to Logan Co., KY, which later became Simpson Co., KY. {RWP}

Bolling, Alexander (b. 3/12/1721, d. 6/11/1767) m. 12/23/1745 Susanna Bolling (his cousin) (b. 6/16/1728). Both were grandchildren of Col. Robert Bolling by his 2nd wife Anne Stith. Their children: Elizabeth (b. 6/24/1747, d. 11/23/1776, m. 1st Peter Jones, m. 2nd Chris. Manlove); Robert (b. 3/24/1751), Stith (b. 5/11/1753), Ann (b. 3/31/1755), John (b. 10/13/1756, d. 11/9/1759), Alexander (b. 12/2/1761), Susanna (b. 12/5/1764) and Sally (b. 3/25/1776, d. 6/127/1773). {VBR:246-7; BPR:291}

Bolling, Alexander (d. ca. 1818) of Dinwiddie Co., son of Alexander (d. 1767) and Susanna (Bolling) Bolling, m. (bond dated 24 Dec 1782, Mary, dau. of John and Mary (Dennis) Pryor. {APP 3:80-1}

Bolling, Drury (b. 21 Jun 1695, d. by 1738) of Prince George Co., son of Robert Bolling, m. Elizabeth, dau. of Francis Meriwether of Essex Co. Frances Bolling, dau. of Drury Bolling dec'd, chose in 1738 as her guardian, Robert Bolling. {GVAT (Genealogies of Virginia Families) II:732; PGR:16}

Bolling, George m. Jane (N). Their dau. Jane b. 31 Dec 1740. {BPR: 288}

Bolling, John (b. 1675, d. 1729) of Bristol Parish, son of Robert and Jane (Rolfe) Bolling, m. (license dated 29 Dec 1697) Mary Kennon, dau. of Richard Kennon. Children: Jane (m. Col. Richard Randolph), John, Elizabeth (m. Dr. William Gay), Mary (m. Col. John Fleming), Martha (b. 1713, m. Thomas Eldridge) and Anne (m. James Murray of Prince George Co.). {HMM:92 (Henrico Co. Court records); GVA (Genealogies of Virginia Families II, Cl-Fi:138); GVAW (Genealogies of Virginia Families) II:260; APP3:28-35; HCW 1:171}

Bolling, John (d. by Mar 1744) was the brother of Alexander Bolling and Anne (m. John Edloe). {SWBC:205}

Bolling, Robert (b. 26 Dec 1646, d. 17 Jul 1709), the immigrant, was son of John and Mary Bolling of Bolling Hall, Yorkshire, England. He m. 1st Jane, dau. of Thomas Rolfe. They had a son John b. 27 Jan 1676. Robert

m. 2nd Anne Stith, dau. of John Stith. Their children: Robert (b. 25 Jan 1682, d. 1749), Stith (b. 28 Mar 1686), Edward (b. 1 Oct 1687), Martha, Anne (b. 22 Jul 1690), Drury (b. 21 Jun 1695), Thomas (b. 20 Mar 1697/8) and Agnes (b. 30 Nov 1700). {GVAW (Genealogies of Virginia Families) IV:567-8; PGM:12; PGW&D (1713-1728):16}

Bolling, Major Robert (b. 1682, d. 1749) of Charles City Co., son of Robert and Anne (Stith) Bolling, m. 27 Jan 1706 Anne Cocke, probable dau. of Richard Cocke, the younger. Their children: Mary/Mary Ann (b. 25 Jan 1708, m. 1727, William Starke (d. 1755), had son Robert Starke), Elizabeth (b. 1709, m. James Munford, had sons Thomas Bolling Munford, Robert Munford, and Edward Munford), Ann (m. John Hall), Lucy (b. 1719, m. Col. Peter Randolph of *Chatsworth*), Robert (b. 30 Oct 1720), Jane (b. 1722, m. Hugh Miller), Mason (dau., b. 14 Aug 1724), Martha (b. 1726, m. Richard Eppes), Susanna (b. 1728, m. Alexander Bolling of Prince George Co.) and Robert (b. 1730, d. 1775, res. Petersburg, VA, m. 1st Martha Banister, m. 2nd 1758, Mary Marshall, dau. of Col. Thomas Tabb of Amelia Co.). {GVA (Genealogies of Virginia Families II, Cl-Fi:104, 124, 138-140; GVAT Genealogies of Virginia Families) IV:2; PGW&D (1710-1713):24; SWBC:205}

Bolling, Robert (b. 3/24/1751), son of Alexander and Susanna (Bolling) Bolling, m. 5/10/1772, Franky Green (d. 3/15/1773). Their son: John b. 3/10/1773, d. 5/1/17--. {VBR:246-7}

Bolling, Robert Jr. of Buckingham Co. m. 1st Mary Burton and m. 2nd bef. 18 Mar 1771, Susannah, dau. of John (d. 1750) and Martha Watson. {HCW 2:51, 54; HCDB (1750-1774):216}

Bolling, Robert of Dinwiddie Co. (d. by Mar 1777) m. Mary (N). Sons: Robert (under 21) and Thomas. {SWBC:40}

Bolling, Robert (d. by Feb 1791) m. bef. 1 Oct 1787 Clara (N). Children: Robert and Susanna (m. (N) Gilliam). {PGR:93; SWBC:50}

Bolling, Robert had a son Robert Stith who d. 1792. {BPR:294}

Bolling, Robert m. Catharine (N). Their children: Rebecca (b. 23 Feb 1793) and Lucy Ann (b. 3 May 1795). {BPR:294}

Bolling, Stith (res. Surry Co. in 1717), son of Robert and Anne (Stith) Bolling, m. Elizabeth, widow of John Hartwell of Surry Co. Stith's will was probated 16 Aug 1727 in Prince George Co. Sons: Stith, Alexander, John and Robert. {GVAW (Genealogies of Virginia Families) IV:568}

Bolling, Stith (b. 5/11/1753, son of Alexander and Susanna (Bolling) Bolling, m. 10/10/1776, Charlotte Edmunds. Their dau. Rebecca B. (b. 2/16/1778), m. Melchijah Spragins, son of Lt. Thomas Spragins of Halifax Co. {VBR:246-7}

Bolling, Thomas m. Seigniora (N). Their children: Rebeccah (b. 18 Mar 1792) and Yelverton de Mallet (b. 10 Dec 1795). {BPR:294, 295}

Bonner, Henry m. bef. 9 Nov 1784, Ann (N). {PGR:114}

Bonner, Jesse (d. 1795) of Dinwiddie Co. m. Rebecca (N). {SWBC:51; BPR:295}

Bonner, John of Martins Brandon Parish gave his son William Bonner, 114 acres in 1727. {PGW&D (1713-1728):171}

Bonner, Richard m. (bond dated 7 Apr 1783) Frances, dau. of Henry and Priscilla Mitchell. {APP1:381}

Bonner, Robert of Wilks Co., GA, heir of William Bonner, in 1790 sold 1/3 of a tract called *Caits*, left to him by William Bonner, dec'd. {PGR:152}

Bonner, Thomas m. Susanna (N). Their son Isham b. 7 Feb 1741/2. {BPR: 288}

Bonner, William m. Silvia, sister of William Williamson. In her LWT (dated 22 Jul 1776) Silvia named dau. Rebecca Tyas and son Williamson Bonner. {PGR:112}

Bonner, William d. by 1791, William Bonner, exec. Probable son: Jesse Bonner. {PGR:145}

Booker, Elinor was fined 50 shillings in 1747 for having a bastard child. Francis Hardyman promised to pay the fine. {CCCR:112}

Booker, John d. by 1739, leaving an orphan son, James. {CCCR:84}

Booker, Richard (d. 27 Aug 1793) of Chesterfield Co. m. Margaret (N). Their dau. Mary Brooks b. 19 Mar 1792, d. 24 Jul 1793. {BPR:293, 294}

Booth, Thomas (d. by 1688) m. Anne (N). Thomas had a son Thomas and dau. Ann who were placed in the guardianship of their father-in-law (*step-father*), Philip Thomas. Thomas also had a son George, bound apprentice to Stephen Samson, shoemaker and tanner, in 1693 and a dau. Mary who removed to Henrico Co. {CCOB (1687-95):19, 135, 159, 213}

Booth, Thomas m. Dorcorrs (N). Their dau. Amie b. 5 Jun 1728. {BPR:282}

Boram, Edmond (d. by 1759). His children, Mary Anne, Benjamin and Edmund were appointed a guardian, Francis Irby. His widow Mary m. 2nd John Robinson. {CCCR:15, 56}

Boreman, James d. by 1718, Matilda Boreman, granddau. {PGW&D (1713-1728):33}

Bosman, John d. by 1827, Mary Bosman, admx. {CCW&D (1725-31):22}

Boseman/Bosman/Bozeman, Harman of Westover Parish (d. 1725-6) m. Mary (N) (d. 1726). Children: John, Harman, Thomas, Frances and Mary. {CCW&D (1725-31):4}

Bosman, John m. by Aug 1754, Hannah (N). {CCCR:128}

Bott. See Batt.

Bottle, Margaret d. Aug 1660. {CCOB 1658-61):270}

Bowen, Robert m. Avis (N). Their children: Lucie (b. 23 Aug 1730) and Ephraim (b. 12 Feb 1731). {BPR:283, 284}

Bowen/Bowyon, William m. Amy (N). Their children: William (b. 2 Dec 1729), David (b. 13 Nov 1731) and Jesse (b. 11 Mar 1734). {BPR:283, 284, 287}

Bowman, William m. Elizabeth (N). Their children: Robert (b. 14 Mar 1728), William (b. 3 Apr 1731) and Peter (b. 30 Dec 1734). {BPR:282, 284, 286}

Bowry, (N) m. Mary, sister of James Gregory. Children: Henry. In her LWT Mary named "son" William Gregory and "son" John Gregory. {CCCR:52}

Bowry, Stephen m. (bond dated 9 Jan 1769), Mary Gregory, widow. {MB:195}

Boyce, Chainey d. ca. 1630? leaving a widow, Joyce and an only son,

Thomas. Joyce m. 2nd Capt. Richard Tye (d. by 1662). {CCOB (1655-58): 17; CCOB (1661-64):355}

Boyce, Taxied/Daniel d. by 1761, Lucy Boyce, extx. {CCCR:148}

Boyce, Thomas of Westover Parish m. bef. 20 Nov 1663, Emelia, granddau. of Richard Craven. {CCOB (1661-64):425}

Boyd, Alexander Sr. of Dinwiddie Co. m. Ann (N). Children: William, James, Richard, Robert, Alexander, and David. By 1824, Ann, James, Robert, and David were dead. {SWBC:51}

Bracy/Brasey, Francis m. Elizabeth (N). Their children: Elizabeth (b. 23 Dec 1724), Thomas (b. 25 Mar 1733) and Samuel (b. 12 Feb 1740). {BPR:281, 287}

Bradford, John, son of Richard and Frances (Taylor) Bradford, m. Rebecca (N). Children: Richard, Frances, Rebecca and Sarah. {VG&B:152-3}

Bradford, Philemon, planter, son of Richard Bradford, sold land ca. 28 May 1726, part of which was purchased by his grandfather, Richard Bradford, dec'd. {CCW&D (1725-31):12}

Bradford, Richard (d. 1716) m. bef. 3 Aug 1688, Frances, dau. of Richard Taylor (d. by 1684) and Sarah (Barker) Taylor. Their children: Richard, John and Ralph. {CCOB (1687-95):26-7; VG&B:152}

Bradford, Richard m. [Anna] (N). Both d. by 1725. Son: Richard. {CCW&D (1725-31):6}

Bradford, Richard son of Richard Bradford, m. bef. 23 Oct 1729, Rachel (N). {CCW&D (1725-31):36}

Bradley, Benjamin (d. by 1768) m. Judith (N). Children: Benjamin, Devorex, James, William, Jesse, Walter, Mary (m. (N) Tomson), Elizabeth (m. (N) Clarke), Rachel (m. (N) Weaver), Ann (m. (N) Moore) and Joice (m. (N) Hughes). {CCCR:5, 10}

Bradley, James d. by 1740, James and Richard Bradley, execs. {CCCR:88}

Bradly, John d. by 1740. His sons: John Bradly, admin. of thes estate and son Drury was bound to Benskin Marston in 1743. {CCCR:89, 101}

Bradley, John (d. 1769-70) m. Mary [Dancy]. Children: John, Dancy/Fancy, Betty Dancy, Anne and Mary (m. James Eppes). James Eppes was guardian of Betty and John Bradley in 1771. {CCCR:21, 37, 60; APP1:911-12}

Bradley, Joseph d. by 1662 leaving a widow who m. 2nd Cuthbert Winson. {CCOB (1661-64):335}

Bradly, Joseph gave 595 acres in 1729/30 to his sons, Benjamin and Thomas. {CCW&D (1725-31):40}

Bradley, Joseph d. by 1750, James Bradley, exec. {CCR:122}

Bradshaw/Bradsho, John m. Anne (N). Their children: William (b. 9 Jun 1719), John (b. 1 Feb 1721/2), Gower (b. 24 Oct 1724), Elizabeth (b. 20 Jul 1727), Phebe (b. 21 Dec 1729) and Benjamin (b. 6 Apr 1732). {BPR:280, 281, 282, 283, 284}

Bragg, Hugh m. Mary (N). Their children: William (b. 20 Mar 1722/3), Elizabeth (b. 8 Jul 1725) and Joel (b. 10 Apr 1729). {BPR:279, 281, 282}

Braine, Edward (d. by 1691) of Charles City Co. m. Sarah (N) (d. by 1692), widow of (1) Thomas Stegge, (2) George Harris and (3) Thomas Grendon. {HCW 1:108; CCOB (1687-95):121, 141}

Brayne, Richard (d. by 1662) m. 1st Elizabeth (N) who inherited property from George Drew. Richard m. 2nd Sarah (N). Richard d. leaving orphans, Richard and Mary. {CCOB (1761-64):363, 385, 466}

Branch, Christopher (b. 1602 in London, d. in VA 1681), son of Lionel and Valentia [Sparke] Branch of London, m. 2 Sep 1619 in St. Peter's, Westcheap, London, Mary Addie, dau. of Francis Addie of County York. They arrived in VA, 1619-20 and settled in Henrico Co. Their children: Thomas (b. 1623, d. 1694, m. Elizabeth (N)), William (b. ca. 1625, d. ca. 1676, m. Jane (N)) and Christopher (b. ca. 1627, d. 1665, moved to Charles City Co.). Grandchildren: Samuel Branch, Benjamin Branch and Christopher Branch. {GVAW I:413; HCW 1:11}

Branch, Christopher, son of Christopher Branch (d. 1681), m. (N)(N). Children: Christopher, Samuel, Mary, Sarah and Benjamin. {APP1:368}

Brand, Richard, brother of Robert (had a son Thomas) and Thomas Brand (had a dau. Elizabeth), m. Elizabeth (N) who m. 2nd Thomas Hollinghurst (d. by 1725). {CCW&D (1725-31):5, 29}

Brandon, Mary had children: John (b. 22 Oct 1740), Charles (b. 1 Mar 1742), Elizabeth (b. 11 Apr 1758), John (b. 4 Oct 1760), Aaron (b. 1 Aug 1762), Judith (b. 16 Jul 1764), Peter (b. 16 Jan 1766) and Gabril (b. 2 Oct 1767). {BPR:289, 293}

Brandy, Peter m. 1741, Frances. Their children, William and Harris (dau.) were bound out in 1741. {CCCR:91}

Brasey. See Bracy.

Bressie, Francis m. bef. 8 Aug 1726, Elizabeth (N). Their dau. Mary b. 3 Aug 1731. {PGW&D (1713-1728):148, 284}

Brewer, John (d. by 1729) m. Mary (N). They had a son John. {CCW&D (1725-31):36}

Brewer, John (LWT dated 4 Oct 1798) m. Usle (N). {Dinwiddie Co. GenWeb; SWBC:51}

Brewer, Joseph m. Margarit (N). Their dau. Mary b. 7 Oct 1725. {BPR:281}

Brewer, Nicholas Jr., son of Nicholas Brewer Sr. of Martins Brandon Parish, m. bef. 10 Aug 1722, Elizabeth (N). {PGW&D (1713-1728):84}

Brewer, Peter m. Letisia (N). Their son James b. 1 Nov 1733. {BPR:286}

Brewer, Sackfeild (d. by 1737), son of Barrett Brewer, m. bef. 7 Jul 1725 Elener (N), dau. of (N) Barrett. Execs.: Elinor and William Brewer. {CCW&D (1725-31):4-5; CCCR:81}

Brewer, Sackville (d. 1744-5), brother of James, William, Catherine and Mary, m. Anne (N). Anne m. 2nd (N) Tatum. {HCW 2:26, 40}

Brewer, William m. by Sep 1743, Frances (N). {CCCR:100}

Brice, William m. Margarett (N). Their daus. Nancy (b. 2 Dec 1766) and Molley (b. 22 Dec 1768). {BPR:293}

Bristow, Thompson m. bef. 2 Jan 1769, Mary, dau. of Warwick Hockaday. {CCCR:20-1}

Broadie, (N) of Petersburg d. 16 Sep 1794. {BPR:295}

Broadway/Brawdiway, Edward/Edm. m. Mary (N). Their children: William (b. 4 Jun 1724) and Edward (b. 7 Dec 1726). {BPR:280, 282}

Broadway/Brawdiway, Thomas m. Letitia (N). Their son John b. 10 May 1720 . {BPR:280}

Broadway/Brawdiway, Thomas was father of Sarah (b. 28 Sep 1733). {BPR:286}

Brockwell, James, brother of Joseph Brockwell, d. 1786-7. {PGR:83}

Brockwell, John m. bef. 24 Jan 1760, Mary, dau. of Joseph Carter. Their son: Carter. {PGR:78}

Brockwell, Thomas m. Jemimah (N). Their dau. Betsey b. 10 Sep 1793. {BPR:294}

Brodnax, Edward (d. by 1749), son of William Bronax, m. 1st (N)(N), m. 2nd Mary Brown and m. 3rd Elizabeth/Betty Hall. Their children: probably Henry, Elizabeth (m. Vivian Brooking), Edward (m. Rebecca Dansy), Ann (probably m. Robert Munford) and Rebecca (m. Alexander Walker). Elizabeth m. 2nd Edward Munford. {CCCR:119; GVAW (Genealogies of Virginia Families) I:463}

Brodnax, William, son of William and Rebecca (Champion) Broadnax, m. Ann Hall, dau. of Thomas Hall of Prince George Co. Their children: Elizabeth (m. William Evans), dau. (m. (N) Wall and had John and William Brodnax Wall), Ann (m. (N) Jackson), Mary (m. (N) Smith), a dau. (m. (N) Power and had Henry Power, William Brodnax Power and John Power), William (b. 26 Nov 1745), John, William Edward (b 1755) and Thomas Hall Brodnax. {BPR:290; GVAW (Genealogies of Virginia Families) I:460}

Brodnax, William (d. Sussex Co. 13 Mar 1775), son of Edward Broanax (d. by 1748), m. bef. 25 Nov 1769, Mary, dau. of Thomas Cowles (d. 1770). Their children: Mary (m. (N) Mulford/Mumford?), Ann, Rebecca, Benjamin (b. 28 Aug 1772), Samuel (b. 24 Mar 1774), William (m. 1793, Ann Brooking, dau. of Vivian Brooking) and Edward (m. Frances Brooking, dau. of Vivian Brooking). Mary, widow of William Brodnax, m. 2nd Richard Gregory, son of Roger Gregory. {CCCR:26-7, 117; GVAW (Genealogies of Virginia Families) I:464}

Brookes, Edward. Catharine Brookes was charged with petit treason in poisoning her husband Edward Brookes - Oct. Court 1789. {W&M, Vol. 23, No. 3 (Jan., 1915): 214-217}

Brooks, George m. Ann (N). Their children: Thomas (b. 20 Feb 1722/3), Martha (b. 31 Mar 1725) and Martha (b. 31 Mar 1725). {BPR:280, 281, 283}

Brooks, John m. by Oct 1760, Martha (N). {CCCR:145}

Brookes, Robert b. ca. 1623. {CCOB (1658-61):219}

Brookes, Robert m. bef. 3 Jun 1692, Anne, only dau. of Hanna Hickman. {CCOB (1687-95):128}

Brooks, Robert m. bef. Nov 1741 Martha (N). Martha d. by 1760, John Brooks, exec. {CCCR:93}

Brooks, Thomas m. Ann (N). Their children: John (b. 21 Dec 1728), Thomas (b. 10 Jun 1731), Amy (b. 17 Feb 1732) and George (b. 28 May 1734). {BPR:282, 284, 285, 286}

Browder, Edmond Sr. of Bristol Parish m. bef. 7 Aug 1721, Elizabeth (N). They probably had son Edmond Browder Jr. (witness to sale of land by Edmond Browder Sr. {PGW&D (1713-1728):74}

Browder, Edmond m. Martha (N) Their children: Handstress (b. 30 Nov 1721), James (b. 24 Aug 1725) and William (b. 31 Oct 1727 or 1728). {BPR:281, 282}

Browder, George m. Elizabeth (N). Their children: Mary (b. 20 Aug 1725), Jeane (b. 29 Dec 1729), Presilia (b. 2 Jun 1735) and Winnie (b. 7 Jan 1741/2). {BPR:281, 283, 286, 288}

Browder, George Andrew of Bristol Parish gave or sold 100 acres to Edmond Browder, Jr. in 1723. {PGW&D (1713-1728):95}

Browder, John m. Elizabeth (N). Their children: William (b. 7 Jul 1723), George (b. 5 Dec 1731), Anne (b. 13 Feb 1733) and Joseph (b. 2 Feb 1741/2). {BPR:280, 285, 286, 288}

Browder, John m. Mary (N). Their children: Mason (b. 30 Jun 1742) and Frederick (b. 22 Feb 1744/5). {BPR:288, 290}

Browder, John Sr. gave his son John Browder Jr., ca. 1760. [missing fragment]. {PGR:80}

Browder, William m. Dorithy (N). Their children: Sarah (b. 22 Dec 1727) and Amy (b. 11 Jul 1733). {BPR:282, 285}

Browder, William m. Margret (N). Their children: Margret (b. 16 Nov 1742) and Susanna (b. 18 Jun 1745). {BPR:289, 290}

Brown, (N) m. Elizabeth (N). Their children, John and Abraham were bound to Jacob Danzee in 1744. {CCCR:102}

Brown, Charles d. by 1740, Samuel Gregory, admin. {CCCR:89}

Brown, Elizabeth, Mulatto, had a son Will Brown, bound to John Jacob Danzee in 1744. {CCCR:103}

Brown, James (b. 24 May 1759, Dinwiddie Co.). He later moved to NC, then TN, then upper LA, then back to TN. In 1832 he was living in Davidson Co., TN. {RWP}

Brown, John m. Elizabeth (N). Their son Richard b. 3 Jul 1721. {BPR:279}

Brown, John m. by Nov 1755, Ann, widow of John Miles the younger. {CCCR:133, 142}

Brown, Marmaduke was father of Ann who was bound out in 1761 and Mary who was bound out in 1762. {CCCR:152, 155}

Brown, Moses (b. 26 May 1752, Dinwiddie Co., possibly the brother of James Brown). He moved to Davidson Co., TN. {RWP}

Brown, Noah Sr. of Martins Brandon Parish m. Elizabeth (N). Their children: Rebeckah (b. 19 Nov 1738), Betty (b. 27 Sep 1740), William (b. 16 Oct 1742), Noah (b. 26 Jan 1744), Jesse (b. 6 May 1747), Burwell (b. 11 Sep 1749) and Boswell (b. 1 May 1752). Noah gave his son Burwell 30 acres in 1776. {BPR:290, 291; PGR:166}

Brown, Noah (d. by Apr 1798) of Dinwiddie Co. m. Martha (N). Children: Lewis (under 21), Burwell, Noah, John, Susanah Baugh (underage in 1798), and Patsy Wingfield (underage in 1798). {SWBC:51}

Brown, Sarah, Mulatto, had a dau. Betty b. 28 Mar 1745. {BPR:290}

Brown, Tabitha was presented in 1739 for having a bastard child.
{CCCR:84}

Brown, Thomas m. Frances (N). Their son Thomas b. 12 Aug 1741.
{BPR: 288}

Brown, Thomas of Martins Brandon Parish (d. 1790) m. (N)(N).
Children: John, Rebecca, Sally, Elizabeth (m. Richard Shackleford),
Nancy, Henry, Lucy, Isham and Lucretia. {PGR:141}

Brown, William m. Anne (N). Their son John b. 30 Aug 1721.
{BPR:279}

Brown, William m. Elizabeth (N). Their son Burwell b. 13 Dec 1741.
{BPR: 288}

Brown, William and servant Probey had twins, Mary and Elizabeth
Brown, b. 20 Jul 1761. {BPR:355}

Brown, William m. (bond dated 28 May 1767) Martha Bassett (Spinster).
{CCCR:14; MB:195}}

Brown, William of Martins Brandon Parish d. by 1789 leaving widow,
Elizabeth, extx. {PGR:126}

Broyely, John m. Rebecca (N). Their dau. Prudence b. 16 Dec 1723.
{BPR:280}

Bruce, James m. Margaret (N). Their dau. Hannah b. 22 Mar 1745/6.
{BPR:290}

Brun, Joseph m. by 1741, Caton (N) who m. 2nd (N) DeWest. Their
children: Caton and Mary Ann. Caton DeWest d. by 1745, Benjamin
Harris, admin. {CCCR:92, 106}

Brunskill, Rev. John made a gift to his dau. Mary in 1739. {CCCR:85}

Bryan, (N) m. Margaret (N). In 1737 Margaret Tanner gave her son
Thomas Bryan and her granddaus., Sarah and Elizabeth Bryan a gift.
{CCCR:78}

Bryan, (N) (d. by 1744), m. Susanna, widow of (N) Johnson. {CCCR:104}

Bryan, Thomas d. by 1744, Elizabeth, widow, extx. {CCCR:104}

Bryan, William m. Mary (N). Their son Thomas b. 29 May 1728. {BPR:282}

Bryerly/Bryally, John m. Rebecca (N). Their children: William (b. 9 Sep 1721) and Dorithy (b. 30 Feb 1726). {BPR:279, 282}

Buchanan, (N) m. bef. 7 Apr 1790, Elizabeth, dau. of Robert Gilliam. {PGR:130}

Buchanan, David (d. 15 Aug 1792). Son: Silias Dunlop Buchanan. {BPR:293}

Buckner, Larrance (d. by 1690) m. Elizabeth (N). {CCOB (1687-95):76}

Buckner, Larrance d. by 1720, Sarah Buckner, admx. {PGW&D (1713-1728):69}

Buckner, William m. bef. (N), widow of George Hunt, who was probably the son of William Hunt. {CCOB (1664-65):569}

Bugg, William m. Mary (N). Their son John b. 1 Feb 1731. {BPR:284}

Bullifant, Charles m. Mary (N) before 1777, at which time he died in the Rev. War. Widow Mary lost her eyesight ca. 1793. {Legislative Petitions – Library of VA website}

Bullington, William m. (bond dated 17 Apr 1790), Frances Bradley. {MB:194}

Bullock, Ishmail m. Bersheba Chiswell (N). Their children: Elizabeth (b. 17 Mar 1721) and Frances (b. 2 Mar 1722). {BPR:282}

Bundy, Richard m. Constance (N). Their dau. Mary b. 25 Dec 1743. {BPR:289}

Burch, Barnaby d. by 1759, Tabitha Burch, admx. {CCCR:141}

Burch, Richard m. Jane (N). Their children: John (b. 7 Mar 1722) and Martha (b. 27 Feb 1725/6). {BPR:279, 283}

Burch, Samuel m. bef. 8 Mar 1725, Mary (N). {PGR:180; PGW&D (1713-1728):142}

Burcher, Maurice/Morris (age 37 in 1673) m. bef. 13 Sep 1677, Joan (N). {CCOB (Fragments):530; CCOB (1677-79):16}

Burchet. See Birchet.

Burge, James (d. 1791) m. Elizabeth (N). Children: Thomas, James (had a son Augustain), Joel (had a son Wood), Hamilton, Wilee, Lucy, Alexander and Thomas Bonner. {PGR:163-4}

Burge, James m. bef. 20 Jan 1790, Lucrecy (N). {PGR:132}

Burge, John (d. by 1693) m. bef. 4 Feb 1677/8, the widow of Samuel Hilman. John d. by 1693 leaving a widow, Mary. {CCOB (1677-79):39; CCOB (1687-95):150, CCCR:74}

Burge/Byrge/Burg/Burges, John m. Frances (N). Their children: Richard (b. 29 Mar 1728), Elizabeth (b. 11 Dec 1729), John (b. 10 Nov 1732) and Frances (b. 7 Jul 1741). {BPR:282, 283, 285, 288}

Burge, Richard m. Constant (N). Their son William b. 23 Mar 1746. {BPR:290}

Burge, Thomas Sr. of Bristol Parish m. Mary (N). Their children: Thomas (b. 31 May 1721), Frederick (b. 5 Nov 1741), Woodie (b. 22 Mar 1743/4) and Alexander (b. 6 Jun 1746). {PGW&D (1713-1728):156-7; BPR:279, 287}

Burge, William m. bef. 9 Jun 1789, Frances (N). {PGR:115}

Burn, David m. Frances (N). Their son David b. 25 Mar 1733. {BPR:285}

Burnet. See Barnet.

Burrow, Dobson (b. c1758, d. 18 Mar 1840, Randolph Co., NC), son of Lucy Burrow. He was brother to Barney Burrow and brother in law to Thomas Yeargin. He entered the Rev. War in Dinwiddie Co. Dobson d. without children. {RWP}

Burrow, James m. Catherine (N). Their children: Mary (b. 11 Nov 1733) and Anne (b. 28 Mar 1742). {BPR:285, 288}

Burrough, John m. Johannah (N). Their son Henry b. 26 Oct 1730). {BPR:283}

Burrow, John (d. by May 1778) of Dinwiddie Co. m. (N) (N). Children: Philip, John, Isabel (m. (N) Henry), and Henry. Granddaus: Bethier

Burrow and Susannah Burrow. {SWBC:51}

Burreys, Joseph m. Mary (N). Their dau. Anne b. 1 Apr 1742.
{BPR:288}

Burrows, Nathanael m. Mary (N). Their dau. Patty b. 22 Sep 1745.
{BPR:290}

Burroughs, Peter d. 1711-12. {PGW&D (1710-1713): 15}

Burroughs/Burrow, Philip Jr. m. bef. 20 Jan 1710, Bethyer/Parthenia,
dau. of John Scott of Weynoake Parish. {PGW&D (1710-1713):4, 20}

Burrow, Philip m. Martha (N). Their son Philip b. 20 Jul 1741. Other
children: Martha (m. (N) Cain), Jerrald, Mary, and Gray. Sons in law:
James Mangum and William Martin. {BPR: 287; SWBC:51}

Burrow, Thomas in 1792 gave land he bought from the execs of Edward
Newell Sr. to James Burrow, David Burrow and Drury Hobbs. [*The
relationship is not obvious.*] {PGR:168}

Burrow, William m. Elizabeth (N). Their dau. Elizabeth b. 5 Feb 1734/5.
{BPR:287}

Bursby, Simon m. Martha (N). Their children: Anne (b. 28 Jan 1725) and
Elizabeth (b. 7 Jan 1729). {BPR:281, 283}

Burton, Abraham m. Mary (N). Their children: Elizabeth (b. Apr 1726),
Abraham (b. 28 Jan 1727), Phebe (b. 11 Sep 1730) and Robert (b. 24
Aug 1732). {BPR:281, 282, 283, 285}

Burton, Charles m. Lovedy (N). Their son Henry b. 17 Jan 1734.
{BPR:286}

Burton, Hesther was presented in 1739 for having a bastard child.
{CCCR:86}

Burton, John m. 1st Catherine (N). Their son John b. 7 Sep 1725.
Catherine d. 10 Sep 1725. John m. 2nd Sarah (N). Their children: Mary
(b. 15 Jun 1728), Martha (b. 25 May 1732) and Rachell (b. 13 Feb 1734).
{BPR:281, 282, 284, 286}

Burton/Berten/Benton, Lazarus m. Winefred (N). Their children: Abram
(b. 17 Dec 1726) and David (b. 16 Sep 1729). {BPR:282}

Burton, Ralph d. by 1744 leaving a widow, Mary Burton. Two of his children, William and James, were bound out. In 1755 James and Elizabeth Burton, orphans of Ralph Burton, chose Mary Sorrel as their guardian. Dau. Sarah was appointed a guardian in 1755. Later in 1758 the name of the guardian was Mary Bullifant. {CCCR:102, 107, 126, 130, 139}

Burton, Robert m. Ann (N). Their dau. Frances b. 11 Oct 1732. {BPR:284}

Burton, William m. by Jul 1753, Susanna (N). {CCCR:128}

Burton, William m. (bond dated 31 Mar 1788), May Baily. {MB:194}

Burwell, Major Lewis, son of Lewis Burwell, m. 1st Abigail Smith (d. 1692), dau. of Anthony and Martha (Bacon) Smith of Colchester, England. Their children: Joanna, Elizabeth, Nathaniel, Lewis, Lucy, Martha, Bacon, Jane and James. Lewis Burwell m. 2nd Martha (Lear) Cole, dau. of Col. John Lear and widow of William Cole. Their children: a dau. who m. Henry Seaton, a son who d. young, Mary (d. young), Lewis, Jane (d. young) and Martha. {CCOB (1687-95):204; APP1:433-4 (See APP1 much more detail on the Burwells.)}

Busby, Simon m. Martha (N). Their children: Drury (b. 11 Dec 1732) and Miles (b. 11 Dec 1732. {BPR:284}

Busby, Thomas m. bef. 29 Oct 1686 Suzanne (N). {PGW&D (1713-1728):25-6}

Busby, Thomas (d. by 1723) of Waynoke Parish m. bef. 4 Mar 1694, Mary (N). Children: Simon, Mary (m. (N) Mallone), Sarah (m. (N) Jones), Elizabeth (m. (N) Brewer) and Lucy. {CCOB (1687-95):200; PGW&D (1713-1728):91}

Butler, (N) m. 1st (N)(N) and m. 2nd Mutus, widow of (N) Newhouse. In her LWT (dated 1710/11, recorded 1713) Mutus Butler named sons: Raize Newhouse and John Butler *(step-son)*. {PGW&D (1710-1713):33}

Butler, Betsey of Petersburg d. 16 Sep 1794. {BPR:295}

Butler, Elizabeth had a son John b. 10 Feb 1725. {BPR:284}

Butler, James of Dinwiddie Co. m. bef. Apr 1760, Tabitha (N). {PGR:78}

Butler, John d. by 1658 leaving a widow, Mary, who m. (N) West. {CCOB (1658-61):151}

Butler, John (d. by 1719), step-son of Mutus Butler, m. bef. 14 Apr 1713, Mary (N). John Butler and wife Mary and Elizabeth Woodley/Woodlief, sold land in 1713 that they inherited from James Wallace. Children: James, Joseph, William, John and Sarah. {PGM:3; PGW&D (1710-1713):33; PGW&D (1713-1728):25-6, 49-50}

Butler, John m. Ann (N). Their children: John (b. 15 Apr 1730), Martha (b. 23 Apr 1732), James (b. 14 Mar 1734) and Ann (b. 25 Sep 1743). {BPR:283, 284, 289}

Butler, John m. Sarah (N). Their children: Elizabeth (b. 23 Jan 1753), Mary (b. 28 Nov 1755), William (b. 11 Nov 1758) and John (b. 6 Jul 1762). {BPR:292}

Butler, John of Dinwiddle Co., Bath Parish, m. bef. 14 May 1759, Sarah (N). {PGR:68}

Butler, Joseph m. Fanny (N). Their dau. Ann b. 8 Dec 1766. {BPR:293}

Butler, Samuel m. bef. Aug 1738, Elizabeth (N). {CCCR:83}

Butler, Sion m. Dionicia (N). Their son Sterling b. 11 Sep 1792. {BPR:294}

Butler, Thomas m. Martha (N). Their son John b. 25 Jun 1740. {BPR:287}

Butler, William m. Elizabeth (N). Their children: Sarah (b. 8 Dec 1714), Joseph (b. 5 Jan 1719) and Peter (b. 20 Oct 1732). {BPR:284, 285, 289}

Butler, William m. Margrett (N). Their children: Martha (b. 24 Sep 1735), Elizabeth (b. 4 Sep 1737), Sarah (b. 30 Jun 1740) and Jesse (b. 2 Aug 1742). {BPR:287, 288}

Butterworth, Charles m. Elizabeth (N). Their children: Charles (b. 18 Apr 1744) and Mary (b. 16 Jan 1743). {BPR:289, 290}

Butterworth, Nicholas m. Ann (N). Their son Charles b. 6 Jan 172-. {BPR:280}

Byrd, William (d. by Feb 1704) m. (N) (N). Children: Mary (youngest dau.), Susan (m. (N) Brain), Ursula (m. Robert Barverly, had son William, d. bef. her father), William Byrd, {SWBC: 31}

Byrd, William, Esq. (b. 28 Mar 1674, d. 26 Aug 1744) m. 1st Mary (d. 9 Nov 1699, in her 47th year), dau. of Warham Horsmanden. William m. 2nd 1706, Lucy Parke, dau. of Col. Daniel Parke. Their children: Evelyn (b. 1707, d. unm., 13 Nov 1737), Parke (b. 1709, d. 1710), Philip William (b. and d., 1712) and Wilhelmina (b. 1715, m. Thomas Chamberlayne of New Kent Co.). William m. 3rd 1724, Maria, dau. of Thomas Taylor of Kensington, England. Their childen: Ann (b. 5 Feb 1725, m. Charles Carter of King George Co.), Maria (b. 1727, m. Landon Carter), William (b. 1728) and Jane (b. 1729, m. John Page). {PGW&D (1710-1713):31; GVAT (Genealogies of Virginia Families) I:312; CCCR:81, 105; W&M Vol. 4, No. 3 (Jan., 1896):144-5}

Byrd, William, Esq. (age 41 in 1770), son of William Byrd, m. 1st Elizabeth Carter (d. 1760). Their children: William (b. 1749), John Carter (b. 1751), Thomas Taylor (b. 1752), Elizabeth Hill (b. 1754, m. 1st James Farley, m. 2nd Rev. John Dunbar, m. 3rd Col. Henry Skipwith) and Francis Otway (b. 1756). William m. 2nd Mary Willing of Philadelphia. Their children: Maria (b. 1761, m. John Page), Ann Willing (b. 1763), Charles Willing (b. 1765, d. 1766), Evelyn Taylor (b. 1766, m. Benjamin Harrison), Abby (b. 1767, m. Judge William Nelson), Dorothy (b. 1769, d. 1770), Charles Willing (b. 1770), Jane (b. 1773, m. Carter Harrison), Richard Willing (b. 1774, d. 1815) and William. {CCCR:24; GVAT (Genealogies of Virginia Families) I:312-15; CCCR:81, 105}

Bywater, Abraham (d. by Jul 1768) was the brother of Robinson Peacock Bywater. {SWBC:205}

Cabanis, Henry (d. by 1720) m. Mary (N). Children: Henry, Mathew and George. {PGW&D (1713-1728):64}

Cabinis, Mathew (d. 1789-90) m. bef. 9 May 1738, Hannah, dau. of Thomas Clay. Their children: Ann, Charles, Matthew, Mary (m. Francis Belcher), John, Phebe, George, Henry, Elijah, Hannah, Elizabeth and Amy Clay. {PGR:7; APP1:648}

Cain, William of Bristol Parish, gave his son William, 50 acres, Negro woman Lucy and Negro girl Amey. {PGR:111}

Calagham/Caligham, Morris d. by 1694, leaving a widow, Sarah who m. 2nd Robert Reives. {CCOB (1687-95):189, 209}

Call, William m. bef. 11 Jul 1759, Elizabeth (N). {PGR:72}

Call, William m. 17 Mar 1787, Hellen Walker. By Rev. John Buchanan. Their son Richard Keith, b. 24 Oct 1792. {BPR:303; HMM:96; PGR:101}

Calloway, Thomas m. by 1665 (N), widow of William Panton. {CCOB (1664-65):544}

Cameron, Rev. John m. Anne Owen (N). Their son Thomas b. 16 Jan 1793. {BPR:303}

Camp, James m. bef. 11 Dec 1739, Elizabeth (N). {PGM:60}

Cannell, Robert m. Katharine (N). Their son Moses b. 8 Feb 17--. {BPR:296}

Capell, Thomas (d. by 1689) m. (N), dau. of Thomas Drew. They had a son Edward. The widow of Thomas Capell m. 2nd Nicholas Mosier. {CCOB (1687-95):60; CCOB (Fragments):522}

Cardwell, Thomas (d. by 1789), probably m. Obedience (N). Children: William, Henry, Jane (d. by Feb 1796) and Elizabeth. {W&M, Vol. 23, No. 3 (Jan., 1915): 216; SWBC:52}

Cargill, Cornelius m. bef. 8 Jul 1712, Mary, widow of Thomas Anderson. {PGW&D (1710-1713): 21}

Cargill, Cornelius and Elizabeth Daniell were parents of William b. 15 Jun 1727. {BPR:297}

Caries, William m. Judith (N). Their dau. Mary b. 11 Dec 1741. {BPR:300}

Carlile, Richard (d. by 1739) m. bef. 7 Nov 1726 Mary, dau. of Samuel and Mary Tatum. Their children: Kasiah (b. 24 Aug 1715), Elizabeth (b. 2 May 1719), Richard and Nathaniel (b. 2 Jan 1721/2). {PGR:41; PGW&D (1713-1728):152; BPR:295, 296; APP 3:267}

Carlile, Richard m. Elizabeth (N). Their children: Elizabeth (b. 22 Aug 1744) and John (b. 9 Mar 1745/6). {BPR:301}

Carlos, John d. by 1746, William Carlos, exec. {CCCR:106}

Carnill, Daniel m. Sandilla (N). Their son George b. 31 Mar 1729. {BPR: 298}

Carsey, (N) m. Susan (N). They had a son John who was indentured to Daniel Massingal, later John Harrison, exec. of Daniel Massingal. {CCOB (1687-95):53}

Carter, Ann was presented in 1758 for having a bastard child. {CCCR:141}

Carter, Charles m. (N) (N). His children: Mildred W. Carter, Anne H. (wife of General Lee, mother of Carter Lee, Anna Lee, Smith Lee, Robert Lee, and Mildred Lee), Bernard Carter, and William Carter. (will of Mildred W. Carter dated 31 May 1807) {Legislative Petitions – Library of VA website}

Carter, Charles (b. 3 Sep 1762, Dinwiddie Co.). After the Revolution, he moved to Mecklenburg Co., VA and lived there about forty years, the moved to Roane Co., TN and lived there about two years, then moved to Smith Co., TN. {RWP}

Carter, Giles made a gift to his son Theodorick in 1741. {CCCR:91}

Carter, John m. (bond dated 12 Jan 1787), Elizabeth Collins. {MB:196}

Carter, Joseph (d. 1721) m. (N)(N). Children: John, Joseph, Richard and Ann. {PGW&D (1713-1728):73}

Carter, Joseph (d. 1760) m. Anne (N). Children: Joseph, John (had a son Joseph), William, Daniel, David (had a son Joseph), Elizabeth, Lucy and Sary (m. (N) Williams), Mary (m. John Brockwell, had son Carter Brockwell) and Anne (m. (N) Williams). One of the daus. m. Peter Williams and had a son Joseph Williams. {PGR:76; SWBC:205}

Carter, Richard m. bef. 25 Oct 1659, Sara (N). {CCOB (1658-61):207}

Carter, Sarah was presented in 1742 for having a bastard child. Received 20 lashes. {CCCR:97, 99}

Carter, Theodorick m. ca. 1772, Elizabeth, widow of Samuel Gregory. {CCCR:16, 144, 165}

Carvell/Carbell, Daniell d. by 1689 leaving a widow, Phebe, admx. {CCOB (1687-95):69}

Case, Richard d. by 1688. Children: son John Case, admin. and Elizabeth. {CCOB (1687-95):41}

Cate, James m. bef. 10 Feb 1791, Mary (N). James gave his son John 250 acres. {PGR:159}

Cate, John, son of James Cate, m. bef. 12 Sep 1791 Winny/Winifred (N). John sold the 250 acres his father (*above*) gave him. {PGR:159}

Caudle, John m. Mary (N). Their children: Elizabeth (b. 17 Jan 1722/3), Thomas (b. 5 Jan 172-), Mary (b. 172-) and David (b. 27 Feb 1729. {BPR:296, 297, 298}

Cavenaugh, Arthur m. ca. 1695, Mary, widow of Thomas Whitmell. {CCOB (1687-95):163, 209}

Cavanist, George m. Mary (N). Their son George b. 30 Jan 1740. {BPR:300}

Chalmers, Henry m. Frances (N). Their dau. Silvia b. 5 Dec 1743. {BPR:301}

Chamberlayne, Thomas (b. ca. 1652, d. 1719), m. 1st Mary (Wood) Bly, dau. of Major Gen. Abraham Wood of Charles City Co. and widow of John Bly. Thomas m. 2nd 1 Jun 1709, Elizabeth Stratton, dau. of Edward Jr. and Mary (Sheppey), Stratton. Their children: Elizabeth (m. Henry Batte) and Dorothy (m. Major Peter Jones). Elizabeth, widow of Thomas Chamberlayne, m. 2nd Gilbert Style/Fyfe. {APP3:167-8, 177-8; HMM:93 (Henrico Co. Court records); GVAW V:761; HCW 2:127, 151, 168}

Chambles, Henry m. Francise (N). Their son Joshua b. 15 May 1741. {BPR:300}

Chambles, John m. Sarah, dau. of Samuel Lee. Their children: dau. Frances (b. 24 Jan 1748/9), Elizabeth, and Peter. {BPR:301; PGW&D (1710-1713):20, 41; PGR:71; APP 3:288-9}

Chamless/Chamnis, Henry (d. 1717) m. Mary, dau. of John Moor. Children: John, Henry, William, Elizabeth, Mary, Ann, Nathaniel and Jacob. Wife mentioned in LWT of Henry but unnamed. Mary m. 2nd Jacob Denhart. {PGW&D (1713-1728):50-1, 68, 69, 143}

Chamlis, Henry m. Frances (N). Their children: Frances (b. 7 Nov 1732) and Mary (b. 26 May 1729). {BPR: 299}

Chamless, John m. bef. 14 May 1728, Elizabeth, dau. of Thomas Taylor of Southwark Parish, Surry Co., planter. {PGW&D (1713-1728):180}

Chambless, William (d. by Aug 1759) m. Agness (N). {SWBC:206}

Chamles, John m. Elizabeth (N). Their son James b. 6 Oct 1744. {BPR:301}

Chancey, William m. (bond dated 5 Jan 1783), Mary Timberlake. {MB:196}

Chandler, William m. Elizabeth (N). Their children: Isaac (b. 15 Apr 1732) and Abraham (b. 26 Feb 1735). {BPR: 299, 300}

Changely, Elizabeth, dau. of Tabitha Changely to be bound out to Thomas Blanks in 1745. {CCCR:107}

Chappell, Benjamin, son of Thomas Chappel, of Prince George Co., dec'd., m. 3rd da., 8th mo., 1754, Agnis Binford, dau. of John Binford of Charles City Co. Their children: Elizabeth (b. 13 Sep 1755, m. Stephen Peebles), Thomas (b. 22 Jan 1758, d. 13 Aug 1793). {HMM:29, 31; APP 3:752-3}

Chappell, James (d. in Sussex Co. 12 Feb 1769, age, 75), son of Thomas Chappell (b. ca. 1650), removed to Surry Co., m. 1st Elizabeth Howell, dau. of Thomas Howell. Elizabeth d. 20 Sep 1744. Their children: James, Thomas, Howell, John, Elizabeth (m. (N) Mason), Mary (m. (N) Gee), Sarah (m. (N) Mason), Rebecca (m. (N) Rorthington), Amy (m. (N) Smith) and Lucretia (m. (N) Carter). James m. 2nd Elizabeth (N) who d. 11 Jul 1762. {GVAW I:730}

Chapell, John, son of Thomas Chappel of Prince George Co. m. – da., 7th mo., 1741, Anne Simmon, widow of Thomas Simmon of the same county and dau. of Godfrey Fowler of Henry Co. {HMM:21}

Chappell, Robert (d. ca. 1724) m. Sarah (N). Children: Robert, Sarah, Mary, John, Ann and James (youngest son). {PGW&D (1713-1728):101}

Chappell, Robert m. Mary (N). Their dau. Anne b. 8 Feb 172-. {BPR:295}

Chappell/Chaple, Robert m. Elizabeth (N). Their children: Abraham (b. 6 May 1729) and Robert (b. 2 Apr 1732). {BPR:297, 298}

Chappell, Samuell d. by 1713, Ann Bolling, his extx. {PGW&D (1710-1713):41-2}

Chappell, Thomas (b. ca. 1612, d. by 1658), Richard son of Capt. John Chappell, master of the *Speedwell*, had a son Thomas and a dau. {GVAW I:729; CCOB (1658-61):159}

Chapell, Thomas (b. ca. 1650, d. 1694-1700), son of Thomas (b. 1612), m. Elizabeth, dau. of James Jones of Prince George Co. Children: Samuel, Thomas, James, Robert and a dau. who m. John Williams. {GVAW I:729; PGW&D (1713-1728):141}

Chappell, Thomas, had a dau. Sarah who m. James Binford.bef. 3 Jun 1678. {CCOB (1677-79:58}

Chapell, Thomas, son of Thomas Chapell of Prince George Co. m. 5th da., 10th mo., 1731, Margarett Hunnicut, dau. of Robert and Margaret (Wyke) Hunnicut of Prince George Co. {HMM:17} GVAW (Genealogies of Virginia Families) III:97-100}

Chapman, (N) m. Sarah, dau. of Henry and Rachel Gee. They had a son Allen. {PGR:170}

Chapman, Charles m. Frances (N). Their children: John (b. 26 Aug 1722) and Sarah (b. 18 Feb 172-). {BPR:296}

Chapman, John m. bef. Oct 1737, Rebecca (N). {CCCR:80}

Charles, Henry (d. by 1758) m. Elizabeth (N). His orphan son, Thomas chose Richard Hales as his guardian. Elizabeth m. 2nd Samuel Gregory. {CCCR:139, 144}

Charles, Thomas (d. by 1754) m. Margaret (N). Grandchildren: Thomas and Mary Charles. Possibly a dau. of Thomas Charles m. Samuel Gregory. {CCCR:127-8}

Charles, Thomas, son of Henry Charles, dec'd., of Charles City Co., m. 10th da., 7th mo., 1768 at Wain Oak Meeting House in Charles City Co., Lydia Ladd, dau. of James Ladd of the same county. Their children: Elizabeth (b. 21/8/1769), Henry (b. 23/7/1771, d. 9/3/1772), Mary (b. 23/11/1775, m. outside the Society of Friends by 7 Aug 1790) and Martha (b. 6/1/1778). {HMM:47, 61, 75}

Charles, William, Rev. War soldier, d.by 1792 leaving John Charles, heir at law. {Legislative Petitions – Library of VA website}

Chavis, Frances - Her/his son William Chavis was bound out in 1755. {CCCR:130}

Chavis, Margaret – Her son George Chavis and dau. Rebecca were bound out in 1761. {CCCR:150, 151}

Cheatham, George m. Nelly (N). Their son Walker b. 2 Apr 1792. {BPR:302}

Cheaves, John (d. by 1759) m. Mary (N), possible widow of William Russell. Son: William and probable dau. Elizabeth. {PGR:80}

Cheaves/Cheives/Cheeves, Thomas (d. by 1760) of Bristol Parish m. Mary (N). Their children: John (b. 3 Aug 1732), Susanah (b. 1 Aug 1734), Sarah (b. 2 Jan 1724/5), Thomas (b. 13 Nov 1738), Elizabeth (b. 15 Sep 1748), Tabitha (b. 27 Sep 1750) and Jemina (b. 1 Apr 1753). {BPR: 299, 300, 301; PGR:74}

Cheves, William m. Mary (N). Their son William b. 22 Dec 1740. {BPR:300}

Chevers, John m. Anne (N). Their son John b. 18 Jan 1741/2. {BPR:301}

Childers, Robert m. Agnis (N). Their dau. Susanna b. 28 Aug 1732. {BPR: 299}

Childs, Walter had a son Peter M. b. 14 Jan 1727. {BPR:297}

Childress, Matthew of Henrico Co. m. by Feb 1755, Sarah (N). {CCCR:130-1}

Childress, Robert m. Agnis (N). Their son John b. 20 Apr 1734. {BPR:300}

Chisnall, Alexander m. Mary (N). Their son Alexander b. 25 Dec 1729. {BPR: 298}

Chrecher, Titus m Hannah (N). She was bapt. 172-. Their children: Mourning (b. 5 Dec 1716), Millesin (b. 25 Jan 1719) and Agnis (b. 24 Aug 172-. {BPR:296}

Christian, Charles m. bef. 30 Jan 1727/8, Elizabeth, dau. of John Hunt. Their children: Elizabeth, Lucy, Susanna, Mary and John. {CCW&D 1725-31:48}

Christian, Charles m. (bond dated 3 Jun 1772), Rebecca Terrill (with Wm. Christian's consent). {MB:194}

Christian, Gideon (LWT probated in Charles City Co. in 1797), son of James Christian (of Thomas Christian, New Kent Co.) m. Susan, dau. of William and Alice (Eaton) Browne. Children: Eaton, Francis, Patrick, William Allen, Anne (m. (N) Hill), Alice (m. Samuel Trower), Fanny and Susanna (m. John Timberlake). {GVAW (Genealogies of Virginia Famiilies) I:781; MB:193, 194}

Christian, James m. Mary (N). Their dau. Mary b. 31 May 1741. {BPR:300}

Christian, James (d. 1747-50). Sons: Joel, Richard and probably James. {CCCR:112, 123; GVAW (Genealogies of Virginia Famiilies) I:783}

Christian, Joel m. bef. 24 Sep 1768, Sarah (N). {CCCR:10}

Christian, Joel, m. bef. 28 Feb 1769, Mildred (N). {CCCR:11}

Christian, John m. (bond dated 3 Feb 1768), Mary, widow of Nathaniel Maynard. Mary was mother of Elizabeth and Ann Maynard. {CCCR:15, 24; MB:195}

Christian, John (d. by 1768) m. Susanna (N) who became guardian of Edmund, Turner, William Brown, Elizabeth and Susanna Christian in 1768-70. {CCCR:28, 55}

Christian, Richard m. bef. Jun 1740, Lucy (N). {CCCR:88}

Christian, Richard of Sussex Co. m. Anne (N). Their dau. Lucy Grice b. 10 Mar 1791. {BPR:302}

Christian, Robert Walker, clerk of Charles City Co., son of Turner Christian, m. widow, Elizabeth Jones (nee Irby). Their children: Virginia (m. Col. James M. Willcox), Robert Walker Jr. (never married), Augustus (never married), Elizabeth (m. her cousin Dr. Edmund Oliver Christian), Richard (m. Martha S. Batte and d. without issue), Philip (never married) and Mary Lightfoot (never married). {GVAW (Genealogies of Virginia Famiilies) I:797}

Christian, Samuel, son of Richard Christian, m. 7 Sep 1768, Lucy (N). Children: Samuel, Richard, Benjamin and Isham. {CCCR:9}

Christian, Thomas m. bef. 30 Jan 1726, Elizabeth (N). {CCW&D (1725-31):19}

Christian, Turner Hunt m. by Feb 1755, Mary (N). In 1761 Turner Hunt Christian of Bedford Co. recorded a deed to William Christian of Charles City Co. {CCCR:131, 151}

Christian, William m. bef. 28 Feb 1769, Elizabeth, dau. of William and Mary Collier. {CCCR:11, 117, 118, 152, 157}

Church, Ann, servant of Thomas Grendon, had a bastard child by a Negro ca. 1678. {CCOB (1677-79):47}

Claiborne, Augustine m. Mary (N). Mary Claiborne of Windsor, Sussex Co. gave her sons Augustine Claiborne of Dinwiddle Co. and Thomas Claiborne of Sussex Co., several slaves in support of her dau. Elizabeth Peterson, wife of Thomas Peterson in 1787. {PGR:83}

Claiborne, Burnell of Dinwiddie Co. m. Hannah (Ravenscroft) Poythress, widow of Francis Poythress . Their children: Martha (b. 19 Feb 1744/5, d. 9 Feb 1825, m. Rev. Devereux Jarrrett), Thomas B. (b. 1 Feb 1747, Dinwiddie Co., d. 1811) and Sallie. {BPR:301; APP 1:619}

Claiborne, Daniel d. by 1790, Mary Claiborne, extx. {W&M, Vol. 23, No. 3 (Jan., 1915): 216}

Claiborne, Thomas B. of Brunswick Co., son of Burnell Claiborne, m. bef. 9 Jun 1789, Mary Clayton. {PGR:118; APP 1:619}

Clanthorne, William, son of William Clanthorne, complained in 1679 that his mother-in-law (step-mother who m. 1st his father and m. 2nd Richard Spencer), was likely to embezzle his inheritance. {CCOB (1677-79):100, 106}

Clark, (N) m. bef. 9 Oct 1771, Rebeckah (N). Son: Nathaniel Hamlin Clark. {CCCR:40}

Clarke, Bolling m. Phebe (N). Their son William b. 26 Jan 1745/6. {BPR:301}

Clarke, Lt. Col. Daniel d. by 1685 leaving sons: Joseph, Thomas and

Edward; and perhaps Daniel. {CCOB (Fragments, 1685):10; CCOB (1687-95):108}

Clarke, Daniel m. by Jun 1743, Martha (N). {CCCR:99}

Clarke, Henry d. by 1738 leaving a widow Rebecca. {CCCR:84}

Clarke, James d. by 1750, Sarah Clarke and William Clarke, execs. {CCCR:120}

Clark, James m. Henrietta Maria, dau. of John and Henrietta Maria (Taylor) Hardiman. They both d. by 1750. Dau. Frances chose John Hardyman as her guardian. A dau. m. Thomas Anderson. {CCCR:121; GVAT (Genealogies of Virginia Families) II:486; IV:536}

Clark(e), John (d. by 1759) m. Elisabeth (N). Their dau. Elisabeth b. 16 Mar 1740. {BPR:300; CCCR:141}

Clark, John m. Margret (N). Their son Daniel b. 17 Mar 1740. {BPR:300}

Clarke, Joseph m. Joice (N) bef. 1724. {SWBC: 32}

Clark, Joseph m. bef. 28 Apr 1730, Elizabeth (N). He and his son Daniel were added to list of tithables in 1737. {CCW&D (1725-31):41; CCCR:80}

Clarke, Joseph m. Elizabeth (N). Their son William b. 6 Jan 1741. {BPR:300}

Clarke, Joseph was presented for committing fornication with Rebecca Hodges. {CCOB (1687-95):69}

Clark, Lewis (b. 22 Apr 1763, Dinwiddie Co., d. 12 Jan 1842, Jackson Co., AL) m. 24 Sep 1800 (bond dated 11 Sep 1800), Sally Rogers (b. ca. 1780), at the home of her father in Dinwiddie Co. They moved to Franklin Co., TN in Mar 1820, and in 1829 they moved to Jackson Co., AL. This was apparently a 2nd marriage for Lewis Clark, since his son Joseph S. Clarke of Lincoln Co., TN, stated he was present at the marriage of his father and Sally Rogers. {RWP}

Clarke, Mary was presented in 1745 for having a bastard child. John Wayless entered as security for the fine. Case dismist. {CCCR:106}

Clarke, Thomas m. bef. 3 Oct 1688, Mary, widow of John Edwards. They probably had a son Edward. {CCOB (1687-95):14, 30, 99}

Clarke, Thomas (d. by Nov 1794) m. Lucy (N) {Legislative Petitions – Library of VA website}

Clarke, William was ordered in 1739 to care for his brother John who was disordered in his senses. {CCCR:85}

Clark, William d. by 1754, Mary Clark, extx. {CCCR:126}

Clarke, William d. by 1761, Rebecca Clarke, admx. {CCCR:150}

Clarke, William m. (bond dated 4 Sep 1781), Ann Leonard (Spinster), dau. of William Leonard. {MB:195}

Clay, Charles m. Mary (N). Their son John b. 2 Jan 1733. {BPR:299}

Clay, John (d. by 1655) m. 1st ca. 1624, Ann (N). Their son: William. John m. 2nd by 1645, Elizabeth (N). Their son: Charles. Elizabeth m. 2nd John Wall. {APP1:643-4; CCOB (1655-58): 24; CCOB (1658-61):245}

Clay, John (d. 1710-12) m. Mary (N). Children: Thomas, John (res. Chowan Co., NC), Charles, Elizabeth and Judith. {PGW&D (1710-1713): 20-1; APP 1:645}

Clay, Thomas (d. 1726) may have m. a sister of Richard Munns. Children: Charles, James, John, Dorothy, Phoebe, Hannah (m. Mathew Cabinis) and Amy (b. 9 Mar 172-). {PGR:7; BPR:296; APP 1:645-6; PGW&D (1713-1728):152}

Clayton, John m. Sarah (N). Their son Isham b. 1 Nov 1727. {BPR: 299}

Clayton, William B., clerk of Charles City Co., m. Lockey Walker. Daus.: Catherine, Elizabeth (m. Bartholomew Dandridge) and Mary A. (m. Robert C. Walker, son of Wyatt and Elizabeth (Christian) Walker). {GVAT (Genealogies of Virginia families) III:106}

Clements, Cornelius d. by 1673 leaving a widow, Ann. {CCOB (Fragments):510-11}

Clements, George, son of Benjamin Clements (son of Benjamin Clements) m. bef. 18 Dec 1754, Lucy Washington, dau. of Thomas Washington of Surry Co. (of Richard Washington). Their children:

Thomas Washington (m. Martha Edwards or Edmunds), James (m. Lucretia Cotton), Elizabeth, Lucy, George and Richard. {GVAT (Genealogies of Virginia Families) I:377, 384}

Clements, George of Southampton Co., son of George Clements (son of Benjamin Clements), sold land in 1787, devised by Benjamin Clements, his grandfather. {PGR:84}

Clements, James, son of George Clements, m. Lucretia Cotton. Their dau. Rebecca m. Richard Moore. A son of James Clements d. 1795. {GVAT (Genealogies of Virginia Families) I:377, 384; BPR:303}

Clemonds, John m. Mary (N). Their children: Prissilla (b. 30 Jun 1750), Mary (b. 16 May 1754), Margret (b. 1 Dec 1757), Elizabeth (b. 25 Dec 1762) and William (b. 28 May 1760). {BPR:301, 302}

Clements, Thomas of Southampton Co., son of George Clements, sold land in 1787, devised by Benjamin Clements, his grandfather. {PGR:84; GVAT (Genealogies of Virginia Families) I:377, 384}

Clements/Clemans/Clemmonds, Thomas Washington/also Washington Clements and also Thomas Clements (b. Prince George Co.) m. Martha Edwards [or Edmunds or Edloe]. Their children: Rebeckah (b. 10 Nov 1733), Freeman (b. 26 Jun 1735), Thomas (b. 12 Dec 1742), Robert (b. 11 Nov 1744), Lockie (dau.) (b. 20 Feb 1748) and Joshua (b. 24 Nov 1752). {GVAT (Genealogies of Virginia Families) I:378; BPR:299, 300, 301, 302}

Clensy, Cornelius m. Sarah (N). Their dau. Anne b. 10 Feb 1733. {BPR:299}

Clifton, Edward, "brother" of William, John and Henry Clark, d. 1726. {CCW&D (1725-31):10}

Clifton, Thomas of Martins Brandon Parish (d. 1724) m. Mary (N). Children: William, Elizabeth and another dau. {PGW&D (1713-1728):127}

Clopton, Robert d. by 1760, Mary Binns, wife of John Binns, admx. {CCCR:144}

Coates, John, age 32 in 1741. {CCCR:93}

Cobb, Robert had a son Oather, b. 1 Jan 1731. {BPR: 298}

The Cocke Family. For the English origins of the Cocke Family, see
GVAW II. See also APP1 for much more detail on the Cocke family.

Cocke, Abraham, son of Stephen (d. by 1711) and Martha (Batte) Cocke,
m. ca. 1729, Charles City Co., Mary Batte (b. 1710, d. 4 Nov 1780), dau.
of William and Mary (Stratton) Batte. Children: Abraham (b. 30 Sep
1730), Peter, Mary (m. Richard Ellis), Agnes (m. Charles Hamlin Jr.),
Stephen, John, Martha (m. Theophilus Lacy), Elizabeth (1st John Cross,
m. 2nd William Sydnor), Thomas and William. {APP1:130, 147-9;
APP3:167}

Cocke, Edward (d. intestate 1726) m. Mary, niece of Abraham Hamlin*.
Children: Martha (m. 1st (N) Pendexter, m. 2nd Thomas Vaughan), Mary
(m. Rabley Vaughn) and Edward. {CCW&D (1725-31):14, 18, 35 (gives
name as Abranas. Haulin)}

Cocke, Benjamin of Prince George Co. m. Mary, dau. of Richard Eppes.
Their children: Elizabeth (d. infant), Dr. Richard, Mary (d. in infancy)
and John (d. in infancy). {GVA (Genealogies of Virginia Families II, Cl-
Fi:711-13)}

Cocke, Benjamin (d. by 1787) m. by Nov 1760, Agathy, widow of
Samuel Harwood and dau. of Robert and Elizabeth (Cocke) Poythress of
Prince George Co. Their children: James (m. Elizabeth Poythress),
Pleasant (m. Mary Noble). {CCCR:145; APP1:130; APP2:325-6;
PGR:106}

Cocke, Bowler (b. 1696, d. 1771 in Charles City Co.), son of Richard and
Ann (Bowler) Cocke, m. 1st Sarah Fleming. Their children: Susanna (b.
1712, d. 1713), Anne (b. 18 Jun 1720), Susanna (b. 6 Nov 1722, d.
1723), Tabitha (b. 25 Sep 1724), Bowler (b. 11 Mar 1726, d. 1772),
Sarah (b. 6 Feb 1728), Elizabeth (b. 15 May 1731), Richard (b. 7 Mar
1733, d. 25 days later) and Charles (b. 9 Sep 1735, d. 4 Aug 1739).
Bowler m. 2nd ca. 1745, Elizabeth Carter, widow of Col. John Carter and
dau. of Col. Edward Hill of *Shirley*. No issue by his second marriage.
{HMM:101; GVA (Genealogies of Virginia Families II, Cl-Fi:119-20,
132, 156); APP:132-3}

Cocke, James d. by 1791, leaving orphans, John and Thomas.
{PGR:153}

Cocke, James Powell (d. 1747), son of Thomas Cocke (d. 1707), m.
1718, his step-sister, Martha Herbert, dau. of John Herbert (d. 1704) of

Prince George Co. and his wife Frances (Anderson) Herbert. Children: Martha and James Powell (m. Mary Magdalene Chastain). Martha Cocke, probably James Powell Cocke's widow, d. by 1757 {GVA (Genealogies of Virginia Families II, Cl-Fi:114-16, 125, 125-8); APP1:128, 138; HCW 2:36, 72}

Cocke, John m. Elizabeth, widow of Littlebury Hardyman and dau. of Peter Eppes (d. 1773). {CCCR:53-4; APP1:870, 911}

Cocke, Littleberry (d. by 1773), Gent., m. bef. 11 Feb 1754, Rebecca Hubbard Edloe, dau. of John and Rebecca (Huberd) Edloe and widow of Henry Soane. Their dau.:Rebecca m. James Bray Johnson. In 1761Littlebury, his wife Rebecca Hubbard Cocke and Mary Tyree recorded a deed to William Kennon. {APP1:847-8, 850-1; CCCR:10, 53, 147; GVAW I:448}

Cocke, Pleasant (d. intestate in 1794, Prince George Co.) m. Mary Noble. Children: Benjamin, George, Ann, Mary, Agnes, Robert and Samuel Cocke, five of whom were underage in 1794. {Legislative Petitions – Library of VA website; APP2:326}

Cocke, Richard (b. ca. 1600, d. 1665), son of John and Elizabeth Cocke of Wallfurlong, parish of Stottesdon, Shropshire, England, m. 1st Temperance (Baley) Browne, widow of John Browne and probable dau. of Sisley Jordan. Richard and Temperance were parents of Thomas (b. 1638, d. 1696-8), Richard the elder (b. 1639, d. 1706) and Elizabeth. Richard m. 2nd Mary Aston, dau. of Lt. Col. Walter Aston. Richard and Mary were parents of John (b. 1647), William Fleming (b. 1655, d. 1693), Richard the younger, and Edward (b. after his father's death). Mary, widow of Richard Cocke, m. 2nd Daniel Clarke of Charles City Co. {GVA (Genealogies of Virginia Families II, Cl-Fi:104-111, 255); APP1:120-2; HCW 1:219-20}

Cocke, Richard (d. 1706), the younger, son of Richard and Mary (Aston) Cocke (d. 1665), m. Elizabeth (N). Their children: Richard, Elizabeth, Martha and John. They probably had dau. Anne (who m. Robert Bolling (b. 1682, d. 1749) of Charles City Co. {GVA (Genealogies of Virginia Families II, Cl-Fi:104, 124, 138); APP1:123}

Cocke, Richard (b. 1672, d. 1720), son of Richard Cocke (d. 1706) m. 1st ca. 1695 Anne Bowler (b. 1674/5, d. 1705), dau. of Col. Thomas and Tabitha (Underwood) Bowler of Old Rappahannock Co. Richard m. 2nd Rebecca (N). Richard and Anne were parents of Bowler, Martha (m. Thomas Adams), Tabitha (m. Ebenezer Adams, res. New Kent Co.) and

John. Children by Rebecca: Richard (b. ca. 1706, Benjamin and Anne (m. William Acrill of Charles City Co.). {HCW 2:156; APP1:125-35; GVA (Genealogies of Virginia Families II, Cl-Fi:104-8, 119-20, 132) *has another dau. Mary who m. (N) Eppes*. [Eppes? (See also HCDB (1750-1774):165]}

Cocke, Richard d. testate by 1749. Jane Cocke, extx. {CCCR:118, 124}

Cocke, Richard d. by 1754, Alice Cocke, admx., who also d. by 1754. {CCCR:129}

Cocke, Stephen (b. 1664, d. by 1711 in Prince George Co.), son of Thomas and Agnes (Powell) Cocke (d. 1698), m. 1st 1688, Mrs. Sarah Marston and m. 2nd May 26th 1694 Mrs. Martha (Batte) Banister, admx. of Rev. John Bannister (d. by 1694) and dau. of Thomas Batte. Children (by Martha): Abraham (b. ca. 1690, d. 1760, settled in Charles City Co. (that part that became Amelia Co.), Batte (d. young), Charles (b. 1735, d. 1739) and Agnes (m. Richard Smith). {APP1:124; GVA (Genealogies of Virginia Families II, Cl-Fi:116, 129-30; HMM:90, 91 (Henrico Co. Court records); HMM:101; CCOB (1687-95):191; PGW&D (1710-1713):10, 40}

Cocke, Thomas (b. 1638, d. 1697), son of Richard and Temperance (Baley) Cocke, m. 1st ca. 1661, Agnes Powell and m. 2nd 1663 Margaret Jones (d. 1718-19), widow of Peter Jones and step-dau. of Major General Abraham Wood and grandmother of Major Peter Jones, founder of Petersburg. Thomas and Agnes were parents of Thomas (1664-1707), Stephen (1666-1717), William (d. 1717)*, James (1667-1721), Agnes (b. ca. 1672, m. Capt. Joseph Harwood of Charles City Co.) and Temperance (b. ca. 1670, m. Capt. Samuel Harwood). Margaret d. 1718. In her LWT she named sons: Abraham (d. by 1718) and Peter Jones. She also named grandchildren: Margaret (m. Edward Goodrich), Mary (m. John Worsham), Joshua, Peter, Robert, William and Francis Wynn; Margaret Jones; and Peter Jones (son of Abraham Jones dec'd.).{GVA (Genealogies of Virginia Families II, Cl-Fi:104-8, 118, 231-2); APP1:122-3; HCW 1:62-4, 229} *Not John as stated on p. 106 of GVA.

Cocke, Thomas, son of Thomas and Agnes (Powell)? Cocke, m. 1st 1687, Mary Brasseur of Nansemnod Co., dau. of John and Mary (Pitt) Brasseur. Their children: Thomas (b. ca. 1687), James Powell, Henry (b. ca. 1696, lost at sea), Brazure, Mary and Elizabeth. Thomas m. 2nd Frances (Anderson) Herbert, widow of John Herbert. Frances m. 3rd Capt. Joshua Wynne. {APP1:123-4; PGW&D (1710-1713):14}

Cogan, John m. bef. 3 Jun 1659 (N), widow of Capt. Richard Tye. {CCOB (1658-61):185}

Coggs, John m. bef. 3 Jan 1684, Elizabeth (N). {CCCR:164}

Coiled, Robert m. bef. 6 Feb 1771, Frances (N). {CCCR:32}

Colbreth, Evin m. Affa (N). Their dau. Martha b. 8 Feb 1740. {BPR:300}

Cole, Edmond d. by 1677. Anne Cole was ordered to pay his note. {CCOB (1677-79):35}

Cole, Robert (d. 1717-18, owning land in Charles City Co.) of Varina Parish, m. Easter (N). Children: Robert (res. in Henrico Co. in 1730), Joseph, Aphara (had a son John) and James. {HCW 1:145; CCW&D (1725-31):42}

Cole, William (d. by 1751) m. Elizabeth (N). Children: William, Richard, and Mary (m. Richard Cary). Philip Edmondson was appointed their guardian in 1755. Elizabeth m. 2nd Philip Par Edmondson in 1756. {CCCR:131; APP1:716-7}

Cole, William, son of William and Elizabeth Cole, m. bef. 3 Feb 1770, Susanna Digges, dau. of William and Frances (Robinson) Digges. Their children: William, Capt. John, Sarah, Mary (m. Thomas Woolfolk), Susannah, Richard, Joseph, Ann (m. Edmund Anderson) and Elizabeth (m. Joseph Holt Irwin). {CCCR:24; APP 1:718-19, 842}

Cole, William (b. 17/18 Jan 1753, d. by 1806) m. Anne (N) (d. 8 Jul 1809 at Petersburg). Their children: perhaps Ann/Nancy and William (b. 22 Jan 1792, d. 1823 in Prnce George Co., m. Elizabeth Poythress Cocke, dau. of John Poythress and Elizabeth Buchanan (Peter) Cocke. {APP 1:721; BPR:302}

Coleby, William d. by 1688. His widow, Joane, m. 2nd William Window. {CCOB (1687-95):22}

Coley, George of Westover Parish, m. bef. 22 Feb 1725/6) Dorcas/Darcis (N). {CCW&D (1725-31):9}

Coley, Isham m. bef. 4 Apr 1771, Hannah (N). {CCCR:36}

Coley, Thomas m. bef. 8 Aug 1730, Anna, dau. of John Rogers. Son: William. {CCW&D (1725-31):42}

Coleman/Coalman, Daniel m. Elizabeth (N). Their children: Benjamin (b. 14 Dec 172-), Martha (b. 20 Nov 1726) and Daniel (b. 24 May 1731) {BPR:297, 298}

Coleman, Francis Sr. m. bef. 13 Jul 1719, Honor (N). Sons: John and Francis. {PGW&D (1713-1728):52-3, 77}

Coleman, Francis Jr. m. bef. 7 Aug 1719, Mary (N). They sold 150 acres in Bristol Parish. Their children: John (b. ca. 1721?), Amy (b. 23 May 17— and William (b. 2 May 1733). {PGW&D (1713-1728):55; BPR:295, 296, 299, 300}

Coleman, John, son of Robert Coleman, m. bef. 8 May 1725, Mary Ligon, dau. of Richard and Mary (Worsham) Ligon. Their dau. Mary Ligon (b. 18 Jul 1731). {PGW&D (1713-1728):138; BPR: 298; APP 2:268-9, 276}

Coleman, Joseph m. Elizabeth (N). Their son William b. 8 Mar 1734. {BPR:300}

Coleman, Robert d. (1675-1688) leaving sons: William, John and Robert (b. by 1664, granted admin. of Warner Coleman's estate and guardianship of his brother, John). {CCOB (1664-65):508; CCOB (1687-95):38; PGW&D (1710-1713):2}

Coleman, William m. Faith (N). Their children: Peter (b. ca. 1721?) {BPR:295}

Coleman/Coalman, William m. Sarah (N). Their children: (N) (b. 18 Aug 1728), Martha (b. 10 Sep 1730), William (b. 23 Jun 1732) and Sarah (b. 20 Mar 1734). {BPR:297, 298, 299}

Coalman, William m. Margaret (N). Their children: Anne (b. 11 Apr 1731) and Margery Lucas (b. 24 Sep 1733). {BPR: 298, 299}

Coalman, William m. Elizabeth (N). Their son Warner b. 20 Mar 1732. {BPR: 299}

Colgill, William m. bef. 15 Sep 1677, Joane/Jane (N). {CCOB (1677-79):20, 21}

Collawn, Charles m. by May 1748, Joanna (N). Charles Collawn d. by 1758, William Collawn, admin. {CCCR:115, 141}

Collawn, (N) m. Elizabeth, sister of Richard Poynter. {CCCR:153}

Colly, Nathaniel m. bef. 10 Oct 1791, Martha, dau. of Robert Batte Sr. {PGR:164}

Collier, Joseph d. by 1744, Elizabeth Collier and William Collier, execs. {CCCR:105}

Collier, Thomas d. intestate by 1741, leaving widow Rebecca who m. 2nd John Minge. {CCCR:90, 97}

Collier, William m. bef. 3 Nov 1773, Agnes Anne (N). {CCCR:60}

Collier, William (d. testate by 1748) m. Mary. Their children: Charles (m. Milly (N), Mildred, William and Elizabeth (m. William Christian). His son William chose William Christian his guardian in 1761. {CCCR:117, 152}

Collup, Thomas m. bef. 10 Mar 1723, Elizabeth (N). {PGW&D (1713-1728):103}

Colvill, Edward m. Tabitha (N). Their dau. Anne b. 10 Aug 1721. {BPR:295}

Comboo, Richard of Westover Parish m. bef. 2 Feb 1724, Ann (N). {CCW&D (1725-31):1}

Conner, John d. by 1745, Elizabeth Curl, heir at law to be summoned to court. {CCCR:106}

Cook, Benjamin m. Frances (N). Their dau. Elizabeth b. 15 Mar 1745/6. {BPR:301}

Cook, John m. Dinah (N). Their son Richard b. 27 Jul 1729. {BPR:297}

Cook, Richard m. Elizabeth (N). Their children: Peter Hannor (b. 28 Feb 17--), Ruth (b. 1 Apr 17--) and Sarah (b. 18 Dec 172-). {BPR:295, 296, 297}

Cook, Richard of Sussex Co. m. Jean (N). Their son Henry b. 22 Aug 1790. {BPR:302}

Cook, Robert m. Winiford/Winifrid (N). Their children: John (b. 29 Sep 1724), Nickols (b. 28 Jul 1731) and Fredirick (b. 15 Dec 1734).

{BPR:297, 298, 300}

Cooper, John d. by 1717, Elizabeth, admx. {PGW&D (1713-1728):25}

Corbett, Richard m. by Nov 1755, Mary (N). {CCCR:43, 133}

Corbin, William m. Rosey (N). Their children: Elizabeth (b. 20 Apr 1760) and Rosey (b. 27 Feb 1764). {BPR:302}

Cordle, John m. Mary (N). Their children: Lucretia (b. 7 May 1727) and Sarah (b. 19 Oct 1732). {BPR:297, 299}

Cordle, Sampson m. bef. Apr 1737, Sarah, dau. of Thompson Gregory. {CCCR:78}

Corney, Rebecca, servant of John Baxter was convicted of having a mulatto bastard and fined, 5 Aug 1689. {CCOB (1687-95):54}

Cornwell, Jacob of Surry Co. m. 6th da., 11th mo., 1745, Elizabeth Crew, dau. of John Crew of Charles City Co., at the meeting house near the White Oak Swamp in Henrico Co. {HMM:23-4}

Cotton, John m. Celah (N). Their dau. Becky b. Apr 1792. {BPR:334}

Cotton, Richard (d. by 1718) m. Susanna, dau. of Francis Wyatt (d. by 1718. {PGW&D (1713-1728):36}

Cotton, William Sr. (d. 1787) of Brandon Parish m. Lucy (N). Children: John, Mary, Smith, William, Frances and Martha. {PGR:94}

Couch, Thomas m. Elizabeth (N). Their son Matthew b. 24 Jul 1725. {BPR:297}

Courtney, Philip (b. ca. 1609) probably m. Joyce (N) (b. ca. 1624). {CCOB (1661-64):454}

Cousens, Charles m. Margery (N). Their children: George (b. 9 Sep 1721) and Anne (b. 8 Jan 1730). {BPR:295, 298}

Covington, Thomas m. Mary (N). Their dau. Catharine b. 16 Feb 1733. {BPR:299}

Cowles, Thomas (d. 1770) m. (N)(N). Children: John, William Marston, Thomas, Martha (m. William Stith), Mary (m. William Broadnax) and

(N) (m. John Coleman). {CCCR:26-7}

Cox, Benjamin m. Frances (N). Their dau. Mary b. 28 Apr 1742. {BPR:301}

Cox, Charles Henry d. by 1748 leaving a widow Mary who m. 2nd William Finch. Daus. of Charles Henry and Mary Cox: Sarah (m. William Lacy), Henryann, Rebecca and Donita. Rebecca and Donita chose William Finch as their guardian. {CCCR:114, 115}

Cox, John m. Lucretia (N). Their children: Sarah (b. 2 Nov 1735) and George (b. 12 Jan 1741). {BPR:300}

Cox, Samuel m. Ellinor (N). Their dau. Elizabeth b. 29 Aug 1759. {BPR:302}

Cozier, John m. Elizabeth (N). Their son Dunnim (b. 28 Jul 1734). {BPR:300}

Crabb, Francis (d. by 1713) m. Sarah (N). Daus.: Frances and Agnes. {PGW&D (1713-1728):1, 4}

Crabb, James of Wynoke Parish d. intestate, by 1694, Sarah his widow. {CCOB (1687-95):174}

Crabb, John d. by 1677, Richard Smith, admin, m. the widow. {CCOB (1677-79):19}

Cradock, (N) (d. by 1656) m. Hester (N). Their children: Robert (age 15 in 1656), Hester and Jone (youngest dau.). {CCOB (1655-58):52}

Craddock, Robert (d. by 1755) m. Sarah (N). Children: Elizabeth, Sarah and Ann. In 1761 Mary Cradocke was granted administration of the estate. {CCCR:38-9, 130, 146}

Craddock, William m. Mary (N). Elizabeth Thompson stipulated in 1769 that following her death, William Craddock and his wife Mary to receive 50 acres devised to said Elizabeth by the will of Ling Thompson dated 1760. {CCCR:17}

Crawley, David (d. ca. 1726, owning land in Prince George Co., Brunswick Co. and land in NC) m. Tabitha (N). Children: George, William and David. {PGW&D (1713-1728):150}

Crawley, William of Amelia Co. d. by 1738, leaving an infant son, William. {PGR:33}

Crew, Abigall, dau. of Joseph Crew, having married a husband, not of the Society, was disowned. Reported 4/12/1743. Disowned -/7/1744. {HMM:22, 25}

Crew, Andrew (son of John Crew) of Charles City m. 12th da., 2nd mo., 1720, Hanah Elyson,, dau. of Robert Elyson of New Kent Co. They married in Charles City Co. {HMM:10}

Crew, Andrew, elder and member of Waynoak Meeting d. 27th da., 6th mo., 1786. {HMM:71, 89}

Crew, Andrew, son of --- Crew, of Charles City Co., m. 11th mo., 1752, Elizabeth Ellyson, widow of Mathew Ellyson of New Kent Co. at the meeting house in Henrico Co. Children of Andrew and Elizabeth Crew: Joseph (twin), b. 16/9/1753; Benjamin (twin), b. 16/9/1753; Andrew, b. 25/2/1755; Hannah, b. 25/6/1757; Elizabeth, b. 3/9/1759. Elizabeth, wife of Andrew Crew, d. 13/7/1779. {HMM:27, 61, 62}

Crew, Andrew. In 1755 Sarah, dau. of Andrew Crew, was reported for her outgoing in marriage to her first cousin. {HMM:30}

Crew, Andrew recorded in 1761 a deed of gift to his son James Crew. {CCCR:151}

Crew, Andrew, son of Andrew and Elizabeth Crew of Charles City Co. m. 6th da., 8th mo., 1776, Mary Binford, dau. of John Binford of afsd. co. They removed to the limits of Rich Square Monthly Meeting, NC ca. 1785. {HMM:55, 69}

Crew, Andrew, son of Gatley Crew, a member of Black Creek Meeting, d. 20/8/1792. {HMM:62}

Crew, Ann had a son Joseph b. 27 Sep 1792. {BPR:303}

Crew, Benjamin (d. 4th da., 9th mo., 1792) m. Margaret (N). Their children: Robert Hunnicutt (b. 5/8/1768), Sarah (b. 7/4/17--), Margaret (b. 14/5/17-), Miriam (b. 28/3/1773), Elizabeth (b. 14/5/1775), Hannah (b. 8/5/1778), Joshua (b. 8/2/1781), Benjamin (b. 24/1/--, d. 22/2/1777), and Benjamin (b. 27/8/1783, d. 25/2/1826). Margaret Crew, mother of the above, d. 14/6/1789. {HMM:62}

Crew, Benjamin, Jr. m. 1787, Mary Ladd. Children of Benjamin and Mary Crew: Chappel, (b. 4th da., 12th mo., 1788, d. 9th da., 7th mo., 1824), Rebekah (b. 15th da., 10th mo., 1791), Exum (b. 28th da., 9th mo., 1793, d. 5th da., 6th mo., 1807), Daniel (b. 8th da., 12th mo., 1795), Isaac (b. 23rd da., 2nd mo, 1799). {HMM:72, 84}

Crew, David, son of John Crew of New Kent Co. m. 1st on 9th da., 11th mo., 1733, Mary Stanley, dau. of --- Stanly. Friends from Cedar Creek Meeting reported that he had walked orderly with them for about a year. Dau. Elizabeth m. ca. 1753 to one not in the Society of Friends (Quakers). In 1757 Sarah Crew of [Black CreekMeeting], dau. of David Crew, was delivered of a child [by another woman's husband], being unmarried [disowned]. David Crew m. 2nd on 4th da., 8th mo., 1754, Mary McGahea, widow of Saml. McGahea of Hanover Co. {HMM:18, 27-8, 31, 32}

Crew, Ellyson (d. aft. Dec 1722) m. Lydia (N). He was the brother of James and John Crew, and the cousin of Andrew Crew. Children: John, William, Ellyson (under 21 at father's death), Sarah, Ann, Lydia, and Mary. {SWBC: 33}

Crew, Ellyson, son of John and Agathy Crew, a member of Wainoak Meeting, b. 17/2/1718, d. 15/12/1772.---, father of the above ---, d. 16/10/---. Hannah Crew, wife of ditto, d. 21(?)/11/1774. {HMM:62}

Crew, Ellyson, son of John Crew of Charles City Co. m. 14th da., 9th mo., 1738, Lydia Lead, dau. of William Lead of the afsd. co. {HMM:20}

Crew, Ellyson had removed within the limits of Rich Square Monthly Meeting, NC by 1781. By 1784, Mary Crew, dau. of Ellyson Crew, had removed to within the verge of Richsquare Monthly Meeting, NC. {HMM:66, 69}

Crews, Edward, brother of James Crews, had an only dau. Sarah (m. (N) Whittingham). {HCW 1:9}

Crews, Francis, brother of James Crews, had a son Matthew. {HCW 1:9}

Crew, Gatley (d. by 1762), son of John Crew, Sr., of New Kent Co., m. 1st da., 9th mo., 1753, Elizabeth Macgahea (d. 7 Nov 1778), dau. of Samuel Macgahea of Hanover Co., dec'd. They m. at Huldah Ladds in Charles City Co. Their children: John, Elizabeth (d. 5 Apr 1779). In 1781 it was reported by Swamp Meeting that John Crew, son of Gatley, declined the attendance of meetings, has frequented loose company and used profane words and walked disorderly in several respects. {HMM:28, 62, 66; CCCR:153}

Crew, Huldah married ca. 1785 to a man outside the Society of Friends - disowned. {HMM:69}

Crew, Jacob m. ca. Feb 1784, Elizabeth Leadbetter. Children of Jacob and Elizabeth Crew: Sally Leadbetter (b. 9/12/1784), Henry (b. 6/8/1786), James (b. 11/9/1790), Micajah (b. 30/4/1793), Susannah (b. 4/11/1795), Jacob (b. 3/2/1798), Cornalius (b. 24/3/1804), Joel (b. 2/5/1807), and Elizabeth (b. 24/10/1810). {HMM:65, 69}

Crews, James d. by 1686. {HCW 1:21}

Crew, James m. Judith (N). In 1759 Judith, wife of James Crew moved to Henrico Monthly from Circular Monthly Meeting. In 1764 Judith, being removed with her family ca. 1764, requested a certificate to Cedar Creek Monthly Meeting. {HMM:35, 40}

Crew, James, son of John Crew of Charles City Co., m. 7th da., 9th mo., 1773, Ann Crew, dau. of Ellyson Crew of Charles City Co., at the meeting house in Charles City Co. In 1781 a certificate was requested for James Crew and wife to Rich Square Monthly Meeting, NC. {HMM;52, 60}

Crew, Jesse and Molly Vaughan married 4th da., 4th mo., 1780 at the meeting house at Wainoak. {HMM;60}

Crew, Jesse m. Margaret (N). Their children: Owin (d. 14th da., 9th mo., -- -), Jesse Milton (b. 11th da., 9th mo., 1817) and Margaret Owen (b. 2nd da., 8th mo., 1819). {HMM:84}

Crew, John m. bef. 4 Aug 1690, Sarah, orphan of Nicholas and Sarah Gattley. [Apparently both John and Sarah were under the age of 21 in 1690.] {CCOB (1687-95):85, 91}

Crew, John (d. by 1761), son of John Crew, of Charles City Co. m. 14th da., 3rd mo., 1717, Agatha Elyson, dau. of Robert Elyson of New Kent Co., at a meeting house in Charles City Co. The LWT of John Crew, was presented in 1761 by John Crew and Ellyson Crew, execs. Liberty was reserved to Agathy Crew, extx. to join in probate. {HMM:8; CCCR:150}

Crew, John m. Sarah (N). Their children: James (b. 25/11/1750), Judith (b. 13/11/1752), Jacob (b. 11/6/1754), John (b. 1/7/1758), Joseph (b. 12/3/1771). John's dau. Judith m. (N) Hubbard. {HMM:61; CCCR:148}

Crew, John, son of Andrew and Judeth Ladd, announced intentioned to marry on 3/11/1748. Denied by the Meeting because of their being first cousins. {HMM:25}

Crew, John, son of Ellyson Crew, dec'd., of Charles City Co. m. 9th da., 11th mo., 1773, Judith Crew, dau. of John Crew of afsd. co., in Charles City Co. {HMM:52}

Crew, John, son of Joseph, took a wife by the priest, to one not of the Society - disowned on 4/1/1755. {HMM:29}

Crew, John Jr. m. his 1st cousin, Meriam Crew. Children of John Crew and Meriam: Eleazer (b. 31st da., 1st mo., 1797, d. 16th da., 11th mo., 1822), Edna (b. 11th da., 12th mo., 1798), John Hunnicutt (b. 26th da., 3rd mo., ---, d. 3rd da., 9th mo., ---), Miriam (b. 23rd da., 11th mo., 1805) and Sarah (b. 5th da., 1st mo., 1808). {HMM:80, 84}

Crew, John (b. 16 Jul 1728, d. 31 Jan 1800) m. Mourning Scott (d. 15 May 1800), sister of Joseph Scott (d. by 1793 in Nansemond Co.). Their children: Robert Crew (moved to England, m. an English woman), Exum Scott Crew (d. by 1793) and Elizabeth. John Crew was appointed guardian to his children, Robert Crew, Exom Scott Crew and Elizabeth Crew, in 1761. {Charles City Co. Newsletter, Sep 1997; HCDB 4:43; CCCR:150}}

Crew, Joseph, son of John Crew of Charles City Co., m. 12 da., 6th mo., 1725, Massey Johnson, dau. of John Johnson of Hanover Co., at the meeting house in Hanover Co. Joseph had a dau. Martha who married outside the Society - disowned. {HMM:14, 34}

Crew, Joseph m. 10th da., 12th mo., 1782, Mary McManners of Charles City County at Waynoak Meeting House. Children of Joseph and Mary Crew: Clarey (b. 20/2/1785), Andrew (b. 11/7/1787), Mary (b. 22/11/1788), Bana (Rana?) (b. 12/11/1791), Elizabeth (b. 21/3/1793), Joseph (b. 25/2/1797) and Ezra (b. 14/3/1799). {HMM:65, 67}

Crew, Josiah and Mary How (New?) announced in 1738 their intentions to marry {HMM:20}

Crew, Josiah. Sarah Crew, dau. of Josiah Crew of Charles City Co. was disowned in 1766 for marrying by a priest to a man not of the Society - 7 da., 6 mo., 1766. {HMM:43}

Crew, Josiah. It was reported in 1796 that Elizabeth Crew [dau. of Josiah Crew, dec'd.] some time past delivered a bastard child. {HMM:80}

Crew, Lydia was delivered of a bastard child ca. 1787. {HMM:71}

Crew, Mary, dau. of Mary Crew had a bastard child ca. 1778. [disowned]. {HMM:57}

Crew, Mary d. 13th da., 3rd mo., (1775) in the 70th year of her age. {HMM:53}

Crew, Micajah, from Cedar Creek Monthly Meeting, son of Joseph Crew of Caroline Co., dec'd., m. 3rd da., 12th mo., 1775, Margaret Ladd, dau. of James Ladd of Charles City Co., at a meeting house in Charles City Co. {HMM:54}

Crew, Mildred m. bef. 7 May 1796, her first cousin contrary to discipline – disowned. {HMM:80}

Crew, Robert of Charles City Co. m. 17th da., 8th mo., 1703, Sarah Crispe (daughter of Mary Howard) of the same co. {HMM:3-4}

Crew, Robert, son of Josiah and Mary Crew, m. 1774 (N)(N) outside the Society of Friends (Quakers) - disowned. In 1779 he submitted a paper condemning his conduct along with recommendations from Friends of Jack Swamp Meeting in NC where he resided and requested a certificate to join him to Rich Square Monthly Meeting in NC. {HMM:52, 58-9}

Crew, Robert m. Nancy (N). Their children: Terrell (b. 17th da., 7th mo., 1795), Faris (b. 14th da., 4th mo., 1797), Pleasant (b. 17th da., 12th mo., 1798, d. 30th da., 8th mo., 1814), Rachel (b. 22nd da., 9th mo., 1800), Robert (b. 2nd da., 8th mo., 1802, d. 10th da., 8th mo., 1825?), Jesse (b. 2nd da., 5th mo., 1804), Catharine (twin with Benjamin), Benjamin (b. 28th da., 4th mo., 1806), Nancy (b. 7th da., 4th mo., 1808), William (b. 3rd da., 12th mo., 1809), Martha (b. 5th da., 2nd mo., 1812) and Edward. Robert Crew, father of the above children, d. 31st da., 3rd mo., 1826. {HMM:83-4}

Crew, Samuell m. Ann (N). They had a dau. b. 18 Aug 17-8. {BPR:297}

Crew, Samuel m. Hannah (N0. Their son David b. 28 Jan 1725.

68

{BPR:297}

Crew, William, son of John Crew of New Kent Co. m. 8th da., 7th mo., 1729, Hanah Sanders of Hanover Co., dau. of John Sanders. {HMM:16}

Cristwell, Barsheba was mother of Luis (b. 18 Aug 1718) and Margaret (b. 16 Aug 1720). {BPR:295}

Croilla, Lawrence, a Mulatto, reputed to have been begotten by Lawrence Croilla, a Spanish Mullato, on the body of Mary Peers, was set free in 1694. {CCOB (1687-95):200}

Crook(e), George of Bristol Parish m. bef. 14 Aug 1716, Elizabeth (N). Their children: Martha (b. 9 Apr 1715), Mary D. (b. 28 Mar 1717), Tabitha (b. 8 Feb 1719), Joseph (b. 28 Aug 1722) and James (b. 27 Jan 1725). {PGW&D (1713-1728):18; BPR: 298}

Crook, Solomon m. Martha (N). Their dau. Martha b. 1 Feb 1740/1. {BPR:300}

Crook, Thomas m. by 1664, Ann (N). {CCOB (1661-64):458}

Crosby, John m. by Apr 1762, Anne (N). {CCCR:154}

Crosland, Jonah d. by 1688 leaving widow, Elizabeth, admx. {CCOB (1687-95):41}

Cross, John (d. ca. 1730) of Westover Parish m. bef. 1 Dec 1730, Jane [Featherstone]. Children: William, Hannah, Mary (m. (N) Cradock), Featherstone, John, Richard, Charles, Elias, Parrish, Judith and Jane. Featherstone was nephew of William Featherstone of Prince George Co. Jane, widow of John Cross, m. 2nd Francis Hardyman. At January Court Charles Bayles, mariner of New England, declared he saw Parrish Cross, one of the defendants in a chancery suit, in New England April 1745. {CCW&D (1725-31):45, 46; CCCR:92, 94, 95, 111}

Cross, Martha Holy had an illegitimate dau. Ann Ford b. 24 Sep 1735. {BPR:300}

Crosse, William (d. by 1689) m. (N) who m. 2nd Edward Woodham. {CCOB (1687-95):62}

Crow, Abraham (b. 29 July 1763, Prince George Co., d. 4 Oct 1848, near Campbell Co., GA), m. 1 Jul 1829, Maria Timmons (b. circa 1799), by

William Hunt, Justice of the Peace in Spartanburg District, SC. When young he went to Northampton Co., NC, then to Brunswick Co., VA. He served as a substitute for several men in the Rev. War. He moved to Rutherford Co., NC in 1784. In 1822 he moved to Spartanburg District, SC. {RWP}

Crowder, Abraham m. Frances (N). Their children: Frances (b. 14 Dec 172-), Febe (b. 3 Jan 1726), Abraham (b. 30 Aug 1730), David (b. 26 May 1733) and Joseph (b. 22 Apr 1741). {BPR:297, 298, 300}

Crowder, Bartholomew m. bef. 9 Mar 1707 Elizabeth (N). Their children: Bartholomew (b. 3 Jun 17--), William (b. 23 Aug 172-), Amy (b. 20 Sep 1725), George (b. 13 Oct 1727) and Richard (b. 13 Oct 1727). {BPR:295, 296, 297; PGW&D (1713-1728):12}

Crowder, Henry m. Mary (N). Their son Richard b. 26 Mar 172-. {BPR:296}

Crowder, Henry m. Amy (N). Their son Henry b. 15 Jun 1729. {BPR:297}

Crowder, John m. Mary ()N). Their children: Thomas (b. 19 Jul 1730), John (b. 11 Sep 1731) and William (b. 1 Oct 1734). {BPR: 298, 299, 300}

Crump, Richard m. bef. Oct 1738, Lucy (N). {CCCR:83}

Crutchfield, Lewis m. (bond dated 29 Oct 1779), Mildred Jamison, spinster. {MB:194}

Crutchfield, William d. by 1744, widow Elizabeth, admx. {CCCR:103}

Cunliffe, John (buried 14 Mar 1660) of Martins Brandon Parish, m. 7 Aug 1660, Johan Mountain. {CCOB 1658-61):270}

Curd, Edward m. Elizabeth (N) by Oct 1778. {SWBC: 29}

Cureton/Cuerton, Francis had a son William who res. Westover Parish in 1717. {PGW&D (1713-1728):28}

Cureton, James and Susanna Heath [relationship?] emancipated several slaves in 1790. [PGR:142}

Cureton, James m. bef. 15 Aug 1791, Betsey (N). {PGR:161}

Cureton/Curiton, John m. Frances (N). Their children: Susanna (b. 19 Jan 17--), Elizabeth (b. 20 Jan 1726) and John (b. 27 Sep 1731). {BPR:296, 297, 298}

Cureton, John m. Mary (N). Their children: John (b. 13 Nov 1757) and Louisey (b. 28 Jan 1760). {BPR:302}

Cureton, John of Prince George Co. gave his son William 100 acres in 1759. {PGR:71}

Cureton, John m. Winifred (N). Their children: Frances (b. 13 Dec 1762) and Charles (b. 20 Sep 1765). {BPR:302}

Cureton, Thomas d. by 1791. Children: Archibald, Jane (m. William Dunn), Elizabeth (m. Nathan Heath), Anne (m. Briggs Rives) and Mary. {PGR:144, 146, 171, 172}

Curry, James d. by 1738, Richard Kennon, admin. {CCCR:82}

Currey, Macom d. by 1660, Alse Currey, widow and extx. {CCOB (1658-61):257}

Curtis, John m. Elliner (N). Their son John b. 22 Feb 1726. {BPR:297}

Curtis, John (b. 1759 or 1760, Dinwiddie Co., d. 7 Aug 1844, Knoxville, TN) m. Dolly Honeycutt (b. c1770) 10 Oct 1794, likely in Chatham Co., NC. Their oldest child was born Jan 1796. John's father died when John was young, and his mother died while he served in the Rev. War. After the war he moved to Orange Co., NC, and later lived in Chatham Co., NC; Sumner Co., TN; Giles Co., TN; White Co., TN; and Bledsoe Co., TN. John mentioned brothers and sisters, but not by name in his pension application. {RWP}

Dabney, William d. by 1790 leaving a son Isham Eppes Dabney, for whom a guardian, William Eppes, was appointed. {W&M, Vol. 23, No. 3 (Jan., 1915): 217}

Daingerfield, John m. by 1789, Elizabeth (N). {W&M, Vol. 23, No. 3 (Jan., 1915): 215}

Dalton, Luke made his indenture for 7 years to John Hodgson on 12 Sep 1730. {CCW&D (1725-31):45}

Dancy, Benjamin d. 1771. In his LWT he named brothers Edward and

Francis Dancy, nephews: William Dancy, Edward Dancy, John Dancy, Benjamin Dancy; and niece: Mary Davidson. {CCCR:33-4}

Dancy Edward m. bef. 31 Dec 1771, Susanna (N). {CCCR:47}

Dancy, Edward (d. 1771) m. Rebeckah (N). Nephew: Hardyman Dancy. {CCCR:34}

Dancy, Edward recorded a deed of gift to his son Francis in 1760. {CCCR:144}

Dancy, Francis (d. by 1772) m. by 1762 Agnes, widow of Isaac Williams. Francis recorded a deed of gift in 1761 to his son Eaton. Francis gave his son William, 300 acres on Kerbys Creek in 1771. {CCCR:34, 44, 149, 153}

Dancy, Hardyman, nephew of Edward Dancy, m. bef. 18 Nov 1771 Frances (N). {CCCR:44}

Dancy, John d. by 1760, John Dancy, exec. {CCCR:144}

Danzie, John Jacob Coignan m. bef. 23 Feb 1769, Elizabeth Rebecca (N), extx. of Temperance Harwood. In 1761 John Jacob Coignan Danzie was appointed guardian to his son John Jacob Coignan Danzie. {CCCR:11, 31, 144, 148}

Dancy, Samuel m. Ann Dancy. Ann d. by 1741, Francis Dancy, admin. {CCCR:94}

Dancy, William d. without issue in 1772. {CCCR:44}

Dandridge, Bartholomew (b. 25 Dec 1737, d. 18 Apr 1785) of New Kent Co., son of John and Frances (Jones) Dandridge, m. bef. 8 Oct 1771, Mary (N). {GVAW (Genealogies of Virginia Families) II:120-1, 128; CCCR:39, 43}

Daniel, (N) probable brother of Thomas Daniel (d. 1712) m. Elizabeth (N). Son: John. {PGW&D (1710-1713): 21}

Daniel (N) (predeceased his wife) m. Lucrese (N) who d. ca. Nov 1787. Their children: Mary, William, Lucrese (probably m. Reuben Tucker), John, Sarah, Thomas and Martha. {PGR:93, 117}

Daniel, Buckner (b. 1761, Dinwiddie Co.) m. (N) (N). He moved to

Davidson Co., NC then to Washington Co., IN ca. 1839 along with his children. In 1838 Hugh Daniel gave an affidavit on Buckner's behalf [no relationship stated]. {RWP}

Daniel, John of Prince George Co., son of John Daniel, m. bef. 8 Jan 1788, Winny (N). {PGR:100}

Daniel, John d. by 1791, leaving an orphan dau. Nancy whose guardian was William Bonner. {PGR:161}

Daniel, John H. of Martins Brandon Parish m. bef. 5 Nov 1790, Anna/Nancy (N). {PGR:142}

Daniel, Joseph (d. 1712) m. Elizabeth (N). Children: Joseph, Rogger, John, Thomas (under age of 21 in 1712) and Elizabeth. {PGW&D (1710-1713):22-3}

Daniel, Reese of Dinwiddie Co., son of John Daniel, m. bef. 16 Dec 1786 Mary (N). {PGR:104; GVAT (Genealogies of Virginia Families) I:514}

Daniel, Thomas m. bef. 27 Apr 1693, Ann, dau. of Francis Ledbetter. {CCCR:72}

Daniel, Thomas (d. 1712), brother of Joseph and John Daniell, m. (N). Children: Sarah, Mary, Ann, Hannah and Rebecca. {PGW&D (1710-1713): 21}

Daniel, William m. (bond dated 18 Jun 1793, Polly Martin, dau. of Martin Martin. {MB:195}

Daux, Walter (d. by 1658) m. Mary, widow of Robert Plaine. Children: Ann and Susan. Mary m. 3rd John Flower. {CCOB (1658-61):148}

Davenport, (N) m. bef. 5 Jan 1789, Rebeckah, sister of Thomas Rosser Rives. {PGR:112}

Davenport, Daniel of Bristol Parish m. bef. 3 Feb 1787, Elizabeth/ Betsey, dau. of Joseph Ledbetter. {PGR:102, 162}

Devonport, George d. by 1739, oldest son, Thomas Devonport, admin. {PGR:450}

Davidson, David d. testate by 1756, Stephen Davidson, exec. Children: Mary (m. Ingram Gill), Sarah (m. Bartholomew Jackson), Lucy (m.

William Adams), Hannah (m. Haley Bleighton), Ezekiel and probably Stephen. {CCCR:136, 154}

Davidson, David b. ca. 1764, d. 15 Dec 1822), enlisted in the Rev War while a resident in Charles City Co. in 1779. He was wounded at the battle of Guilford. In April 1819 he was living in Halifax County, VA. He m.15 Nov 1792, Maza Phillips (b. ca. 1761. By 1844, she was living in Franklin Co. Children: Solomon (b. ca. 1811), John (b. ca. 1816), Ritter [Harriet] (b. ca. 1814), Polly (b. ca. 1797, m. (N) Jenkins), Lucy (b. ca. 1800, m. (N) Jenkins), Moses (b. ca. 1812), and Rebeccah (b. ca. 1793, m. (N) Loyd). {RWP}

Davidson, Ezekiel d. by 1762, Philemon Davidson, exec. {CCCR:153}

Davidson, Solomon d. by 1772 leaving a widow Mary. {CCCR:48}

Davis, Christopher of Surry Co. (d. 1722) m. Elizabeth (N). Children: John (eldest son), Christopher, Hugh, Elizabeth and Frances. {PGW&D (1713-1728):87, 88}

Davis, Edward (d. by Jan 1758) of Dinwiddie Co. m. Lucy (N). Children: William, Edward, Joshua, Charles (all underage); and daus. Eliza, Susannah and Sarah Davis. {SWBC:52}

Davis, John, son of Christopher Davis (d. 1722) m. Mary (N). {PGW&D (1713-1728):88}

Davis, John of Bristol Parish m. bef. 31 Dec 1759, Elizabeth (N). {PGR:79}

Davis, Mary d. by 1745. Hezekiah Davis, her son, was bound to Thomas Johnson. {CCCR:109}

Davis, Mer. was appointed guardian to his dau. Charity ca. 1690. {CCOB (1687-95):82}

Davis, Ralph d. 22 Jul 1751. {W&M Vol. 4, No. 3 (Jan., 1896):143}

Davis, Robert d. by 1713. {PGW&D (1713-1728):1}

Davis, Robert of Wyanoke Parish m. bef. 8 Jul 1717, Elizabeth (N). {PGW&D (1713-1728):28}

Davis, Samuel d. by 1791, widow Sarah. Their son Samuel b. 26 Jan

1792. {BPR:303; PGR:158}

Davis, Shepherd m. Martha (N). Their dau. Polly Baugh b. 17 Dec 1792. {BPR:303}

Davies, Thomas, age 22 in 1660. {CCOB (1658-61):232}

Davis, Thomas d. by 1688 leaving widow, Mary, admx. {CCOB (1687-95):24}

Davis, William m. Maxey (N). Their children: Mary (b. 22 Apr 1747), Thomas Jones (b. 1 Nov 1752), Samuel (b. 23 Mar 1757), Shepherd (b. 28 Jun 1759) and Elizabeth (b. 22 Mar 1744). {BPR:303}

Davison, David d. by 1688, leaving widow, Sarah. {CCOB (1687-95):16}

Dawson, Thomas (d. by 1742) m. by Mar 1741, Elizabeth (N). {CCCR:94, 95}

Day, Ambrose d. testate by 1747, Elizabeth Day, extx. {CCCR:114}

Day, Edward m. by Aug 1758, Joyce (N). {CCCR:140

Day, James m. Levina (N). Their dau. Lucy Ann Kimbow b. 20 Apr 1793. {BPR:304}

Day, John m. bef. Oct 1740, Elizabeth (N). {CCCR:89}

Day, Joseph m. bef. Dec 1685 Dorcas (N). {CCOB (Fragments, 1685):2, 3}

Day, Joseph d. by 1744, Mary Day and George Minge, execs. Mary Day d. by 1761, James Bullifant, admin. {CCCR:105, 147}

Day, Mary recorded a deed in Apr 1761 to her dau. Alle Day. {CCCR:148}

Day, William (b. ca. 1761, d. 29 Jan 1837), m. (N) (N), who was also b. ca. 1761. Children: one son and two daus. {RWP}

Dean, John d. by 1740, Sarah Dean and Jones Dean, execs. {CCCR:88}

Dearden/Derden, Richard m. bef. 18 Nov 1719, Mary, widow of John

Williams. {PGW&D (1710-1713):3, 13, 22; PGW&D (1713-1728):142, 172}

Debnam, Mordecai m. by Nov 1760, Ann (N). {CCCR:145}

Delony, Lewis d. by 1750. Execs.: Henry Delony and Elizabeth Delony, widow of Lewis. Lewis Delony was appointed guardian of Lucy, Mary, Elizabeth and William, orphans of Lewis Delony. Elizabeth, widow of Lewis Delony, m. 2nd Bernard Major the younger ca. 1754. {CCCR:124, 125, 129}

Denhart, (N) (d. by 1788) m. Rebecca (N). In her LWT Rebecca Denhart named children: Shadrick Denhart, Mary (m. (N) Lanthrope), Silvey (m. (N) Tayton), Lucy Denhart and Elizabeth (m. (N) Drewry); and grandchildren: James Drewry, Mary Denhart and Patsy Moore Denhart. {PGR:125}

Denheart, Drury d. by 1787, Mary Denheart, extx. Daus.: Sarah, Amey and Elizabeth. {PGR:81, 111}

Denhart, Jacob m. bef. 8 Mar 1725, Mary, widow of Henry Chamless/Chamnis. {PGW&D (1713-1728):50-1, 68, 69, 143}

Dennis, Gower, son of Richard and Mary Dennis, m. 1st Susannah (N). Their dau.: Susanna (b. 14 Oct 1736). Gower m. 2nd Frances (N). Their son: Joseph (b. 26 Feb 1738/9). {APP3:56}

Dennis, Richard (d. 1724-5), son of (N) and (N) (Royall) Dennis and grandson of Katherine (Banks) Royal Isham, m. bef. 6 Mar 1710/11 Mary (N). Children: Henry (d. testate ca. 1726 without issue), Richard, Gower, Sarah (m. William Waddill of New Kent Co.), Elizabeth (b. ca. 1700, m. William Hayes of Henrico Co.), Mary (m. [John] Waddill), Martha (m. 1st Thomas Hales/Hail, m. 2nd Pridgin Waddill), Ann and Tabitha. {APP3:48, 56-7; CCW&D 1725-31:2; HCW 1:22-3, 154, 156}

Dennis, Richard, son of Richard and Mary Dennis, settled in Amelia Co., m. bef. 3 Sep 1736, Dearest (N). Children: Henry, John, Richard, Mary, Elizabeth and Sarah (m. John Royall). {APP3:56}

Dennis, William m. (bond dated 5 Mar 1764) Jane Parish, dau. of William Parish. {MB:194}

Denton, John m. Margaret (N). Their children: Polly Baugh (b. 17 Dec 1792) and Rebeccah Hathorn (b. 9 Sep 1791. {BPR:303}

Derden. See Dearden.

Deven, Thomas m. bef. 3 Apr 1689, (N), widow of William Stroud. {CCOB (1687-95):46, 60}

Dew, John d. by 1716, Elizabeth Dew, admx. {PGW&D (1713-1728):16}

Dewell, John (d. 1714) m. Jean/Jane, widow of (N) Price. Dau.: Mary. Jane m. 3rd Edward Johnson. {PGW&D (1713-1728):4, 62, 141}

Dibdall, John m. Jone (N). He gave his grandson, John Dibdall, son of Richard and Sara Dibdall, a bay mare filly, a heifer, a lamb and other animals, in 1659. {CCOB (1658-61):180}

Dibdall, Richard (d. by 1660), son of John Dibdall, d. leaving a widow, Sara. Sara m. 2nd Thomas Marston of Chickahomely. {CCOB (1658-61):260; CCOB (1661-64):312}

Dispain, Ann was presented in 1746 for having a bastard child. {CCCR:110}

Dixon, Anthony Tucker (d. by Aug 1808) m. (N) (N). He was the brother of Carver Dixon. {SWBC:33}

Dobson, William with consent of his wife made a gift to his two step-sons, Jarvis and Robert Winkfield. {CCOB (1677-79):16\\37}

Dodson, William m. Mary (N). Their dau. Aggy Franklin b. 11 Jan 1793. {BPR:303}

Doelittle, William, buried 1 Mar 1660. {CCOB 1658-61):270}

Dollin, William (b. ca. 1620) m. Rebecca (b. ca. 1636). {CCOB (1658-61):207}

Donald, Robert d. by 1745, Rebecca Donald, extx. {CCCR:106}

Doram, Patrick m. Jane (N). Ther son William b. 172-? {BPR:297}

Dove, John m. bef. 4 Nov 1729, Susanna (N). {CCW&D (1725-31):36}

Downman, Rawleigh Porteus (d. by Jun 1801) of Dinwiddie Co. m. Ann (N). Children: Frances and Charlotte Downman. His brother, Robert

Downman (father of Frances and Elizabeth Downman). {SWBC:53}

Drayton, Roger and Sarah Drayton d. by 1715. Francis and Peter
Poynthress were appointed guardians of Roger's orphans. {PGW&D
(1713-1728):42-3; GVAW (Genealogies of Virginia Families) IV:176}

Drew, (N) m. Frances (N), widow of (N) Netherland. They had a dau.
Elizabeth (youngest dau.) m. Philip Lymbry. {CCOB 1676-79:9, 50}

Drew, Lt. Col. Thomas, brother of George Drew (res. in England), on 10
Nov 1665 recorded a gift of slaves to his dau., Dorothy (m. Hubert
Farrell). {CCOB (1664-65):559; CCOB (Fragments):521}

Drinkard, (N) m. Mary, widow of (N) Thompson. In her LWT (dated
1771) Mary named children: William Rollison Drinkard, Elizabeth
Brewer, Mary Prewett, William Thompson and granddau. Molly
Thompson. {CCCR:38}

Drinkwater, John d. 1692 leaving a son John and another son (younger)
and widow Mary who m. 2nd John Sledge. {CCOB (1687-95):151;
CCCR:71}

Dudley, Camp m. Elizabeth (Clements?) (d. 1762-4). In her LWT
Elizabeth named children: Elizabeth, Lydia, Mary, Thomas Dudley,
Grace (m. Thomas Morris) and Lucy (may have m. Samuel Harris). In
LWT Elizabeth also mentioned "husband Camp" who left her 3 Negroes:
Jack, Dick and Dinar. She also mentioned son Thomas' uncle Benjamin
Clements in Southampton Co. {PGM:15; SWBC:206}

Dudley, John m. bef. 21 Jan 1788 Betsey (N). {PGR:107}

Duffey, John m. bef. 13 Feb 1738, Ann (N). {PGR:32}

Dugger, John (b. 1749, Surry Co., VA, d. 23 Mar 1834, Sumner Co., TN)
enlisted in the Rev. War while residing in Dinwiddie Co. He m. 4 Nov
1771, Frances (N). Their second child, Leonard Dugger, was born 4 Nov
1773. Their seventh child, Flood Dugger, was b. 20 Jan 1788. {RWP}

Dugger, Leonard (b. 4 Nov 1773, d. c1817), son of John and Frances
Dugger, m. 1st 12 Jan 1791, Rhodia (N), and m. 2nd 12 Jan 1801,
Elizabeth Taylor (b. 1773, sister of Benjamin Taylor). Children by
Rhodia: Jarrott (b. 8 Feb 1792, m. 25 Aug 1811, Polly W. Adams, and
had children: Elizabeth (b. 11 (?) 1812), Joseph (b. 21 Feb 1814),
Leonard W. (b. 12 Sep 1815), William Ferguson Dugger (b. 4 Apr

1817)); Wesley (b. 30 Apr 1793, m. Letty (N) 15 Jul 1816), Polly (b. 14 Dec 1795), twins Betsey and John (b. 14 Nov 1797 who m. 24 Aug 1820 Holly McAdam). Children by Elizabeth (2nd wife): Nancy (b. 5 Sep 1801, d. 10 Jul 1820, m. John Johnson 27 Aug 1818, their son: Leonard D. (b. 24 Sep 1819)). {RWP}

Duglas, Thomas (d. by 1688) m. Joane (N). Dau. Elizabeth (m. Edmund Irby). Widow Joane m. 2nd Edward Hues. {CCOB (1687-95):15, 91}

Duke, Edmond of Cumberland Co. sold 100 acres in 1771, given him by his father James Duke. {CCCR:45}

Duke, Capt. Henry (d. by 1718) m. Elizabeth, dau. of Capt. John Taylor. {PGW&D (1713-1728):52, 164}

Duke, James d. by 1755, Mary Duke and Joab Mountcastle, execs. Mary Duke, orphan of James Duke chose Richard Corbett as her guardian. {CCCR:132, 139}

Duke, Marston, son of Thomas and Elizabeth (Marston) Duke m. Sarah (N). They res. in Hanover Co. in 1730. {CCW&D (1725-31):40}

Duke, Thomas m. Elizabeth (d. 1729), dau. of Thomas Marston. In her LWT Elizabeth named children: Marston Duke, Susanna (m. Michael Sherman), Sarah (m. John Lice) and Mary Duke. {CCW&D (1725-31):38}

Duke, William (d. by 1678) m. bef. 3 Jun 1673 Hannah (N), widow of William Bird. {CCOB (1677-79):40; CCOB (Fragments):525, 531}

Dunn, Morris (d. by 1733) m. Elizabeth Larrance, widow of John Larrance. {PGR:178}

Dunn, Nathaniel (d. by 1789)m. bef. 9 Oct 1788, Betty, widow of Thomas Thweatt. Betty m. 3rd (agreement dated 5 Aug 1789) Thomas Galt.{PGR:88, 141}

Dunn, Thomas m. bef. 8 Apr 1789, Lucy, sister of James Green. Their son Lewis Burwell b. 22 Oct 1792 and probably others. Lucy m. 2nd (bond dated 6 May 1804), Capt. William Wills (d. by 1823). {PGR:115; BPR:303; APP 2:309}

Dunn, William Jr. m. bef. 4 Jan 1791, Jane, dau. of Thomas Cureton. {PGR:144}

Durand, Mary b. 1 Jun 1776, bapt. 1793. {BPR:303}

Earth, Abraham d. by 1694. Children: Abraham, Sarah and Elizabeth. {CCOB (1687-95):188}

East, Thomas d. by 1659 leaving an orphan dau. Jane who was bound to Morgan Jones. {CCOB (1658-61):217, 244}

Eaton, John of York Co. gave 170 acres in Prince George Co. to his dau. Sara and her husband John Woodland of Warwick Co. in 1713. {PGW&D (1713-1728):1}

Eaton, John (d. ca. 1719) m. (N)(N). Son: Samuel and William. {PGW&D (1713-1728):53}

Edgar, William m. Jane (N). Their dau. Elizabeth b. 6 Feb 1780. {BPR:343}

Edloe, Henry Lound (d. by 1740), son of John and (N) (Blanks) Edloe, m. Jane Browne, dau. of William Browne of Surry Co. Jane d. by 1741. Their children: Henry, Philip, William, Jane, Rebecca, John and Mary. In 1749 their daus. Jane and Rebecca chose Philip Edloe as their guardian. William Hunt Edloe (res. in Charles City in 1750) was probably a son. In 1746 the LWT of Henry Edloe was presented by Francis Tyree. Dau. Jane chose Benjamin Dancy as her guardian in 1750. In 1750 Benjamin Dancy was also appointed guardian to orphans John and Mary Edloe, orphans of Henry and Jane Edloe. {GVAW:II:241; CCCR:88, 90-1, 110, 119, 122; APP 1:848-9}

Edloe, John (d. by 1749) m. bef. 14 Jun 1729, Rebecca Huberd, dau. of Matthew Huberd of York Co. Their children: John, Sibella and Rebecca Hubbard Edloe. John m. 2nd 1699, Mrs. Martha Hatcher. {CCW&D (1725-31):35-6; CCCR:119; APP1:847-8; GVAW (Genealogies of Virginia Families): II:239}

Edloe, John, son of John Edloe, m. bef. 13 Mar 1744, Ann Bolling, sister of John Bolling. Children: John and Elizabeth (m. by Oct 1761 (N) Cocke). {CCCR:115, 128; APP1:850; PGM:12-13}

Edloe, John "of the River" (d. by 1759) m. by Mar 1747, his cousin Sibella Edloe. Their children: Rebecca (m. Parker Hare of Chesterfield Co.), Martha (d. by 1785), Tabitha (m. William Barret of James City Co.) and Alice. Sibella m. 2nd Park Bailey of Chesterfield Co. In 1762 Martha, orphan of John Edloe, Gent., chose William Acrill her guardian. Tabitha chose William Edloe, her guardian. {CCCR:114, 142, 156, 157; APP1:851-2}

Edloe, John, son of John and Ann (Bolling) Edloe, m. 1st by Oct 1761, Martha (N) and m. 2nd 1775, Anne Bailey. {CCCR:151; APP 1:850}

Edloe, John (b. 1777, d. 27 Apr 1833), son of William and Ann Edloe, m. Ann Armistead Allen (d. 1833), dau. of Col. William Allen of Claremont. {GVAW II:241; APP 1:852}

Edloe, Philip (d. by 1754), brother of Matthew and Henry Edloe (d. by 1726) m. Mary (N). Children: Rebecca, Sarah, Ann, Elizabeth and ?John. {CCW&D (1725-31):21; CCCR:127; APP 1:847}

Edloe, William, Gent., son of Henry Lound Edloe, m. by Oct 1762, Anne (N). Children: William, Henry and John. {CCCR:157; APP 1:852}

Edloe, William Hunt d. by 1748, probable son of Matthew and Martha (Hunt) Edloe. John Edloe, heir at law. {CCCR:117; APP 1:848}

Edmondson, Philip Par m. 1756, Elizabeth, widow of William Cole. {CCCR:24; APP1:716}

Edmunds, John d. by 1689. His admx. (widow?) m. bef. 5 Aug 1689, Thomas Clarke. {CCOB (1687-95):53}

Edmunds, William m. Sarah (N). They had a dau. Elizabeth. Sarah m. 2nd John Lanier. {CCOB (1687-95):48, 53}

Edwards, Benjamin of Bristol Parish m. bef. 5 Apr 1792, Ann (N). Both d. by 1806. Probable children: (N) (m. William Davenport), Patsy (m. Uriah Adams) and Jane Edwards. {PGM:38}

Edwards, Charles d. by 1761, John Stokes and Bridget Edwards, execs. {CCCR:148}

Edwards, John (d. by1688) m. Mary (N). Mary m. 2nd Thomas Clarke. {CCOB (1687-95):14, 30, 39}

Edwards, John (d. 1770) m. Tabitha (N). Children: Isaac and Ann. {CCCR:28}

Edwards, Lewis m. Mary (N). Their dau. Mary Danforth b. 4 Jan 1793

(1792?). Mary, wife of Lewis Edwards, d. 30 Oct 1792. {BPR:304}

Edwards, Sarah was fined in 1737 for having a bastard child.
{CCCR:79}

Edwards, Thomas d. by 1712, leaving widow, Mary Edwards. Thomas
was father of Frances who m. Samuell Lee. {PGW&D (1710-1713): 20,
41}

Edwards, William m. (prenuptial agreement dated 2 Jul 1659) Margaret,
widow of William Stadword (d. leaving orphans, William and Joice).
{CCOB (1658-61):194}

Edwards, William d. by 1726, Elizabeth Edwards, admx. {CCW&D
(1725-31):11}

Edwards, William (d. by 1802) m. bef. 7 Jul 1792, Mason (N) who m. 2nd
Henry Wilkerson. William's probable children: John, William, Joseph,
Mary (m. Hamlin Baird) and Rebecca (m. (N) Baird). {PGM:10}

Eelbank, Daniel d. by 1739, Ann Eelbank, extx. {PGR:41; CCCR:98}

Eldridge, Thomas (d. 4 Dec 1754, Surry Co.) m. 1st Martha Bolling (d.
1749), dau. of John Bolling. Their children: Sarah (m. George Rives),
John, Jane, Mary (m. Thomas Branch), Judith (twin of Mary, m. James
Ferguson), Rolfe and Martha (m. John Harris). Thomas m. 2nd Elizabeth
Jones, dau. of James Jones (d. 1743). Their son: Howell. {PGR:75;
GVAT (Genealogies of Virginia Families) I:648; GVAW (Genealogies
of Virginia Families) II:260-1}

Elerbee, Edward purchased land in 1688 which he conveyed to his son
Thomas Elerbee which he sold in 1729. {CCW&D (1725-31):39}

Ellington, John Jr. m. bef. 14 Aug 1739, Sabina (N). {PGR:51}

Elliott, Robert d. by 1760. His sons, Henry and John, were bound out.
{CCCR:145}

Ellis, John d. by 1738. His dau. Martha chose Margery Gillam to be her
guardian, John Gillam, security. {PGR:16}

Ellis, John Jr. m. bef. 8 Aug 1738, Lucy (N). {PGR:15}

Ellyson, Benjamin, son of William Ellyson. 4/9/1762. it is reported that

Benjamin Ellyson [son of Willm. Ellyson] and Sarah Wooddy [dau. of Micajah Wooddy] had in a disorderly manner and contrary to the discipline of Friends (Quakers), procured a certificate and took each other in marriage at the Swamp Meeting being first cousins [disowned]. {HMM:38}

Ellyson, Cecilia. 6/4/1782. Informed that Cecilia Ellyson has lately been delivered of a bastard child. {HMM:67}

Ellyson, Gerrard (d. Chesterfield Co., ca. 1770), son of Gerard Robert Ellyson, m. bef. 10 Jun 1755, Sarah (N). {HCDB (1750-1774):64; GVAT (Genealogies of Virginia Families) I:687}

Ellyson, Gererd and his wife Elizabeth produced certificate from monthly meeting held at Caroline on 6/2/1762. Elizabeth Ellyson, wife of Gerrard Ellyson, d. 9/10/1783. {HMM:37, 63}

Ellyson, Gerrard Robert m. bef. 5th da., 8th mo., 1780, Sarah (N). {HMM:57, 60, 69}

Ellyson, Gidion m. Margery (N). Their children: William (b. 1/10/1758), Gidion (b. 26/11/1760), Zachariah (b. 6/10/1762, went to Goose Creek Monthly to reside in 1786), Mary (b. 1/5/1765), Margery (b. 15/12/1767), Miriam (b. 1/12/1769) and Jonathan (b. 21/1/1774). {HMM:62; HMM:70}

Ellyson, Isaiah (d. 7th da., 8th mo., 177-), son of William and Jane Ellyson of New Kent Co., m. 6th da., 11th mo., 1766, Cisilia Wooddy, dau. of Micajah and Cisilia Wooddy of Hanover Co., in Hanover Co. Their children: Annaritta (b. 2/9/1779), Jessee (b. 10/11/1767) and Hannah(?) (b. 19/4/1773). {HMM:44, 62}

Ellyson, John, elder and member of Black Creek meeting d. 28th da, 9th mo, 1786. {HMM:63, 71}

Ellyson, John, son of Robert Ellyson of New Kent Co. m. 7th da., 5th mo., 1772, Agnes Woodson, dau. of Charles and Agnes (Parsons) Woodson of Henrico Co., at Curles Meeting House. "Whereas John Ellyson some years ago purchased a Negro contrary to discipline and did not properly condemn his ... but as he has granted all his 6 Negroes their liberty and recorded manumissions, his restrictions are removed." {HMM:50, 67; APP3:741-2, 792

Ellyson, John and family removed to the back parts of North Carolina within the limits of Deep River Monthly Meeting sometime before Jul 1786. {HMM:70}

Ellyson, John m. Elizabeth (N). They had a son Samuel, b. 11/7/1784. On 2 Dec 1786 Elizabeth Ellyson informed the (Quaker) meeting that she intended to remove to within the limits of Western Branch Monthly Meeting and requested a certificate for herself and son Samuel. {HMM:59, 63, 70}

Ellyson, Joseph, son of Robert Ellyson of New Kent Co. m. 6th da., 3rd mo., 1744, Mary Benford, dau. of John Benford of Charles City Co., in Windoak, Charles City Co. Their dau. Agnis m. Moore Bell. {HMM:23, 34-5, 42, 65, 81, 83}

Ellyson, Josiah. His dau. Henrietta married a man not of the (Quaker) Society by 1793. {HMM:77}

Ellyson, Mathew, son of Robert Ellyson of New Kent Co. and Elizabeth Lead, dau. of William Lead of Charles City Co. m. 17 da., 9 mo., 1737. {HMM:19}

Ellyson, Robert. 2/5/1767. Mary Ellyson, dau. of Robert[and Sarah] Ellyson of New Kent Co. was disowned for marrying by a priest to a man not a member of the Society. {HMM:44}

Elyson, Robert (son of Robert Elyson) of Newkent County m. 8th da., 1st mo., 171-, Sarah Crew, dau. of John Crew of Charles City County, at William Lead's house 8/1/171?. {HMM:8}

Ellyson, Susanna. Informed 4/6/1768 that Susanna Ellyson had absconded from her mother's house in a scandalous manner with intention of marriage with a man not of the Society]. {HMM:46}

Ellyson, Thomas of Prince George Co. m. 6th da., 2nd mo., 1731, Elizabeth Crew, dau. of Robert Crew of Charles City Co. Thomas d. by 1757 leaving an orphan child. No suitable provisions were made for the orphan child of Thomas Ellyson, dec'd. John Crew, Jr. took the orphan of Thomas Ellyson at his house and sent him to school. John Crew also reports that he has agreed to schooling several of the orphans of John Bates agreeable to last monthly (Quaker) meeting. {HMM:17, 31, 33}

Ellyson, Thomas (d. 4th da., 1st mo., 178-) of New Kent Co., m. 16th da., 12th mo., 1778, Agness Ellyson, dau. of Gideon Ellyson of the same county. Children of Thomas and Agness Ellyson: Susanna (b.

26/1/1780), Martha (b. 24/7/1781), Mary (b. 15/11/1783) and Agness (b. 12/8/1785). {HMM:57, 58, 63}

Elyson, William, son of Robt. Elyson of New Kent Co. m. 5th da., 4th mo., 1722, Agnis Johnson, dau. of John Johnson of Hanover Co. {HMM:11}

Ellyson, William (d. 22/5/1779), son of Gaird [Gerrard] Robert Ellyson of New Kent Co. m. 8th da., 10th mo., 1734, Jane/Jean Saunders, dau. of John Saunders of Hanover Co. Jane Ellyson, wife of the said William, d. 10/1/1780.{HMM:18, 63}

Ellyson, William, son of William Ellyson, m. 10th da., 6th mo., 1762, Molly Johnson, dau. of Nathan Johnson of New Kent Co at Swamp Meeting House in Hanover Co. Their children: Orina (b. 27th da., 10th mo., 17--), Albanah (b. 10th da., 12th mo., 1769) and Mary b. 13th da., 1st mo., 1772. Mary Ellyson, widow of William, d. 17th da., 10th mo., 1786 - Member of Black Creek Meeting. {HMM:37, 62, 63}

Ellyson, William, elder and member of Black Creek Meeting died 24th da, 8th mo, 1786. {HMM:71}

Elmore, Charles m. 20 May 1786, Mary Glenn. By Rev. John Buchanan. {HMM:95}

Emery, Charles d. by 1761, William Emery, admin. Martha Emery, widow, relinquished her right to administer the estate. {CCCR:149}

Emery, John d. by 1770, Mary Emery, admx. {CCCR:28}

Eppes Family. Many of the Eppes family resided in Prince George, Henrico, Chesterfield and Surry counties. For more detail on the family, see APP1.

Epes, Amey d. by 1789. {PGR:119}

Eppes, (N) m. Christian (N) (d. aft. Feb 1799). Children: Archibald, Robertson, William (all three underage), dau. Christian Gilliam, dau. Polly Eppes, and son Richard. {SWBC:207}

Eppes, Edmund (d. by 1755), son of Littlebury Epes, m. Henrietta Maria Hardyman, dau. of John and Henrietta Maria (Taylor) Hardyman. Their children: Mary (m. Grief Randolph), Henrietta Maria, Frances, James and Ann. {APP1:870-1; CCCR:133}

Eppes, Lt. Col. Francis (b. ca. 1628, d. 1678), son of Capt. Francis Eppes of Charles City Co., m. 1st (N)(N) and m. 2nd Elizabeth, widow of William Worsham of Henrico Co. Son Francis (b. 1659, d. ca. 1719) was by his 1st wife. Francis and Elizabeth were parents of William (b. 1661), Lt. Col. Littlebury of Charles City Co., Mary (m. 1st bef. Jun 1685, John Hardyman of Charles City Co., m. 2nd Major Charles Goodrich) and Anne. {GVA (Genealogies of Virginia Families II, Cl-Fi:709-12); APP1:857-9; GVAW I:454; HCW 1:13; CCOB (1677-79):15}

Epes, Francis (d. by 1739) of Hopewell, son of William and Sarah (widow of William Jones and dau. of Caesar Walpole) Epes, m. Susanna Moore, dau. of William Moore (d. 1756). Their children: William, Francis, Daniel, Richard and Sarah. {PGR:47; APP1:860, 864-5; PGR:47}

Eppes, Francis (b. 1747, d. 4 Jul 1808), son of Richard and Martha (Bolling) Eppes, m. bef. 30 Apr 1771, Elizabeth (b. 24 Feb 1752, d. 10 Jun 1810), dau. of John Wayles. Their sons: Richard and John Wayles Eppes. {CCCR:39, 53; APP 1:893-4}

Epes, Hamlin (d. by Dec 1774) of Dinwiddie Co. m. (N) (N). Had children, not named. His brother, Francis Epes. {SWBC:53}

Eppes, Isham (b. bef. 1700, d. 1760 in Dinwiddie Co.), son of William Eppes, m. bef. 11 Sep 1733, Amey (Goodwyn) Scott, widow of John Scott Jr. and dau. of Thomas and Mary Goodwyn. Their children: Amey, Francis, William, Isham and Frederick. {PGR:178; APP1:870}

Eppes, James, probable son of Littlebury and (N) (Llewellyn) Eppes, d. by 1740, Edmund Eppes, admin., probable brother. {CCCR:87; APP 1:862}

Eppes, James, son of Edmund and Henrietta Maria Hardyman Epes, m. bef. 17 Apr 1769, Mary, dau. of John Bradley (d. 1769-70). {CCCR:21; APP1:871, 911-12}

Epes, Joel of Prince George Co. sold 400 acres to Francis Epes of Ameila Co. in 1788, land devised to Joel by John Epes' will. {PGR:110}

Epes, Col. John (b. 1626, d. by 1689), son of Francis and Mary Epes m. Mary Kent. Children: Francis, John, William, Edward and Daniel. Their son John was exec. of his father's estate. {CCOB (1687-95):48; APP1:856-7}

Epes, John of Westover Parish (d. by 1718), son of Thomas and (N) (Wyatt) Epes, m. Mary Epes, dau. of John and [Mary] Epes. Children: John, Nathaniel, Thomas and three others [probably John, Nathaniel, Thomas, Francis, William and one other.] {PGW&D (1713-1728):36-7, 82; APP1:859}

Eppes, Lt. Col. John of Charles City Co., son of Capt. Francis or Richard Eppes of Charles City Co., m. bef. 9 Jun 1712, Mary Epes. Children: William and Richard. {GVA (Genealogies of Virginia Families II, Cl-Fi:709-12); APP 1:864; PGW&D (1710-1713): 19}

Eppes, John (d. by 1725) m. Tabitha Peterson (d. by 1726). They d. leaving a son John who chose Benjamin Harrison as his guardian. {CCCR:80; APP 1:872}

Eppes, John m. Susanna (N). Their dau. Lucretia b. 7 Feb 1791. {BPR:304}

Eppes, Lewellin (d. by May 1758) m. Angelica (N). Children: sons Temple and Peter; daus. Elizabeth, Ann, Mary, and Angelica. Grandchildren: Angelica Wilkinson and Joseph Royall (son of Littlebury Royall). {SWBC: 34}

Eppes, Littlebury (d. by 1737), son of Francis Epes, m. ca. 1689, (N) Llewellyn, dau. of Daniel Llewellyn. Their child: Llewellin. Littlebury m. 2nd (N)(N). Their children: Edmund, James, Mary (m. Peter Tatum) and Littlebury. {CCCR:78; APP 1:862-3; APP 2:850, 852}

Eppes, Littlebury, son of Littlebury Eppes, m. (N)(N). Children: Mary (m. David Mason of Sussex Co.) and Thomas (m. Elizabeth (N). {APP 1:871, 912; PGM:17}

Eppes, Mary was presented in 1745 for having a bastard child. {CCCR:108}

Eppes, Peter (d. 1773), son of Lewellin and Angelica (Bray) Eppes, m. Elizabeth, dau. of John Hardyman. Children: Peter, John Temple/Temple, Elizabeth (m. 1st Littlebury Hardyman, m. 2nd John Cocke) and Angelica (m. John Holt). {CCCR:53-4; APP1:870, 911}

Eppes, Peter (b. 9 Mar 1759, Dinwiddie Co.). {RWP}

Eppes, Richard (?) m. Mary Cocke (d. testate 1771-2). Their children: Elizabeth (m. Samuel Harwood), Mary Ann (m. Dr. William Torborn) and Richard. {APP1:872, 917-8; CCCR:8, 42}

Eppes, Richard (d. 8 Jul 1792) of City Point, Prince George Co., son of Richard Eppes (son of Lt. Col. John Eppes), m. Christian, dau. of Archibald and Elizabeth (Fitzgerald) Robertson or dau. of William Robertson of Petersburg. Their children: Richard (d. unm.), Archibald (d. unm.), Robertson (d. unm.), Thomas (d. unm.), William (m (N) Gregory of Chesterfield Co. and died without issue), Elizabeth (m. (N) Maitland of Scotland), Christian (m. William Gilliam) and Mary (m. Benjamin Cocke of Prince George Co.). {GVA (Genealogies of Virginia Families II, Cl-Fi:711-12); PGM:18; APP 1:918-919; BPR:304}

Epes, Robinson [Robertson?] d. by 1805. Possible heirs: William Epes, Christian Gilliam, Polly Epes and Archibald Epes. {PGM:36-7}

Eppes, Thomas Jr. (b. ca. 1630, d. by 1679), son of Thomas Epes (d. by 1737), m. (N), dau. of Anthony Wyatt. {CCOB (1664-65):633; CCOB (1677-79):113}

Eppes, Thomas (d. by 1737), m. bef. 4 Jun 1679, Elizabeth (N). Mary Eppes presented the will. Thomas was father of Thomas and John. {CCCR:81; APP 1:859; CCOB (1677-9):106}

Epes, Thomas (d. 1779-80 without issue), son of Littlebury Epes, m. Betty/Elizabeth (N), possibly the dau. of Hartwell Cocke. Hartwell's dau. Elizabeth was sister of Martha Cocke who m. 1st Thomas Clements Jr. and m. 2nd Daniel Coleman. In his LWT Thomas Epes named his sister-in-law, Martha Coleman. Also named was sister Mary Mason (had daus. Mary and Rebecca, and son Thomas). Elizabeth, dau. of Hartwell Cocke, m. (bond dated 22 Dec 1788) as his second wife, William Taliaferro of Caroline Co. {PGM:17; APP 1:169, 871, 912; SWBC:208}

Epes, William (d. by 1727) m. bef. 3 Mar 1691, Sarah, dau. of Caesar (d. 1678) and Elizabeth (Nance) Walpole and widow of William Jones. Sarah's mother Elizabeth m. 2nd James Wallis. Children of William and Sarah Epes: Mary (m. John Bevill of Chesterfield Co.), Francis, Sarah and William. {CCOB (1687-95):122; APP1:860; PGM:16; PGW&D (1713-1728): 14, 159}

Epes, William (d. 16 Nov 1710), son of Francis Epes, m. Elizabeth (N). Their children: Francis, John, Isham, William and Littlebury. {APP1:862; PGW&D (1710-1713):5; PGM:7}

Epes, William m. bef. 4 Feb 1801, Palmer (N). {PGM:8}

Evans, Ann was presented in 1738 for having a bastard child; case dismissed. {CCCR:82}

Evans, Benjamin (d. 1711) of Martins Brandon Parish m. Sarah (N). Their children: Benjamin, Rebecca and Mary (m. Charles Lucas). Sarah d. 1711. In her LWT she mentioned children, Benjamin, Rebecca and Mary; and also dau. Sarah mother of William, Larence, Elizabeth and Henry Backnall. {PGW&D (1710-1713):8, 12; PGW&D (1713-1728):128}

Evans, Benjamin m. bef. 4 Jun 1729, Faith (N). {CCW&D1725-34}

Evans, Charles of Bartie Precinct, Albemarle Co., NC, m. bef. 4 Sep 1704, Sarah (N) (d. by 1727). {CCW&D (1725-31):25, 46}

Evans, Elizabeth d. by 1739, Stephen and Robert Evans, execs. {PGR:62}

Evans, John, age 24 in 1673. {CCOB (Fragments):518}

Evans, John Sr. m. bef. 2 Apr 1690, Mary (N). In 1690 John Evans Sr. gave 90 acres to Robert Hix and Winnifred his wife, "son and daughter in law." {CCCR:67}

Evans, John m. bef. 9 Jan 1715, Sarah (N). {PGW&D (1713-1728):14}

Evans, Lucy was charged of having a bastard child in 1742. Charges dismissed. {CCCR:96}

Evans, Ludwell d. by 1738, Elizabeth, his widow. {PGR:2}

Evans, Mary, age 26 in 1673. {CCOB (Fragments):518}

Evans, Peter m. bef. 24 Mar 1691, Mary, widow of Curtis Land. {CCOB (1687-95):125}

Evans, Stephen, son of John Evans, m. Elizabeth (N). In 1711/12 Stephen gave his son John, land inherited from his father John. {PGW&D (1710-1713): 17}

Evans, Thomas (d. by 1757) of Westover Parish, Charles City Co. m. 1734-6, Susanna, widow of Joseph Cole. {GVAT III:415; HCW 1:199}

Everitt, John m. bef. 4 Oct 1689, Elizabeth (N). {CCOB (1687-95):66}

Everitt, John was named by Bernard Sykes as his father-in-law in 1690. {CCOB (1687-95):77}

Ezell, Buckner of Sussex Co. m. Elizabeth (N). Their son Richard b. 15 Aug 1791. {BPR:304}

Fano, Richard d. by 1755 leaving orphans, Mary and Susanna who were bound out. {CCCR:133}

Farley, John of Henrico Co. gave his son John half of his land at Blackwater, 75 acres, in 1692. {CCCR:71-2}

Farne, Henry m. Ann (N) bef. Feb 1671. Their son, Francis (under 21 in 1671). Ann's will dated 1673 mentions "if my loving husband Henry Farne be dead or never come back..." {SWBC:34}

Farrar, Col. William (d. 1676) of Henrico Co., son of William and Cicely Farrar and brother of Capt. John Farrar m. Mary (N). Children: William, Thomas, John, Martha (m. Walter Shippey of Charles City Co.) and Cicely. {GVA (Genealogies of Virginia Families II, Cl-Fi:749); APP1:929-30; HCW 1:1}

Farrell, Brian (d. 1716) m. Elizabeth (N). Son: Hubbert. {PGW&D (1713-1728):19}

Farrell, Hubbert, exec. of Thomas Winter (d. by 1677), m. by 1673, Dorothy (d. 18 Jan 1673), dau. of Thomas Drew (d. by 1673). Hubert d. by 1677. {CCOB 1676-79:8; CCOB (Fragments):521; W&M Vol. 4, No. 3 (Jan., 1896):147}

Farrell, William (d. ca. 1718) m. Sarah (N). {PGW&D (1713-1728):37}

Fear, James d. by 1741, admx. Elizabeth, widow. {CCCR:91}

Ferguson, Andrew, a free man of color (b. Jul 1765, Dinwiddie Co., son of a free man, Andrew Ferguson and a woman of color), m. (N) (N). Both died in 1855 (she d. first, he left no heirs). He was living in Monroe Co., IN in 1838. {RWP}

Fernando/Fernendo, Benjamin m. Mary (N). Their children: Sarah (b. 16 May 1764) and Ann (b. 21 Sep 1766). {BPR:304}

Finn, Francis Lisenburg m. Sarah (N). Their children: Thomas Francis (b. 25 Apr 1753), William (b. 12 Jan 1756), Joel (b. 8 Aug 1758), John (b.

18 May 1761), Rosey (b. 13 Oct 1763) and David (b. 7 Aug 1765).
{BPR:304}

Fenn, Joel m. Mary (N). Their children: Daniel Baugh (b. 12 Apr 1791)
and Richard (b. 28 Jun 1789). {BPR:305}

Fenn. John (d. 23 Apr 1843), of Prince George Co., m. 7 Sep 1798, Sarah
(N) (b. ca. 1781) by Beverly Booth. They had children (unnamed).
{RWP}

Featherstone, Edward m. Sarah (N). Their children: Lucy (b. 20 Jun
1791) and Martha Edwards (b. 3 Sep 1792). {BPR:305}

Fetherstone, William m. bef. 3 Oct 1689, Mary, widow of Henry
May/Mayes. William Fetherstone "unlawfully departed the county" ca.
1695.{CCOB (1687-95):61, 74}

Fetherstone, William d. ca. 1718, leaving 150 acres to his son William
(m. Frances (N)). {CCW&D (1725-31):19-20}

Fewqua. See Fuqua.

Field, Dr. James (d. ca. 1789), physician in Bristol Parish, later res. in
Edinburgh, m. Margaret, dau. of John Shaw (d. by 1771), merchant in
Edinburgh. {PGR:114}

Field, John d. by 1695 leaving an orphan, William, who was put
apprentice to Robert Cradock with the consent of his mother on 3 Jun
1695. {CCOB (1687-95):208}

Field/Beddingfield/Benningfield, Theophilus of Prince George Co. m.
(bond dated 19 Sep 1783), Martha widow of Henry Simmons. {APP2:
599}

Finch, Adam m. by Mar 1757, Mary, dau. of James Thomson and
granddau. of James Thomson, dec'd. {CCCR:137}

Finch, Brothers was appointed William Finch as his guardian in 1746.
{CCCR:110}

Finch, Brothers (d. by 1767) m. Sarah, dau. of Rabley Vaughan.
Children: Edward, William, Sarah, Martha and Elizabeth, all minors in
1767. {CCCR:3, 29, 30, 44, 57}

Finch, Henry d. by 1754, Edward and John Finch, execs. Frances Finch possible dau. [CCCR:129}

Finch, Henry d. by 1798, leaving a widow, Sarah. {PGM:25}

Finch, William m. by 1747, Mary, probable widow of Charles Henry Cox. {CCCR:114}

Finch, William (d. by 1773) m. Agnes (N). Children: William, Henry, Edward, Fanny (m. John Lamb). Sons-in-law: Malcolm Grant, John Lamb, John Stubblefield, John Cosby and Benjamin Walker. In her LWT (dated 21 Mar 1771) Agnes named son William Finch and "all my children," unnamed. {CCCR:46; 51}

Finn. See Fenn.

Fisher, John K. m. Elizabeth (N). Their son Daniel b. 2 Jun 1792. {BPR:304}

Fitz, Henry m. bef. 14 Aug 1739, Ann (N), admx. of Nicholas Vaughan. {PGR:51}

Fitz, Robert W. (b. 1755 or 1756, Dinwiddie Co.). He lived in Lunenburg, Mecklenburg, and Halifax counties, VA. {RWP}

Fitz-Gareld, John m. Anne (N). Their son John b. 25 Jul 1741. {BPR:309}

Fitz Rock. See Rock.

Flack, Andrew (d. 1767-9) m. Mary (N). Children: George, Andrew, Mary, Mildred, Susanne (m. (N) Pharoan/Pharoah), Nancy Anderson and Rebecca. Granddau.?: Molly Pharoah. {CCCR:12}

Fletcher, James m. bef. 13 Oct 1717, Mary dau. of Richard Atkins. Their children: Richard and Sarah Fletcher. {PGW&D (1713-1728):34-5}

Fletcher, James predeceased his widow Rebeckah who d. by 1789. {PGR:123}

Fletcher, Michael m. bef. 14 Sep 1660, (N), widow of William Garrett. {CCOB (1658-61):246}

Flewellen, Hannah was presented in 1743 for having a bastard child.

{CCCR:98}

Flewellin, William (b. 21 Apr 1754, Prince George Co). He was living in Halifax Co., NC when called into service of the Rev. War. He later lived in Robertson Co., TN, then Carroll Co., TN. {RWP}

Florday, (N) m. bef. 11 Jul 1713, Susan, widow of Daniell Mallone. {PGW&D (1710-1713):35}

Flower, John m. (prenuptial agreement dated 24 May 1658), Mary, widow of (1) Robert Plaine and (2) Walter Daux. {CCOB (1658-61):148}

Floyd, Charles (d. 1768-9) m. Sarah Moseley, dau. of Arthur Jr and Martha (Cocke) Moseley and. Children: Martha (m. Arthur Moseley) and Mary (m. [John] Miller). {CCCR:13: APP1:138, 197; HCDB 2:18}

Floyd, Penelope d. by 1758, John Hudson, exec. {CCCR:141}

Flyn, Laughlin m. bef. 26 Oct 1738, Elizabeth (N). {PGR:25}

Fontain, Rev. Peter recorded a deed of gift to his son Peter and to his grandson, Peter Winston in 1748. Rev. Fontain d. by 1757, Sarah Fontain and Peter Fontain, execs. {CCCR:116, 138}

Forshaw, Hugh d. by 1656 leaving widow, Elizabeth and son Henry who was apprenticed to Phillip Ellyott and son Daniel, apprenticed to Cornel Clemence. {CCOB (1655-58): 59, 60}

Foster, Alice d. testate by 1738. {PGR:13}

Foster, Benjamin m. bef. Feb 1689, Juhan (N). {CCCR:66-7}

Foster, Benjamin, wheelwright, m. bef. 5 Dec 1718, Elizabeth (N). {PGW&D (1713-1728):41, 100}

Foster, Benjamin d. by 1739, Alice Foster who also d. by 1739. {PGR:40}

Foster, Edward d. by 1677 leaving widow Hester. {CCOB 1676-79:1}

Foster, Seth m. by 1790, Ann, extx. of John Gary and John King. {W&M, Vol. 23, No. 3 (Jan., 1915): 216}

Fowler, Alexander d. by 6 Jun 1664, Mary Fowler, extx. {CCOB (1664-65)}

Fowler, Marke m. Mary (N). Their son Matthew b. 4 Jan 1730. {BPR:338}

Fowler, Samuel d. by 1690, leaving a son Samuel. {CCOB (1687-95):97}

Fraser, Simon (d. 28 Oct 1792) m. Elizabeth (N). Their dau. Ann Laughton b. 18 Jan 1792. {BPR:304, 305}

Fraser, Thomas m. Ann Loughton (N). Their dau. Maria Deas b. 3 Jul 1792. {BPR:305}

Freeman, John d. by 1694, leaving widow Barbara. Their children: Elizabeth and Hannah. {CCOB (1687-95):175, 188}

Freme, Capt. John (d. by 1655) m. Mary, widow of William Laurence. In 1655, Mary Freme, contemplating marriage, made provisions for her children [*probably all by William Laurence*]: Arther, William, James (m. Mary (N)), Sarah, Jonne and Ann (m. 1st John Bishop, m. 2nd Francis Redford). Mary m. 3rd Edward Fitzgarrett/Fitzgerald, m. 4th (N) Rose and m. 5th William Leedford. William Justice m. Mary, one of the daus. of Capt. John Freme bef. 11 Jul 1662. {CCOB (1655-58): 23, 43, 52; CCOB (1658-61):156; CCOB (1661-64):345, 360; CCOB 1676-79:16}

Froughton, William d. by 1721, Elizabeth Froughton, admx. In 1725 Elizabeth and James Froughton (son?) sold 25 acres on James River in Martins Brandon Parish. {PGW&D (1713-1728):79, 140}

Frost, John (d. by 1689) m. Elizabeth, dau. of Christopher Batty. John was probably father of Martha (bound to William Frost in 1693), Joseph and John (bound to James Batty in 1693). Elizabeth m. 2nd bef. 5 Jan 1690 Robert Williams. {CCOB (1687-95):63, 95, 160}

Fuglar, John d. 1769-70), son of Richard Fuglar, m. Sarah, dau. of Elizabeth West and sister of Stephen, John and Joice West. In his LWT John Fugler named wife Sarah, brother Richard and his son John; nephew Richard, son of Henry Fuglar; sister Mary Brown and her dau. Lucy; and sister Lucy Partin and her dau. Elizabeth Wyatt Partin. In her LWT Sarah Fuglar named son Henry Young; brothers: Stephen and John West; sister, Joice West; mother Elizabeth West; and brother John West's children: William, Mary and Ann. {CCCR:22, 40-1}

Fuglar, Richard m. by Nov 1744, Mary (N). Their children: John, Richard, Mary (m. (N) Brown), Lucy (m. (N) Partin. {CCCR:22, 40-1, 104}

Fuqua/Fewqua, Giles (d. by 1771) m. Elizabeth (N). Children: John, Giles, Joseph, Samuel, William, Hannah (m. (N) Rook), Elizabeth (m. (N) Johnson) and Dianah.{CCCR:35}

Fuqua, Randolph d. by 1802, Lydia Fuqua, admx. {PGM:11}

Galbreath, Angus m. Isabel (N). Their dau. Katharine b. 23 Oct 1742. {BPR:310}

Galbreath, Duncan m. Barbara (N). Their son Daniel b. 31 May 1743. {BPR:310}

Galbreath, William m. Margret (N). Their dau. Mary b. 15 Aug 1743. {BPR:310}

Gallimore – The orphans, Ann, Samuel, Elisabeth, Elionar and William Gallimore were ordered to be bound out in 1762. {BPVB:65}

Galloes, John m. bef. 15 (Oct 1679, (N), widow of Mathew Rushing. {CCOB (1677-79):114}

Galloway, Sarah was mother of dau. Hubbard Johnson who was bound out in 1755. {CCCR:130]

Gamlin, William m. Mary (N). Their son William b. 24 Jul 1727. {BPR:307}

Ganaway, Duke/Marmaduke d. by May 1747, Hannah Ganaway, widow and admx. Hannah Ganaway d. by 1755. Their son Marmaduke and dau. Frances were bound out in 1755. {CCCR:112, 130, 131}

Gardiner, John d. by 1745, Charles Clarke and George Read, execs. {CCCR:108}

Garner, William m. bef. 16 Jun 1677, (N), widow of John Harwood. {CCOB 1676-79:1}

Garrat, John (d. 1729) of Westover Parish, m. Elizabeth (N). Children: William and Richard. Dau.-in-law: Sarah Spell. {CCW&D (1725-31):36-7}
Garret, John m. Susanna (N). Their children: Anne (b. 22 Sep 1721),

Susanna (b. 1 Sep 1723), John (b. 10 Jul 1726), Isack (b. 9 Dec 1729), Thomas (b. 6 Dec 1730?), Abraham (b. 3 Jul 1729), Thomas (b. 6 Dec 1730) and Stephen (b. 9 Apr 1733). {BPR:305, 306, 307, 308, 309}

Garrett, William d. by 1660 leaving a widow who m. 2nd Thomas Douglas. {CCOB (1658-61):240}

Garrett, William m. bef. 31 Jan 1726, Ann (N). {CCW&D (1725-31):18-19}:

Gary, Boyce and her son James Gary sold 173 acres to Thomas Lewis in 1788. {PGR:100}

Gary, Josiah m. bef. 10 Jun 1788, Sarah (N). Their dau. Elizabeth b. 16 Dec 1791. {PGR:103; BPR:311}

Gary, Richard m. Hannah (N). Their children: Elizabeth (b. 2 Dec 1741), John (b. 4 Dec 1743) and Richard (b. 9 Sep 1745. {BPR:310}

Gary, Richard m. Mary (N). Their dau. Nancy Harrison b. 10 May 1792. {BPR:311}

Gary, William (d. ca. 1716) of Westover Parish m. Sarah (N). Children: William, Sarah, Mary, Elizabeth, John and Richard. {PGW&D (1713-1728):16}

Gary, William d. by 1759 (LWT dated 1745). Sons: Josiah, John and Thomas (d. by 1759). {PGR:68}

Gary, William (d. by 1791) m. Sarah Cate who m. 2nd Henry Tench. {PGR:161}

Gates, William m. Susannah (N). Their children: Edward (b. 6 Nov 1727) and Mary (b. 26 Feb 1732). {BPR:307, 309}

Gattley, Nicholas d. by 1677 leaving widow Sarah and dau. Sarah (m. John Crew). Widow Sarah m. John Smith (d. by 3 Mar 1690). {CCOB (1677-79:1; CCOB (1687-95):85, 91, 103}

Geddy, James Jr. m. Euphan (N). Their dau. Elizabeth Kid b. 14 Feb 1793. {BPR:311}

Gee, (N) m. Hannah (N). In 1728 Hannah Gee gave her son Henry Gee, 300 acres in Martins Brandon Parish. {PGW&D (1713-1728):180}

Gee, Charles of Martins Brandon Parish d. by 1788. His widow Mary d. 1788. In her LWT dated 1788 she named sons: Charles, John (b. 18 Jan 1744/5), Henry. She named daus.: Boyer Powell, Sary (b. 22 Aug 1743, m. John Rives), Elizabeth Potts, Mary Gee and Rebecca Parham. {PGR:108; APP 3:263; BPR:310}

Gee, Charles m. Susannah (N). Their children: Charles (b. 9 Apr 1792) and Thomas b. 21 Nov 1793. {BPR:311}

Gee, Henry (d. several years bef. 1791) m. Rachel (living in 1791) (N). Their children: sons Charles, John, and James (underage in 1791), and daus.: Elizabeth, Winny (m. John Daniel) and Sarah (d. several years bef. 1791, m. Charles Chapman). {PGR:170; SWBC:208}

Geers, Robert d. by 1756, Dorothea Geers, admx. {CCCR:135}

Gent, Jane had a son James Williams b. 21 Aug 1745. {BPR:310}

Gent, Thomas d. by 1689 leaving a widow, Sarah. {CCOB (1687-95):75, 90}

Gent/Ghents, Thomas m. Mary (N). Their children: Abraham (b. 7 Jul 1722) and Thomas (b. 8 Dec 1741). {BPR:306, 310}

Gent/Jent, William m. Mary (N). Their children: Anne (b. 4 Apr 1721), Moses (b. 15 May 1723) and Jane (b. 26 Jul 1725). {BPR:305, 306, 322}

Gerarl, John m. Anne (N). Their dau. Anne b. 17 Jun 1745. {BPR:310}

Gibbs, Cornelius m. Susanna (N). Their children: Richard (b. 22 Jun 1724), Susanna (b. 31 Jan 1726), Lucie (b. 15 Apr 1728) and Thomas (b. 14 Mar 1730). {BPR:308}

Gibbs, John m. Mary (N). Their children: Mary (b. 18 Sep 1716), Elizabeth (b. 6 Oct 1718), John (b. 30 Apr 1719), Ann (b. 23 Dec 1723), Agnis (b. 6 Oct 172-), Susannah (b. 1 Dec 1728), Phebe (b. 1 Sep 1730) and Mathew (b. 25 Sep 1732). {BPR:305, 306, 307, 308}

Gibbs, John of Chesterfield Co. m. Martha (N). Their children: John (b. 7 Mar 1792) and Martha (b. ca. 1792). {BPR:311}

Gibbs, Matthew d. by 1711, Anne Gibbs, admx. {PGW&D (1710-1713):9}

Gibbs, William m. Martha (N). Their children: John (b. 17 Dec 1744) and Pattie (b. 12 Nov 1750). {BPR:310}

Gibson, Edward of Charles City Parish, m. Anna (N). Daus.: Rebecca and Tabitha (m. (N) Ellet). {CCW&D (1725-31):22}

Gibson, George m. bef. 16 Apr 1664, Mary (N). {CCOB (1661-64):478}

Gibson, Gibby (d. 1726/7) m. Fran: (N). Gibby was father of Frances (m. George Smith), Gibby, Edward and George. {CCW&D (1725-31):15, 20-1}

Gibson, Hubberd m. bef. 11 Dec 1704, Mary (N). Their son Edward res. in NC in 1721. {PGW&D (1713-1728):78}

Gibson, John d. by 1657 leaving a dau. Elizabeth. {CCOB (1655-58):131}

Giles, Abraham d. by 1677 leaving a widow Rebecca. {CCOB 1676-79:3}

Gill, Erasmus m. Sarah (N). Their dau. Lucy Jones b. 7 Sep 1792, d. Sep 1792. {BPR:311}

Gill, Ingram m. by Aug 1761, Mary, dau. of David Davidson. {CCCR:151; 154}

Gill, Joss: m. Elizabeth (N). Their dau. Ann b. 30 May 1723. {BPR:306}

Gill, Richard (d. by 1743) m. Sarah, widow of (N) Blanks. Nicholson Blanks the son of (N) Blanks, sought compensation from Richard Gill for lumber removed from his father's farm and later from Sarah; both refused. In 1750 Sarah Gill was summoned to answer a petition of Elizabeth Minge to show cause why she should not deliver up the estate of her dec'd. husband. Sarah Gill d. by 1760, William Gill, admin. In 1761 Matthew Rogers and Anne his wife and Samuel Harwood and Elizabeth his wife vs. William Gill, admin. of Sarah Gill, dec'd., and Richard Gill and James Pearman and Sarah his wife in a chancery case. Suit dismissed by consent. {CCCR:100-1, 122, 148}

Gill, Stephen m. Martha (N). Their children: William (b. 6 Jan 1721/2) and Amy (b. 30 Aug 1729). {BPR:305, 307}

Gilley. See Gilly.

Gilliam, Charles m. Frances (N). Their children: Josiah (b. 30 Mar 1730), Elizabeth (b. 7 May 1732) and Joshua (b. 20 Mar 1733). {BPR:308, 309}

Gilliam, Epaphroditus m. by Nov 1755, Priscilla (N). Epaphroditus Gilliam d. by 1761, William Green Munford, exec. {CCCR:133, 149}

Gilliam, Harris m. Frances (N). Their children: Rebecca (b. 18 Jul 1721), William (b. 29 Jan 1723), John (b. 18 Apr 1726), Amie (b. Apr 1728), Harris (b. 8 Sep 1730) and James (b. 13 May 1733). {BPR:305, 306, 307, 308, 309}

Gillam, Hinshea (d. 1733/4) of Surry Co. m. bef. 3 Apr 1690, Fortune, dau. of Walter and Anne (Browne) Flood. {CCOB (1687-95):76; APP 1:997}

Gillam, Jeffrey, son of William Gillam (d. by 1669) and brother of Richard Gillam, res. Charles City Co. in 1692. {CCCR:74}

Gilliam, Jeffry (d. 1768-9)) m. (N)(N). Children: Richard, Ann, Jeffry, Mary and Judith (m. (N) Drake). {CCCR:10}

Gilliam, Jeffry, son of Jeffry Gilliam, m. bef. 1 Jan 1772, Sarah (N). {CCCR:42, 58, 64}

Gillam, John (d. by 1739) m. Ann (N). Their children: John (b. 2 May 1712 or 1713), Elizabeth (b. 16 Jan 1714 or 1716) and probably Mary who m. John West. {BPR:306, 307; PGR:62; PGW&D (1713-1728):74}

Gilliam, John (b. 1712, d. 1772) m. Elizabeth Poythress, dau. of Robert and Elizabeth (Cocke) Poythress. Their children: Robert (m. 1760, Lucy Skelton (b. 1743), William (d. ca. 1800), m. 30 Apr 1789, Christian Eppes), John (b. 1742, d. 1801, m. Jane Henry), Jane (m. Charles Duncan of Chesterfield Co.) and Anne (m. Nathaniel Harrison). {APP 1:130, 155}

Gilliam, John m. Elizabeth (N). Their children: John (b. 13 Dec 1725), Lucy (b. 17 Dec 1727) and William (b. 29 Nov 1744). {BPR:307, 310}

Gilliam, John, the Elder, gave his son John Gilliam, the younger, several slaves in 1789. {PGR:127}

Gilliam, John the Younger (d. 1790), of Bristol Parish m. Mary, dau. of Nathaniel Harrison. Children: Mary and Jenny. {PGR:135}

Gilliam, John, the Elder (d. 1801), son of John and Elizabeth (Poythress) Gilliam, m. Jane Henry, dau. of Rev. Patrick Henry. Children: Walter Boyd Gilliam and Mary Poythress Gilliam. In his LWT John named trustees incluing Reuben M. Gilliam to maintain Elizabeth Arthur (daughter) for life. {PGR:176; APP 1:155; SWBC:208}

Gilliam, Robert m. 1760, Lucy (b. 1743, d. by 1784), sister of Meriweather Skelton of Hanover Co. In her LWT Lucy named children: John Gilliam, James Skelton Gilliam, Reuben Meriweather Gilliam, James S. Gilliam, Elizabeth, Jane Meriweather, Meriweather Skelton, Susanna Barthurst and Anne. {PGR:124; APP1:155}

Gilliam, William (d. ca. 1800), son of John and Elizabeth (Poythress) Gilliam, m. 30 Apr 1789, Christian Eppes, dau. of Richard and Christian (Robertson) Eppes. Their children: Elizabeth (b. 26 Oct 1792) and John (b. 15 Apr 1795). {APP1:155, 918; BPR:311}

Gillis, John d. by 1657. His children: Grace and John, both appointed guardians, George Atkins and William Dollin, respectively. {CCOB (1655-58):107}

Gilley, Edward Jr. m. bef. 3 Oct 1678, Mary, dau. of Roger Wamsley. Their dau.: Mary. {CCOB 1676-79):75, 102}

Gilly, John d. by 1742, Edward Gilly, exec. {CCCR:96}

Glascock, Robert m. Rachel (N). Their son John b. 3 Feb 1722. {BPR:306}

Glass, John m. by April 1746, Elizabeth (N). {CCCR:109}

Glass, Joshua m. Sarah (N). Their children: John (b. 10 Oct 1726), Elizabeth (b. 15 Apr 1728), Sarah (b. 24 Jan 1729), Joshua (b. 26 Apr 1731) and Mary (b. 17 Feb 1732). {BPR:307, 308}

Glidwell, Robert m. Elizabeth (N). Their children: Nash (b. 19 Jun 1721), Susan (b. 13 Nov 172-) and Robert (b. 23 Oct 1722). {BPR:305, 307}

Glidwell, Elizabeth had a son Tarance Lamb Glidewell b. 14 Jan 1733. {BPR:309}

Glidwell/Gloydwells, Nash m. Martha (N). Their son Peter b. 9 Oct 1741. {BPR:310}

Glover, Edward m. bef. 14 Apr 1789, Rebecca (N). {PGR:114}

Goeing, Phillis was presented in 1739 for having a bastard child. {CCCR:86}

Golighty, Christopher m. bef. 12 Jun 1739, Frances [?Shands, dau. of Thomas Shands]. {PGR:46; GVAT (Genealogies of Virginia Families) III:276}

Golightly, Hugh of Bristol Parish m. bef. 9 Oct 1727, Jane (N). Their children: Mary (b. 24 Jul 1720), Thomas (b. 27 May 1725) and John. {PGW&D (1713-1728): 170; BPR:305, 306}

Golightly, John had a son Hugh Lee b. 27 Sep 1725. {BPR:306}

Golloford, Nicholas m. bef. Dec 1737, Mary, admx. of John Hood. {CCCR:81}

Good, John m. bef. 5 Jan 1690, (N), admx. of John Barker. {CCOB (1687-95):99}

Good, John m. ca. 1690, Elizabeth, widow of John Tatem. {CCOB (1687-95):24, 81}

Good, Peter m. bef. 5 Dec 1678, Naomy, widow of Theo. Benningfield. {CCOB 1676-79:9, 57, 80}

Good, Robert Jr. m. bef. Jun 1737, Agnes (N). {CCCR:78}

Good, Thomas m. by Nov 1750, Lucy (N). {CCCR:122}

Goodall, (N) m. Rebecca (N). Their son William was bound out to Edward Brodnax in 1739. {CCCR:84}

Goodall, John m. bef. Nov 1739, Mary (N). {CCCR:86}

Goodey, John m. Susannah (N). Their children: Sarah (b. 18 Jul 1790) and Elizabeth Cain (b. 15 Oct 1791). {BPR:311}

Goodgame, David and Joshua Goodgame of Martins Brandon Parish, sold 289 acres to David Wallace in 1733. {PGR:179}

Goodgame, David (d. by 1791) m. Elizabeth (N). {PGR:151}

Goodgar, Thomas m. bef. 15 Sep 1673, Elizabeth (N). {CCOB (Fragments):544}

Goodrich, Benjamin d. by 1761 leaving an orphan Frances who chose Benjamin Bradley her guardian and a dau. Elizabeth who chose John Dancy as her guardian. Later in 1762 Frances chose John Dancy as her guardian. {CCCR:149, 153}

Goodrich, Charles (d. ca. 1723) m. bef. 10 Dec 1712, Mary, widow of Col. John Hardyman. Probable sons: Edward and Charles. {PGW&D (1710-1713):28; GVAT (Genealogies of Virginia Families) II:23}

Goodrich, Charles (d. ca. 1728), probable son of Charles Goodrich (d. ca. 1723), m. (N)(N). Children: Anne (m. John Hamlin), Sarah and Lucy. {GVAT (Genealogies of Virginia Families) II:23}

Goodrich, Capt. Edward (d. by 1720, owning land in Prince George and Surry cos.) of Prince George Co., probable son of Charles Goodrich, m. bef. 10 Feb 1711, Margaret (N) (d. by 1723). Children: Mary, Benjamin Elizabeth and Edward. {PGW&D (1710-1713): 16; PGW&D (1713-1728):67-8, 97; GVAT (Genealogies of Virginia Families) II:23}

Goodwyn, Joseph, son of Thomas Goodwyn, m. Miss Peterson (b. Isle of Wight Co.). Children: possibly John, Joseph (m. Mary Coleman), Braddock (m. Elizabeth Brown), Esau (m. S. Sturdivant), Peterson (twin with Joseph, m. Elizabeth Peterson), possibly a son, Burwell Goodwyn. {W&M Vol. 6, No. 2, Supplement (Oct. 1897):104-114}

Goodwyn, Matthew m. Ann (N). Their children: John (b. 20 Apr 1740), Burwell and Susannah (b. 17 Dec 1736). {BPR:309; GVAW (Genealogies of Virginia Families) II:727}

Goodwynne, Thomas d. by 1711. Probable dau.: Grace. {PGW&D (1710-1713):5, 23}

Goodwyn, Thomas gave 150 acres in 1721 to John Scott Jr. who m. Amy, dau. of Thomas Goodwyn. {PGW&D (1713-1728):71}

Goodwyn, Thomas m. Martha Thweatt, dau. of John Thweatt (d. by 1759). Their children: Thomas, Matthew, Joseph, Tabitha (b. 25 Jan 1721), David (b. 27 Aug 1722), Amy and James (m. Judith Thweatt). {BPR:305, 306; GVAW (Genealogies of Virginia Families) II:727}

Goodwyn, Thomas (d. ca. 1781 from wounds received in the Rev. War, left heir at law, Harman D. Beadles. {Legislative Petitions – Library of VA website}

Gordon, Alexander d. by 1791. {PGR:166}

Gordon, James, son of James and Mary Gordon, m. 30 Jun 1774, Ann Payne, dau. of Col. John Payne of Goochland Co. Ann d. 16 Mar 1798. {GVAT (Genealogies of Virginia Families) II:26, 27; PGM:11}

Gough, Rebecca d. by 1694, William Gough, exec. {CCOB (1687-95):186}

Gower, William d. by 1695 leaving a widow, Ann Gower. {CCOB (1687-95):213}

Gower, William of Brunswick Co., planter, m. Ann (N). Their children: William (b. 30 Apr 1725) and Elizabeth (b. 18 Mar 1726). {PGW&D (1713-1728):149; BPR:307}

Gracie, Archibald m. Hester (N). Their dau. Sarah Rogers b. 14 Dec 1791. {BPR:310}

Grammer, Grief (d. 1787) of Bristol Parish, brother of John Grammer, m. Polly (N). Children: Sally, Martha and the child yet unborn at the time his LWT was written. Execs.: John Grammer and James Cureton. {PGR:92, 147}

Grammer, John m. Priscilla (N). Their dau. Mary Wright b. 30 Jan 1792. {BPR:310}

Grammer, John (d. 1789) m. Lucy (N). Children: Peter, John, Frances (m. (N) Livesay), Angelina, Sally, Lucy and Jackabinah. {PGR:127}

Grammer, Joseph m. Elizabeth (N). Their children: Peter (b. 11 Oct 1744) and Joseph (b. 14 Mar 1745/6). {BPR:310}

Grammer, Timothy (d. 1787) of Martins Brandon Parish m. Prisiller (N). Children: William, James, Jeremiah, John, Nancy and Joseph. In his LWT Timothy devised to wife Prisiller Grammer's son, Paton Grammer, 1 shilling. {PGR:88}

Granger/Grainger, Benjamin m. Anne (N). Their children: John (b. 24 Dec 1726), Joseph (b. 10 Feb 1727), Benjamin (b. 21 Feb 1730), Frances

(b. 2 Sep 1731) and Edith (15 Jun 1734). {BPR:307, 308, 309}

Granger, Joseph gave his "son-in-law," Daniel Jackson, 100 acres in 1727. {PGW&D (1713-1728):175}

Grant, John (d. by Apr 1801) of Dinwiddie Co. m. (N) (N). Children: Aaron (had son John Grant), Stephen, Burwell, Lucy (had dau. Sally Grant). {SWBC:53}

Grantham, James m. Jean (N). Their dau. Delilah Peterson, b. 17 Dec 1792. {BPR:311}

Gray, Alexander m. Mary (N). Their dau. Ann b. 20 May 1734. {BPR:309}

Green, Abraham m. by Nov 1742, Elizabeth (N). {CCCR:96}

Green, Burrell m. bef. 11 Dec 1721, Anne Poythress, dau. of Francis and Rebecca (Wynne) Poythress. {PGW&D (1713-1728):77; GVAW (Genealogies of Virginia Families):IV:175}

Green, Burwell m. Mary (N). Their children: Burwell (b. 25 Aug 1741) and William Randolph (b. 26 Mar 1743). {BPR:310}

Green, Francis Burwell m. bef. 27 May 1789 Mary (N). {PGR:119}

Green, George m. Rosamond (N). Their children: Mary (b. 24 Feb 1721) and Ann (b. 1 Feb 1729). {BPR:307, 308}

Green, Henry m. Elizabeth (N). Their children: John (b. 10 Jan 1724), Dorcus (b. 27 Sep 1726) and Winnifrid (b. 17 Mar 1731). {BPR:306, 307, 308}

Green, John m. Abigall, dau. of Thomas Tippett. Their children: Mary (b. 9 Aug 1722), Ann (b. 12 Jan 1725), Margret (b. 15 Feb 1727), Jemima (b. 28 Jul 1731) and Martha (b. 1741). {BPR:306, 307, 308; OP; KGDB3:40; KGOB1721-1724:61)

Green, John m. Esther (N). Their son Jonathan b. 29 Dec 1732. {BPR:309}

Green, John m. bef. 4 Feb 1801, Anne (N). {PGM:8}

Green, Luis m. Frances (N). Their son Peter b. 16 Oct 1720. {BPR:305}

Green, Lewis, Sr. gave his son Lewis Green Jr. ½ of his title to a grist mill on Easterly Run in Martins Brandon Parish. {PGW&D (1713-1728):89}

Green, Luis m. Susanna (N). Their dau. Susanna b. 14 Jul 1723. {BPR:306}

Green, Peter m. Mary (N). Their dau. Martha b. 27 May 1728. {BPR:307}

Green, Richard m. Elizabeth (N). Their son? Ann b. 25 Feb 1733. {BPR:309}

Green, Walker (d. by 1726) m. Martha (N), widow of (N)(N). Walker was father of Wilson and James. Mrs. Martha Green d. by 1769. {CCW&D (1725-31):16; CCCR:43}

Greene, William m. bef. 3 May 1661, (N), widow of David Ramsey. {CCOB 1658-61):271}

Green, William d. by 1662 leaving a son William. {CCOB (1661-64):342}

Green, William m. Amey (N). Their dau. Martha b. 8 May 1734. {BPR:309}

Green, William (d. 1790) of Martins Brandon Parish m. Elizabeth (N). Children: Frederick and Ann. Elizabeth Green and Francis B. Green, execs. of William Green. {PGR:130, 132, 150, 169}

Green, William Irby m. Mary (N). Their son William Irby b. 30 Dec 1730. {BPR:323}

Greenaway, Edward d. by 1689 leaving a widow Sarah, admx. {CCOB (1687-95):61}

Greenhill, Joseph m. bef. 1 May 1723, Frances (N). {PGW&D (1713-1728):102}

Greeshon, James of Westover Parish m. bef. 5 Nov 1719, Margaret (N). {PGW&D (1713-1728):57}

Gregory, (N) m. bef. 9 Jun 1716, Elizabeth, dau. of John Nance (d. 1716). {PGW&D (1713-1728):21}

Gregory, John m. bef. Sep 1738, Elizabeth, admx. of Turner Hunt. {CCCR:83}

Gregory, John was granted admin. of the estate of his son Thomas in Jun 1749. {CCCR:118}

Gregory, John (d. by Sep 1777) m. Martha (probably Mumford). Children: Richmond and John Mumford Gregory. John was the brother of William Gregory. Execs. of John's will: wife and William Green Mumford. {SWBC:36}

Gregory, John m. (bond dated 3 Aug 1774), Elizabeth Maynard. {MB:194}

Gregory, John Sherman (d. by 1762) m. bef. by Jun 1761 Mary (N). John S. Gregory d. leaving orphans, John, Ann (minor in 1773), Mary, Samuel and William. Guardians: William Green Munford, William Gregory and Stephen Bowry. {CCCR:37, 149, 158}

Gregory, Richard Jr.* (b. 12 Jan 1758, d. 20 Dec 1844) of the town of Petersburg, son of Roger and Mary Cole (Claiborne) Gregory, m. 1st 20 Sep 1777, Mary (Ward) Broadnax and m. 2nd 6 Jul 1789, Elizabeth Wilkinson. Richard gave Patsey Gregory, youngest dau. of Roger Gregory, a Negro girl, Claressey. * addressed as Jr. to distinguish him from his uncle, Richard Gregory. Richard Gregory Jr. gave his brother-in-law (*step-brother*), Herbert Gregory, a Negro girl, Milly. In 1790 Richard Gregory Jr. gave his brother-in-law (*step-brother*) Francis Gregory a Negro boy, Will. {APP3:496-7; PGR:143, 145}

Grigory, Richard m. Elizabeth (N). Their children: Wilson (b. 28 Sep 1791) and Harriott (b. 27 Oct 1792. {BPR:310, 311}

Gregory, Roger (b. 12 Feb 1761, d. 1811), son of Roger and Mary Cole (Claiborne), m. Sarah Southerland. Roger was father of youngest dau., Patsey. {APP3:496-7; PGR:143}

Gregory, Samuel (d. 1768), brother of John Gregory, m. by May 1760, Elizabeth, widow of Henry Charles. Children: William and Sarah (m. Nicholas Holt). Elizabeth m. 2nd Theodorick Carter. {CCCR:16, 144, 165; SWBC:36}

Gregory, Sarah d. by 1762, John Gregory, admin. {CCCR:154}

Gregory, Sylvanus d. by 1761, leaving orphans: Wilson Gregory chose

William Green Munford his guardian; Jane Gregory chose Sylvanus Gregory who is also appointed guardian of James Gregory, orphan of Sylvanus. {CCCR:146}

Gregory, Thomas (d. by 1655) m. Jane (N). Their son: Thomas. Jane m. 2nd (N) Parsons. {CCOB (1655-58): 42, 69, 70}

Gregory, Thomas m. Jane (N). Their dau. Lucey b. 9 Jul 1734. {BPR:309}

Gregory, Thomas d. by 1679, Joyce, wife and extx. {CCOB 1777-79):118}

Gregory/Grigory, Thomas (d. by 1724) m. Elizabeth, dau. of John Nance. Their children: Nance (b. 10 Nov 1720/1), John (b. 30 Jan 1722), John (b. 1 Jan 1723) and Mary (b. 9 Sep 1724). {BPR:305, 306; CCW&D (1725-31):1}

Gregory, Thomas d. by 1737 leaving a dau. Sarah (m. Sampson Cordle) and other children who were bound out. {CCCR:78; PGR:55}

Gregory, Thomas (d. 1773), m. Lucy (pregnant when LWT of Thomas was written). In his LWT he named brothers John, William and Samuel Gregory and brother-in-law John Gregory. {CCCR:50}

Gregory, William, son of Samuel Gregory (d. 1768), m. bef. 4 Oct 1769, Miriam (N). Children: Samuel and Elizabeth. {CCCR:16, 165}

Gregory, William gave his father Samuel Gregory a Negro girl Hannah and his part of the personal estate of Martha Green, dec'd., in 1768. {CCCR:6}

Gregory, William (d. by Aug 1776) m. (N) (N). Children: William (underage in 1776). {SWBC:36}

Gregory, William m. (bond dated 24 Jul 1764) Ann Royster (Spinster). {MB:193}

Grendon, Thomas (d. 1683-5) of Westover Parish, son of Thomas (son of Thomas) and Elizabeth Grendon, m. Sarah (N), widow of (1) Thomas Stegge, Jr. and (2) George Harris. Sarah m. 4th Edward Braine. {CCCR:159; APP 2:225-6; SWBC:37}

Gresset, James d. by 1740, Thomas Gresset, exec. {CCCR:89}

Grey, Capt. Francis m. ca. 1640, Grace (N). Dau.: Elizabeth. The court approved their separation because of his ill treatment in 1665. At this point they had six children, three of whom were married. {CCOB (1664-65):491, 569, 576}

Grey, Peter m. Mary (N) who d. by 1661. {CCOB (1661-64):294}

Grice, Aristotle d. by 1740, Jeffrey Murrell and Richard Christian and Richard's wife Lucy, admins. {CCCR:88}

Grice, Edward, brother of William Grice, d. by 1727. {CCW&D (1725-31):22}

Griffin, Richard m. bef. 3 Jun 1692, Elizabeth (N), admx. of Jacob Bayly. {CCOB (1687-95):127, 138}

Griffin, Richard m. Mary (N). Their children: Ralph (b. 16 Feb 1725), John (b. 22 Jun 1727) and William (b. 21 Nov 1740). {BPR:306, 307, 309}

Griffith, (N) (d. by 1727), m. Elizabeth (d. by 1728). Children: Thomas (d. without issue, Martins Brandons Parish, ca. 1728), John (had a son William), Joannah, William and Richard. In her LWT Elizabeth also named granddau., Susannah Short, dau. of William and Elizabeth Short. PGW&D (1713-1728):177, 180}

Griffith, Richard d. by 1719, Elizabeth Griffith, admx. {PGW&D (1713-1728):53-4}

Griffith, William (d. ca. 1727), son of Elizabeth Griffith, m. Katherine (N). Son: Thomas. {PGW&D (1713-1728):176, 180}

Grigg, Abner, son of William Grigg, m. Mary (N). Their son William b. 6 Mar 1740. {BPR:309}

Grigg, Burwell/Burrell, son of Jesse and Amey Grigg, m. (N)(N). Their dau. Susanna m. 1st 22 Jan 1788, James Eppes and m. 2nd (N) Walker. {APP 1:875}

Grigg, James m. Frances (N). Their children: Elizabeth (b. 24 Apr 1726) and James (b. 7 Jan 1729). {BPR:307}

Grigg, Jessey, son of William Grigg (d. ca. 1726), m. Amey (N). Their son Burrell/Burwell b. 28 Apr 1741. {BPR:309}

Grigg, William of Bristol Parish m. bef. 4 Jun 1711, Susan (N). Children: William and James. {PGW&D (1710-1713):9; PGW&D (1713-1749-50}

Grigg, William (d. ca. 1726, predeceasing his mother and father), son of William and Susan/Susanna Grigg and brother of James Grigg. m. Elizabeth (N). Children: Abner, Jesse, Lewis, Burrell and Susanna/Susan (b. 11 Jun 1720). {PGW&D (1713-1728):149-50; BPR:306}

Gross, Solomon m. bef. Apr 1738, Joanna (N). {CCCR:82}

Gubbins, Hugh was buried 11 Oct 1660. {CCOB 1658-61):270}

Gulson, John of Martins Brandon Parish m. bef. 13 Jul 1714, Mary (N). {PGW&D (1713-1728):3}

Gundry, John m. bef. 1 May 1655, Ann (N). {CCOB (1658-61):274}

Gunn, James m. bef. 15 Sep 1677, (N), widow of Jeremy Woodhall. {CCOB (1677-79):20}

Gunn, James m. by Jun 1744, Isabella (N). {CCCR:103}

Gunter, Thomas m. Martha (N). Their children: John (b. 19 Oct 1723) and Mary (b. 17 Dec 1724). {BPR:306, 307}

Hacker, John, late of Lyme House, county Middlesex, England, d. by 1657 leaving widow Elizabeth and son John, minor. {CCOB (1655-58):124}

Hackney, Thomas m. Sarah (N). Their children: William (b. 28 Sep 1725), Frances (b. 20 Jan 1729) and John (b. 9 Mar 1734). {BPR:313, 315, 317}

Haddon, Francis m. Frances (N). Their children: Lucy (b. 15 Jul 1743), Edward (b. 8 Apr 1745) and Mary (b. 13 May 1748). {BPR:318, 319}

Haddon, Francis m. Becky (N). Their son Peterson b. 8 Mar 1792. {BPR:321}

Hair, Thomas m. Ann (N). Their children: Daniel (b. 18 Dec 1760), James (b. 7 Apr 1762) and Mary (b. 14 Nov 1763). {BPR:320}

Hailes, (N) d. by 1771 leaving orphans James Green Hailes and Susanna Hailes to whom were appointed a guardian, Richard Hailes. {CCCR:37, 56}

Hales, John d. by 1743, John Hales, exec. {CCCR:98}

Hales, Richard d. by 1743, leaving an orphan Richard who was appointed John Hales as his guardian. {CCCR:101}

Hales, Thomas (d. by 1728) m. Martha Dennis, dau. of Richard and Mary Dennis. Their son: Richard who was bound to John Hales Jr. in 1740. Martha m. 2nd Pridgen Waddill. {APP3:48, 56-7; CCW&D 1725-31:2; HCW 1:22-3, 154, 156; CCCR:81, 89}

Haley, James (d. by 1714) m. (N)(N). Children: William, Elizabeth (m. Walter Jeffreys), Sarah (m. Peter Talbott), Jane and Johannah, all children-in-law (*step-children?*) of John Middleton of Martins Brandon Parish. {PGW&D (1713-1728):6, 56}

Halford, Tobias d. by 1678, Ann Halford, widow. {CCOB (1677-79):40}

Hall, Edward m. Elizabeth (N). Their children: John (b. 1 Oct 1721), Richard (twin, b. 1 Oct 1721) and Patrick (b. 4 May 1724). {BPR:312, 314}

Hall, Elisha of New Kent Co. m. bef. 31 Oct 1783, Carolina Carter, under the guardianship of Charles Carter of Shirley in Charles City Co. {HCDB 1:26}

Hall, Hugh (b. 1733, res. in Dinwiddie Co., d. 1771), son of John and Ann (Bolling) Hall, m. Mary Dixon. {GVAW (Genealogies of Virginia Families) II:837)

Hall, Instant m. bef. 10 Oct 1712, Mary (N). Their children: James (b. 3 Jan 1701/2), Judith (b. 17 Jun 1705), Instant (b. 28 Oct 1707), John (b. 18 Jan 1709/10), Frances (b. 20 Jul 1716), George (b. 20 Jan 1718/19) and William (b. 22 Apr 1721). On 12 Dec 1738 William Hall, one of the orphans of Instance Hall, dec'd., chose his brother John Hall as his guardian. {PGW&D (1710-1713):27; PGR:27; BPR:312}

Hall, Instance m. Elizabeth (N). Their dau. Mary Herbert Stith b. 20 May 1792. {BPR:321}

Hall, James m. Ruth (N). Their children: Frances (b. 8 Feb 1725), (N) (b. 27 Nov 1726), Theodrick (b. 27 Nov 1726) and John (b. 2 Mar 1728). {BPR:314, 315}

Hall, Joel Stirdevent, son of Mary Hall, b. 30 Jul 1760. {BPR:320}

Hall, John, "sometime of Virginia," and brother of Hugh Hall, his eldest brother, of island of Barbados, d. by 1714 when his widow, Prudence Hall was living in West Ham, County Essex, England. Their son John d. by 1714. {PGW&D (1713-1728):15}

Hall, John m. Martha (N). Their children: John (b. 3 Feb 1742) and Anne (b. 22 Jun 1745). {BPR:318, 319}

Hall, Oswin d. by 1660 leaving a widow Jane and their children: Jane, Anne and Hellena. {CCOB (1658-61):247}

Hall, Robert d. by 1738, Elizabeth Ravenscroft and John Hall, execs. {PGR:36}

Hall, Thomas of Prince George Co. m. in 1739, Molly, dau. of Major Henry Power of James City Co. {GVAW (Genealogies of Virginia Families) I:460}

Hall, Thomas m. bef. 10 Oct 1787, Fanny (N), res. in Warren Co., NC. In 1787 they sold 140 acres in Bristol Parish to Instance Hall. {PGR:103}

Hall, William, son of Mary Hall was apprenticed to Henry Wilson bef. 1738. {PGR:23}

Hall, William m. bef. 12 Feb 1739, Frances, probable widow of John Sykes. {PGR:65}

Hall, William m. Elizabeth (N). Their dau. Salley b. 14 Feb 1792. {BPR:320}

Hall, Willis d. by 1787, father of William Hall. {PGR:152, 155}

Hallom/Hallam, Robert (d. by 1661), from Burnham, County Essex, England, brother of William Hallom, m. ca. 1630, Ann, widow of John Price. Dau.: Sara m. Samuel Woodward. Ann m. 3rd Daniel Llewellyn. {APP 2:231-2; CCOB (1655-58):56; CCOB (1658-61):275}

Hallom, Thomas (d. by 1656) m. Margaret (N). They had a son Thomas. Margaret m. 2nd bef. 20 Apr 1657, William Mason. {CCOB (1655-58):103; APP2:232}

Hallford, Tobias d. by 1677, Ann, widow and admx. {CCOB (1677-79):19}

Hamilton, Andrew of the town of Petersburg d. 8 Mar 1794. {BPR:321}

Hamleton, David m. Elizabeth (N). Their children: John (b. 22 Aug 1728) and Ann (b. 5 May 1730). {BPR:315}

Hamelton, George d. by 1739, execs., his sons, William and Marmaduke. {PGR:45}

Hamlet, John m. bef. 3 Apr 1731, Sarah (N). {CCW&D (1725-31):47}

Hamlet, Richard had a son Maurice, bapt. 4 Apr 1660. {CCOB 1658-61):270}

Hamlet, Richard d. by 1661, leaving widow, Elizabeth and son Richard. Elizabeth m. 2nd Feacro Labelle. {CCOB (1658-61):264; CCOB (1664-65):588}

Hamlet, Richard m. by Apr 1743, Ann (N). In 1750 Richard Hamlet recorded a deed of gift to his son John Hamlet. {CCCR:98, 1213}

Hamlet, Thomas made a gift to his son Thomas in 1738. {CCCR:84}

Hamlet, Thomas recorded a deed of gift to his son George in 1756. {CCCR:136}

Hamlet, William d. testate by 1750, William Hamlet, exec. {CCCR:122}

Hamlin, Charles d. by 1695 leaving an orphan, Mary Hamlin who chose Nicholas Haynes as her guardian. {CCOB (1687-95):203}

Hamlin, Charles m. bef. 13 Mar 1738, Martha ()N). {PGR:35}

Hamblin, Hubbard (d. bef. the death of his wife) m. Lucy (N). Their son John was father of Susan. {PGR:86}

Hamlin/Hamblin, Capt. John m. bef. 3 Aug 1688, Elizabeth (d. by 1720), dau. of Richard Taylor and sister of Capt. John Taylor and Richard Taylor (d. by 1694). Children: John, William, Hannah, Lucy, Sarah, Elizabeth (m. (N)(N)) and probably Richard. {CCOB (1687-95):26-7, 197; PGW&D (1713-1728):65, 86; GVAW (Genealogies of Virginia Families) V:488-9}

Hamlin, John (d. ca. 1725, owning land in Isle of Wight Co.) of Martins Brandon Parish, son of Capt. John Hamlin, m. Ann, dau. of Charles

Goodrich. Children: John, Peter, Charles, Hubbard, William, Ann and Mary (m. John Irby). In his LWT John also named "brothers," Thomas Ravenscroft and William Hamlin as trustees. {PGR:61; PGW&D (1713-1728):97, 130, 146; GVAW (Genealogies of Virginia Families) V:489}

Hamlin, Capt. Peter d. by 1711. {PGW&D (1710-1713): 18}

Hamlin, Richard (d. by 1718), probable son of Capt. John Hamlin, m. Ann Harrison, dau. of Thomas and Elenor Harrison. Their children: Thomas, Martha, Richard, Elizabeth and Sarah (m. Francis Eppes). {PGW&D (1713-1728):40; GVAW (Genealogies of Virginia Families) V:489}

Hamlin, Stephen d. by 15 Sep 1692 leaving an orphan, Charles, placed in the care of Abraham Hamlin and later bound to Capt. John Hamlin to learn trade of carpenter. {CCOB (1687-95):136, 154}

Hamlin, Thomas m. bef. Dec 1687 (N), widow of Anthony Wynd. {CCOB (1687-95):2}

Hamlin, Thomas m. Pheboe (N). Their children: Peter (b. 6 Aug 1732) and Anne (b. 21 Aug 1733). {BPR:316, 317}

Hammond, John m. Elizabeth (N) Their children: Ruth (b. 8 Feb 1730) and John (b. 17 May 1733). {BPR:315, 317}

Hancock, Thomas and Mary Hancock d. by 1696. {CCOB (Fragments, 1696):90}

Handy, William d. by 1745, Mary Handy, widow and admx. {CCCR:106}

Handson, Richard d. by 1679. Son: Daniel Warriner. {CCOB 1676-79):86}

Hansil, William m. (bond dated 7 Aug 1780, Judith Crew. {MB:195}

Hardey, John m. Rachell (N). Their son James b. 29 Feb 1740/1. {BPR:318}

Hardaway, Drury, son of Joseph Hardaway, m. Anne (N). Their son Benjamin Stith b. 30 Dec 1791. {BPR:320; GVAW (Genealogies of Virginia Families) II:837}

Hardaway/Hardway, James, brother of John Hardway (d. by 1664), had a son John as of 1664. {CCOB (1664-65):497}

Hardeway, James m. Frances (N). They had children, including dau. Sarah who received a gift from Susan Hardeway. The widow Frances Hardeway m. 2nd James Batty. {CCOB (1687-95):71}

Hardaway/Hardway, John d. by 1693 leaving orphans: John (age 15 in 1693) and others. John chose his brother-in-law Henry Hatcher of Henrico Co. as his guardian. {CCOB (1687-95):149}

Hardaway/Hardiway, John m. Frances, dau. of Samuel Markam. Their children: James Markam (b. 21 Jan 1729), Jeane (b. 21 Mar 1731), Thomas (b. 20 Sep 1734), Kerenhappuck (b. 27 Jan 1741) and Ainsworth (b. 30 Jun 1742). {BPR:315, 317; PGR:1, 29}

Hardaway, Joseph m. Ann (N). Their children: Lucey (b. 25 May 1755), Drury (b. 13 Aug 1756), Mason (dau., b. 6 Feb 1758) and Ann (b. 24 Sep 1759). {BPR:319; GVAW (Genealogies of Virginia Families) II:837}

Hardaway, Thomas m. 1st Jane, probable dau. of Col. Drury Stith. Their children: James (b. 10 Jul 1719), Jane (b. 26 Mar 1721), William (b. 12 Jun 1723), Frances (b. 4 Apr 1725), Joseph (b. 9 Mar 1728), Drury (b. 2 Apr 1733) and possibly Stith. Thomas m. 2nd m. Agnis Thweatt. Their children: Susannah (b. 27 Sep 1740, m. Peter Manson) and Agnes (b. 30 Mar 1749, m. Peter Manson, widower of her sister). {APP 1:259; BPR:312, 313, 316, 318, 381; GVAW {Genealogies of Virginia Families) II:843}

Hardaway, Thomas m. Sarah Jones, sister of Ludwell Jones. Sarah d. in 1761 leaving a son Thomas Hardaway, Jr. {W&M, Vol. 23, No. 3 (Jan., 1915): 217}

Harding, Anne had a son Charles who was to serve Mrs. Hodges beginning in 1688 until age 21. {CCOB (1687-95):21}

Hardey, John m. Rachell (N). Their son Richard b. 20 Aug 1741. {BPR:318}

Hardyman, Francis (d. by 1741) , probable son of Col. John Hardyman, m. 1st bef. 14 Dec 1721, Sarah, dau. of John Taylor. Francis m. 2nd Jane, widow of John Cross. Richard Kennon and David Stokes were execs. of the LWT of Francis Hardyman. His widow, Jane Hardyman, was appointed guardian to their children, James and Mary Hardyman. Francis was father of Francis, John, Henrietta Maria (m. James Clark), Littlebury, James and Martha. John Hardyman was appointed guardian of his brother Littlebury in Feb 1741. Jane Hardyman d. by 1743. Subsequently, Richard Kennon was appointed guardian to James Hardyman. {GVAT (Genealogies of Virginia Families) IV:536; PGW&D (1713-1728):78, 100, 136; CCCR:92, 94, 100; GVAW II:863}

Hardyman, Francis (d. 1763) m. by Mar 1756, Mary (N). Children: William, Francis, John, James, Sarah and Lucy. {CCCR:1, 135}

Hardyman, Col. John (d. 18 Sep 1711 in Prince George Co.), Justice of Charles City Co., m. Mary, dau. of Francis Epes. John Hardyman was admin. of the estate. Children: John and probably: Francis, James, Littlebury, and William. Mary m. 2nd Major Charles Goodrich. {APP 1:863; PGW&D (1710-1713): 18, 28; GVAW (Genealogies of Virginia Families) II:862}

Hardyman/Hardiman, John, son of Col. John Hardyman, m. bef. 10 Oct 1721, Henrietta Maria, dau. of John Taylor. {GVAT (Genealogies of Virginia Families) II:486; IV:536; PGW&D (1713-1728):76, 85}

Hardyman, John d. by 1738, leaving a orphan dau., Ann. {PGR:35}

Hardyman, Littlebury of Martins Brandon Parish (d. by 1728), probable son of Col. John Hardyman, m. Judith (N). {PGW&D (1713-1728):152, 153}

Hardyman, Littlebury (d. 1771), brother of John Hardyman, m. Susanna (N) (d. by 6 Nov 1771). Children: Littlebury Hardyman, Susanna Stith Hardyman (appointed a guardian, William Green Munford, in 1773, m. Daniel Jones), Frances/Fanny Hardyman (m. John Binford of Northampton Co., NC) and Lucy Hardyman (m. Col. John Bradley). {CCCR:38, 57, 65; GVAW ii;864}

Hardyman, Littlebury, son of Littlebury Hardyman, m. (bond dated 12 Apr 1784), Elizabeth, dau. of Peter Eppes (d. 1773). Elizabeth m. 2nd John Cocke. {CCCR:53-4; APP1:870, 911; MB:194}

Hardman/Herdman, Robert d. by 1659 leaving a son Robert (b. ca. 1638). {CCOB (1658-61):203}

Hardy, John gave his dau. Elizabeth Eppes 2 Negroes, Phillis and Hall on 4 May 1768. {CCCR:5-6}

Hare, Parker m. by Apr 1760, Rebecca (N). {CCCR:143}

Hargrave, Jessee, son of Samuel and Martha Hargrave of Caroline Co., m. 10th da., 9th mo., 1776, Mary Pleasants, dau. of John and Agness Pleasants of Henrico Co., at Picquenocque, Henrico Co. {HMM:55, 57}

Hargrave, Samuel, son of Joseph Hargrave, dec'd., of Surry Co., and Elizabeth Charles, dau. of Thomas Charles, dec'd., of Charles City Co., m. 9th da., 2nd mo., 1790 at Waynoak Meeting House. Their children: Thomas (b. 21st da., 11th mo., 1790), Anna (b. 28th da., 8th mo., 1793), Charles (b. 19th da., 10th mo., 1795), Joseph (b. 2nd da., 10th mo., 1797), Lemuel (b. 20th da., 10th mo., 1799), Mary, Martha (b. 15th da., 6th mo., 1801) and Jane (b. 16th da., 3rd mo., 1809). {HMM:74, 76, 84}

Hargrave, Thomas m. Sarah (N). Their dau. Elizabeth Ann Hargrave b. 14th da., 9th mo., 1821. {HMM:84}

Harmond, Henry m. bef. 5 Aug 1679, (N), widow of John Ludwell. {CCOB (1677-79):111}

Harman, Henry m. bef. 15 Sep 1690, Alice, widow of Robert Shorte. {CCOB (1687-95):91; CCCR:67}

Harmer, Thomas m. Anne (N). Their dau. Anne b. 2 Mar 1745/6. {BPR:319}

Harper, Joseph m. Susannah (N). Their son George b. 24 Dec 1732. {BPR:316}

Harris, (N) (d. by 1749) m. Martha (N). Their son Edward was bound out in 1749. {CCCR:118}

Harris, Benjamin of Martins Brandon Parish d. by 1739 leaving widow Elizabeth. {PGR:62}

Harris, Elizabeth was presented in 1760 for having a bastard child. In May 1760 her son, David Harris was bound out. {CCCR:143, 144}

Harris, George d. by 1673, leaving widow, Sarah. {CCOB (Fragments):510}

Harris, Mary was presented on 8 Apr 1739 for havaing a bastard child. {PGR:41}

Harris, Richard m. Elizabeth (N). Their son Richard b. 18 Feb 1740/1. {BPR:318}

Harris, Robert of Martins Brandon Parish m. bef. 12 Jun 1787, Fatha (N). {PGR:84}

Harris, Thomas, son of Benjamin Harriss, dec'd., of Hanover Co., m. 6th da., 3rd mo., 1787 Chlotilda Ladd, dau. of James Ladd at Charles City Co. Meeting House. {HMM:71}

Harris, Timothy m. Ann (N). Their son Timothy (b. 1 Aug 1720), George (b. 27 Feb 1723) and Edward (b. 27 Mar 1726). {PGW&D (1713-1728):106; BPR:312, 313, 314}

Harris, William d. 8 Mar 1687/8, age 35. {W&M Vol. 4, No. 3 (Jan., 1896):148}

Harris, William had a dau. Ann, b. 7 Mar 1729. {BPR:315}

Harrison, (N) m. bef. 15 Sep 1677, Rebecca (N). In 1677 Rebecca Harrison assumed a fine imposed on her son, Gabriel Harrison. {CCOB (1677-79):22}

Harrison, Benjamin (d. 10 Apr 1710) m. Elizabeth Burwell (d. 30 Dec 1734), 2nd dau. of Col. Lewis Burwell. Children: Benjamin and Elizabeth. Benjamin deeded land to his son Benjamin in 1693. {CCOB (1687-95):169; APP 1:435; W&M Vol. 4, No. 3 (Jan., 1896):146}

Harrison, Benjamin (d. 12 Jul 1745), son of Benjamin and Elizabeth (Burwell) Harrison, m. bef. 12 Jun 1730, Ann Carter, dau. of Robert Carter of Lancaster Co. Their children: Ann (m. William Randolph of Henrico Co.), Elizabeth (m. Peyton Randolph), Benjamin, Robert, Henry (d. young), Lucy (m. Capt. Edward Randolph m. 2nd Robert Neck), Henry, Carter Henry/Carter, Hannah, Nathaniel, Charles, and a dau. killed by lightning, 1745. {CCW&D 1725-31:43; APP 1:440-1; APP1:441-2; CCCR:120} See APP1 for much more detail on this family.

Harrison, Benjamin, son of Col. Nathaniel Harrison, m. Evelyn Taylor, dau. of Col. William Byrd. {W&M Vol. 6, No. 3 (Jan., 1899):235}

Harrison, Benjamin of Martins Brandon Parish, son of James Harrison, d. ca. 1790. Nephews: John Harrison, Thomas Harrison, James William Harrison. Niece: Elizabeth Stainback soon to marry in 1789 Benjamin's nephew William Faun. {PGR:142}

Harrison, Charles (b. at Berkeley, Charles City Co., d. 12 Dec 1793) m.
Mary Claiborne (b. 19 Jan 1744/5, d. 25 Jul 1775), dau. of Augustine
Claiborne. Their children: Augustine (d. infant), Charles, Mary Herbert
(m. John Herbert Peterson), Benjamin Henry (d. 1811, m. Elizabeth
Herbert Butts), Anne Carter (m. Matthew Maury Claiborne) and
Elizabeth Randolph (b. 1 Jul 1775 in Surry Co., m. Daniel Claiborne).
{APP 1:633-4}

Harrison, Collier, son of Robert and Elizabeth (Collier) Harrison, m.
Christian, dau. of James Shields of York Co. and widow of David Minge.
{GVAW (Genealogies of Virginia Families, III:691}

Harrison, Edmund m. Mary (N). Their children: Martha Ann (d. 1794)
and Mary Murray (b. 1793, d. 1794) {BPR:321}

Harrison, Gabriel m. Grace (N). Their son Arthur b. 15 Jan 1720/1.
{BPR:312}

Harrison, Henry of Sussex Co. m. Elizabeth (N). Their son Peyton b. 3
Mar 1792. {BPR:320}

Harrison, James of Martins Brandon Parish m. bef. 14 Sep 1790, Mildred
(N). {PGR:139}

Harrison, John d. by 1656 leaving a widow who m. John Tate. {CCOB
(1655-58): 50}

Harrison, John m. bef. 13 Nov 1739, Elizabeth (N). {PGM:56}

Harrison, Katherine was presented in 1739 for having a bastard child.
{PGM:57}

Harrison, Lemuel (d. 1787) of Prince George Co. m. Susanna (N).
Lemuel gave his brother, William Harrison of same, 50 acres, in 1787.
{PGR:82}

Harrison, Col. Nathaniel (d. 1 Oct 1781, age 78) m. 1st 23 Aug 1739,
Mary Digges (d. 12 Nov 1744 in her 27th year), dau. of Cole and
Elizabeth (Power) Digges. Children: Mary (m. John Gilliam, the
Younger who d. 1790), Elizabeth (m. Major John Fitzhugh), Nathaniel
(b. 25 May 1739, d. 13 Jun 1740), Digges (b. 22 Oct 1741, d. 12 Nov
1741) and Benjamin (b. 13 Feb 1742/3, d. 7 Aug 1807, m. 1st Anne
Randolph, m. 2nd (N)(N), m. 3rd Dec 1789, Evelyn Taylor Byrd). Col.
Nathaniel Harrison m. 2nd bef. 15 Feb 1748, Lucy, dau. of Robert Carter

and widow of Henry Fitzhugh. No issue by this marriage. {PGR:135, 165; APP 1: 840-1; W&M Vol. 6, No. 3 (Jan., 1899):235}

Harrison, Richard of Martins Brandon Parish m. bef. 23 Apr 1719, Frances (N). {PGW&D (1713-1728):56}

Harrison, Richard m. Elizabeth (N). Their son Benjamin b. 25 Jan 1745. {BPR:319}

Harrison, Richard (d. by 1791, perhaps by 1787) m. Rebecca (N). Sons: William, Alexander, Shadrach, Peyton, Theodorick, Ishmael (res. Sussex Co. in 1787) and Charles. In 1787 Ishmael Harrison of Sussex Co. conveyed to Theodorick Harrison of Prince George Co., 25 acres, part of a tract given to Ishmael by his father, Richard Harrison. {PGR:103, 107, 126, 163}

Harrison, Robert (d. by 1775), son of Benjamin and Anne (Carter) Harrison, m. bef. 17 Dec 1763, Elizabeth Collier. Their son Collier, m. Christian, dau. of James Shields of York Co. and widow of David Minge. {CCCR:13; APP 1:441}}

Harrison, Robert (d. ca. 1788) of Martins Brandon Parish m. Mary (N). Children: Robert, Duke, Sally (m. Thomas Mattox), Mary and Susanna (m. Jesse Binford whom her father referred to as "infamous fellow"). {PGR:110, 130, 171}

Harrison/Harnison, Thomas (d. by 1720) m. bef. 30 Jul 1686, Ellinore, probable widow of James Blaymore. Children: Ann (m. Richard Hamlin) and Elizabeth (m. Robert Hall). Grandchildren: Thomas Hamlin, Martha Hamlin, Richard Hamlin, Elizabeth Hamlin, John Hall, Thomas Hall and Sarah Hall.{CCOB (1687-95):31, 37; GVAW (Genealogies of Virginia Families) V:489; PGW&D (1713-1728):4, 61}

Harrison, Thomas d. by 1791, Ann Harrison, admx. and apparent widow. {PGR:162}

Harrison, William was father of Elizabeth who received a gift of a heifer on 3 Aug 1665. {CCOB (1664-65):575}

Harrison, William deeded land to his brother, James Harrison in 1694. {CCOB (1687-95):174, CCCR:77}

Harrison, William Sr. of Wayanock Parish, gave his son Thomas, 150 acres on 5 Mar 1711/12 and to son Richard he gave 682 acres. {PGW&D

(1710-1713): 17}

Harrison, William Sr. (d. 1712) of Waynoak Parish, brother of James, m. Rebecca (N). Children: William, Richard, Sarah (m. (N) Hobbs), Hannah, Rebecca (m. John Woodlief/Woodley), Thomas, Elizabeth (m. (N) Norwood); grandsons: Thomas Harrison, Benjamin Harrison, Henry Harrison, Richard Harrison (son of William), William (son of Richard), John (son of Richard). {PGW&D (1710-1713):30-1; PGR:11; APP 3:708}

Harrison, William m. Frances (N). Their dau. Mary b. 11 Jul 1732. {BPR:316}

Harwell, John m. Susan (N). Their dau. Lucainna b. 18 Oct 1725. {BPR:314}

Harwell, John m. Elizabeth (N). Their children: Sarah (b. 22 Apr 1725) and Thomas (b. 29 Mar 1727). {BPR:314}

Harwell, John [Jonathan?] m. Rebeckah (N). Their children: James (b. 9 Jun 1727), William (b. 20 Aug 1729) and Anne (b. 18 Mar 1732). {BPR:314, 315, 3167}

Hartwell, Michael d. by 1756. His sons, James and William, were bound out. {CCCR:137}

Harwell, Peter m. Barbara (N). Their son Randolph b. 22 May 1745. {BPR:319}

Harwell, William m. Elizabeth (N). Their children: Thomas (b. 27 Mar 1742) and John (b. 4 Mar 1745/6). {BPR:318, 319}

Harvey, Sir John m. bef. 11 May 1649, Elizabeth, widow of Capt. Richard Stephens and dau. of Capt. Abraham Piersey. {VG&B:146}

Harvey, William m. Elizabeth (N). Their son William b. 9 Apr 1744. {BPR:319}

Harwell. See Hartwell.

Harwood, John d. by 1677, leaving a widow who m. 2nd William Garner. {CCOB 1676-79:1}

Harwood, Capt. Joseph of Charles City Co., brother of Samuel Harwood,

m. Agnes, dau. of Thomas and Agnes (Powell) Cocke. Their children: Thomas, Joseph, Samuel, Agnes and Joyce. {GVA (Genealogies of Virginia Families II, Cl-Fi:104-8, 118, 231-2); APP1:122-3, 125; HCW 1:62-3; CCOB (1687-95):170}

Harwood, Peter m. Barbara (N). Their dau. Mary b. 5 Aug 1743. {BPR:318}

Harwood, Samuel m. Joyce (N). They had sons Robert, Joseph and Samuel. Joyce m. 2nd by 1693, (N) Meldrum. Joyce d. by 1693, Andrew Meldrum and Samuel Harwood, execs. {CCOB (1687-95):164; CCCR:78}

Harwood, Capt. Samuel (d. by 1737) of Charles City Co., brother of Joseph Harwood, m. 14 Jun 1694, Temperance Cocke, dau. of Thomas and Agnes (Powell) Cocke. Son: Samuel. Temperance Harwood d. by 1756. John Jacob Coignan Danzie and his wife Elizabeth, were admins. of her estate. {HMM:91 (Henrico Co. Court records); GVA (Genealogies of Virginia Families II, Cl-Fi:104-8, 118); APP1:125; HCW 1:62-3, CCOB (1687-95):170; CCCR:136}

Harwood, Samuel, only son of Samuel Harwood of Westover Parish, m. (prenuptial agreement dated 16 Sep 1728), Martha Taylor, dau. of Daniel Taylor (owning land in Blissland Parish, James City Co.). {CCW&D (1725-31):31}

Harwood, Samuel Jr. m. bef. Apr 1738, Amedia (N). {CCCR:82, 90}

Harwood, Samuel (d. by 1745) m. by Dec 1741 Agnes/Agatha (N), extx. of his will. Catherine, orphan of Samuel Harwood, chose Benjamin Cocke as her guardian. Son Travis chose John Jacob Danzie as his guardian. Agathy m. 2nd Benjamin Cocke. {CCCR:93-4, 108, 121}

Harwood, Major Samuel m. Margaret (d. 1793-4), dau. of John and Ann (Cocke) Waddrop. Margaret m. 2nd Benjamin Edmundson of Charles City Co. {APP 2:323}

Harwood, Thomas d. by 1739, leaving a son Samuel and widow who m. 2nd Isaac Hill. {CCCR:85}

Harwood, Travis m. bef. 15 Apr 1769, Elizabeth (N). {CCCR:17}

Harwood, William m. Elizabeth (N). Their son David b. 28 Jan 1742/3. {BPR:318}

Hatch, John (d. 1722), merchant, was father of Nicholas. {PGW&D (1713-1728):85}

Hatcher, William m. Margret (N). Their son John b. 13 Jul 1733. {BPR:317}

Hatley, John m. bef. 3 Jun 1692, Elizabeth, relict and admx. of ? {CCOB (1687-95):128}

Hatley, John m. by 1724, Hannah (N). {CCW&D (1725-31):1}

Hatt, William (d. by 11 Jan 1720/1) m. Sarah Hamlin, dau. of Richard and Ann (Harrison) Hamlin. Dau. Sarah. Sarah, widow of William Hart, m. 2nd Francis Epes. {APP 1:868-9 (states William and Sarah were childless); PGW&D (1713-1728):68}

Hattaway, David m. Mary (N). Their son Edmund b. 31 Jan 1734. {BPR:317}

Hatton, Thomas m. Ann (N). Their dau. Delilah Ann b. 29 Mar 1793. {BPR:321}

Hawks, Abram m. Lucy (N). Their son John b. 7 Dec 1742. {BPR:318}

Hawks, Frederick (b. 22 Jan 1752, Dinwiddie Co.). After the war he moved to Warren Co., NC, then Madison Co., GA. {RWP}

Hauks, Jeffry m. Sarah (N). Their son John b. 10 Feb 1721. {BPR:312}

Hawks, John m. Christian (N). Their son Frederick b. 22 Jan 1750/1. {BPR:319}

Hawkes, Joshua m. bef. 8 Aug 1738, Angelica (N). {PGR:12}

Hawks, Thomas (b. 5 May 1752, d. 6 Jun 1835) m. ca. Dec 1785, Margaret (N) (b. ca. 1752) by Parson Harrison. They were the parents of two children, not named. {RWP}

Hawkins, Edward m. Eleanor (N). Their son Thomas Boon b. 3 May 1720. {BPR:316}

Hawkins, Edward m. Jane (N). Their son Isham b. 15 Jan 1740. {BPR:317}

Hawkins, John m. Ruth (N). Their son Harbud b. 22 Dec 1740.
{BPR:317}

Hawkins/Hankings, Mical m. Agnis (N). Their children: John (b. 7 Jan
1721), Jane (b. 7 Aug 1723), David (b. 3 Jun 1727), Joshua (b. 25 Jul
1725) and Elizabeth (b. 7 Jun 1731). {BPR:314, 315}

Hawkins, Richard m. Mary (N). Their dau. Lucy b. 14 May 1742.
{BPR:318}

Hawkins, Solomon m. Lucy (N). Their dau. Hannah b. 15 Dec 1733.
{BPR:317}

Hawkins/Hawkings, Thomas m. bef. 18 May 1696, Elizabeth, dau. of
Thomas Hart. CCW&D (1725-31):30}

Hawkins, Thomas (d. 1758) m. Mary who m. 2nd John Potter. Thomas'
eldest son was Matthew. {PGR:109}

Hawkins, William m. Martha (N). Their children: Drury (b. 25 May
1733) and William (b. 9 Mar 1734). {BPR:316, 317}

Hawthorn, Isham d. by 1802, Ursula Hawthorn, extx. {PGM:11}

Hayes, William (b. ca. 1700, d. 1733) m. bef. 9 Nov 1724, Elizabeth,
dau. of Richard Dennis (d. 1724-5). Children: Richard, Henry and Mary.
{APP3:48, 56-7; CCW&D 1725-31:2; HCW 1:22-3, 154, 156}

Haygood, William m. bef. 12 Jun 1690 Jeane (N). {CCOB (1687-95):81}

Haynes, Christopher m. (bond dated 30 Mar 1791) Anne Young.
{MB:193}

Heath, Abraham m. bef. 9 Jun 1677, Elizabeth (N). Both were execs of
the LWT of Sarah Savage. {CCOB (1677-79):4}

Heath, Benjamin m. bef. Nov 1741, Sarah (N). {CCCR:93}

Heath, David d. by 1787, Nathan Heath, exec. {PGR:93}

Heath, Drury (d. 16 Dec 1792) m. Elle (N). Their son Armistead b. 25
Dec 1792. {BPR:321}

Heath, Elizabeth, servant of Edd. Fitzgerrald, committed fornication and bore a child in 1656. {CCOB (1655-58): 58}

Heth, Jesse m. Agnes (N). Their son Williamson Bonner b. 16 Feb 1792. {BPR:320}

Heath, Joseph m. bef. Sep 1796, Edith, widow of Joseph Williams. {PGM:23}

Heath, Nathan m. bef. 4 Jan 1791, Elizabeth, dau. of Thomas Cureton. {PGR:144}

Heath, Thomas m. Selah (N). Their son William Rives b. 6 Sep 1791. {BPR:321}

Heeth, William m. bef. 10 Mar 1715, Elizabeth (N). {PGW&D (1713-1728):15}

Heath, William of Surry Co. m. bef. 3 Jul 1738, Elizaberth (N). {PGR:11}

Heth, William m. Elizabeth (N). Their children: Dolly Agness (b. 19 Mar 1789, d. 31 Oct 1791) and Anne (b. 28 Nov 1791). {BPR:320}

Heth. See Heath.

Heathcote, Michael of the town of Petersburgm. Mary (N). Their son Edward b. 29 Dec 1791, d. Oct 1792. {BPR:320}

Hemans, John m. Elizabeth (N). Their children: Elizabeth (b. ca. 1724) and Mary (b. 1 Feb 1723/4). {BPR:313}

Hendrick, William m. by Jul 1755, Martha (N). {CCCR:132}

Herbert, Buller/Bullard, son of John and Frances (Anderson) Herbert, m. Mary Stith. Their children: John (b. 4 Apr 1724), Ann (b. 21 Mar 1726/7) and Mary (m. .(N) Claiborne) {BPR:313, 314; GVAW (Genealogies of Virginia Families) III:14}

Herbert, John (d. 17 Mar 1704, in his 46th year), son of John Herbert, apothecary of London, m. Frances, dau. of John Anderson of Prince George Co. Frances m. 2nd Peter Wynne. In her LWT Frances (d. 1727) only named her Herbert children: Martha (m. James Powell Cocke), Richard and Buller Herbert; and dau.-in-law Mary Herbert. {GVAT (Genealogies of Virginia Families) III:14; IV:532-3; GVAW

(Genealogies of Virginia Families) III:14; PGW&D (1713-1728):158}

Herbert, Richard (d. by 1731), son of John Herbert (d. 1704), m. Phebe (N). Children: Frances (b. 6 Oct 1729) and John. {HCW&D 1:176; GVA (Genealogies of Virginia Families II, Cl-Fi:114-16, 125, 125-8); APP1:128, 138; BPR:315}

Herrington, William m. Prudence (N). Their children: Mary (b. 3 Aug 1739), William (b. 15 May 1742) and Betty (b. 11 Oct 1744). {BPR:320}

Heylins, Richard m. Winnifred (N). Their dau. Hannah b. 17 Apr 1741. {BPR:318}

Higdon, Daniel (d. by 1735) m. (N)(N). Children: Daniel (res. NC), John (under the age of 21 in 1738), Elizabeth, Ann and Sarah. Grandson: Francis Spiller (*son of Sarah?*) {PGR:19, 175}

Higgledy, John m. bef. 3 Mar 1690, Ann (N). {CCCOB (1687-95):102}

High, Gardner (b. 1753, Dinwiddie Co., d. 5 Jan 1837, Anson Co., NC) m. Rachel Gibbs (b. Brunswick Co., VA, d. 25 Dec 1844) in Brunswick Co., VA. After their marriage, they moved to Montgomery Co., NC, and later moved to Anson Co., NC ca. 1812. Children, grandchildren, and great-grandchildren were mentioned, but not named. {RWP}

High, John m. Mary (N). Their children: David (b. 2 Mar 1725), Susanah (b. 12 Apr 1727), Elizabeth (b. 17 Jun 1729) and Thomas (b. 22 Sep 1731). {BPR:314, 315}

Hill, Aaron of Pasquotank in NC m. 10th da., 12th mo., 1737, Margaret Chappel of Prince George Co. {HMM:20}

Hill, Col. Edward d. by 1661, leaving a son Capt. Edward Hill. In 1661/2 there was a dispute between Capt. Edward Hill and Mrs. Hannah Hill (*his mother or step-mother?*). {CCOB (1661-64):370, 376}

Hill, Edward d. 30 Nov 1700 in his 63rd year. {W&M Vol. 4, No. 3 (Jan., 1896):147}

Hill, Edward m. Frances (N). Their children: Mary (b. 15 Sep 1728) and Edward (b. 22 Jan 1734). {BPR:314, 317}

Hill, Francis, m. bef. 18 Feb 1678/9, (N), widow of William Minchen/Minthan. {CCOB (1677-79):93, 112}

Hill, Isaac m. bef. Sep 1739, (N), widow of Thomas Harwood. {CCCR:85}

Hill, John of Westover Parish m. bef. 11 Oct 1715 Mary (N). {PGW&D (1713-1728):10}

Hill, John Sr. (d. 1718) m. Ann (N). Children: John and others. {PGW&D (1713-1728):40}

Hill, John m. bef. 12 Mar 1722, Frances (N). Their son Liewes b. 12 Aug 1729. {PGW&D (1713-1728):81; BPR:315}

Hill, John m. Elizabeth (N). Their son James b. 17 Jul 1726. {BPR:314}

Hill, John m. Ann (N). Their dau. Ann b. 19 Sep 1732. {BPR:316}

Hill, Micall m. Elizabeth (N). Their son Micaell b. 20 Feb 1720/1. {BPR:312}

Hill, Michael m. Susanna (N). Their dau. Elizabeth (b. 18 Jul 1743) and Amie (b. 27 Apr 1746). {BPR:318, 319}

Hill, Capt. Thomas m. Mary, dau. of Capt. Abraham Piersey. Mary m. 2nd Thomas Bushrod. {VG&B:146}

Hill, Turner m. by Nov 1755, Sarah (N). Turner was father and guardian of Rebecca, Thomas, Mary and Susanna HilL, 1768-1770. Lucy Hill was appointed guardian of Susannah Hill in 1773. {CCCR:29, 59, 133}

Hill, William m. Amy (N). Their children: William (b. 14 Feb 1731) and Frances (b. 2 Jan 1728). {BPR:308, 314, 316}

Hilliard, John (LWT dated 1711) was father of Robert and William. {CCW&D (1725-31):28-9}

Hilliard, Richard (d. 1773-4) m. (N)(N). Children: Elizabeth, Mary, William, John, Joab, Amy (m. (N) Binns) and David. Grandson: Joseph Hilliard. Son-in-law (*step-son*?): William Lennard. {CCCR:62}

Hiland, William m. Lucy (N). Their son Robert b. 15 Apr 1793. {BPR:321}

Hilman, Elizabeth, widow, d. by 1688. John Mekenny, kinsman, admin.

{CCOB (1687-95):26}

Hilman, John, brother of Samuel Hilman, d. by 1688 leaving a widow.
{CCOB (1687-95):35}

Hillman, Samuel, brother of John Hillman, d. by 1688 leaving daus.
Dorothy and Elizabeth Hillman alias Symons. The widow of Samuel
Hilman m. John Burge bef. 4 Feb 1677/8. {CCOB (1677-79):39; CCOB
(1687-95):35}

Hines, Charles of Dinwiddie Co. d. by 1789, leaving orphans, Elizabeth
and Patty, who were appointed a guardian, Joseph Turner, Jr. {W&M,
Vol. 23, No. 3 (Jan., 1915): 216}

Hinton, Christopher d. by 1688 leaving a widow Rebecca. {CCOB
(1687-95):12}

Hinton, Christopher m. Margaret (N). Their children: John (b. 29 Jul
1722, d. Oct 1724), Thomas (b. 31 Jan 1723/4), James (b. 25 Jan 1729),
Christopher (b. 2 Dec 1731) and Robert (b. 14 Apr 1734). {BPR:312,
313, 315, 316, 317}

Hinton, Samuel (d. by 1789) m. Katherine (N). {W&M, Vol. 23, No. 3
(Jan., 1915): 216}

Hitchcock, John m. bef. 12 Jun 1690, Mary Glover, widow. {CCOB
(1687-95):61, 85}

Hitchcock, Ussery m. Mary (N). Their son John b. 21 Mar 1741/2.
{BPR:318}

Hix, Joseph (d. by 1756) m. by Feb 1750, Susanna (N). They deeded
some property to Pride Hix in 1750. {CCCR:124}

Hix, Robert m. bef. 2 Apr 1690, Winnifred (N). In his deed John Evans
Sr. named Robert Hix and Winnifred his wife, "my son and daughter in
law." {CCCR:67}

Hix, Robert m. bef. 9 Mar 1726, Frances (N). {PGW&D (1713-
1728):157}

Hix, Thomas d. by 1748, Lucy Hix, extx. {CCCR:115}

Hobbs, Alexander d. by 1802, Edmund Hobbs, exec. {PGM:11}

Hobbs, Benjamin of Martins Brandon Parish m. Frances (N). {PGR:162}

Hobbs, Benjamin m. Molly (N). Their dau. Sarah b. 11 Mar 1789. {BPR:320}

Hobbs, Burwell m. bef. 27 Mar 1801, (N), widow of John T. Lee. {PGM:27}

Hobbs, Edward (d. ca. 1792), brother of Bernard Hobbs, m. Rosanna (N). Son: Collin Straughan Hobbs. {PGR:165}

Hobbs, Jesse m. bef. 12 Jun 1787 Mary (N). {PGR:87}

Hobbs, John Sr. (d. by 1711) of Waynoak Parish m. (N)(N). Children: Mary, William and Robert. {PGW&D (1710-1713):8}

Hobbs, Mary d. by 1790. {PGR:143}

Hobbs, Robert (d. 1718) of Waynoak Parish m. Sarah (N). Children: Robert, John, William, Sarah, Rebecca, Frances, Elizabeth and Mary. {PGW&D (1713-1728):37}

Hobbs, William probably m. Sarah (N) who was extx. and d. by 1738, Richard Hobbs, exec. of her estate. {PGR:4}

Hobbs, William m. Mary (N). Their children: Edward (b. 29 Dec 1742), Sarah (b. 22 Apr 1744) and Jesse (b. 6 Jun 1746). {BPR:318, 319}

Hobbs, William gave to his son-in-law (*step-son?*) William Birchett his plantation in 1787. William Hobbs was father of three or more daus., the third dau. being Frances who m. Henry Mitchell. {PGR:89, 144}

Hobby, Thomas m. Johanna (N). Their children: Elizabeth (b. 26 Dec 1723) and Johannah (b. 14 Mar 1725). {PGW&D (1713-1728):138-9; BPR:313, 314}

Hobby, Thomas m. Mary (N). Their dau. Mary b. 29 Jan 1720/1. {BPR:312}

Hockaday, Warwick (d. by 1769) m. Mary (N). Sons: James, Elizabeth, Mary (m. Thompson Bristow), William, Warwick and Samuel Hockaday. {CCCR:20-1}

Hodges, John/Jon. d. by 1688 leaving widow Ellianore, probably his 2nd wife. Daus.: Mary (m. (N) Land) and Elizabeth (m. (N) Donavill). Elianore removed from the county by 1690. {CCOB (1687-95):27, 92}

Hodges, Thomas m. Elizabeth (N). Their dau. Anne b. 19 Jun 1734. {BPR:317}

Hoe. See Hooe.

Hogg, Jesse of Charles City Co. received 25 acres from his uncle James Vallentine prior to 19 Jan 1796. {HCDB 5:12}

Hogg, John. On 5 Mar 1796 it was reported at the Henrico Monthly Meeting that John Hogg had married a woman not of the Society, was an overseer of slaves and had neglected attendance of meetings. {HMM:80}

Hogwood/Hogwool, Francis of Martins Brandon Parish was father of Francis (bapt. 12 Nov 1660). {CCOB 1658-61):270; W&M 4, No. 3 (Jan., 1896):168}

Holland, Francis m. bef. 21 Apr 1727, Eleanor, widow of William Jackson. {PGW&D (1713-1728):160, 164}

Holloway, (N) (d. by 1728) was father of Charles, John and Edward. {PGW&D (1713-1728):178-9}

Holloway, Edward m. bef. 14 May 1728, Katherine, dau. of Thomas Taylor of Southwark Parish, Surry Co., planter. {PGW&D (1713-1728):180}

Holdsworth, Charles m. bef. 3 Apr 1694, Elizabeth, extx. of William Phillips. {CCOB (1687-95):173}

Holsworth, John m. bef. 8 Oct 1771, Agnes (N). {CCCR:39}

Holdsworth/Housworthy/Houldsworth, Walter of Martins Brandon Parish m. 1st Mary (N) and m. 2nd 11 Oct 1660, Naomie Davis. Walter was father of Mary (bapt. 16 May 1660). His wife, Mary, was buried 11 May 1660. {CCOB 1658-61):270; W&M 4, No. 3 (Jan., 1896):168}

Holloway, Taylor (b. c1769) entered the Rev. War in Dinwiddie Co. He moved to New Hanover Co., NC. {RWP}

Hollinghurst, Thomas (d. by 1725), m. Elizabeth, widow of Richard

Brand. Elizabeth d. 1728. {CCW&D (1725-31):5, 29, 31}

Holmes, Peter d. by 1652 leaving an orphan son, Richard who was bound to William Worsham in 1652. {CCOB (1658-61):203}

Homes, Samuel m. Anne (N). Their children: Mary (b. 29 Nov 1725), Isack (b. 16 Nov 1727) and Samuel (b. 27 May 1731). {BPR:314, 315}

Holt, John m. bef. 14 Dec 1780, Angelica, dau. of Peter and Elizabeth (Hardyman) Eppes. {CCCR:53-4; APP1:870, 911}

Holt, Joseph (d. by 1772) m. (N)(N). Children: John, Joseph, Nicholas and Thomas. {CCCR:45}

Holt, Nicholas (d. by 1770) m. bef. 2 Dec 1768, Sarah, dau. of Samuel Gregory. Their children: Samuel, Martha and William. Their guardian in 1770-3 was Thomas Holt. {CCCR:16, 48, 56-7}

Holt, William, merchant of Williamsburg m. (marriage settlement dated Oct 1761), Mary Edloe. {CCCR:21, 157}

Homes. See Holmes.

Hood, John d. by 1694 leaving widow Elizabeth. Their sons: John, Thomas and Giles. Elizabeth m. 2nd John Blackborn. {CCOB (1687-95):179, 188}

Hood, John d. by 1737, Nicholas Gollioford and his wife Mary, admins. {CCCR:81}

Hood, Thomas m. Jane (N). Their children: William (b. 14 May 1711), Anne (b. 26 Jul 1721), Johanna (b. 7 Nov 1723), John (b. 1 Oct 1728) and Sarah (b. 21 Feb 1733). {BPR:312, 313, 314, 317}

Hood, Thomas d. by 1756, Elizabeth Hood, admx. {CCCR:137}

Hood, William m. Margery (N). Their children: Martha (b. 8 May 1732) and Abraham (b. 11 Dec 1734). {BPR:316}

Hood, William, Mulatto son of Mary Hood, was bound out in 1758. {CCCR:140}

Hooe, Rice (d. by 1655) arrived in VA ca. 1618, age 20, m. Sarah (N). Son: Rice. {APP 1:337-8; CCOB (1655-58): 21, 27, 28}

Hooe, Rice (b. ca. 1636, d. bef. 1 Oct 1694), son of Rice Hooe, the immigrant, m. 1st Susanna (N), widow of Richard Nicholas and m. 2nd 1689 Ann, widow of Thomas Howard. {APP 2:338-9; CCOB (1658-61):236, 253}

Hope, Thomas of Petersburg d. 3 Nov 1792. {BPR:320}

Hopkins, James m. (bond dated 17 Jan 1763), Elizabeth Marston. {MB:196}

Hore, James m. bef. Nov 1740, Martha (N). {CCCR:89}

House, James m. (N)(N). Their son William b. 25 Dec 1723. {BPR:313}

Howard, Benjamin (d. by 1725) of James City Co., brother of Allen Howard, m. Martha (N). Martha Howard d. by 1740. {CCW&D (1725-31):7; CCCR:87}

Howard, John m. bef. 4 Dec 1689, Margaret, adm. of Richard Clarke. {CCOB (1687-95):72}

Howell, (N) m. bef. 9 Jun 1789, Sally, sister of Isham Thomas. Dau. Ann. {PGR:126}

Howl, James d. by 1750, Elizabeth and Absalom Howl, execs. {CCCR:123}

Howell, John d. by 1679, son John Howell, admin. {CCOB 1676-79):86}

Howlett, William m. (bond dated 6 May 1797), Lucy Roper. {MB:195}

Hubard, George, son of John Hubbard of Caroline Co. m. 6th da., 1st mo., 1743, Judeth Crew, dau. of John Crew of Charles City Co. {HMM:22}

Hubbard, George, son of George Hubbard, dec'd. of Charles City Co., m. 8th da., 3rd mo., 1791, Priscilla/Priscillar Ladd, dau. of Amos Ladd, dec'd., at Waynoak Meeting House. Their children: Exum (b. 22nd da., 5th mo., 1794), Amos (b. 22nd da., 8th mo., 1796), Sarah (b. 25th da., 8th mo., 1798), Robert (b. 12th da., 1st mo., 1801), Elizabeth (b. 14th da., 2nd mo., 1803), Mary Ann (b. 21st da., 3rd mo., 1805) and George (b. 20th da., 12th mo., 1806). {HMM:75, 84}

Hubbard, George m. Elizabeth (N). Their children: William (b. 29th da., 2nd mo., 1812) and James (b. 2nd da., 3rd mo., 1814). {HMM:84}

Hubbard, John. 2/8/1777. Curles Meeting reports that John Hubbard has some thoughts of going to some of the upper settlements of Friends in NC and requested a certificate. In 1789 it was reported that John Hubbard having removed some years ago within the limits of Deep River Monthly Meeting, NC, married the dau. of a Friend (Quaker) in a disorderly manner. {HMM:56, 73}

Hubbard, Joseph, b. 27th da, 5th mo, 1819. {HMM:84}

Hubbard, Judith. It was reported in 1762 that Judith Hubbard, sister of Agatha Johnson aided her sister in her disorderly marriage [found not culpable]. {HMM:38}

Huberd, Mathew (d. Feb-Mar 1724/5) m. (N)(N). Children: two daus. {CCW&D (1725-31):2}

Hubbard, Sarah, dau. of George Hubbard of Charles City Co., was delivered of a bastard child bef. 1777 (disowned). {HMM:55}

Hubbard, Stephen married by a priest to a woman not of the Society [disowned 1/1/1774]. {HMM:51}

Huccaby, James m. Mary (N). Their children: Sam (b. 19 May 1721) and Ann (b. 9 Oct 1723). {BPR:313}

Hudson, Hall of Bristol Parish m. Elizabeth (N). Their children: Isaac (b. 7 Jul 1723), Mary (b. 12 Sep 1724), Joshua (b. 9 Jun 1727), Benjamin (b. 15 Jan 1728) and Joakim (b. 11 Feb 1733). {PGW&D (1713-1728):93, 143; BPR:313, 314, 317}

Hudson, Irby d. by 1743, Penelope Floyd, extx. {CCCR:98}

Hudson, Isaac m. Anne (N). Their dau. Mary b. 2 Feb 1732. {BPR:316}

Hudson, James m. Phebe (N). Their children: William (b. 11 Jan 1722), James (b. 13 Jun 1725), Richard (b. 18 Jul 1729) and Frances (28 Jan 1732). {BPR:312, 313; BPR:315, 316}

Hudson, James m. Mary (N). Their son James b. Aug 1724. {BPR:313}

Hudson, John (d. by 1761) m. Elizabeth (N). They had a son William. {CCCR:8, 147}

Hudson, Richard m. Martha (N). Their children: Obedience (b. 7 Jul

1720), Mary (b. 9 Oct 1724) and Charles (b. 14 Apr 1729). {BPR:312, 313, 314}

Hudson, Robert m. Sina (N). Their dau. Obedience b. 9 Jun 1742. {BPR:318}

Hudson, Robert m. Margret (N). Their dau. Anne (b. 31 Jul 1744). {BPR:319}

Hudson, Thomas of Bristol Parish m. Elizabeth (N). Their children: Heuen (b. 4 Aug 1724), Thomas (b. 1 Feb 1724), Tabitha (29 Mar 1728) and Elizabeth (b. 9 Mar 1731). {CCCR:90; PGW&D (1713-1728):159; BPR:313, 314, 316}

Hudson, Thomas d. by 1738, Elizabeth Hudson, admx. who m. 2nd Israel Robinson. Ca. 12 Feb 1739 Elizabeth Peterson Smith, admx. of the estate of Thomas Hudson, returned a further inventory of Hudsons's estate. {PGR:32, 45, 64}

Hudson, William and Charity Smith had a dau. Elizabeth b. 18 Oct 1732. {BPR:316} [married?]

Hudson, William, son of Elizabeth Hudson, m. bef. 4 Jan 1769, Betty (N). On 15 Sep 1768 William Hudson sold a Negro girl Sally to Ann Hudson. {CCCR:9}

Hudson, William (d. by Feb 1790) of Dinwiddie Co. was brother of Irby Hudson (father of Irby and Sally), Tuttle Hudson, and Penelope Hudson. {SWBC:54}

Hues, Anne, servant to Richard Bland, was convicted in 1691 of having a bastard child. {CCOB (1687-95):107}

Hughes/Hues, Edward m. bef. 3 Oct 1690, Joane, widow of Thomas Duglas. Edward m. 2nd Elizabeth, widow of Rineer Anderson. {CCOB (1687-95):15, 91, 95, 130}

Hughes, Thomas d. by 1660 leaving an orphan, Katherine. {CCOB (1658-61):262}

Hulme, William of Martins Brandon Parish m. bef. 9 May 1727, Ann (N). {PGW&D (1713-1728):162}

Hulme/Hulem/Hulone, William m. Mary (N). Their children: (N) (b. 29

Jan 1732) and William (b. 13 Apr 1734). {BPR:316, 317}

Humbles, (N) m. Elizabeth (N). Their sons: Jesse and Obadiah. {CCCR:115}

Humphris, Robert m. Jane (N). Their dau. Catherine b. 20 Jul 1730. {BPR:315}

Hunnicutt, Glaister (b. 27 Apr 1732, d. 13 Apr 1781), son of Wyke and Sarah (Glaister) Hunnicutt, m. Jane, dau. of Thomas and Mary (Jordan) Pleasants. Their children: Thomas Pleasants (b. 24 Aug 1757, d. 10 Mar 1758), Mary (b. 5 Jan 1760, m. John Bottom), Sarah (b. 14 Jul 1761, m. 1st Josiah Jordan, m. 2nd Hubbard Williams), Pleasant (b. 24 Jul 1763), Glaister (b. 11 Mar 1766) and Jane (b. 31 Dec 1769). {APP2:385; GVAW (Genealogies of Virginia Families) III:107}

Hunnicutt, Glaister (b. 11 Mar 1766, d. 1815-19), son of Glaister and Jane (Pleasants) Hunnicutt, m. ca. 1787, Rebecca Hunnicutt, dau. of Robert Wyke and Priscilla (Binford) Hunnicutt. {HMM:39; GVAW III:99; APP2:385}

Hunnicutt, John, son of Robert and Margaret (Wyke) Hunnicutt, m. 1st (N)(N) They had a son John (m. Mary Butler). John m. 2nd Feb 1743/4, Elizabeth (N) of Nansemond Co. Their children: Elizabeth (m. James Bates) and James (m. Rebecca, dau. of Joshua Pretlow of Sussex Co. {GVAW III:100; HMM:22}

Hunnicut/Honeycut, Peter, son of Robert and Margaret (Wyke) Hunnicutt, desired a certificate on 7/7/1728 in relation to marriage to the monthly meeting at Pequimons, NC. He m. (N)(N). Children: Robert and William. ({HMM:16; GVAW III:97-8}}

Hunnicut, Robert of Prince George Co. m. Margaret Wyke, dau. of Peter and Huldah (Ladd) Wyke of Prince George Co. Their children: Wyke (b. ca. 1701), Peter (b. ca. 1703), Huldah (m. Francis Newby), Mary (m. Jesse Newby), Robert, Margaret (m. Thomas Chappel), John and William. {GVAW III:94, 97-100; HMM:12, 16; PGR:66}

Hunnicutt, Robert, son of Peter Hunnicutt, m. Ann Simmons. Their children: Mary (b. 1755, m. William Ladd), Martha (b. 24 Sep 1757, m. Chappel Binford of Prince George Co.), Jane (b. 18 Mar 1759, d. 2 Nov 1759), Peter (b. 11 May 1763, d. 18 May 1763), Elizabeth (b. 18 Jun 1764), Sarah (b. 5 Nov 1766) and Thomas (b. 22 May 1769, m. Mary (N)). {GVAW III:98}

Hunnicut, Robert (d. 13 Feb 1782), son of Robert Hunnicut of Prince George Co., m. 1st 10th da., 5th mo., 1733, Sarah Lead, dau. of William Lead of Charles City Co. Their children: Robert Wyke, William, Sarah (m. (N) Nixon), Huldah (m. (N) Simmons) and Margaret (m. Benjamin Crew). Robert m. 2nd Oct 1772, Agnes Chappel by whom he probably had Miriam (m. Joseph Butler), Benjamin and John. {HMM:18; GVAW III:98-9; PGR:91-2}

Hunnicutt, Robert Wyke (d. 1768), son of Robert and Sarah (Lead) Hunnicutt, m. Feb 1764, Priscilla Binford. Children: Samuel (b. 1766) and Rebecca (b. 1768, m. Glaister Hunnicutt). {HMM:39; GVAW III:99}

Hunnicutt, William (d. by 1769), son of Robert and Margaret (Wyke) Hunnicut, m. Miriam Murdaugh, dau. of John and Miriam (Jourdan) Murdaugh. Children: Jesse, Robert, Thomas, Miriam, Margaret and Anne. Miriam, widow of William Hunnicutt, m. 2nd John Pleasants. {GVAW III:100; APP2:376, 395; HMM:48}

Hunnicutt, William, son of Peter Hunnicutt, m. Mary, dau. of James Butler of Dinwiddie Co. {GVAW III:98}

Hunnicutt, Wyke (b. ca. 1701, d. 1768), son of Robert Hunnicutt and Margaret (Wyke) Hunnicutt, m. Sarah, dau. of Joseph and Mary (Palin) Glaister of Pasquotank, NC. Their children: Sarah, Glaister, Mary, Robert, Ruth and Wyke. {GVAW III:103-4}

Hunt, (N) (d. by 1694) m. Ann (N). Their son: William. Ann m. 2nd (N) Harris. {CCOB (1687-95):174}

Hunt, George m. bef. Dec 1687 Martha, orphan of Anthony Wynd (d. by 1687). {CCOB (1687-95):2}

Hunt, George d. by 1722, Susanna Hunt, admx. {HCW 2:161; CCW&D (1725-31):3}

Hunt, John (d. ca. 1731) m. (N)(N). Dau.: Elizabeth (m. Charles Christian). A son who probably predeceased his father, was father of Lucy and Elizabeth Hunt. {CCW&D (1725-31):48}

Hunt, Samuel and Ann Lamboth Davis were parents of Rossey Hunt, b. 7 Aug 1760. {BPR:319}

Hunt, Turner d. by 1738, Elizabeth, admx. Elizabeth m. 2nd John

Gregory. {CCCR:83}

Hunt, William (b. 1599, d. 11 Nov 1676), a Frenchman, settled at Kesmons warehouse on James River, Charles City Co. Children: George, John, William, Mary (b. 15 May 1695, m. 1st Robert Minge, m. 2nd William Allen, m. 3rd Field Jefferson) and (N) who m. John Macon. {GVAT (Genealogies of Virginia Families) I:286; II:459-60} One source claims William who d. 1676, m. Tabitha (N). It seems more likely that William, son of William (d. 1676) m. Tabitha (N) who d. by 1717. {CCW&D (1725-31):3}

Hunt, William (LWT dated 1 May 1714 in Surry Co.), son of William Hunt (d. 1676) m. Tabitha (N) who d. by 1717. Children: Mary, George and John. {GVAT (Genealogies of Virginia Families) I:286; II:459-60}

Huntley, John (d. by 1658) m. bef. 3 Feb 1657, Milliscent, dau. of Capt. William Rothwell. {CCOB (1655-58):130, 131; CCOB (1658-61):152}

Hutchings, Boswell b. 10 Jun 1759, Dinwiddie Co. {RWP}

Hutchins, Nicholas, son of Strangeman Hutchins of Goochland Co., m. 3rd da., 6th mo., 1764, Sarah Ladd, dau. of John Ladd, dec'd., of Charles City Co., at Wainoak Meeting House. By 1771 Sarah Hutchins had moved within the limits of Circular Monthly Meeting. {HMM:49, 52}

Hutchins, Thomas of Goochland Co. m. 5th da., 3rd mo., 1780, Susanna Ladd of Charles City Co. {HMM:59, 66}

Huxe, Thomas of Martins Brandon Parish m. bef. 3 Aug 1664, Barbara (N) and was father of Mary (bapt. 13 June 1660). {CCOB 1658-61):270; CCOB 1664-65):505}

Hux, Thomas m. by 1665, Goody (N). [Nickname for Barbara?] {CCOB (1664-65):606}

Hye, John m. Mary (N). Their son Joseph b. 28 Mar 1721. {BPR:312}

Imray, John (d. 1788), brother of William Imray of Inverness (d. by 1788) and Jean Burnet (d. by 1788) of the Parish of Strachan, near Aberdeen. In his LWT John also named nephew James Imray of Aberdeen. {PGR:104-5}

Indian woman, slave, Patt, owned by William Eaton in 1738, was mother of Patt, Phebe, Hall and Pompey. {PGR:14}

Ingram, Richard (d. 1726) m. Sarah (N). In his LWT Richard named nephews, John, Richard and Joseph Hicks. {PGW&D (1713-1728):156}

Innes, Col. James m. Elizabeth (N) bef. Oct 1778. His dau., Anne m. Peyton Randolph. {SWBC: 29}

Irby, (N) d. by 1772 leaving orphans: Hardyman, John and Elizabeth to whom were appointed a guardian, Peter Royster. {CCCR:57}

Irby, Edmund m. bef. 3 Apr 1688, Elizabeth, dau. of Thomas Duglas. {CCOB (1687-95):15}

Irby, Edmund (d. by 1733) m. Ann, sister of Richard Blunt. Children: William, Edmund, John, Charles, Douglas, James and Elizabeth. In his will Edmund provided that if his wife died before Elizabeth was of age, then Elizabeth to be left in her Aunt Mary Knott's care. {PGR:178}

Irby, Elizabeth d. by 1761. Elizabeth Irby [dau.?] was summoned in1761 to declare if she would take administration of the estate. {CCCR:6, 147}

Irby, John, son of William Irby (d. by 1720) m. bef. 3 Apr 1726, Mary Hamlin, dau. of John Hamlin. {CCW&D (1725-31):13; PGR:61; PGW&D (1713-1728):97, 130, 146; GVAW (Genealogies of Virginia Families) V:489}

Irby, Joshua m. by 1708, Elizabeth (N). {PGW&D (1713-1728):157}

Irby, Joshua m. (N)(N). Their dau. Wilmoth b. by 1732. {BPR:324}

Irby, Littlebury, brother of William Irby, m. by Jul 1761, Elizabeth (N). {CCCR:150, 154}

Irby, Thomas Douglas of Martins Brandon Parish m. bef. 12 Jun 1759, Elizabeth (N). {PGR:69}

Irby, William d. by 1687 leaving sons: Joshua and William. {CCOB (1687-95):5}

Irby, William d. by 1720, sons: William and John Irby, execs. {HCW 2:156; CCW&D (1725-31):13}

Irby, William m. bef. 1 Oct 1766, Elizabeth (N). Elizabeth Irby d. by 1761, William Irby, admin. {CCCR:3, 148}

Irby, William d. by 1800, leaving children Mary I. and William R. Irby
(b. ca. 1798 and under the guardianship of Francis H. Irby). {Legislative
Petitions – Library of VA website}

Irwin, Francis m. Mary Ann (N) by Oct. 1778. {SWBC: 29}

Ivey, George of Waynoak Parish, Prince George Co. m. Elizabeth
Langley, dau. of William Langly, Elizabeth River Parish, Norfolk Co.
Elizabeth d. by 1819. In her LWT she named children: George Ivie,
Henry Ivie, John Ivie, Gilbert Ivie, Adam Ivie (had a dau. Elizabeth),
Elizabeth Ivie and Susan (m. (N) Hays). {PGW&D (1713-1728):59-60;
GVAW (Genealogies of Virginia Families) III:128}

Ivy/Ivie, George of Surry Co., son of George Ivey, m. bef. 8 Feb 1719,
Ruth (N). {PGW&D (1713-1728):59}

Ivy, Thomas m. Elizabeth (N). Their children: Ann (b. 28 Jan 1730),
Elisabeth (b. 25 Nov 1732), Absolem and David. {BPR:323, 325;
GVAW (Genealogies of Virginia Families) III:129}}

Jackson, Ann was presented in 1748 for having a bastard child. In 1750
Mary Fontain Jackson, dau. of Ann Jackson was bound to Edward Major.
{CCCR:115, 123}

Jackson, Bartholomew m. by Apr 1762, Sarah, dau. of David Davidson.
{CCCR:154}

Jackson, Daniel m. Elizabeth (N). Their children: Elizabeth (b. 2 Jun
1731) and Joseph (b. 5 Feb 1733). {BPR:324, 325}

Jackson, David m. by Apr 1762, Mary, dau. of John Miles. {CCCR:154}

Jackson, James (d. ca. 1711) of Prince George Co. m. Susanna (N) (d. by
1715). Susanna devised land to Thomas Collup. {PGW&D (1710-1713):
17; PGW&D (1713-1728):16}

Jackson, James m. bef. Jun 1737, Elizabeth (N). {C CCR:78}

Jackson, James d. by 1739, Charity Ireland, extx. {CCCR:85}

Jackson, Jeremiah m. (bond dated 16 Dec 1799), Nancy Bell, dau. of
John Bell. {MB:195}

Jackson, Joseph (d. by Jan 179-) of Dinwiddie Co. m. (N) (N). He was brother of Abner Jackson. {SWBC:54}

Jackson, Thomas (d. 1712-13) of Martins Brandon Parish, m. Ann (N). Children: William, John, Edward, James, Elizabeth and Sarah. {PGW&D (1710-1713):35}

Jackson, Thomas m. Judith (N). Their son Neptune b. 30 Nov 1730 at sea. {BPR:323}

Jackson, Turner (d. by 1770) m. (N)(N). Children: Thomas, John, Turner, Martha, Caty and Sarah. Sister-in-law: Sarah Major. {CCCR:26}

Jackson, William (d. 1720) m. Martha (N). Dau. Sarah and perhaps a son? {PGW&D (1713-1728):62}

Jackson, William (d. ca. 1727) of Martins Brandon Parish, smith, m. Eleanor (N). Children: Joshua and William. Eleanor m. 2nd Francis Holland. {PGW&D (1713-1728):160, 164}

Jacob(s), Thomas m. Tabitha (N). Their children: Thomas (b. 14 Nov 1731) and John (b. 26 Apr 1734). {BPR:324, 325}

James/Jeems, George? of St. Eustatius Island, planter, m. bef. 11 Jul 1793, Ann, sister of Abraham Lucas and Elizabeth Peniston of Prince George Co. Their children: Catherine, Anne, Sarah, John, Mary, Adriana, Cornelia, Peter and George. {PGM:19}

James, Richard d. by 1677. His widow m. 2nd William Sherwood. {CCOB 1676-79:6}

James, Richard m. Elizabeth (N). Their dau. Elizabeth b. 8 Feb 1724/5. {BPR:322}

James, Richard m. Mary (N). Their dau. Mary b. 2 Jan 1728/9. {BPR:323}

James, Sarah, servant to John Drayton, had a bastard child ca. 1678. {CCOB 1676-79):79}

Jane. See also Jean.

Jane, Joshua m. Elizabeth (N). Their son Moses b. 1 Jul 1734. {BPR:325}

Jarrett/Jerrard/Gerrard, Henry d. by 1689, leaving sons: Fernando (age 20 in 1689) and Nicholas. {CCOB (1687-95):65, 68, 127}

Jarrard, Nicholas, planter, m. bef. 13 Dec 1715, Elizabeth (N). {PGW&D (1713-1728):13}

Jarrett, Robert (d. by 1761), son of Robert Jarrett, m. Sarah Bradley, dau. of Joseph Bradley. Children: Mary (b. 10 Jul 1721, m. Walter Clopton), David (b. 23 Dec 1723), Robert (b. 26 Dec 1724), Susanna (b. 16 Nov 1727), Joseph and Rev. Devoreux (b. 6 Jan 1733, d. 29 Jan 1801). {CCCR:150; GVAT (Genealogies of Virginia Families) II:429; GVAW (Genealogies of Virginia Families) I:854}

Jasper. See Jesper.

Jean. See also Jane.

Jean/Jane, John (d. by 1710) m. bef. 19 Jan 1673, Elizabeth (N). Elizabeth m. 2nd John Wicket. {PGW&D (1710-1713):2, 6}

Jean(s)/Jane, Philip (d. by 1719) m. bef. 9 Dec 1717, Elizabeth (N). {PGW&D (1713-1728):31, 54}

Jeffries, Anne d. Oct 1792. {BPR:326}

Jeffreys, Walter m. Elizabeth Haley (d. by 1714). Their son: Thomas. {PGW&D (1713-1728):56}

Jenkins, Levi m. (bond dated 3 Jan 1775) Mary Waldrop. {CCMB:193}

Jinkins, William m. Mary (N). Their son John Hall b. 13 May 1768. {BPR:326}

Jennings, William d. by 1694, leaving a widow, Ann. {CCOB (1687-95):200}

Jasper/Jesper, (N) m. Elizabeth (N). Their children, Anthony, Robert and Lucy were bound to Joseph Day. {CCCR:101}

Jasper/Jesper, Mary, a Mulatto, was mother of Sarah and Henry who were bound out in 1746. {CCCR:110}

Johnson, Barnes m. by Nov 1761, Susanna (N). {CCCR:152}
Johnson, Edward of Martins Brandon Parish (d. ca. 1725) m. Jane,

widow of (1) (N) Price and (2) John Dewell. {PGW&D (1713-1728):4, 62, 141}

Johnson, Elizabeth d. testate by 1749. {CCCR:117}

Johnson, Hubbard was father of Sarah b. 18 Nov 1766. {BPR:326}

Johnson, Jacob d. by 1755, Francis Johnson, admin. {CCCR:133}

Johnson, James m. by Jun 1746, Ann (N). {CCCR:110}

Johnson, James Bray of James City Co., son of Col. Philip and Elizabeth (Bray) Johnson, m. (prenuptial agreement 8 Jun 1773) Rebecca Cocke, dau. of Littleberry and Rebecca Hubbard (Edloe) Cocke. They had a dau. Eliza. {CCCR:10, 58; APP1:847-8, 850-1; GVAW I:448}

Johnson, John m. (N), dau. of Jane Morris. They had a dau. Mary Ann. {CCW&D (1725-31):39}

Johnstone, John m. Elizabeth (N). Their children (son) (b. 21 Jan 1722/3), Isaac (b. 22 Jan 1722/3), William (b. 25 Oct 1724), John (b. 4 Mar 1726) and Dianah (b. 16 May 1732). {BPR:322, 324}

Johnson, Squire, son of Benj. Johnson of Hanover Co., dec'd., m. 4th da., 8th mo., 1744, Agathy Crew, dau. of John Crew of Charles City Co., at a meeting house in Charles City Co. [The minutes show that the marriage occurred circa 8th mo. 1743.] In 1762 Agatha Johnson, widow of Squire Johnson, and dau. of John Crew, dec'd. of Charles City Co., was disowned, having joined in marriage by a priest to a man (Brazure Williams) not of the Society (Quakers). {HMM:22, 38; MB:194}

Johnson, Thomas m. bef. Nov 1737, Susanna (N). Their dau. Lucretia Johnson bound out in 1744. {CCCR:80, 104}

Johnson, William m. Joan/Johannah (N). Their children: Ann (b. 8 Jun 1710), Martin (b. 13 Nov 1713), William (b. 16 Dec 1717 and Grace (b. 31 Oct 1721). {BPR:322, 323}

Jolley, Boling (b. c1766, Dinwiddie Co.) m. (N) (N) Chatham Co., NC [date unknown]. After the Revolution, he moved with his father from VA to Chatham Co., NC. By 1842, he was living in Morgan Co., IL. {RWP}

Jones, (N) m. bef. 4 Feb 1677/8, Mary A., widow of (N) Mansfield. {CCOB (1677-79):37}

Jones, (N) m. Elizabeth (d. by 1738). Their son Stephen was bound out to Thomas Blanks in 1738. {CCCR:82}

Jones, Abraham d. by 1689 leaving widow who m. 2nd John Banister. The widow m. 3rd James Wallace. {CCOB (1677-79):58; CCOB (1687-95):70, 190, 191}

Jones, Abraham (d. by 1719) had a son Peter (1719). {PGM:5}

Jones, Abraham m. Sarah (N). Their children: Abraham (b. 16 Feb 1720), Ann (b. 11 May 1724), Henry (b. 9 Jan 1727), William (b. 19 Feb 1730) and Peter (b. 2 Nov 1733) {BPR:321, 322, 323, 325}

Jones, Abraham m. bef. 10 Sep 1720, Sarah Batte, dau. of Henry and Mary (Lound) Batte. Their son Thomas (d. by 1773) m. Lucy Watson, dau. of Joseph and Anna (Stratton) Watson of Henry Co. {APP3:166-7, 177; CCCR:73; PGW&D (1713-1728):72-3}

Jones, Abram m. Sarah (N). Their son John b. 14 Dec 1742. {BPR:325}

Jones, Callam/Calhoun (d. 20 Mar 1808, in his 40th year) m. Paulina/Polina (d. 9 Oct 1819, dau. of Col. Turner Southall. {HMM:19; GVA (Genealogies of Virginia Families II, Cl-Fi:136; V, R-Z:339, 342-3); GVAT (Genealogies of Virginia Families) III: 332; APP 1:185-6; HCW2:99}

Jones, Daniel m. (prenuptial agreement dated ca. 1774) Susanna, dau. of Littlebury Hardyman. {CCCR:65}

Jones, Daniel m. Mary (N). Their children: Phillip (b. 6 Jul 1733) and Mordica (b. 22 Jul 1741). {BPR:325}

Jones, David, age 63 in 1657. {CCOB (1655-58):104}

Jones, Elizabeth was presented in 1738 for having a bastard child and left the county. {PGR:26, 44}

Jones, Hamelton d. by 1791 leaving land to his brother William Jones. {PGR:153}

Jones, Holmes of Sussex Co. m. Susannah (N). Their son John Holmes b.

20 Mar 1791. {BPR:320}
Jones, James m. bef. 5 Dec 1693, Sarah, widow of James Mumford.
James Jones d. 1719 leaving widow Sarah. In his LWT James mentioned
wife's two sons (unnamed), son: James; daus.: Mary Dardin, Elizabeth
(probably m. Thomas Chappel) and Rebecca; grandchildren: Elizabeth
Glover, Jane Cooke (dau. of John Cooke), James Jones and Thomas
Chappell. {PGW&D (1713-1728):47-8; CCOB (1687-95):166, 172, 176}

Jones, James (d. ca. 1725), son of James Jones m. bef. 16 Jan 1710/11,
Rebecca (N). Children: James, David, Robert, Elizabeth (m. (N) Glover),
Rebecca, John and Richard. In his LWT James also named his "mother-
in-law" Sarah Jones. {PGW&D (1710-1713):3; PGW&D (1713-
1728):137}

Jones, James (d. 1742), son of James Jones (d. 1725, of Martins Brandon
Parish, (son of James Jones (d. 1719)), m. Sarah, dau. of Capt. Howell
and Elizabeth Blunt Edmunds Howell. {GVAT (Genealogies of Virginia
Families) I:648}

Jones, James m. Mary (N). Their children: Mary (b. 5 Jul 1731) and
Ursula (b. 28 Jul 1733). {BPR:324}

Jones, John, brother of Mary and Ann Jones, d. by 1657 leaving a widow,
Mary, extx. {CCOB (1655-58):104}

Jones, John d. by 1662, leaving his orphan children in the hands of his
father, David Jones. {CCOB (1661-64):343}

Jones, John m. bef. 5 Aug 1689, (N), widow of Robert Jones. {CCOB
(1687-95):57}

Jones, John m. bef. 5 Aug 1689, admx. of William Stringer. {CCOB
(1687-95):58}

Jones, John m. Susan/Susaner (N). Their children: Elizabeth (b. 27 Jan
1726) and Eleonar (b. 20 Aug 1729). {BPR:322, 323}

Jones, John m. Elizabeth (N). Their children: Anne (b. 29 May 1742) and
Betty (b. 24 Dec 1744). {BPR:325}

Jones, Ledbetter m. Martha (N). Their children: Elizabeth (b. 7 Jan
1721/2), Frances (b. 19 Jul 1725), Amy (b. 19 Jul 1725) and Ann (b. 15
Jan 1727). {PGW&D (1713-1728):96; BPR:321, 323}

Jones, Ludwell (d. by Apr 1760) of Dinwiddie Co. was the son of (N) and Mary Jones. Siblings: William Jones, Lucy Worsham, Frances Tucker (m. Isaac Tucker, her sons Berryman and Colston Tucker), and Sarah (m. Thomas Hardaway, their son Thomas Hardaway). {SWBC:54}

Jones, Morgan d. by 1673, leaving a widow, Morriall Jones. {CCOB (Fragments):513}

Jones, Paul (d. testate 1720) m. Mary (N) (d. testate 1725). Children: John, Robert and Elizabeth. {PGW&D (1713-1728):69, 142}

Jones, Capt. Peter, son of Abraham Jones, m. bef. 3 Dec 1694, Mary (N). Peter had a son Robert (res. in Surry Co. in 1727). In his LWT (dated 1721) Peter named wife Mary; sons: Abraham, Peter, William, Thomas, John, Wood; and daus.: Ann, Margaret, Martha and Mary who m. Peter Jones (sic). {CCOB (1687-95):193; PGM:2, 5; PGW&D (1713-1728):46, 153-4}

Jones, Peter m. Mary (N). Their children: Frederick (b. 4 Dec 1720), Samuell (b. 12 Aug 1720), William (b. 25 Mar 1725), Cadwalter (b. 19 Jun 1728) and Peter (b. 28 Mar 1731). {BPR:321, 323, 324}

Jones, Peter m. Dorithy (N). Their children: Ridly (b. 5 Aug 1728), Ridlie (b. 9 Aug 1730), Elizabeth (b. 19 Mar 1731), Margrett (b. 14 Aug 1733) and Dorothy (b. 29 Jan 1744/5). {BPR:323, 324, 325, 326}

Jones, Peter (d. 1/18/1771) m. Elizabeth (b. 6/24/1747, d. 11/23/1776), dau. of Alexander and Susanna (Bolling) Bolling. Elizabeth m. 2nd 11/24/1771, Chris. Manlove. {VBR:246-7}

Jones, Philip m. Amy (N). Their children: Lucrece (b.11 Mar 1726), William (b. 23 Sep 1728) and David (b. 4 Mar 1734). {BPR:322, 323, 325}

Jones, Rev. Richard m. Martha Llewellyn, dau. of Daniel and Ann Llewellyn. Their son: Richard. {APP 2:849-50}

Jones, Richard, son of Rev. Richard and Martha (Llewellyn) Jones, m. 1st Amy [Batte]. Their children: Richard, Daniel, Thomas, Robert, William, Lewellin, Martha (m. (N) Evans) and Mary. Richard m. 2nd 15 Feb 1692/3, Rachel Ragsdale. {APP2:851-2; CCOB (1687-95):175}

Jones, Richard of Prince George Co. m. bef. 10 Aug 1713, Mary (N). {PGW&D (1710-1713):34}

Jones, Richard m. Sarah (N). Their children: Peter (b. 17 Nov 1720) , Edward (b. 18 Apr 1722), Daniel (b. 30 Oct 1723) and Ptu. (dau., b. 19 Feb 1725). {BPR:321, 322}

Jones, Richard m. Margrat (N). Their children: Batte (b. 30 Dec 1729) and Rebecca (b. 28 Dec 1731). {BPR:323, 324}

Jones, Capt. Richard had a son Thomas (1719). {PGM:5}

Jones, Robert (probably b. 1624, d. 1688-90) of Martins Brandon Parish m. Elizabeth (N). Children: Elizabeth, Paul, and Thomas. {CCCR:67-8, 162}

Jones, Robert m. bef. 16 Jan 1710/11, Hester (N). {PGW&D (1710-1713):3}

Jones, Robert Jr. (d. 1727, predeceasing his father) of Batte Precinct, NC, son of Robert Jones Sr. Eldest son: Thomas. {PGW&D (1713-1728):168}

Jones, Stephen (b. c1763, Dinwiddie Co., d. 3 Jan 1834) m. Mary Gibbs (b. ca. 1765) 28 Dec 1782, Bedford Co., VA where the couple later resided. {RWP}

Jones, Thomas m. (N)(N). Their dau. Prissilla b. by 1723. {BPR:322}

Jones, Thomas m. Amy (N) (possible dau. of Thomas and Elizabeth Parham). Their children: Nathaniel (b. 17 Apr 1731), and Rachel (b. 12 Feb 1732, m. William Holt). {BPR:324; APP 2:861}

Jones, Thomas m. Easter (N). Their dau. Amey b. 30 Nov 1734. {BPR:325}

Jones, Thomas m. Tabitha (N). Their son Thomas b. 21 Jul 1740. {BPR:325}

Jones, Thomas (d. by 1790) m. Susanna (N). Children: Elizabeth (m. William Tucker), Mary, Rebecca, Ann, Martha, Sarah and Green. {W&M Vol. 23, No. 3 (Jan., 1915): 214-218}

Jones, Thomas m. Lucy Watson, dau. of Joseph and Anna (Stratton) Watson of Henrico Co. Their children: Joseph (b. 23 Apr 1749, d. 7 Feb 1824), Ann (b. by 1751), Lucy (m. William Bragg), Mary (m. Robert Massenburg), Sarah (m. (N) Gillespie) and Elizabeth. {BPR:326; APP

3:167, 177}

Jones, William m. bef. 4 Jun 1688, Sarah, dau. of Cesar Walpole (d. by 1688). {CCOB (1687-95):18, 43}

Jones, William m. Judith (N). Their children: William (b. 8 Apr 1730), James (b. 3 Jun 1732) and Judith (b. 22 Jul 1742). BPR:315, 324, 326}

Jones, William m. Mary (N). Their children: Lucy (b. 9 Oct 1722), Benjamin (b. 8 Feb 1725), Benjamine (b. 19 Feb 1726), Richarda (dau., b. 18 Nov 1731), Richard (b. 12 Nov 1732), William (b. 21 Jan 1733) and Berriman (b. 18 Mar 1733. {BPR:322, 324, 325}

Jones, William m. Frances (N). Their children: Rebeckah (b. 16 Jan 1726), Mary (b. 30 Jun 17219) and Peter (b. 11 Feb 1731). {BPR:322, 323, 324}

Jones, William m. Mary (N). Their children: Pelletiah (b. 27 Jul 1729), Ludwell (b. 6 Mar 1731) and Sarah (m. Thomas Hardaway). {BPR:316, 323; W&M, Vol. 23, No. 3 (Jan., 1915): 217}

Jones, William Jr. had a son Frederick b. by 1751. {BPR:326}

Jones, William d. 1786-7 leaving widow Sarah (N). Son: David Goodgame Jones. {PGR:87, 151}

Jordan, Benjamin (d. by 1775) m. 16 Dec 1741, Lydia Pleasants, dau. of Thomas and Mary (Jordan) Pleasants. Their children: Robert, Benjamin and Thomas. {CCCR:95, 118; APP2:371, 376}

Jordan, Edward d. by 1688 leaving widow Hannah. {CCOB (1687-95):41}

Jordan, Edward, son of Edward? Jordan, chose to live with his uncle Samuel Eale in 1695. {CCOB (1687-95):213}

Jordan, Josiah (d. by 1802) m. 18 Sep 1780 Sally/Sarah Hunnicuttt. Children: Jane, Josiah Jr. and (N) who m. Joseph Heath. Sally m. 2nd Hubbard Williams. {PGM:9, 29}

Jordan, Samuel m. Milson (N). Their children: Edward (b. 2 Feb 1742/3) and Mary (b. 30 Apr 1745). {BPR:326}

Justis, John, son of Mary Wade, m. bef. Sep 1739, Mary (N).

{CCCR:85}

Justice, Justinian m. by 1688 (N), admx. of John Browne. Justinian made a gift to his son John in 1741. {CCOB (1687-95):13; CCCR:92}

Justis, Justinian Sr. m. by Feb 1748, Priscilla (N). Justinian recorded a deed of gift to his son Justinian Jr. in 1748. {CCCR:117}

Justice, William (b. ca. 1623) m. bef. 3 Oct 1662, Mary, dau. of Capt. John Freme. {CCOB (1658-61):166; CCOB (1661-64):345, 360}

Keeling, George m. several years bef. 18 Aug 1784, Mary Ann, dau. of Edward Avery. Their children: Edward Avery, Elizabeth, Lucy, Mary, Sarah, Leonard and Ann Avery Keeling. {PGR:118}

Keeth, Cornelias m. Elizabeth (N). Their children: John (b. 24 Dec 1724) and Samuel (b. 13 Dec 1725). {BPR:327}

Kally, William m. Mary (N). Their dau. Mary b. 22 Sep 1725. {BPR:327}

Kelly, William m. Sarah (N). Their dau. Mary b. 22 Sep 1725. {BPR:327}

Kemp, John m. Ann (N). Their children: John (b. 9 Apr 1710) and Jane (b. 11 May 1713). {BPR:327}

Kennell, Robert m. Catharine (N). Their son John b. Dec 1722. {BPR:327}

Kennon, John m. Hannah (N). Their son William b. 5 Jun 1742. {BPR:328}

Kennon, Col. Richard (b. 15 Apr 1712, d. 1761), son of Col. William Kennon, m. by Feb 1750, Ann Hunt, dau. of William Hunt. They recorded a deed of gift to their son William in 1758. {CCCR:124, 140; GVAT (Genealogies of Virginia Families) I:292}

Kennon, Richard m. Agnis (N). Their children: Elizabeth (b. 12 Dec 1720), Ann (b. 30 Nov 1722), Robert (b. 14 Apr 1727), Mary (b. 29 Jan 1728) and Martha (b. 30 Aug 1731). {BPR:326, 327, 328}

Kennon, William m. Anne (N). Their children: Richard (b. 15 Apr 1712), William b. 9 Feb 1713), Francis (b. 3 Sep 1715), Henry Isham (b. 22 Apr

1718) and John (b. 20 Dec 1721). {BPR:327}

Kenny, (N) m. Margaret who gave her dau. Jane Kenny, household items and a mare in 1773. Dau. Jane Kenny was probably the same Jane Bolling Kenny who m. (bond dated 15 Apr 1781), John Lefrane. {CCCR:62; MB:194}

Kent, Thomas b. ca. 1670, bapt. 1721/1. {BPR:326}

Keown, Eleanor had children: Milly (b. 12 Feb 1785), John Reading (b. 25 Jun 1790) and Elizabeth Reading (b. 4 Apr 1792). {BPR:328, 329}

Kersey, Ann d. by 1727, George Kersey, admin. {CCW&D (1725-31):24}

Kigan, Dennis/Daniel m. 8 Aug 1660, Phebie Banks, Martins Brandon Parish. {CCOB 1658-61):270; W&M 4, No. 3 (Jan., 1896):67-168}

Kileress, Robert m. Jane (N). Their son Nimrod b. 28 Jul 1728. {BPR:327}

Kimbal, Joseph m. Sarah (N). Their dau. Sarah b. 20 Feb 1725. {BPR:327}

King, Charles m. Anne (N). Their children: Olive (b. 30 Dec 1720), John (b. 4 Jan 1723/4), Ann (b. 3 Oct 1726) and Martha (b. 5 Dec 1728). {BPR:326, 327, 328}

King, Henry m. bef. 3 Apr 1689, Mary, widow of David Williams. {CCOB (1687-95):46, CCCR:74}

King, Henry m. Mary (N). Their children: Mary (b. 12 Jul 1720), Sarah (b. 31 Jan 1723) and Rebeckah (b. 1 Jul 1725). {BPR:326, 327}

King, John m. Hannah (N). Their son John b. 22 Aug 1724. {BPR:327}

King, Julian m. Elizabeth (N). Their son William b. 18 Oct 1742. {BPR:328}

King, William m. Judith (N). Their dau. Ann b. 11 Nov 1734. {BPR:328}

King, William m. Jane (N). Their son James b. 18 Dec 1740). {BPR:328}

Kington, Nicholas was father of John Kington, beaten by his master, Robert Hudson in 1738. {PGR:17}

Kinton (Hinton?), John m. Hannah (N). Their dau. Molly b. 21 Jan 1740. {BPR:328}

Kirby, John m. Elizabeth (N). Their son John b. 18 Apr 1741. {BPR:328}

Kirkland, John (b. c1754, Prince George Co., raised in Dinwiddie Co., d. 1837, Mercer Co., KY) m. (N) (N). Son, John Kirkland. Charles Kirkland gave an affidavit in 1833 [no relationship stated]. {RWP}

Kirkland, Joseph gave his son Hartwell, a Negro slave James in 1790. {PGR:129}

Knight, Josiah m. Milly (N). Their dau. Polly Cheatham b. 15 Feb 1793. {BPR:329}

Knight, Stephen m. Leah (N). Their children: Betsy (b. 9 Dec 1791) and Billy Stephens (b. 2 Jul 1793). {BPR:329}

Lacy, Henry m. (bond dated 22 Jan 1787) Lucy Duke Timberlake. {MB:193}

Lacy, Isaac m. (bond dated 15 Sep 1791), Elizabeth Walker. {MB:194}

Lacy, Thomas Batts (d. 1771-3) m. bef. 29 Apr 1769, Anthany (N), dau.-in-law (*step-dau.*?). of Francis Dancy. Children: Henry, Isaac, Angelica and John, all apparently minors in 1771. {CCCR:14, 63}

Lacy, William m. by Mar 1747, Sarah (N). William and his wife Sarah and Richard Graves and his wife Dionysia of James City Co., conveyed land (?) to William Finch in 1761. {CCCR:114, 151}

Ladd/Lead, Amos m. bef. 13 Jun 1711, Mary, dau. of Nicholas and Elizabeth (Childress) Perkins. They had a son Constant (d. by 1766). {GVAT II:816}

Ladd, Amos (d. 8th da., 5th mo., 1791), son of John Ladd, dec'd., of Charles City Co. m. 11th da., 1763, Sarah Binford, dau. of Thomas Binford, dec'd., of Henrico Co., at the Curles Meeting House. Their children: Mary (b. 14/5/1765), John Kinsey(b. 7/8/1767, d.

14/11/1788(?)), Thomas (b. 16/10/1769), Priscilla (b. 2/8/1772), Sarah (b. 4/8/1775, d. 6/1/1795), Amos (b. 21/9/1775), Elizabeth (b. 20/1/1781), Susanna (b. 26/1/1783, d. 13/9/1783) and Deborah (b. 6/1/1785). {HMM:39, 63, 64, 75}

Ladd, Gererd, son of Wm. Ladd of Charles City Co., disowned on 2/2/1760, having married by a priest (minister) to a woman not of the Society. {HMM:35, 57, 58}

Ladd, Huldah. 7/10/1786. Certificate prepared for Hannah Ladd and her five children: Thomas, Judith, John, Amos and Joseph Ladd, to Black Water and Burleigh Monthly Meeting. {HMM:70}

Lead, James (d. 1770), son of Wm. Lead of Charles City Co. m.18th da., 11th mo., 1726, Judath Elyson, dau. of G. Robt. Elyson, New Kent Co. Their children: Jesse, James, John, William, Lydia (m. Thomas Charles), Elizabeth, Anna, Margret and Sarah (m. (N) Crew). James Ladd gave his son William land at the head of Herring Creek in 1760. {CCCR:2, 30-1, 152; HMM:15, 49}

Ladd, James (d. 19th da., 9th mo., 1776 in his 41st year) m. Sarah (N). Their children: Peter (b. 2/1/1763), Mary (b. 14/4/1765, d. 4/10/1818), Rebecca (b. 8/11/1767, d. 2/9/1770(?) and James Binford (b. 11/2/1770). {HMM:63}

Ladd, James. Children of James and Isabella Ladd: Clotilda (b. 11/3/1768), Benjamin (b. 3/10/1769, d. 10/9/1779), Ann (b. 29/3/1771), James Denson (b. 23/1/1774, d. 14/1/1814), Joseph (b. 18/7/1776), Mary, (b. 25/3/1779), Benjamin Whitehead (b. 21/4/1782), Isaac (b. 14/8/1787, d. 1/7/1789) and Isabella (b. 12/6/1792). {HMM:64}

Ladd, James D., m. Jane (N) of Black Water Monthly Meeting. Their children: Evan (b. 3rd da., 8th mo., 1796), Oliver (b. 16th da., 6th mo., 1798), Anne (b. 21st? da., 8th mo., 1800), Anna Maria (b. -da, 4th mo., 1809). {HMM:79, 80, 85}

Ladd, Jessee of Charles City Co. married sometime bef. 7/12/1771 by a priest to a woman not of the Society [disowned]. (Reference is made to his children.) In 1793 Elizabeth Ladd, dau. of Jesse Ladd requested to be joined in membership in Henrico Monthly Meeting. {HMM:49, 77}

Lead/Leed, John d. by 1681. {HCW 1:10}

Ladd, John. 2/2/1777. John Ladd of Mecklenburg Co. requested a certificate so as to join himself and family to Blackwater and Burleigh Monthly Meeting. [He was visited but it was found that he frequently had taken strong drink to excess and not worthy of a certificate but it also appeared that he seemed sincerely to condemn his past conduct.] {HMM:55}

Ladd, John m. Unity (N). Their children: Guili/Gulielma (b. 11/3/1769, m. ca. 1788 outside the Society of Friends), Rachel (b. 7/1/1771, b. 10/10/--), Elizabeth (b. 29/11/1772), Benjamin Harris (b. 18/6/1774), Margaret (b. 8/9/1776), Unity Smith (b. 8/7/1780), Mary (b. 9/10/1782), Sarah (b. 1/4/1785) and John (b. 25/5/1787). John Ladd, father of the above, d. 20/3/1816. {HMM:64, 73}

Lead, John, son of William Lead, and Mary Crew, dau. of John Crew, announced their intentions to marry on 3/2/1724. Later Mary Crew did not appear to explain her public pretensions of marriage and not proceeding any further. On 6/24/1724 a letter was read from Mary Crew explaining her putting a stop to the proceedings in marriage to John Lead. Later the marriage was on track as John Lead, son of William Lead and Huldah his wife of Charles City Co., Virginia, m. 10th da., 9th mo., 1724, Mary Crew, dau. of John Crew and Sarah his wife. {HMM:13, 14}

Ladd, Joseph (d. 7/8/1771), son of John Ladd, dec'd. of New Kent Co., m. 10th da., 9th mo., 1767, Mary Binford, dau. of Thomas Binford, dec'd., of Henrico Co., at Curles Meeting House. Their children: Sarah (d. 7/8/1771) and Betty Kinsey (d. 11/8/1771). Mary m. 2nd (N), outside the Society of Friends and disowned. {HMM:45, 57, 64}

Ladd, Judith, Elder and member of Waynoak Meeting, d. ?/?/1785. {HMM:89}

Ladd, Peter m. Sarah (N). Their children: Henry (b. 2nd da., 4th mo., 1787), Delila (b. 12th da, 4th mo., 1790), Levi (b. 12th da., 11th mo., 1791), Elizabeth (b. 13th da., 7th mo., 1793), Deborah (b. 27th da., 2nd mo., 1796), Peter (b. 13th da., 9th mo., 1798) and Leadbetter (b. 2nd da., 10th mo., 1800). Sarah, mother of the above children d. 7th da., 3rd mo., 1803. {HMM:77, 85}

Ladd, Sarah. 2/11/1799. Certificate for Sarah Ladd (late Binford) from Black Water Monthly Meeting. {HMM:82}

Ladd, Thomas, son of William Ladd of Charles City Co., dec'd. m. 8th da., 12th mo., 1761, Ann Ellyson, dau. of Thomas Ellyson of Chesterfield Co., in Charles City Co. {HMM:36, 37}

Ladd, Thomas, son of William Ladd, late of Mecklinburg Co. married bef. 7/12/1771 by a priest to a woman not of the Society [disowned]. {HMM:49}

Ladd, Thomas of the city of Richmond, son of Amos Ladd, dec'd., of Charles City Co. m. 7th da., 8th mo., 1799, Ann Bell, dau. of Nathan Bell of Henrico Co. at the meeting house in city of Richmond. {HMM:88}

Ladd, Thomas Senr. d. 4/12/1785. {HMM:63}

Ladd, William of Charles City Co., Huldah (N). Their children: James (b. 22/10/1703, d. 19/9/1770), Hulda (b. 13 Apr 1712, m. 1737, Peter Peebles) and Jacob. {HMM:35, 46, 62; GVAW III:97}

Ladd/Lead, William son of William Lad of Charles City Co. m. 10th da., 12th mo., 1730, Ursula Ellyson, dau. of Jarerd Robert Ellyson of New Kent Co. Their children: Ursula (m. outside the Society of Friends by 1759), Millicent (m. by 1768 outside the Society of Friends and disowned), Elizabeth, Hulda, Jacob and James. {HMM:17, 47}

Ladd, William Jr. m. 1773, Mary (N), former member of Blackwater Monthly Meeting, later a member of Wain Oak Meeting. Children of William and Mary Ladd: Robert (b. 14/7/1774), Armelia (b. 27/12/1776, d. 12/9/1780), Ann (b. 16/2/1779), Martha (b. 19/11/1781), Elizabeth (b. 4/8/1783), Mary (b. 27/2/1790, d. 16/10/1822) and Sarah (b. 31/10/1792). William Ladd, father of the above, d. 17/7/--. Mary Ladd, wife of Wm. Ladd, dec'd., d. 30/9/1822. {HMM:51}

Ladd/Lead, William, son of John Ladd/Lead m. bef. 4th da., 1st mo., 1755, Sarah Ladd, his first cousin by a priest [a hireling minister]. bef. 4/1/1755. Disowned by the Society of Friends. {HMM:29, 30, 67}

Ladd/Morgan 6/12/1783. Informed that Mary Morgan late Ladd(?) was removed by marriage to within the verge of Rich Square Monthly Meeting, NC. {HMM:68}

Laine, William of Westover Parish d. by 1725. {CCW&D (1725-31):7}

Lamb, (N) m. Ruth (N). Their son John was bound out in 1738 to James Jackson. {CCCR:84}

Lamb, John m. (bond dated 26 Nov 1770), Fanny Finch (Spinster), dau. of William Finch. {MB:195}

Lamport, Daniel d. by 1738, Ann Lamport, admx. {CCCR:83}
Land, Curtis d. by 1688, leaving widow Mary, admx. Mary may have been a dau. of John Hodges. {CCOB (1687-95):20, 27}

Land, Robert of Sussex Co. m. Martha (N). Their dau. Patsey b. 6 Oct 1791. {BPR:334}

Landford, Euclid of Sussex Co. m. Elizabeth (N). Their children: Betsy (b. 19 Oct 1789) and Henry (b. 16 Dec 1791). {BPR:334}

Lane, Christopher m. Mary (N). Their dau. Elizabeth b. 2 Aug 1735. {BPR:332}

Lang, James m. Elizabeth (N). Their dau. Ellen (b. 20 Dec 1766, d. 4 Aug 1767) and Elizabeth (b. 9 Jul 1768). {BPR:333}

Linear, (N) m. bef. 8 Apr 1789, Patsey, sister of James Green (LWT dated 1781) and Lucy Green (m. Thomas Dunn). {PGR:115}

Lajon [Ligon?], Francis m. Jane (N). Their dau. Jane b. 28 Aug 1722. {BPR:329}

Lanier, John. His young dau. Katharine d. accidentally ca. May 1665. {CCOB (1664-65):565}

Lanier, John (b. 1655, d. 1717/18) m. bef. 3 Apr 1689, Sarah, widow of William Edmunds. Children: Robert, John, Sampson, Sarah Brewer and Nicholas (had a son John). {CCOB (1687-95):48, 53; GVAT (Genealogies of Virginia Families) II:566; PGW&D (1713-1728):46}

Lanier, John m. Catharine (N). Their dau. Rebecca Dressony b. 5 Jun 1791. {BPR:334}

Lanier, John m. Anne (N). Their son Isham Randolph b. 5 May 1793. {BPR:334}

Lanier, Mrs., wife of (N) Laniere of the town of Petersburg, d. 1794. {BPR:334}

Lanier, Nicholas of Brunswick Co., son of John Lanier, m. bef. 2 Apr 1728, Mary (N). {PGW&D (1713-1728):179}

Lanier, Robert, son of John Lanier, m. Pricilla Washington, dau. of

Richard and Elizabeth (Jordan) Washington. {GVAT (Genealogies of Virginia Families) I:384; GVAW (Genealogies of Virginia Families) III:310} Lanier, Sampson (b. ca. 1682, LWT probated in Brunswick Co. 1742/3), son of John Lanier, m. bef. 1724, Elizabeth Washington, dau. of Richard Washington and sister of Pricilla and Thomas Washington. Their children: Arthur, Thomas, Lemuel, Sampson, Richard, Elizabeth (m. George Burch) and James. {GVAT (Genealogies of Virginia Families) I:384; II:568}

Lanthrope, Alexander (d. 1785-90) m. bef. 4 Jan 1791, Rebecca (N). Children: Ledbetter, Jesse, Mary and Sarah.{PGR:148, 172}

Lanthrop, John (d. 1718) m. Margaret (N). Children: Joseph, John, Elizabeth, Mary, Ann, Francis, John, Margaret and Isabel. {PGW&D (1713-1728):44}

Lanthrop, John m. Anne (N). Their children: Thomas (b. 30 Dec 1727) and Margrat (b. 21 May 1730). {BPR:331}

Lantrop, John m. Elizabeth (N). Their children: Mary (b. 25 Oct 1742) and Peter (b. 2 Apr 1745). {BPR:333}

Lantroop, Joss/Joshua m. Mary (N). Their son John b. 27 Oct 1724. {BPR:330}

Lantrope, Joseph m. Mary (N). Their children: Joseph (b. 16 Dec 1726), Mary (b. 24 Nov 1728) and William (b. 13 Jan 1730). Mary, wife of Joseph Lantrope, d. 10 Dec 1732. {BPR:330, 331}

Lanthrope, Joseph of Prince George Co. gave his son John, 120 acres in 1759. {PGR:70}

Lantrop, Thomas m. Hannah (N). Their son Shadrach b. 14 Dec 1750. {BPR:333}

Lard, Francis m. Nancy (N). Their son Peter Singleton b. Nov 1791. {BPR:334}

Laughey, Abraham and Susanna Marshall were convicted in 1663 of fornication. {CCOB (1661-64):420}

Lawrence, John d. by 1711 leaving a widow Elizabeth who m. Morris Dun. {PGW&D (1710-1713): 18; PGR:178}

Lawrence, William d. by 1659 leaving a son Arthur (d. young) and widow (extx.) who m. 2nd Peter Plumer. {CCOB (1658-61):203}
Laurence, William m. Mary (N). Mary was mother of James Laurence (m. Mary (N)) and Sarah (m. John Bishop). William was probably father of Arthur (d. by 1663), James and William. Mary m. 2nd Capt. John Freme (d. by 1655), m. 3rd bef. Jun 1656, Edward Fitzgarrett and m. 4th (N) Rose. In 1677 she intended to marry 5th William Leedford. {CCOB (1655-58): 23, 43, 52; CCOB (1651-64):405; CCOB (1677-79):16}

Laurence, Winny, a free Mulatto, had a son Francis Littlepage b. 20 Jun 1791. {BPR:384}

Laws, William m. Elizabeth (N). Their children: Mary (b. 11 Feb 1719), John (b. 29 Mar 1722). {BPR:329}

Laws, William m. Elishaba (N). Their children: James (b. by 1725), Joss (b. 27 Jan 1716), William (b. 20 Feb 1718), Mary (b. 1 Feb 1719), John (b. 29 Mar 1722), Elizabeth (b. 17 Mar 1725 and Littleberry (b. 23 Jun 1733). {BPR:330, 332}

Lawson, Benjamin had a son Benjamin b. by 1750. {BPR:333}

Lead, William made gifts to his sons, John, William and James in 1741. {CCCR:92}

Ledbetter, (N) m. bef. 16 Jul 1759, Ann, sister of Edward Woodlief of Bristol Parish. {PGR:70}

Ledbetter/Leadbetter, Francis m. Ann (N). Their children: Osbun (b. 14 Feb 1740) , Mary (b. 5 Dec 1742) and Woodie (b. 5 Apr 1745). {BPR:332, 333}

Leadbetter, Francis gave his dau. Ann, wife of Thomas Daniell 100 acres in 1693. {CCCR:72}

Leadbetter, Henry d. by 1684, leaving a son William. {CCCR:164}

Leadbetter, John of Bristol Parish and his wife Elizabeth gave to Francis Coleman Jr. and his wife Mary, 150 acres in 1713. {PGW&D (1710-1713):40}

Ledbetter, John m. bef. 1 Mar 1721/2, Mary (N). {PGW&D (1713-1728):79}

Ledbetter, John m. Frances (N). Their son William b. 19 Feb 1720/1

Ledbetter, Joseph of Bristol Parish, brother of Wood Ledbetter, was father of Elizabeth who m. by 1787, Daniel Davenport. {PGR:102, 111}

Ledbetter, Richard m. Johannah (N). Their son Drury b. 24 Nov 1734. {BPR:332}

Ledbetter, Richard m. Han--- (N). Their son William b. 22 Mar 1740. {BPR:332}

Ledbetter, William m. Rebecca (N). Their dau. Mary b. 28 Dec 1721. {BPR:329}

Leath, Peter d. by 1759, Peter and Abigail Leath, admins. His slaves were divided among Arthur Leath, James Leath, Jessee Leath, Lewis Leath and Joel Leath. {PGR:73, 136}

Leath, Thomas m. bef. 15 Mar 1792, Sarah (N). {PGR:169}

Lee, Anne d. 4 Feb 1743/4. {BPR:333}

Lee, Catharine had a son Joshua b. 11 May 1734. {BPR:332}

Lee, Daniel m. Elisabeth (N). Their children: Roland (b. 6 May 1741) and Drury (b. 31 Aug 1744). {BPR:332, 333}

Lee, Daniel of Bristol Parish m. bef. 21 Nov 1785, Sarah (N). {PGR:160}

Lee, Edd. drownd in Wards Creek ca. Jun 1658. {CCOB (1658-61):154}

Lee, Henry of Bristol Parish, m. bef. 8 Apr 1718, Ann (N). {PGW&D (1713-1728):33}

Lee, Hugh Sr. of Bristol Parish m. bef. 29 Apr 1692 Ann, dau. of Samuel and Mary Tatum. {CCCR:72; PGW&D (1713-1728):3; APP 3:261-2, 266}

Lee, Hugh m. Mary (N). Their children: Thomas (b. 11 Nov 1721) Susanna (b. 10 Feb 1723/4). Mary d. 8 Jan 1734/5. {BPR:329, 330, 332, 372}

Lee, Jesse of Halifax Co., NC, m. bef. 8 Apr 1760, Judith (N). On 8 Apr 1760 they conveyed 100 acres in Prnce George Co. to Nathaniel Lee Jr. of Bristol Parish. {PGR:78}

Lee, Jesse m. Polly Marcum (N). Their son Samuel b. 1 May 1793. {BPR:334}

Lee, John d. by 1689 leaving a widow, Judith. They probably had a son John A., b. ca. 1687. {CCOB (1687-95):54, 135}

Lee, John m. Catharine (N). Their children: Mary (b. 21 Jan 1721/2) and probably Elizabeth (b. ca. 1726?). {BPR:329, 380}

Lee, [John] (d. by 1787) m. Margret. They had a son Joseph. {PGR:94}

Lee, John T. d. by 1801. His widow m. 2nd Burwel Hobbs. {PGM:27}

Lee, Lucy was presented in 1738 for having a bastard child. {CCCR:82}

Lee, Matthew m. (N)(N). Their children: Sarah (b. 26 Aug 1721) and Amy (b. 25 Dec 1722). {BPR:330}

Lee, Matthew m. Anne (N). Their children: Mary (b. 30 May 1725) and Thomas (b. 6 Dec 1731). {BPR:330, 331}

Lee, Mathew d. by 1738. His children, Thomas and Elizabeth Lee, were bound out. William Chamlis was appointed his guardian. {PGR:3, 16}

Lee, Nathaniel Sr. m. bef. 29 Dec 1791, Sarah (N). {PGR:170}

Lee, Nathanael m. Rebecca (N). Their dau. Mary b. 11 Mar 1742/4. {BPR:333}

Lee, Peter m. Tabitha (N). Their dau. Martha b. 16 Oct 1731. {BPR:331}

Lee, Samuel (d. 1759) m. bef. 12 Jan 1713, Frances, dau. of Thomas Edwards. Children: Frances (b. 23 Oct 1720, m. (N) Williams by whom she had dau. Amy), William (d. 29 Sep 1723), Samuel (b. 30 Apr 1725), William, Ann (m. (N) Baugh by whom she had Mary and Samuel Lee Baugh), Mary (m. Shands Raines by whom she had Ephraim and Sarah), Sarah (b. 20 Mar 1731, m. John Chambliss by whom she had Frances, Elizabeth, Peter) and Thomas (b. 22 Apr 1733, had a son Samuel). {PGW&D (1710-1713):20, 41; PGR:71; APP 3:288-9; BPR:301, 329, 331, 332}

Lee, Samuel (d. ca. 1760) of Prince George Co., son of Samuel Lee (d. 1759), m. Mary (N). Son: Peter. Widow Mary m. 2nd Jacob Temple who res. in SC in 1786. {PGR:84; APP 3:288-9}

Lee, Samuel d. by 1808. Heirs: Lodowick Lee, Thomas Lee, Chappell Lee and Richard Lee. {PGM:41}

Lee, Thomas, son of Samuel Lee (d. 1759) m. (N)(N). Son: Samuel (d. ca. 1801, m. 1st (N)(N), m. 2nd Susanna Bonner). {APP3:288; PGR:71; PGW&D (12710-1713):20, 41}

Lee, Thomas m. Sarah (N). Their children: Thomas (b. 12 Jan 1726) and Burrill (b. 30 Aug 1733). {BPR:330, 332}

Lee, Thomas m. Mary (N). Their children: Frederick (b. 1 Feb 1744/5) and Burwell (b. 3 Dec 1750). {BPR:333}

Lee, William m. Anne (N). Their dau. Anne b. 22 Apr 1742. {BPR:333}

Leeth, John m. Rebacah (N). Their dau. Elisabeth b. 22 Jan 1749. {BPR:332}

Leeth/Leath Peter m. Abigaell (N). Their children: Elizabeth (b. 19 Oct 1722), Frances (b. 2 Nov 1723), Sarah (b. 8 Mar 1727) and Mary (b. 5 Apr 1729). {BPR:329, 330, 331}

Leeth/Leith, Thomas m. Ann (N). Their children: Peter (b. 22 Sep 1722) and Charles (b. 23 Aug 1725). {BPR:329, 330}

Lefrane, John m. (bond dated 15 Apr 1781) Jane Bolling Kenny. {MB:194}

Leigh, Samuel m. Susannah (N). Their son Thomas b. 21 Oct 1791. {BPR:334}

Leigh, John Taylor m. Sarah (N). Their dau. Mary b. 18 Jul 1792. {BPR:334}

Leonard, John of Waynoak Parish m. bef. 11 Aug 1719, Elizabeth (N). {PGW&D (1713-1728):53}

Lenard, John m. Mary (N). Their children: Mary (b. 20 Aug 1731), Thomas (b. 18 Mar 1733), John (b. 30 Jan 1731 (sic), Patrick (b. 31 Jul 1734) and Winifred (b. 3 Jun 1743). {BPR:328, 331, 332, 333}

Lenoye, Thomas m. Mourning (N). Their son Thomas b. 11 Aug 1741. {BPR:332}

Lessenbury, Edmund m. bef. 8 Jul Mary (N). {PGR:145}

Lester, Ann (b. ca. 1696, d. by 1756). Son: Dionysius. {CCCR:41, 93, 135}

Lester, Dionysius, son of (N) and Ann Lester, m. bef. 4 Dec 1771, Susannah (N). {CCCR:41, 135}

Lester, Elizabeth was presented in 1745 for having a bastard child. It was ordered that process be issued against Nicholas Blanks at the suit of the Church Wardens. Nicholas Blanks to pay 50 shillings fine. {CCCR:106, 120}

Lester, William d. ca. 1728) m. Jane (N). Children: John, Moses, Lucy, Obedience, Rebecca and Elizabeth. CCW&D (1725-31):31}

Letherland. See also Netherland.

Letherland, Robert m. (N), bef. 4 Jun 1655, admx. of William Barker. {CCOB (1655-58): 42}

Leveret, John m. Sarah (N). Their dau. Sarah b. 2 Nov 1734. {BPR:332}

Lewelin, Thomas m. Anne (N). Their son Jesse b. 11 Mar 1733. {BPR:332}

Lewis, (N) of Bristol Paraish m. Agnes (N). In her LWT (dated 1787) Agnes named sons: Edward, Thomas, William and John Lewis; and dau.: Mary Lang and Ann Quinichett. {PGR:119}

Lewis, David (d. 2 Jan 1831, brother of Jesse Lewis and Ruel Lewis (of Brunswick Co., VA)) m. ca. 24 Dec 1791, Mary Flanders (d. ca. 11 Oct 1844) by Rev. Jesse Lee, a Baptist minister, in Dinwiddie Co. Children: Miles Lewis (b. ca. 1787), John B. Lewis (b. ca. 1802), William Lewis, and Dicy, wife of Grief Hardaway of GA. {RWP}

Lewis/Liewes, Edward (d. by 1739) m. Martha (N). Their son Edward b. 3 Oct 1728. Martha m. 2nd John Manson. {PGM:55; BPR:331}

Lewis, George m. Katharine (N). Their dau. Mary b. 3 Jun 1743. {BPR:333}

Lewis, George m. by Aug 1762, Frances (N). {CCCR:156}

Lewis, Herbert (b. ca. 1759, d. 15 Jan 1841, Chatham Co., NC), enlisted in the Rev. War in Dinwiddie Co. {RWP}

Lewis, John m. Mary (N). Their children: Elizabeth (b. 21 Nov 1705), Mary (b. 12 Jun 1707), Ann (b. 16 Apr 1710), John (b. 26 Sep 1711), William (b. 22 Apr 1713), Frances (b. 11 Feb 1715-16), Susan (b. 11 Apr 1718) and Thomas (b. 29 Apr 1720). {BPR:330}

Lewis, John had a son Ephraim b. 30 Dec 1742. {BPR:333}

Lewis, John (d. by 1756) m. (N)(N). Children: John, Thomas (had a son John), Mary Ann and Susanna. {PGR:175}

Lewis, John m. Frances (N). Their dau. Rebeccah Parham b. 8 Apr 1792. {BPR:334}

Lewis, John d. by 1801 leaving a widow (N). {PGM:27}

Lewis, Joseph m. Mary (N). Their dau. Obedience b. 15 Nov 1741. {BPR:33}

Lewis, Philip d. by 1655, Ann Lewis, widow and admx. {CCOB (1655-58):42}

Lewis, Thomas m. bef. 3 Mar 1690, (N), widow of Richard Titmarsh. {CCOB (1687-95):102}

Lewis, Thomas (d. by 1714) m. Susan (N). {PGW&D (1713-1728):4}

Luis, Thomas m. Mary (N). Their dau. Elizabeth (b. 27 Jul 1722. {BPR:330}

Liewes, Thomas had a son John b. 3 Aur 1730. {BPR:331}

Lewis, Thomas (d. by 1725) m. (N)(N). Son: John and grandchildren: Edward and Ann Lewis. {PGW&D (1713-1728):136}

Lewis, Thomas, brother of Honour Woodleif, d. 1725 leaving a dau. Elizabeth. {PGW&D (1713-1728):138-9:140-1}

Lewis, Thomas m. Elisabeth (N). Their children: Elisabeth (b. 16 Jan 1732) and James (b. 28 May 1741). {BPR:331, 332}

Lewis, William m. Elizabeth (N). Their dau. Joanah b. 7 Jul 1732. {BPR:331}

Lewis, William, son of William Lewis, was ordered to be bound out, in 1741. {BPVB:103}

Lide/Loyd, John m. bef. Oct 1737, Sarah (N). {CCCR:80}

Lide/Loyd, Robert (d.ca. 1724) of Wilmington Parish m. Elizabeth (N). Children: John and Sarah (m. Joseph Wade). {CCW&D (1725-31):3}

Loyd, Thomas (d. 1717) m. Jean/Jane (N). Children: Catern, Elizabeth, Thomas and Francis. {PGW&D (1713-1728):33}

Liffsay, William m. Mary (N). Their son Joseph b. 20 Mar 1743. {BPR:333}

Liggon, (N) m. bef. 25 Feb 1717/18, Elizabeth, sister of Mathew Anderson, Jr. of Bristol Parish. {PGW&D (1713-1728):35}

Ligon, Matthew m. Elizabeth (N). Their children: Thomas (b. 7 Feb 1724/5), and Elizabeth (b. 9 Feb 1727). {BPR:330, 331}

Lygon, Richard, son of Thomas Lygon (d. ca. 1675), m. Mary, dau. of William Worsham. {GVAT (Genealogies of Virginia Families I:648; GVAW (Genealogies of Virginia Families): III:504}

Ligon/Lygon, Thomas (d. ca. 1675) m. by 1649, Mary (d. 1702-4), dau. of Thomas and Adria (Hoare) Harris. Their children: Thomas (b. ca. 1651, d. 1678, unm.), William (b. ca. 1653), Johan (m. Robert Hancock), Richard, Matthew (b. 1659, d. by 1689 without issue), Hugh (b. ca. 1661, m. 1st Elizabeth Walthall, m. 2nd 1711-13, Jane (Pew) Price, widow of John Price and dau. of Henry and Jane (Womack) Pew) and Mary (m. Thomas Farrar). {APP2:265-269, 830; HCW 1:2, 86; CCOB 1676-79:14}

Liggon, Thomas (d. by 1705) m. 15 Mar 1697, Elizabeth Worsham, dau. of Capt. John Worsham. Their children: Thomas, Phebe (m. Henry Walthall of Chesterfield Co.), Mary and Elizabeth (m. James Anderson of Prince George Co.). Elizabeth, widow of Thomas Liggon, m. (N) Marshall. {HMM:92 (Henrico Co. Court records); APP2:271, 277-8; HCW 1:92}

Liggon, William m. bef. 10 Sep 1720, Elizabeth, dau. of Henry and Mary (Lound) Batte. William and Elizabeth res. in Henrico Co. in 1721. {CCCR:73; APP 3:166; PGW&D (1713-1728):72-3, 75}

Lightfoot, Francis, son of Philip Lightfoot, d. 7 Jan 1727, leaving a son and dau. {CCW&D (1725-31):25; GVAW (Genealogies of Virginia Families) III:409}

Lightfoot, Philip (LWT dated 1708) m. Alice Corbin, dau. of Henry Corbin of Middlesex Co. Sons: Philip and Francis (d. 7 Jan 1727). {GVAW (Genealogies of Virginia Families) III:409}

Lightfoot, Philip (d. 30 May 1748), son of Philip Lightfoot, m. bef. 28 May 1726, Mary, dau. of William and Anne Armistead and widow of James Burwell. {CCW&D (1725-31):12; GVAW (Genealogies of Virginia Families) III:409, 425, 426}

Lile(s), John m. Anne (N). Their children: Martha (b. 28 Jun 1724) and John (b. 23 Mar 1726). {BPR:330}

Lile, John m. Elizabeth (N). Their son William b. 3 Jul 1732. {BPR:331}

Limbry, John (d. 1713) of Prince George Co., probable son of Phillip Limbry, m. Elizabeth (N). Daus.: Mary (m. Robert Wilkins), Rebeckah (d. unm. testate, 1720) and Elizabeth. John gave his dau. Mary 138 acres in 1712. {PGW&D (1710-1713):25, 39-40, 62-3; PGR:28, 75}

Limbry/Lymbry, Phillip m. Elizabeth (d. by 1677), youngest dau. of (N) and Frances Drew. Their children: John, Elizabeth and a child that d. young. Philip m. 2nd Jane (N). Phillip d by 1677 and his widow Jane m. 2nd Elias Osborne (d. by 1690). According to Frances Drew, the children (her grandchildren), were mistreated by Elias Osborne. {CCOB 1676-79:9, 26; CCOB (1687-95):87, 98}

Linear. See Lanier.

Linzey/Linzie, Martha was presented in 1743 for having a bastard child. Ordered to receive 25 lashes. She paid the fine and case dismist. {CCCR:98, 107}

Lister, Thomas m. Ann (N). Their son William b. 7 Jul 1734. {BPR:332}

Livesay, John (d. ca. 1720) m. Joan (N). Children: John, Thomas, William, Elizabeth (m. (N) Ledbetter), Mary, Rebecca, Sarah, Hannah and Susannah. {PGW&D (1713-1728):64}

Livesay, Thomas of Martins Brandon Parish m. bef 8 Jun 1790, Ann (N). {PGR:136}

Livesay, William d. by 1800. Legatees (probably his children): William, Jemima, Susannah, Randolph, Mary, Hubart, Thomas, Drury, Milly and Silvy Livesay. {PGM:27}

Locket, Benjamin m. Winnifrit (N) who d. 25 Nov 1729. {BPR:331}

Lockett, Thomas m. Elizabeth (N). Their dau. Hannah b. 28 Dec 1722. {BPR:329}

Lockley, William m. Frances Margret (N). Their dau. Henritta b. 9 Apr 1733. {BPR:332}

Loftus/Loftis, William m. Elizabeth (N). Their children: Thomas (b. 27 Aug 1733), Ann (b. 2 Aug 1728) and William (b. 11 May 1731). {BPR:328, 331}

Long, Walter m. bef. 11 Apr 1738, Mary, widow of John Vincent. {PGR:3; PGW&D (1713-1728):174}

Longman, Robert d. by 1655, leaving a widow, Mary. They had a dau. Mary. Mary, widow of Robert Longman, m. ca. 1656, Thomas Mallory. {CCOB (1655-58): 42, 47}

Love, Amoss m. Mary (N). Their dau. Winifred b. 7 Oct 1750. {BPR:333}

Lovesy, William m. Jane (N). Their son William b. 14 Mar 1730. {BPR:331}

Lovesay, William m. Mary (N). Their son Frederick b. 19 Dec 1745. {BPR:333}

Lovett, John m. Sarah (N). Their children: Elizabeth (b. 4 May 1730), John (b. 14 Jan 1732) and Mary (b. 20 Mar 1734). {BPR:331, 332}

Loffsett, John m. Keziah (N). Their dau. Mille b. 15 Nov 1745. {BPR:333}

Lowe, John of Carolina m. bef. 4 Oct 1727, Sarah (N). {PGW&D (1713-1728): 170}

Lowe, Thomas m. bef 1664, (N), dau. of John Wilson. Their son: William. {CCOB (1661-64):457, 458}

Lowman, John (age 40 in 1673) m. bef. 3 Apr 1673, Joane (N) (age 37 in 1673). {CCOB (Fragments):517}

Loyd, William of Westover Parish d. by 1724. {CCW&D (1725-31):1}

Lucas, Charles of Surry Co. m. bef. 5 Feb 1724, Mary, dau. of Benjamin Evans. {CCCR:93; PGR:45; PGW&D (1713-1728):128}

Lucas, Roger of Martins Brandon Parish was father of William (bapt. 16 May 1660). {CCOB 1658-61):270}

Lucas, Walter had a son William, bapt. 26 May 1660. {W&M 4, No. 3 (Jan., 1896):67-168}

Lucas, William m. bef. 14 Apr 1789, Frances, dau. of Nathaniel Raines (d. 1789). Their son: Henry. {PGR:120}

Lucie, Elizabeth was presented in 1665 for having a bastard child. William Avery paid her fine. {CCOB (1664-65):801}

Lucy, Robert (d. 1687) m. bef. 19 Nov 1677, Sarah, widow of Richard Taylor. Robert and Sarah gave son Richard Lucy in 1677/8. Orphan Mary Lucy chose Capt. John Taylor her guardian in 1694. Sarah m. 3rd Capt. James Bisse. Sarah d. by 1694. {CCOB (1677-79):48; CCOB (1687-95):26-7, 103, 112, 193, 199}

Ludwell, John (patented land in VA in 1663, d. by 1679, probably without issue), son of Thomas and Jane Ludwell, m. (N)(N) who m. 2nd Henry Harmond. {CCOB (1677-79):111; GVAW (Genealogies of Virginia Families) III:471}

Lundy, James of Isle of Wight Co. m. bef. 7 Oct 1717, Elizabeth (N). {PGW&D (1713-1728):29}

Luscomb, Jonas m. bef. 3 Dec 1677, (N), widow of Thomas Balleston. {CCOB (1677-79):35}

Lyell, William (alias Joseph) m. bef. 6 Feb 1801, Anne, dau. of Richard Stewart. {PGM:8}

McCarter, William m. Susannah (N). Their son David b. 6 Oct 1791. {BPR:343}

Maccloud, Daniel m. Susanah (N). Their son William b. 10 Mar 1740. {BPR:341}

MacCraw, Samuel m. by Feb 1760, Alice (N). {CCCR:142}

McCormack, John d. by 1747, Mary McCormack, widow and admx. {CCCR:113}

Macculloch, David m. Elizabeth (N). Their dau. Elizabeth b. 23 Jul 1741. {BPR:341}

Mikedermond, Micail m. Catharine (N). Their son Micail b. 25 Feb 1733. {BPR:340}

McDearmon, Richard m. Eleanor (N). Their son William b. 18 May 1732. {BPR:339}

Machen, George Wale m. Mary (N). Their son Henry b. 7 Mar 1780. {BPR:343}

Machen, Thomas m. Sally (N). Their dau. Mary Wales b. 8 Jun 1791. {BPR:344}

Machie, William m. Susana (N). Their son Vadrey b. 23 Dec 1734. {BPR:340}

McCholler, David m. Elizabeth (N). Their dau. Anne b. 29 Jul 1735. {BPR:341}

Mackdaniell, Ann had a base born child, John, b. 21 Aug 1722. {BPR:335}

Mackey, Michael m. Elizabeth (N). Their dau. Sarah b. 16 Dec 1730. {BPR:338}

MacDowal, James m. Elizabeth (N). Their children: Benjamin (b. 27 Sep 1742) and Benjamin (b. 27 Sep 1742). {BPR:342}

McDowell, William m. Susanna (N). Their son James b. 20 Jan 1793. {BPR:344}

McFarlane, Elizabeth of Chesterfield Co. buried 16 Oct 1792. {BPR:344

McKenny, John of Sussex Co. m. Rebeccah (N). Their son John b. 4 Mar 1791. {BPR:343}

McKenny/Mackinne/Mackinney, Morgan (d. by 1726) m. bef. 7 Oct

1723, Sibella/Sybellah (N). Their children: Morgan (b. 7 Jun 1722), John (b. 12 Feb 1723/4) and James (b. 7 Feb 1725). {PGW&D (1713-1728):95, 147; BPR:335, 336, 337}

Maclain, John, son of John Maclain was bound to William Lester in 1743 to learn trade of ship carpenter. {CCCR:101}

Maclin, William of Surry Co. m. bef. 4 Jan 1726, Kathrine, dau. of Sackfeild Brewer (d. by 1699). {CCW&D (1725-31):18, 42}

MacLaud, Daniel m. Susanna (N). Their dau. Margret b. 8 Jan 1742/3. {BPR:342}

McLeod, John m. Isabella (N). Their son John b. 18 Jan 1793. {BPR:344}

McMurdo, Charles J., m. Elizabeth (N). She d. 13 Sep 1792. Their children: Martha (b. Sep 1792), Anne and Elizabeth. {BPR:344}

MacNeil, Malcom m. Catharine (N). Their dau. Catharine b. 12 Feb 1741/2. {BPR:341}

Madder, Thomas (d. by 1659) m. Elizabeth, widow of (1) Peter Moyles and (2) Nicholas Poole. Elizabeth m. 4th Francis Treham. {CCOB (1655-58): 56; CCOB (1661-64):371}

Maddox, Robert m. by Nov 1755, Mary (N). {CCCR:134}

Magahe, Samuell, son of William Magahe of Hanover Co., m. 19th da., 2nd mo., 1722, Mary Lead, dau. of William Lead of Charles City Co. {HMM:11}

Magnar, Charles. His wife was accused of having a child by Negro Jack. {CCOB (1664-65):559}

Maitland, David of Blandford m. Susanna/Susan Ann (b. 1776, d. 19 Feb 1799), dau. of Joshua Poythress. Their children: Elizabeth Agnes (b. 23 Apr 1793) and Mary Currie (d. 26 Jan 1795). {BPR:302, 344, 345}

Maitland, Robert m. Susan (N). Their son David Currie b. 2 Nov 1796, d. Oct 1797. {BPR:345}

Maitland, William m. Elizabeth (N). Their son Alexander Campbell b. 2 Aug 1795, d. 25 Oct 1796. {BPR:345}

Major, Bernard m. by Nov 1754, Elizabeth, widow of Lewis Delony. Elizabeth d. by 1761, Bernard Major Jr., exec. Children: Barnard, Mary

Emery, Joice (m Stephen West), Samuel, John, and Martha Marrable. Son in law, Thomas Griffith. Grandchildren: John, Betty Major, Sarah, and Stephen West (children of Stephen West); Harwood Major, Joice Harwood Major, Elizabeth Major (dau. of Barnard Major), Barnard Major, Turner Jackson and Sarah Jackson. {CCCR:124, 125, 129; SWBC:41}

Major, Lt. Col. Edd. d. by 1656 leaving a widow, Susanna who was dau. of Lt. Col. Walter Aston. {CCOB (1655-58): 47, 77}

Major, Edward m. bef. Jun 1737, Sarah (N). {CCCR:78}

Major, Edward m. by Jul 1755, Elizabeth (N). {CCCR:132}

Major, John m. bef. 16 Dec 1724, Sarah (N). Dau. Sarah. {CCW&D (1725-31):1}

Major, John Sr. d. 1768. In his LWT he named brother James' son John and his dau. Sarah. {CCCR:6}

Major, Nicholas d. by 1728. Children: Edward, Nicholas, Barnard and Elizabeth (m. (N) Brand). CCW&D (1725-31):32}

Major, Samuel (b. 10 Aug 1760, Dinwiddie Co., d. 24 Jun 1842, Dinwiddie Co.) m. ca. 12 Mar 1800, Nancy Perkins (b. ca. 1777). William Perkins was a surety on the marriage bond. Elizabeth P. Major, relationship not stated, made oath that Nancy was the widow of Samuel Major. Samuel and Nancy had numerous children, unnamed. {RWP}

Malcolm, John d. 23 Jun 1792, buried St. Paul's churchyard. {BPR:344

Mallone, Daniel d. by 1713 leaving a widow Susan who m. (N) Floriday. Daniel and Susan probably had a son Daniel Malone. {PGW&D (1710-1713):35}

Mellone, Daniel m. Mary (N). Their dau. Mary b. 20 Mar 1719/20. {BPR:334}

Malone, Margaret had a son Patrick Smith, b. 27 Feb 1744/5. {BPR:342}

Mallone, Nathaniel of Surry Co. had a son William in 1724. {PGW&D (1713-1728):107}

Molone, Nathaniel m. Mary (N). Their son Daniel b. 15 Sep 1732.

{BPR:340}

Mallone/Melone, William m. Ann (N). Their children: Lucrecee (b. 11 Jan 1726) and Reuben (b. 26 Sep 1741). {BPR:337}

Mallory, Capt. Francis, Gent. (d. ca. 1719, owning land in Prince George and Surry cos.) m. bef. 14 Jul 1713, Elizabeth (N). Children: Elizabeth, Ann, John, Mary, Martha, Francis and the child yet to be born in 1718/19. {PGW&D (1710-1713):36-7, 53; PGW&D (1713-1728):59}

Mallory, Thomas (age 30 in 1665) m. ca. 1656, Mary, widow of Robert Longman. {CCOB (1655-58): 42, 47; CCOB (1664-65):635}

Maine, Edward d. by 1711, George Maine, admin. {PGW&D (1710-1713):5}

Man, Francis m. Elizabeth (N). Their children: Lucy (b. 20 Apr 1722) and Robert (b. 7 Feb 1732). {BPR:335}

Man, John m. Mary (N). Their children: Agnis (b. 31 May 1728), Ann (b. 29 Aug 1729) and Mary (b. 28 Feb 1733). {BPR:337, 338, 340}

Man, John m. Elizabeth (N). Their son William b. 11 Dec 1744. {BPR:342}

Man(n), Samuel m. Elizabeth (N). Their children: John (b. 23 Dec 1733) and Elizabeth (b. 28 Jan 1743/4). {BPR:340, 342}

Man, Thomas m. Prissilla (N). Their son Thomas b. 24 May 1721. {BPR:335}

Man, Thomas m. Jane (N). Their children: Thomas (b. 4 Jun 1725) and Priscilla (b. 13 Dec 1725). {BPR:336}

Mander, James m. bef. 3 Sep 1730, Alice (N). {CCW&D (1725-31):45}

Mane(?), Richard and his wife (N) bound her two sons, James and Thomas Charles Matthews to Isaac Coleson in 1688 to learn the trade of carpenter. {CCOB (1687-95):22}

Manfull, Thomas d. by 1679. His widow, Elizabeth, m. 2nd William Simons. {CCOB (1677-79):108}

Manlove, Chris. m. 11/24/1771, Elizabeth, dau. of Alexander and Susanna (Bolling) Bolling. Their children: Jane Manlove (b. 10/8/1772), Rebecca Bolling Manlove (b. 4/24/1774, d. 7/8/17--), and Thomas Bolling Manlove (b. 11/4/1776). {VBR:246-7}

Manlove, Christopher m. bef. 1795, Mary Epes, dau. of John Sturdivant Sr. Their children: Ann and probably John and Robert. {PGM:19; APP2:239; PGR:92, 177}

Mansfield, (N) (d. by 1677) m. Mary A. (N). Their children: Maxmillian, Thomas and Easter. {CCOB (1677-79):37}

Mansell, Richard gave his mother, Moriall Mansell, 60 acres at *Merchants Hope*. {CCOB (Fragments):512}

Manson, John m. Martha, widow of Edward Lewis. Their children: Peter (b. 24 Dec 1733), possibly Nathaniel and Jane. {PGM:55; BPR:340; APP 1:253}

Marchbank, George m. Ann (N). Their son Joseph b. 4 Oct 1733. {BPR:340}

Markam, Samuel (d. by 1737) m. Mary, dau. of James Batty. Their children: James (d. a minor) and Frances (m. John Hardaway). Their children: Mary (m. Edward Smith), Susanna (m. Richard Smith) and Jemima (m. John Scott). Mary, widow of Samuel Markam, m. 2nd William Parsons by whom she had Joseph Parsons and William Parsons Jr. {PGR:1, 29}

Marks, Edward m. Sally (N). Their dau. Polly b. 24 Jul 1793. {BPR:344}

Marks, Israel (d. by 1718), m. Elizabeth, dau. of Richard Pigeon. {PGW&D (1713-1728):38, 44}

Marks, John m. bef. 11 Dec 1739, Lucy (N). {PGR:60}

Marks, John m. Martha (N). Their son, Lewis Lanier, b. 6 May 1792. {BPR:344}

Marks, Mathew (d. 1719) m. (N)(N). Dau.: Mary (m. (N) Davonport). In his LWT, dated 15 Aug 1719, Mathew named Edward Marks, minor son of Edward Marks; Israel Marks; John and Edward Robyson; and John Marks, son of Israel Marks {PGW&D (1713-1728):54-5}

Marks, William m. Elizabeth (N). Their dau. Johanna b. 3 Aug 179-. {BPR:344}

Marrable, Benjamin m. bef. 16 Dec 1769, Judith (N). {CCCR:34}

Marrable, Charles (d. by Nov 1778) m. Ann (N). Children: Amy Drinkard, Agnes Collier, Martha Major, Edward, William, Benjamin, Hartwell, John, George, and Abraham. Charles was the brother of Henry Hartwell Marrable (dec'd.). {SWBC:41}

Marrable, William m. (bond dated 1 Jan 1772) Susannah Weaver (spinster), dau. of Joseph Weaver. {MB:193}

Marshall, George (d. ca. 1673) m. Ann (N) who m. 2nd John Barker. {CCOB (Fragments):546}

Marshall, John d. by 1688, leaving a widow Joane. {CCOB (1687-95):20}

Marshall, John m. 1st bef. 4 Oct 1689, Elizabeth (N) and m. 2nd bef. 4 Dec 1689, Susan (N). {CCOB (1687-95):66, 73}

Marshall, John m. bef. Nov 1754, Ann (N). {CCCR:129}

Marshal, Samuel m. by Jan 1746, Jane (N). {CCCR:111}

Marshall, William m. Ann (N). Their children: Robert (b. 23 Dec 1729), Elisabeth (b. 13 Jul 1731) and Anne (b. 28 Jan 1733). {BPR:338, 339, 340}

Marston, Benskin (d. by 1750), son of William and Frances Marston of James City Co., m. Elizabeth, dau. of Henry Soane. Richard Kennon and Elizabeth Mossom, execs. Elizabeth, widow of Benskin Marston, m. 2nd Rev. David Mossom. {CCCR:123, 131, 134; GVAW (Genealogies of Virginia Families) I:724-5; III:418}

Marston, John Soane (d. by 1771), probable son of Benskin Marston, m. by Jul 1762 Judith (N). He d. leaving as widow, Judith Marston. His son John Marston was appointed a guardian, Henry Duke, in 1773. {CCCR:31-2, 57}

Marston, Thomas m. (prenuptial agreement dated 13 Sarah Dibdall, widow of Richard Dibdall. {CCOB (1661-64):312}

Martin, Christopher m. bef. 15 Aug 1739, Susanna (N). {PGM:55}

Martin, James d. by 1790. In his LWT he mentioned relatives in Scotland, namely the grandchildren of Elizabeth Martin, married to John Dier; his sister and Ann Martin and brother Peter Martin; and dau. Jean Greasett. Letters of administration were granted to David and Alexander Martin. {PGR:136-7}

Martin, John d. by 1719, Mary Martin, admx. {PGW&D (1713-1728):52}

Martin, John m. Rachail (N). Their son Zacariah b. 22 Jan 1729. {BPR:338}

Martin, Matthew m. Elizabeth (N). Their dau. Lucy b. 25 Sep 1741. {BPR:341}

Martin, William m. Elisabeth (N). Their children: Richard (b. 27 Aug 1733) and William (b. 28 Nov 1734). {BPR:340, 341}

Martin, William m. Sarah (N). Their son Joel b. 18 Mar 1740/1. {BPR:341}

Martin, William m. Isabel (N). Their dau. Anne b. 30 Aug 1741. {BPR:341}

Mason, James (d. by 1679) m. by 1678, Mary, widow of Roger Wamsley. Mary d. by 1679. {CCOB 1676-79):76, 102, 103, 113}

Mason, John of Sussex Co. m. Lucy (N). Their dau. Lucy Massenburg b. 26 Oct 1791. {BPR:343}

Mason, William m. bef. 20 Apr 1657, Margaret, widow of Thomas Hallom. {CCOB (1655-58):103; APP2:232}

Massy/Massie, Richard m. Ann (N). Their children: Ann (b. 14 Jun 1722), Sarah (b. 27 Nov 1723), John (b. 14 Feb 1725), Richard (b. 14 Feb 1725) and Tabitha (b. 8 Jan 1729). {BPR:335, 336, 338}

Masters, (N) d. by 1657, leaving a widow Margery. {CCOB (1655-58):133}

Mathes, Joseph/Josep m. Eleonore/Hellen (N). Their children: Amey (b. 9 Dec 1724) and Joseph (b. 17 Jan 1729). {BPR:336, 338}

Matthis, Thomas m. (bond dated 9 Feb 1788), Rebecca Moody. {MB:193}

Matthews, Henry m. Mary (N). Their son Michal b. 27 Dec 1729. {BPR:338}

Matthews, James m. (N)(N). Their dau. Frances b. 28 Apr 1722. {BPR:335}

Matthews, Joseph m. Eleanore (N). Their dau. Martha b. 8 Jan 1731). {BPR:339}

Matthews, Thomas (b. 30 Dec 1763, Charles City Co.), lived in Charles City Co. when he was called into service of the Rev War. He remained there until 1798 when he moved to Edgecombe Co., NC. In 1818, he moved to Brunswick Co., VA. His brother lived in Nottoway Co., VA. Brother Wm. B. Matthews was in Prince George Co. in 1837. {RWP}

Mattox, Joseph of Charles City Co., m. 1 Apr 1702 Mary, widow of Thomas Jefferson and dau. of William and Jane Branch. {HMM:93; GVAW (Genealogies of Virginia Families) I:415; III:409}

Maule, Ebenezer of Henrico Co., earlier from Gunpower Monthly Meeting, Baltimore Co., MD, m. 10th da., 9th mo., 1793 Sarah Ladd, dau. of Amos Ladd, dec'd., of Charles City Co., at meeting house in Charles City Co. Relations at the wedding: James Ladd, George Hubboard, Jesse Terrell, James D. Ladd, Joseph Ladd, Priscilla Hubbard, Mary Ladd, Rachel Ladd, Margaret Ladd, Nancy Terrell, Elizabeth Ladd, Margaret Crew, Susanna Binford, Salley Thornton and Frances Jackson. {HMM:77, 86}

Mayes, Gardiner m. Elizabeth (N). Their dau. Mary Gardiner b. 13 Oct 1726. {BPR:337}

May, George m. Anna (N). Their son Richard b. 3 Sep 1792. {BPR:344}

May/Mayes, Henry d. by 1688, leaving a widow, Mary who m. 2nd William Fetherstone. {CCOB (1687-95):26, 61}

Mayes, Henry m. bef. 7 Jan 1716, Elizabeth (N). Their son Richard b. 1 Apr 1724. {PGW&D (1713-1728):22; BPR:336}

Mayes, John d. by 1689, Martha Mayes, admx. {CCOB (1687-95):61}

Mays, John m. Julian/Julia (N). Their children: John (b. 29 Feb 1719), Martha (b. 8 Jun 1722), Anne (b. 13 Feb 1725), James (b. 18 Mar 1727) and Sarah (b. 13 Dec 1730). {BPR:335, 336, 337, 338}

Maise/May, John m. Mary (N). Their children: Elizabeth (b. 30 Sep 1722), Mary (b. 2 Jun 1724), William (b. 11 Jun 1725), James (b. 6 Feb 1726), George (b. 19 Jul 1728), Dorithy (b. 9 Dec 1728), Elisabeth (b. 2 Oct 1730), Lucy (b. 26 Jan 1730 [*1731/2?*]) and William (b. 28 Dec 1732). {BPR:335, 336, 337, 338, 339}

Mayes, John m. bef. 8 Aug 1738, Sarah (N). Their son Frederick b. 2 Feb 1741/2. {PGR:13; BPR:341}

May, John (d. by 1760, clerk of Bristol Parish, m. Agnes Smith (b. 9 Apr 1722, d. 1805-6), dau. of Richard and Agnes (Cocke) Smith. Their children: Betty (b. 16 Nov 1740), Richard (b. 20 Dec 1742 or 1743), John (b. 20 Dec 1744, killed by Indians 20 Mar 1790), Stephen (b. 15 Nov 1745), David (b. 15 May 1747), Agnes (b. 6 Sep 1749, m. 1st Abraham Cocke, m. 2nd Thomas Hayes), William (b. Oct 1752, 1825-6), George (b. 6 Feb 1756, d. 26 Apr 1822) and Lucy (m. Joel Bott). {BPR:341, 342; APP 1:129, 141-2}

Mayes/Maise, Mathew, planter, m. bef. 12 Dec 1715, Elizabeth (N). Their children: Drury (b. 15 Jan 1727) and Delilah (b. 20 Jul 1733). {PGW&D (1713-1728):12; BPR:337, 340}

May, Thomas m. Jeane (N). Their dau. Lucy b. 8 Jan 1729. {BPR:338}

Mayse/Mays, William of Bristol Parish m. bef. 3 Dec 1712, Mary [Mattox]. Children: Mattox of Brunswick Co., William of Bristol Parish, Prince George Co. and Joseph of Brunswick Co. {PGW&D (1710-1713):31; PGW&D (1713-1728):4; PGM:14}

Mayes, William m. Elizabeth (N). Their children: Priscilla (b. 22 Aug 1725) and Johanna (b. 14 Sep 1732). {BPR:336, 339}

Maylard, James (d. by 1728) m. bef. 5 Jul 1726, Mary, dau. of Henry Dyer. {CCW&D (1725-31):13}

Maylard, Pyness d. by 1727, Dionisia Maylard, admx. {CCW&D (1725-31):24}

Maynard, Crawley m. (bond dated 27 May 1791), Elizabeth Merry, dau. of David Merry. {MB:193}

Maynard, Capt. Henry d. by 1727. {PGW&D (1713-1728):172}

Maynard, Nathaniel (d. by 1769) m. by Aug 1760 Mary (N) by whom he had daus. Elizabeth and Ann Maynard. Mary m. 2nd John Christian (appointed guardian of the children). {CCC R:15, 28, 145}

Maynard, Nathaniel m. (bond dated 21 Dec 1789) Elizabeth Mathews. {MB:193}

Maynard, William d. by 1757, John Maynard, exec. {CCCR:137}

Meacham, Jeremiah m. Milly (N). Their children: Jamy Cate (b. 26 Oct 1791) and Jemimah Wyat (b. 16 Mar 1793). {BPR:343, 344}

Meacham, Joshua d. by 1678. Children: Elizabeth and Mary. {CCOB 1676-79):67}

Meacham, Elizabeth of Surry Co., widow, in 1710 conveyed a tract of land in Westover Parish, Prince George Co., 100 acres, to Edward Goodrich. {PGW&D (1710-1713):5}

Mead(e), David (b. 1760, d. 1830) of Presque Isle m. 1 Mar 1789, Elizabeth Randolph, dau. of Richard and Ann (Meade) Randoph. By Rev. John Buchanan. David Meade of Prince George Co. had a niece, Susanna Eldridge of Buckingham Co. to whom he gave a number of slaves in 1790. {HMM:97; GVAW IV:244; HCDB 3:19}

Meadland, John m. Jane (N). Their children: Susanna (b. 13 Dec 1741) and Jane (b. 23 Mar 1743/4). {BPR:341, 342}

Meadows, Daniel m. Jane (N). Their son Isham b. 16 Feb 1740/1. {BPR:341}

Meanlan, Richard m. Mary (N). Their dau. Hannah b. 13 Nov 1741. {BPR:341}

Mercer, Thomas m. bef. 3 Jan 1684, Mary (N). {CCCR:164}

Mercy/Marsey, Richard m. bef. 13 Sep 1721, Anne, dau. of William Pettypool. Their children: William and Martha. {PGW&D (1713-1728):157, 161}

Merredeth, David m. by Jun 1749, Mary (N). {CCCR:118}

Meredith, John had a dau. Pleasant who d. 18 Jan 1793. {BPR:344}

Merredith, Lewis d. by 1743, Elizabeth Merredeth and Elizabeth Willard, extxs. {CCCR:98}

Merredith, Sampson (d. ca. 1720) m. Elizabeth (N). Children: Samson, Elizabeth, Lewis and Thomas. {PGW&D (1713-1728):69-70}

Merredeth, Samson d. by 1744. His widow Ann, m. John Bachurst. {CCCR:102, 104}

Meredith, William m. Anne (N). Their dau. Lettice b. 23 Sep 1792. {BPR:344}

Merry, David m. bef. 1 Jul 1772, Elizabeth (N). Elizabeth, dau. of David Merry m. Crawley Maynard. {CCCR:46; MB:193}

Merry, Ramsey m. bef. Nov 1739, Joice (N). {CCCR:86}

Merimon, Francis m. Margaret (N). Their dau. Anne b. 26 Jun 1724. {BPR:336}

Merrymoon/Merrimoon, John of Prince George Co. m. 12th da., 10th mo., 1736, Hanah Patison, widow of Wm. Patison of the same co. In 1764 they res. in Amelia Co. Their dau. Sarah was disowned for marrying out and keeping bad company and committing whoredom and proving with child - then got married by a priest (hireling minister]. {HMM:19, 40}

Meuse, John m. Sarah (N). Their son Matthew b. 27 Feb 1733. {BPR:340}

Micabin, Margaret had a son John Bass b. 26 Jul 1720. {BPR:334}

Mice/Mize, Jeremiah of Brunswick Co., planter, m. bef. 8 May 1727, Grace (N). Their children: Robert (b. 10 May 1721) and Joshua (b. 10 Mar 1726). {PGW&D (1713-1728):160; BPR:337}

Middleton, (N) m. bef. Mar 1759, Mary, dau. of Thomas Perry. They had a son James. {CCCR:142}

Middleton, George m. Kathrine (N). Their son John Middleton Jr. d. by 1720. {PGW&D (1713-1728):62}

Middleton, James d. testate by 1739, leaving a widow Rebecca

Middleton. {CCCR:85}

Middleton, John of Martins Brandon Parish (d. 1722) m. by 1714 Elizabeth (N). Children: John, James and Mary. John's children-in-law (*step-children*?): William, Elizabeth, Sarah, Jane and Johannah, children of James Haley (d. by 1714). {PGW&D (1713-1728):6, 86}

Middleton, Elizabeth d. testate by 1743. {CCCR:100}

Miles/Mils, David m. Jane (N). Their children: David (b. 17 Apr 1727), Frances (b. 21 Jun 1729), Thomas (b. 29 Dec 1731) and John (b. 27 Apr 1734). {BPR:337, 338, 339}

Miles/Milles, Hugh m. Jane (N). Their children: Anne (b. 13 Mar 1742/3), Robert (b. 28 Mar 1742/3) and Jane (b. 21 Feb 1747/8). {BPR:342}

Miles, Isham of Cumberland Co. sold 180 acres in Westover Parish to Miles by his grandfather, John Miles. {CCCR:8}

Miles, James m. (bond dated 3 May 1784), Mary Thompson. {MB:194}

Miles, John d. by 1748, John Miles, exec. Ann Miles granted admin. of the estate of John Miles in 1750. Children: William, Judith (m. John Ridlehurst) and Mary (m. David Jackson). Dau. Judith chose Mordecai Debnam as her guardian in 1762 and m. 1764, John Ridlehurst. {CCCR:116, 123, 133, 153, 154; MB:196}

Miles, John in 1768 sold 150 acres which was given to him in the LWT (dated 1748) of his grandfather, John Miles, dec'd. and William Miles of Cumberland Co. sold 200 acres given to him by the LWT of his grandfather, John Miles. {CCCR:4}

Miles, Judith was presented in 1758 for having a bastard child. {CCCR:141}

Miller, Hugh m. Jane, dau. of Robert and Ann (Cocke) Bolling. Their dau. Anne b. 13 Mar 1742/3. {BPR:342; GVAW (Genealogies of Virginia Families) I:392}

Minge, David (d. 1779-81), son of John Minge (d. by 1772), m. Christian/Christiana Shields, dau. of James Shields of York Co. Children: John, George William Hunt, Rebecca Jones (m. John Dandridge), Ann Shields (never m.) and Judith Bray (m. Edmund Christian). Christian m.

2nd Collier Harrison, son of Robert Harrison. {GVAW (Genealogies of Virginia Families, III:691}

Minge, George (d. by Jan 1782) m. Mary (N). Dau., Sarah m. Freeman Walker, had children (unnamed)). {SWBC:41}

Minge, George William Hunt (LWT dated 1808), son of David Minge, m. Frances Dandridge. Children: Mary, David and George. {GVAW (Genealogies of Virginia Families, III:691}

Minge, James of Charles City Co., probable son of James Minge of Martins Brandon Parish, Charles City Co. (that part that became Prince George Co.) m. Amadea/Amy, dau. of Robert Harrison of York Co. Son: Valentine. {GVAW (Genealogies of Virginia Families), II:158; III:691}

Minge, John Sr. d. by 1746, Elizabeth Minge, extx. Elizabeth Minge d. by Mar 1759, Elizabeth and John Minge, execs. {CCCR:112, 113, 142}

Minge, John (d. by 1772, in Charles City Co., probable son of John Minge (d. by 1746), m. ca. 1742, Rebecca, widow of Thomas Collier. In his LWT John Minge left dau. Mary 1280 acres in Granville, NC and to his son David he left land in Halifax Co., NC. {CCCR:45, 90, 97}

Minge, John (LWT dated 3 Jul 1801) m. Nancy (N). Children: John Minge, Charles Minge, Elijah Minge, Jensy Jones Minge and Nathan Minge. {Dinwiddie Co. GenWeb}

Minge, Valentine (d. by 1725), son of James Minge (d. by 1716) was father of John and George; also probably: Martha (m. George Baskerville), Tabitha and Robert. {CCW&D (1725-31):8; GVAW (Genealogies of Virginia Families, II:158; III):691}

Minor, Peter (d. bef. 1807, Dinwiddie Co.). He was entitled to 300 acres of bounty land for his service in the Rev. War, which was assigned to Thomas D. Harris, by Erasmus Gill, admin. of Minor's estate. {RWP}

Minson, John m. (bond dated 28 Jan 1797) Ann Whitlock Wills. {MB:194}

Minthen, William d. by 1679. Dau.: Issabella. The widow of William Minthen m. 2nd Francis Hill. {CCOB (1677-79):93}

Minter, John (d. by 1655) m. Elizabeth (N). His dau. Mary was bound to Ralph Poole in 1657 until age 15. Mary d. 1660. {CCOB (1655-58):15,

131; CCOB 1658-61):270}

Mitchell, Archelus m. (bond dated 27 Nov 1763), Mary Gregory (spinster), dau. of John Gregory. {MB:196}

Mitchell, Edward of Bristol Parish m. bef. 23 Feb 1724, Margaret (N). {PGW&D (1713-1728):99, 160}

Mitchell, Henry of Sussex Co. m. 1st Tabitha, dau. of Thomas and Elizabeth Archer Branch. Their children: Henry (b. 7 Aug 1735), Nathaniel, Thomas and Addie (b. 20 Jun 1743). Henry m. 2nd Sarah (N). {BPR:341, 342; GVAW (Genealogies of Virginia Families) I:422}

Mitchell, Henry m. bef. 4 Jan 1791, Frances, 3rd dau. of William Hobbs. {PGR:144}

Mitchell, Peter m. Elizabeth (N). Their children: Joshua (b. 26 Feb 1718), Daniel (b. 26 Sep 1722) and Frances (b. 28 Oct 1725). {BPR:335, 336}

Mitchell, Rease/Reaps (b. 13 Feb 1758, d. 12 Mar 1803) of Bristol Parish m. 30 Dec 1783, Susanna Rives. Their son Thomy Branch b. 20 Oct 1791. {BPR:344; PGR:172; APP 1:381}

Mitchell, Robert and his sons, Robert the younger and Henry, sold 100 acres on the Appomattox River in Bristol Parish in 1723. {PGW&D (1713-1728):91}

Mitchell, Thomas m. Hannah (N). Their son Joab b. 11 Feb 1722. {BPR:335}

Mitchell, Thomas m. Ann (N). Their children: John (b. 26 May 1704), Thomas (b. 19 Apr 1705) and Francis (b. 18 Jun 1708). {BPR:335}

Mitchell, Thomas of Bristol Parish m. Barbary, dau. of Samuel and Mary Tatum. Their children: Mary (b. 18 Aug 1713), Barbary (b. 8 Mar 1715/16), Nathaniel (b. 4 Dec 1717), Peter (b. 3 Jan 1719), Samuel (b. 16 Jun 1722) and John. {BPR:335; PGW&D (1713-1728):128, 153; APP 3:267 (does not include son John)}

Mitchell, Thomas m. bef. 14 Apr 1789, Ann, dau. of Capt. Nathaniel Raines. Sons: Henry and Hartwell. Thomas d. 27 Jul 1826 in Thomas Co., GA. {PGR:120; GVAW (Genealogies of Virginia Families) II:729}

Mitchell, Thomas of Sussex Co. m. Rebecca (N). Their son Tazewell b.

16 Aug 1794. {BPR:345}

Mitchell, William m. bef. 11 Aug 1718, Katherine (N). {PGW&D (1713-1728): 36-7}

Mixon, William m. Elizabeth (N). Their son Michaell b. 15 Apr 1727. {BPR:337}

Mobberly, Edward of Martins Brandon Parish d. by 1727. In his LWT he named dau. Rebecca Mobberly in Prince George's Co., MD; Sarah Bilbro and Mary Rivers, dau. of Robert Rivers. {PGW&D (1713-1728):172}

Montfort. See Munford.

Monger, Joshua d. by 1745, Henry Taylor, exec. {CCCR:109}

Moody, Frances gave a Negro named Joan to her dau., Sukey Bonner Temple [or Sukey Temple Bonner). {PGR:97}

Moodie, Humphry m. Elizabeth (N). Their dau. Jane b. 30 Mar 1742. {BPR:341}

Moody, Robert m. Anne (N). Their children: John (b. 18 May 1723), Laurana (b. 29 Jan 1731), Frances (d. 1732) and Daniel (b. 2 Dec 1734). {BPR:335, 339, 340, 341}

Moody, Samuel (d. 1772) m. Sarah (N). Children: Samuel, Thomas, David, Sarah, Rebecca and Mary. {CCCR:48}

Moody, Thomas d. by 1656 leaving a widow (extx.) who m. Francis Redford. CCOB (1655-58): 69}

Moody, Thomas d. by 1771. Sister: "Faris." Children?: Henry, Philip, Lucy (m. (N) Hill), Elizabeth, Mary and Martha. {CCCR:47}

Mooney, John m. Ann (N). Their dau. Jane b. 13 Dec 1735. {BPR:341}

Mooney, Timothy was father of Timothy who was bound out in 1738. {PGR:36}

Moor, Alexander m. Ruth (N). Their son William b. 14 Sep 1731. {BPR:339}

More, George Hunt m. Frances (N). Their children: James (b. 18 Mar 1727) and Elizabeth (b. 1 Jan 1729). {BPR:337, 338}

Moor, James m. Mary (N). Their children: Priscilla b. 1 Jun 1722. {BPR:335}

More, James m. Leah (N). Their son Daniel b. 11 Feb 1732. {BPR:339}

Moore, James m. Mary (N). Their son Robert b. 23 Jan 1734. {BPR:341}

Moore, James (b. ca. 1750) enlisted in the Rev. War from Dinwiddie Co. He later moved to Pendleton Co., KY. {RWP}

Moore, John m. Tabitha Pace, dau. of Richard Pace. {VG&B:153}

Moore, John of Bristol Parish m. in Jul 1692 Elizabeth, dau. of Seth Perkins by Mr. Charles Anderson of Westover Parish. This marriage was charged as unlawful. John Moore was father of Seth (b. 9 Apr 1692). {CCOB (1687-95):179; PGW&D (1710-1713): 15; BPR:336}

Moor, John m. Catharine (N). Their children: John (b. 8 Dec 1720), John (b. 1721), Sara (b. 20 Mar 1723), James (b. 18 Aug 1726), Phebe (b. 22 Oct 1728) and Betty Rutherford (b. 25 Jun 1731). {BPR:334, 335, 336, 337, 338}

More, John m. Mary (N). Their children: Lucia (b. 24 May 1729) , George (b. 23 Nov 1732), John (b. 9 May 1735) and Wood (b. 27 Mar 1741). {BPR:337, 339, 340, 341}

Moor, John, not able to bring up his dau. Mary in a Christian-like manner, Mary was bound out in 1760. {CCCR:144}

Moore, John m. Mary (N). Their son Joseph b. 20 Jan 1767. {BPR:343}

More, Jonathan m. Sarah (N). Their children: Jonathan (bapt. 23 Sep 1732) and David (b. 13 Apr 1733). {BPR:339, 340}

Moore/More, Mark m. Elizabeth (N). Their children: Mark (b. 26 Jul 1723) and Mark (b. 10 Jun 1726). {BPR:336}

Moore, Rebecca was presented in 1745 for having a bastard child. To receive 25 lashes. {CCCR:108, 110}

Moore, Richard had a son John in Surry Co. (1721). {PGM:2}

Moore, Richard of Bristol Parish (d. ca. 1727) m. Elizabeth (N).
Children: John, Benjamin, William, Thomas (predeceased his father, had
a son Thomas), Mary (m. (N) Lewis), Elizabeth (m. (N) Baugh), Samuel
and Roger. Grandson: George Rives. {PGW&D (1713-1728): 169}

Moore, Richard of Prince George and Sussex counties m. Rebecca, dau.
of James and Lucretia (Cotton) Clements. Their children: Eliza, Francis
and John. {GVAT (Genealogies of Virginia Families) I:377, 384}

More, Roger m. Elizabeth (N). Their children: Susannah (b. 27 Apr
1729), Thomas (b. 20 Sep 1730), Roger (b. 8 Dec 1732) and Mary (b. 11
May 1742). {BPR:337, 338, 339}

Moor/More, Samuel m. Mary (N). Their children: Mary (b. 26 Dec
1719), Elizabeth (b. 13 Oct 1722), Richard (b. 9 Feb 1723/4), William (b.
6 Jul 1726) and Mary (b. 29 Apr 1731). {BPR:334, 335, 336, 3390}

Moore, Sharkey of Bristol Parish m. bef. 13 May 1760, Mary (N).
{PGR:79}

Moor, Thomas d. by 1719, Ann Moor, extx. {PGW&D (1713-1728):51,
73}

More, Thomas m. Elionar/Eleonore (N). Their children: Margret (b. 13
Apr 1729) and Avis (b. 27 Mar 1733). {BPR:337, 340}

More, William, son of Wm. More of North Carolina in Pequimans, m.
15th da., 7th mo., 1724, Martha Odum, dau. of Abraham Odum of Prince
George Co. {HMM:13}

Morecock/Morcock, Thomas (d. by 1740) m. bef. 2 Feb 1731, Elizabeth
(N). In 1748 their son Thomas Morecock chose Francis Dancy as his
guardian. {CCCR:11, 87, 114}

Morecock, Thomas, son of Thomas Morecock, m. by Oct 1761, Mildred
(N). {CCCR:152}

Morgan, Phillip m. Mary (N). Their children: Rhuben (b. 11 Nov 1725),
Phillip (b. 15 Dec 1730) and John b. 30 Nov 1731). {BPR:336, 338, 339}

Morgan, Robert gave his son Robert Morgan, Jr. of Charlotte Co. 50
acres in 1771. Robert d. 1773. In his LWT he named son Robert; daus.:
Susannah, Sarah (m. (N) Strange), Frances (m. (N) Green), Amy (m. (N)
Jones) and Tabitha. Granddau.: Elizabeth McCarter. {CCCR:43, 59}

Morgan, Samuel m. Mary (N). Their children: Elizabeth (b. 20 Apr 1732) and John (b. 26 Apr 1734). {BPR:339, 340}

Morland/Moreland/Moorland, John m. Dorithy (N). Their children: Mary (b. 23 Sep 1726), Jean (b. 21 Sep 1728) and Martha (b. 12 Sep 1740). {BPR:336, 337, 341}

Morrimont, Francis m. Margaret (N). Their dau. Rosamund b. 26 Jul 1719. {BPR:334}

Morris, Henry m. Martha (N). Their children: Martha b. 2 Jun 1725. {BPR:336}

Morris, Henry m. Susanah/Susan (N). Their children: Elizabeth (b. 6 Oct 1726) and Henry (b. 3 Mar 1728). {BPR:337}

Morris, Hercules (probably res. Dinwiddie Co.) m. Jane (N). Their dau. Ann b. 1 Aug 1762. {GVAW (Genealogies of Virginia Families II:138}

Morris, John m. Elizabeth (N). Their son John b. 24 Nov 1734. {BPR:341}

Morris, William (d. by 1690) m. bef. 24 Jan 1687, Sarah, admx. of John Smith. {CCOB (1687-95):7, 8, 79}

Morris, William m bef. 3 June 1689, Elizabeth. They bound out their son, Thomas, to John Unite until age 21. {CCOB (1687-95):52}

Morris, William d. by Dec 1689. {CCOB (1687-95):75}

Morris, Winifred, spinster, made her indenture to John Hodgson, merchant, for 7 years in 1730. {CCW&D (1725-31):46}

Morrison, David d. 7 Nov 1787, Prince George Co. leaving orphans (unnamed). {Legislative Petitions – Library of VA website}

Morison, John and his wife Ann and David Morison sold 400 acres of land in 1787. {PGR:90}

Morrison, John (d. ca. 1790) m. Ann Poythress Bland, dau. of Richard Bland. Ann was pregnant in 1785. In his LWT John refereed to his five sisters (unnamed) and brothers, Alexander, Theodorick and David. Ann m. 2nd Peter Woodlief. {PGR:137; GVAW (Genealogies of Virginia

Families): IV:205}

Morrison, William, admin. de bonis non of Alexander Morrison the elder, m. Anne (N). {PGM:8}

Moseby, Edward m. 1st ca. 1688, Sarah Woodson, dau. of Robert Woodson. Their children: John, Robert, Agness (m. John Binford of Prince George Co.), Hezekiah, Jacob, Joseph, Richard and Benjamin. Edward m. 2nd 10th da., 9th mo., 1716 Mary Watkins, widow of Henry Watkins at the meeting house near Curles. {APP3:715-6, 721; HMM:7}

Moseby, Joseph (d. ca. 1727), son of Edward and Sarah (Woodson) Mosby, m. Sabrina (N). Joseph and Sabrina had a dau.: Mary. {PGW&D (1713-1728):163; APP 3:715, 722}

Mosier/Mozier, Nicholas m. bef. 3 Jun 1673, (N), widow of Thomas Capell and dau. of Thomas Drew. {CCOB (1687-95):60; CCOB (Fragments):522}

Mosier, Nicholas (d. 1728) m. (N), probable widow of Thomas Brand. Nicholas was father of Nicholas, Edward and Bernard. In his LWT Nicholas named "dau.-in-law," Elizabeth Brand, probably dau. of his wife by her previous husband. {CCW&D (1725-31):5, 31}

Mosher, Samuel d. by 1693, his "cousin," Nicholas Mosher, exec. {CCOB (1687-95):169; CCCR:75}

Mossom, Rev. David (b. 25 Mar 1690, d. 4 Jun 1767) of St. Peter Parish, New Kent Co. m. 1st Elizabeth (N) who d. 28 Jan 1737. He m. 2nd 20 Jul 1740, Mary (Major), widow of Henry Claiborne. Their children: Mary (b. 6 Sep 1741), Robert (b. 13 May 1744). Mary, widow of Rev. Mosson, d. 23 Nov 1745. Rev. Mosson m. 3rd 6 Jul 1755 (marriage contract Feb 1755) Elizabeth Marston of Westover Parish, Charles City Co., widow of Benskin Marston and dau. of Henry Soane. Elizabeth d. 2 Apr 1759. {Mossom Bible; CCCR:131; GVAW I:724-5; III:815-816}

Mountcastle, Joab d. 1770-3) m. Anne (N). Children: John, David, William, Benjamin, Edmund, Joseph, Richard, Henry, Mary (m. (N) Lawed) and Elizabeth (probably m. James Fear). {CCCR:50-1}

Moyle, Peter d. by 1656 leaving Elizabeth, his widow and extx. They had son Peter and two other children. In 1656 Elizabeth m. 2nd Nicholas Poole, m. 3rd Thomas Madder and m. 4th Francis Treham. {CCOB (1655-58): 56; CCOB (1661-64):371, 391}

Mudgett, Thomas of Martins Brandon Parish m. 1st Ellinor (buried 15 Mar 1660) and was father of Elizabeth (bapt. 9 Jan 1660). Thomas m. 2nd bef. 3 Apr 1663, (N), dau. of Francis Grey. Thomas d. by 1678, Sarah Mudgett, widow and admx. {CCOB 1658-61):270; CCOB (1661-64):381; CCOB (1677-79):47}

Muir, Francis m. bef. 10 Apr 1787, Mary, probable niece of Ann Isham Gordon (d. 1790). Their children: Mary Muir, William Poythress Muir, Margaret Muir. {PGR:88, 131}

Mulatto slave, Betsey, owned by the estate of James Field, had a dau. Clarissa Birchett, b. 25 Feb 1792. {BPR:305}

Mulatto slave Dorcas, owned by John Thweatt, had a son Edward, b. 17 Dec 1792. {BPR:379}

Munford/Monfort, Edward m. bef. 25 Apr 1769, Betty, widow of Edward Broadnax. They res. in Halifax Co., NC in 1769. Son: William. {CCCR:13, 51; GVAW (Virginia Families) I:464}

Montfort, James on 12 Apr 1665 acquitted his father-in-law (*step-father*), Morgan Jones of all claims. {CCOB (1664-65):546}

Munford/Mumford, James d. by 1690 leaving a widow, Sarah. His dau. Wilmott was bound in 1690 to Mrs. Elizabeth Peobles, wife of William Peobles. Edward Munford, age 14 in 1690, probable son of James Munford, chose Anthony Wyatt Jr. as his guardian. Sarah m. 2nd James Jones. {CCOB (1687-95):79, 85, 96, 166}

Munford, Major James (d. 1754 in Amelia Co.), Gent., son of Robert Munford, m. 1727-8, Elizabeth Bolling, dau. of Robert Bolling. Their children: Martha (b. 29 Sep 1728), James (b. 16 Sep 1732), Susanna (b. 29 Mar 1734), William, Robert, Thomas and Edward. Elizabeth probably m. 2nd Col. John Bannister. {PGR:13; GVAT (Genealogies of Virginia Families) II:740, 746; BPR:337, 339, 340}

Mumford, Jeoffry d. by 1678, Mary Mumford, widow and admx. Mary m. 2nd Thomas Blanks. {CCOB (1677-79):50, 108}

Munford, Jeffrey d. by 1737, Ann Munford, extx. Ann Munford d. by 1743. Jeffry was probably father of William Green Munford. {CCCR:83, 100; GVAT II:744}

Munford, Robert (d. 1735), son of James Munford, m. Martha Kennon, dau. of Richard Kennon of Henrico Co. Their children: Mary (m. David, son of Freeman Walker), James, Robert and Edward (b. 1 Nov 1726). {GVAT (Genealogies of Virginia Families) II:733-4; PGW&D (1710-1713):32; PGR:57; BPR:337}

Munford, Capt. Robert (d. Dec 1744) of Bristol Parish, son of Robert Munford (d. 1735), m. Anna Bland, dau. of Richard Bland. Children: Robert, Theodorick (b. 21 Feb 1741/2) and Elizabeth (b. 22 Sep 1734, m. Rev. Archibald McRoberts). Anna m. 2nd George Currie. {PGR:177; GVAT II (Genealogies of Virginia Families):742; BPR:340, 341; SWBC:211}

Munford, Robert, son of Major James Munford, res. Amelia Co., later Halifax Co., m. (bond dated 11 Feb 1755), Anne Brodnax, probable dau. of Edward Brodnax of Charles City Co. {GVAG II (Genealogies of Virginia Families):740}

Munford, Robert (1766-1800), son of William Green Munford, m. Margaret W. Harwood, dau. of Major Samuel and Margaret (Woddrop) Harwood. Children: Samuel, Robert and Margaret Ann (b. after her father's death, m. John Sinclair). Sons, Samuel and Robert removed to Gloucester Co. where they died. {GVAT (Genealogies of Virginia Families II): 745}

Munford, William d. by 1761. His orphans, William, John and Joseph were bound out. {CCCR:150}

Munford, William Green (d. 1786), probable son of Jeffrey Munford (d. by 1738) m. bef. 4 Jan 1769, Ann (N). Children: Robert, John, Stanhope, William Greene, Mary (m. John Lightfoot) and Elizabeth. {CCCR:9; GVAT (Genealogies of Virginia Families II): 745}

Murcollow/Maccollo, David m. Elizabeth (N). Their children: John (b. 14 Dec 1725), Mary (b. 7 Jun 1727), David (b. 28 May 1729) and Ja--- (b. 29 Sep 1731). {BPR:336, 337, 339}

Murray, James m. Anne (N). Their children: James (b. 10 Jul 1743), John (b. 13 Sep 1744), Anne (b. 8 Feb 1748/9), Margaret (b. 8 Feb 1748/9), William (b. 6 May 1752), Mary (b. 22 Feb 1754) and Thomas (b. 13 Jan 1757). {BPR:342, 343}

Murrell, Jeffrey d. by 1754 leaving an orphan son, William who chose Francis Johnson as his guardian. Dau. Lucy chose John Sherman Gregory

as her guardian in 1754. In 1755 son Thomas chose a guardian.
{CCCR:129}

Nance, Daniel m. bef. 8 Apr 1717, Elizabeth (N). Their children: Phebe
(b. Oct 1712), Elizabeth (b. 6 Jul 1719), Elinor (b. 9 Sep 1722) and Lucy
(b. 24 Dec 1730). {PGW&D (1713-1728):24; BPR:345}

Nance, Daniel m. Mary (N). Their dau. Elizabeth b. 19 Jun 1728.
{BPR:346}

Nance, James m. by Nov 1745, Mary (N). {CCCR:108}

Nance, John (d. by 1716) m. Sarah (N). Children: John, Richard, Susan,
Elizabeth (m. Thomas Gregory), Elin (m. Cesar Warpole), John and
Dorothy. {PGW&D (1713-1728):21}

Nance, John m. Jane (N). Their children: Elinor (b. 25 May 1721) ,
Thomas (b. 22 Sep 1723/4), Richard (b. 24 Jan 1726) and William (b. 12
Jul 1728). {BPR:345, 346}

Nance, John m. bef. 6 Dec 1770, Nance (*sic*), dau. of Rabley Vaughan.
{CCCR:44}

Nance, John m. Martha (N). Their son Giles b. 4 May 1735. {BPR:346}

Nance, Richard of Bristol Parish m. bef. 8 Aug 1721, Mary (N). Their
children: John (b. 15 Dec 1723), Nathaniel (b. 9 Dec 1731) and Anne (b.
15 Jan 1741/2). {PGW&D (1713-1728):74; BPR:345, 346, 347}

Nance, Richard m. Mary (N). Their children: Elizabeth (b. 7 Nov 1726)
and Leanord (b. 15 Dec 1730). {BPR:346}

Nantzs, Thomas m. Priscilla (N). Their dau. Sarah b. 19 Oct 1745.
{BPR:347}

Nance, William m. Ann (N). Their children: Thomas (b. 29 Feb 1735)
and Sarah (b. 30 Jan 1742/3). {BPR:347}

Nance, Zacharias/Zachariah (d. 1771-2) m. bef. 5 Nov 1771, Susanna
(N). Children: James, John, Elizabeth, William, Susannah and Zachariah.
{CCCR:42}

Nash, John m. Mary (N). Their son Johney b. 4 Nov 1758. {BPR:347}

Neal/Neel, Thomas m. Margret (N). Their children: Mary (b. 31 Mar 1721), dau. (b. 1723), Thomas (b. 1 Sep 1712), Sarah (b. 5 Jan 1727) and Thomas (b. 4 Jul 1730). {BPR:345, 346}

Neal/Neel, Thomas m. Mary (N). Their dau. Frances b. 7 May 1725. {BPR:345}

Following are slaves for which a connection to parent (usually mother) was evidenced.

Negro Abby, owned by John Thweatt, had a dau. Notise, b. 25 Jan 1792. {BPR:378}

Negro Aggy, belonging to Richard Booker, had a dau. Aggy b. 12 Sep 1790. {BPR:293}

Negro Aggy and her children, Peggy, Jonathan, Aggy, Pegg, Patt, Mazey and Lucy were owned by Edmund Ruffin in 1789. {PGR:153}

Negro Aggy, owned by John McLeod, had a dau. Louisa, b. Mar 1790. {BPR:343}

Negro, Amy and Tabby her child – owned by Bathurst Skelton, 1773. {CCCR:61}

Negro Amy, owned by John Grammar, was mother of Hannah Scott, b. 27 Sep 1792. {BPR:311}

Negro Anaky and her dau. Fanny were owned by Joseph Williams in 1787. {PGR:117}

Negro Beck, and her son, Isham, given by Mary Finnie to Thomas Harris Sr. in 1791. {PGR:148}

Negro Beck and her son Bob, owned by John Gilliam (d. by 1801). {PGR:176}

Negro Beck, owned by Mrs. Lucy Newsum, had a dau. Cressy, b. 15 Mar 1792. {BPR:347}

Negro Bess and her children, Harry and Saray, owned by Thomas Goodwyn of Surry Co. in 1724. {PGW&D (1713-1728):107}

Negro Bess, owned by James Boisseau, had a dau. Nancy (b. 12 Jun 1755) and Hannaball (b. 29 Jan 1758). {BPR:292}

Negro Bet, owned by Robert Birchett, had dau. Milly b. 20 Nov 1789. {BPR:294}

Negro Betty and her children, Lucy and Frank – owned by Littlebury Cocke, 1774 – CCCR:64}

Negro Betty, owned by John Thweatt, had a son Thom, b. 25 Nov 1791. {BPR:378}

Negro Betty and her sons Billy and Bristol (b. 14 Mar 1792), owned by John Gilliam of Princ George Co. in 1789. {PGR:127; BPR:311}

Negro, Bob m. Nuthy and their children: Robin, Polly and Harry – owned by Hon. William Byrd, 1772. {CCCR:54-5}

Negro, Carpenter Charles and his dau. Patt, owned by Hon. William Byrd, 1772. {CCCR:54-5}

Negro, Carpenter Jack and his wife Kate, and Sarah and Charles, their children – owned by Hon. William Byrd, 1772. {CCCR:54-5}

Negro Cate, owned by John Thweatt, had a dau. Charlotte, b. 9 Apr 1791. {BPR:378}

Negro Chloe, owned by James Boisseau, had a son Peter b. 31 Jul 1756. {BPR:292}

Negro, Cook Charles and his sons Charles and Frank – owned by Hon. William Byrd, 1772. {CCCR:54-5}

Negro Cressy, owned by Richard Taylor, had a son Aleck, b. 1 Mar 1792. {BPR:378}

Negro, Black Charles the carpenter and his wife Nanny, owned by Hon. William Byrd, 1772. {CCCR:54-5}

Negro Cooper Godfry and his dau. Evy, owned by Hon. William Byrd, 1772. {CCCR:54-5}

Negro Eliza and her children: Jack, Margret and Nelly, owned by Edmund Ruffin (d. by 1791). {PGR:159}

Negro Elsey, owned by Reasmus Gill, was mother of Erasmus, b. 22 Apr 1792. {BPR:311}

Negro Fanny and child Filly, owned by Edmund Ruffin (d. by 1791). {PGR:159}

Negro Fanny, owned by David Maitland, had a son Joshua, b. 1 Feb 1791. {BPR:344}

Negro Hannah and her dau. Charlotte, owned by Edward Avery in 1784. In his LWT Edward gave Charlotte her freedom and 50 acres, a bed, furniture and a cow and calf. {PGR:118}

Negro, Hannah, owned by William Call, had a dau. Jeany b. 24 Apr 1792. {BPR:302}

Negro Isabell and her dau. Fanny (to have her freedom at age 20, owned by Richard Stewart (d. ca. 1791). {PGR:152-3}

Negro Isabel and her children: Betty, Beck, Mack, Mason, Harry and Cresse, were owned by Edmund Ruffin (d. by 1791) {PGR:159}

Negro, Jack White m. Beck. Their children: Hannah, Sally, Johney and Charles – owned by Hon. William Byrd, 1772. {CCCR:54-5}

Negro Jamey and wife Suckey and Betty and Jamey his children – owned by Hon. William Byrd, 1772. {CCCR:54-5}

Negro Jeanie, owned by Zachariah Shackleford, had a son Johnny, b. 16 Jun 1792. {BPR:370}

Negro Jinny and child Dwella were owned by David Morrison of Greensville Co. in 1788. {PGR:103}

Negro Judy and child Esther were owned by David Morrison of Greensville Co. in 1788. {PGR:103}

Negro Judy, owned by Anthony Sidner, had a son John Taylor, b. 18 Dec 1791. {BPR:370}

Negro Kame and her children, Tom, Lusey and Phebe, owned by John Sturdivant in 1793. {PGM:19}

Negro Jeany, belonging to David Buchanan, had a son William b. Dec

1791. {BPR:293}

Negro, Jene, owned by Mrs. Jane Cocke in 1771, was mother of dau. Silvey. {CCCR:40}

Negro Jenny and her children, Bett and Moses – owned by Peter Eppes – 1773. {CCCR:55}

Negro Jenny, owned by William Robertson, had a son Thomas b. 4 Jan 1792. {BPR:361}

Negro Joe and Statia his wife and Aggy and Beck his children – owned by William Byrd, 1772. {cccr:54-5}

Negro Judith and her children, Sylvia and Sarah – owned by Littlebury Cocke, 1774 – CCCR:64}

Negro Judith and her children, Nancy, Joe and Stephen, owned by Capt. James Clark ca. 1788. {PGR:112}

Negro, Judy and King her child – owned by Bathurst Skelton, 1773. {CCCR:61}

Negro Lego and her children, Lucy and Ned, owned by John Sturdivant in 1793. {PGM:19}

Negro Letty, belonging to Sarah Brown, had a dau. Charlotte, b. 29 Dec 1791. {BPR:293}

Negro Little Aggy, owned by Erasmus Gill, was mother of Fanny, b. 2 1792. {BPR:311}

Negro Little Annecey, owned by James Bell in 1771 was mother of Charles. {CCCR:40}

Negro Liza, owned by Simon Fraser, had a son Arthur, b. 8 Mar 1792. {BPR:304}

Negro Lucy (d. by 1791) and her children, Fanny, Lucy and Patricia, owned by Richard Stewart (d. ca. 1791). {PGR:152-3}

Negro Megg and her children, Harriet and Phebe, owned by John Sturdivant in 1793. {PGM:19}

Negro Michael and his wife Aggy, owned by Hon. William Byrd, 1772. {CCCR:54-5}

Negro Milly and her children, Harry, Bob, Cyrus and Daphney, owned by John Sturdivant in 1793. {PGM:19}

Negro Milly and her child, Kesiah, were owned by Edward Avery Sr. in 1788. {PGR:115}

Negro Molly and her children: Sally, Aron, Joanna and Ephraim, owned by Edmund Ruffin (d. by 1791). {PGR:159}

Negro, Nancy the seamstress and Billy and Fanny, her children – owned by Hon. William Byrd, 1772. {CCCR:54-5}

Negro Nancy, owned by Edmund Harrison, had a dau. Peggy, b. 15 Feb 1792. {BPR:320}

Negro Nancy, owned by Alexander Glass Strachan, had a son William Allfriend, b. 13 Jan 1792. {BPR:370}

Negro Nanny and her 3 children, Jim, Steven and Isaac, owned by Thomas Woodlief in 1787. {PGR:99}

Negro Nanny, owned by William Robertson, had a son Tim, b. 28 Aug 1791. {BPR:361}

Negro Old Siss and her dau. Siss, owned by Martha Cock in 1713. {PGW&D (1710-1713):40}

Negro Page, owned by Thomas G. Peachy, had a son, Lotty Williams, b. 1 Jul 1792. {BPR:355}

Negro Parson and wife Nelly – owned by Hon. William Byrd, 1772. {CCCR:54-5}

Negro Patt, owned by James Boisseau, had sons Charles (b. 28 Mar 1755) and Anthony (b. 26 Oct 1758). {BPR:292}

Negro Pegg and her son Harry, owned by David Meade in 1791. {PGR:157}

Negro Peg, owned by John Verell, had a dau. Peg, b. 4 Mar 1792.

Negro Peninah, owned by William Gilliam was mother of Betsy Philipps, b. 4 Mar 1792. {BPR:311}

Negro Pheaby and her children, Sue and Moll, owned by Richard Stewart (d. ca. 1791). {PGR:152-3}

Negro Phebe and her children, Betty and Anthony – owned by Peter Eppes, 1773. {CCC R:55}

Negro Quoy and Beck and Rachel his children – owned by Hon. William Byrd, 1772. {CCCR:54-5}

Negro Roger and his wife Jiny, owned by Edmund Irby (LWT dated 1733). {PGR:176}

Negro Rose and her children: Hannah, Moses, Sukey and Eliza, owned by Edmund Ruffin (d. by 1791). {PGR:159}

Negro Sall and her children, Sukey and Lucy – owned by Littlebury Cocke, 1774 – CCCR:64}

Negro Sall and her child Phebe, owned by James H. Baird in 1791. {PGR:147}

Negro Sarah and her child, Zaga – owned by Littlebury Cocke, 1774 – CCCR:64}

Negro Sarah, owned by John Verell, had a dau. Lucetta, b. 24 Feb 1792. {BPR:382}

Negro Siss and her grandson Ned (blind) were ordered by the LWT of Lessenbury Williams to be maintained out of his estate. {PGR:151}

Negro Stoakes and Effy his wife – owned by Hon. William Byrd, 1772. {CCCR:54-5}

Negro Suck, owned by Robert Birchett, had a son Thomas b. 10 Jul 1789. {BPR:294}

Negro Suckey, owned by Robert Birchett, had dau. Lid, b. 31 Aug 1789. {BPR:294}

Negro Sucky and her dau. Jane owned by Edward Avery in 1784. {PGR:118}

Negro Sucky and her children, Poll and Answil, sold by Peyton Scarbrough to Isaac Donaldson in 1789. {PGR:135}

Negro Sue and her child Bob, owned by John Sturdivant in 1793. {PGM:19}

Negro Sukey and her children, James and Tom – owned by Peter Eppes. {CCCR:54-5}

Negro Sukey and her children, Aaron, Little Phebe, Charlotte and Ned, owned by John Sturdivant in 1793. {PGM:19}

Negro Suke and her sons, Allen and Wilson, given by Mary Finnie to Thomas Harris Sr. in 1791. {PGR:148}

Negro Susy, owned by John Causy, was mother of Augustus Caesar, b. 25 Nov 1792. {BPR:303}

Negro Sylvia and her children, Charles, Ned Belzey, owned by Richard Stewart (d. ca. 1791). {PGR:152-3}

Negro Tina, owned by Frank Eppes had a dau. Elizabeth Hall b. 27 Jan 1792. {BPR:304}

Negro Tom, son of Amey was sold by Joel Epes, otherwise called Joel Dillihay to Eppes Temple, both of Prince George Co. {PGR:103}

Negro Usey and her children, Peter, Amey and Lucy were owned by Edmund Ruffin in 1789. {PGR:153}

Negro Ussey and her children: Patty, Priscilla, Peter, Amy, Lucy, Ritter and Marian, owned by Edmund Ruffin (d. by 1791). {PGR:159}

Negro Violet and her son Jack, owned by David Meade in 1791. {PGR:157}

Negro Watt, and Eli his dau, owned by Hon. William Byrd, 1772. {CCCR:54-5}

Nelson, Robert probably m. Susan Robinson, dau. of Speaker Robinson. His daus: Susan, Mary, and Ann Nelson. (will of Mildred W. Carter dated 31 May 1807). {Legislative Petitions – Library of VA website; {GVAW (Genealogies of Virginia Families) II:93}

Netherland, Robert m. bef. 4 Jun 1655, Frances, widow of William Barker and dau. of James Ward. They had a son Robert. Frances m. 3rd Lt. Col. Thomas Drew. {CCOB (1655-58): 42; CCOB (1661-64):465; CCOB 1676-79:9, 50; VG&B:149}

Netherland, Robert, son of Robert and Frances (Ward) Netherland, d. by 1688, leaving widow Elizabeth. {CCOB (1687-95):19, 27}

Nevil, John m. Margret (N). Their son James b. 1 Jul 1733. {BPR:346}

New, (N) m. Elizabeth (N). Elizabeth New gave (recorded 4 Feb 1729) household items to her grandsons, Robert Adams, son of Henry Adams and to Peter Gilly, son of Francis Gilly. {CCW&D (1725-31):39}

Newby, Francis, son of Gabriall Jr. and Mary Newby of Pequimans Monthly Meeting, NC, m. 7th da., 12th mo., 1722, Huldah Hunicut, dau. of Robert Hunicut of Prince George Co.. {HMM:12; GVAW III:98}

Newell, Edward (d. 1791) m. Katherine/Katy (N). Children: Rebeccah, James, Benjamin, Peter, Mary and Elizabeth. {PGR:162}

Newell, Edward d. by 1800, leaving Lucy Newell as guardian of his children. {PGM:9}

Newhouse, Raise m. Ann (N). Their children: Thomas (b. 1 Sep 1712) and Elinor (b. 25 May 1721). {BPR:345}

Newhouse, Thomas (d. by 1711) m. Mutus (N). Son: Raize. Mutus m. 2nd (N) Butler. {PGW&D (1710-1713): 16-17, 33}

Newman, Richard m. Mary (N). Their dau. Ann b. 30 Mar 1741. {BPR:347}

Newton, Anna, servant to John Taylor, convicted of having a bastard child Apr 1689 and second time in 1690. William Warren paid her fine. {CCOB (1687-95):46, 86}

Nicholas, Richard d. by 1660, leaving a widow, Susanna and dau. Susanna. Widow Susanna m. 2nd Rice Hoe. {CCOB (1658-61):236, 253}

Nipper, John m. Ann (N). Their dau. Martha b. 19 Nov 1726. {BPR:346}

Noble, Robert m. Elizabeth (N). Their son Mark b. 18 May 1727. {BPR:346}

Noblet, John d. by 1679. His widow m. 2nd Michael Talbott. {CCOB (1677-79):101}

Norden, Susanna d. by 1739. {CCCR:86}

Norman/Norment, Charles, son of Samuel Norman of Henrico Co. and Elizabeth his wife, m. 7th da., 12th mo., 1797 Ann Vaughan, dau. of William S. Vaughan, late of Charles City Co., dec'd., and Hannah his wife, with consent of parents, at the meeting house near Curles in Henrico Co. Their dau. Eliza b. 23rd da., 8th mo., 1800. {HMM:81, 85, 88}

Norman, James m. bef. 8 Jul 1778, Molly (N). Sons: Pleasant and John. {HCDB 1:13}

Norman, Mildred. 3/3/1792. Mildred Norman married a man not of the (Quaker) Society - disowned. {HMM:76}

Norman/Norment, Samuel m. Elizabeth (N). Their children: Charles (b. 14th da., 7th mo., 1777), Samuel (b. 11th da., 5th mo., 1782), Betsy G. (b. 23rd da., 3rd mo., 1784), Ann (b. 13th da, 11th mo., 1786) and John (b. 9th da., 8th mo., 1789). In 1793 Samuel and Elizabeth Norman condemned their consenting to their daughter's disorderly marriage. {HMM:77, 85}

Norten, Francis d. by 1717, leaving a widow, Mary. {PGW&D (1713-1728):28}

Norton, Thomas m. Agness (N). Their children: Thomas (b. 23 Jan 1755), Sarah (b. 21 Oct 1756), Patty (b. 19 Oct 1758), Frances (b. 1 Jun 1760) and William (b. 22 Apr 1762). {BPR:347}

Norton, William m. Ann (N). Their children: James (b. 2 Oct 1721) and Mary (b. 9 Jan 1723/24. {BPR:345}

Nowell, John m. bef. 5 Mar 1660/1, Lydia Perkins, dau. of Nicholas and Mary Perkins. {GVAW IV:30; GVAT II:814}

Nowlin, Richard (d. 1715) of Martins Brandon Parish m. Elizabeth (N). {PGW&D (1713-1728):12}

Nunnally, Daniel (b. 26 Sep 1762 or 1763, Dinwiddie Co., brother of William Nunnally). {RWP}

Nunally, Richard m. (N)(N). Their dau. Obedience b. 26 Nov 1728. {BPR:346}

Nunally/Nunneley, Thomas of Bristol Parish m. Elizabeth (N). Their children: Peter (b. 3 Jan 1723/4), Thomas (b. 1726), John (b. 4 Dec 1728), Daniel (b. 28 Mar 1731), Mary (b. 1 Feb 1732/3) and Zachariah (b. 19 May 1735). {PGW&D (1713-1728):101; BPR:345, 346}

Nunnally, Walter d. by 1712. {PGW&D (1710-1713): 15}

Nunnally, William b. 1755, Dinwiddie Co., brother of Daniel Nunnally. {RWP}

Odlum, Abraham m. bef. 4 Apr 1728, Sarah (N). {PGW&D (1713-1728):177}

Ogbern/Ogburn, (N) m. Suckey, dau. of Elizabeth Sherman (d. by 1787) and sister of Reuben Griffis and dau. of John Griffis? Children: Betsey, Benjamin, Polly and Nancy. {PGR:86, 95}

Ogleby, Jane was presented in 1758 for having a bastard child. {CCCR:141}

Ogilby, Nicolas m. Elizabeth (N). Their dau. Catharine b. 22 Mar 1741/2. {BPR:348}

Ogilby, Richard m. bef. 11 Dec 1739, Lydia (N). {PGM:60}

Oliphant, John d. 1 Nov 1793. {BPR:349}

Oliver, Drury m. 1st Anne (N). Their children: Elizabeth (b. 8 Jun 1718), John (b. 11 Jul 1720) and William (b. 26 Jul 1722). Drury m. 2nd Amy (N). Their children: Martha (b. 25 Nov 1724/5, d. 27 Sep 1726), Martha (b. 27 May 1727) and Mary (b. 8 Mar 1728). Drury m. 3rd Elizabeth (N). Their dau. Ann b. 4 Sep 1734. {BPR:347, 348}

Oliver, Isaac m. Elizabeth (N). Their children: Mildred (b. 15 Oct 1742), Thomas (b. 19 Oct 1743) and William (b. 7 Jul 1746). {BPR:348, 349}

Oliver, James m. Anne (N). Their dau. Mary b. 6 Sep 1745. {BPR:348}

Oliver, Thomas m. Anne (N). Their son John b. 18 Apr 1728. {BPR:348}

Oliver, William d. by 1695 leaving a widow Elizabeth. {CCOB (1687-95):203}

Organ, David m. Elizabeth (N). Their dau. Jean b. 2 Apr 1793. {BPR:349}

Osborne, Elias (d. by 1690) m. bef. 14 Apr 1657, Jane, widow of Phillip Limbry. Jane had daus., Dorothie and Frances. In 1678 Elias gave notice that no person should trade, buy, sell, etc. with his wife Jane. {CCOB (1655-58):95, 96; CCOB 1676-79:9, 52; CCOB (1687-95):87}

Osborne, Elias d. by 1713 leaving a widow Elizabeth. Elizabeth m. 2nd (N) Avery. {PGW&D (1710-1713):34; PGW&D (1713-1728):17}

Osborne, John m. Jane (N). Their son John Harrison b. 19 Jul 1794. {BPR:349}

Overberry, James m. Ann (N). Their son Abraham b. 26 Aug 1725. {BPR:348}

Overbury, James m. Elizabeth (N). Their dau. Lucy b. 29 Jul 1733. {BPR:348}

Overby/Overberry, Nicolas m. Jane (N). Their children: James (b. 5 Sep 1720), Adam (b. 28 Jul 1720) and Mary (b. 9 Aug 1725). {BPR:347, 348}

Overby, Peter m. Ann (N). Their children: Nico: (b. 1 Sep 1722) and Peter (b. 30 Jul 1727). {BPR:347, 348}

Overby/Overbury, Richard m. Dina (N). Their children: Robert (b. 18 Apr 1722), Martha (b. 8 Dec 1723), Jaminah (b. 26 Jan 1727), Rubin (b. 12 Aug 1731), Thomas (b. 1 Jul 1734) and Thamar (dau., b. 1 Jul 1734). {BPR:347, 348}

Overby, William m. Margaret (N). Their dau. Frances b. 20 Feb 1721. {BPR:347}

Owen, (N) m. Mary (N). Both d. by 1688. Sons: Walther (under age in 1688) and William. Their older brother also d. by 1688. {CCOB (1687-95):28}

Owen, David m. bef. 4 Dec 1689, (N), widow of Edward Jordan. {CCOB (1687-95):72, 82}

Owen, David d. by 1729, Hannah Owen, admx. {CCW&D (1725-31):41}

Owen, Edward m. Joyce (N). Their dau. Elizabeth b. 26 Feb 1740. {BPR:348}

Owen, George m. by Jul 1743, Elinor (N). {CCCR:99}

Owen, Howard m. Margaret (N). Their children: Elizabeth (b. 24 Jul 1726), John (b. 1 Aug 1728) and Thomas (b. 2 Jul 1730). {BPR:348}

Owen, Lanceford m. Elizabeth (N). Their son William b. 23 Dec 1734. {BPR:348}

Owen, William m. bef. Sep 1739, Hannah (N). {CCCR:85}

Pace, Richard, son of George (d. by 1658) and Mrs. Mary (Macocke) (d. by 1658) Pace, m. bef. 13 Mar 1662, Mary (N). Children: George, Richard, Thomas, John, James, Elizabeth, Anne and Sarah. Mary m. 2nd Nicholas Whitmore. {APP 2:766-7; CCOB (1658-61):179; CCOB (1661-64):327; CCOB (1687-95):131}

Parham, (N) m. Phebe (N). They had a son James and dau. Phebe (b. 9 Oct 1725). Phebe m. 2nd Thomas Pluckrose and possibly m. 3rd Christopher Hudson. {CCOB (1687-95):23; BPR:350}

Parham, Edward m. Mary (N). Their children: Sarah (b. 16 Dec 1730) and Anne (b. 14 Mar 1732). {BPR:352, 353}

Parham, Ephraim (d. by Jun 1779) of Dinwiddie Co. m. Ann (N). Children: Betsey, Nicholas, Thomas, and Joan. Ann prob. m. next (N) Pegram. {SWBC:57}

Parham, Gower m. Archer (N). Their children: Elisabeth (b. 20 Oct 1732), William (b. 2 Jul 1733) and Mary (b. 23 Dec 1741). {BPR:352, 354}

Parham, James m. bef. 10 Sep 1720, Rachel, dau. of Henry and Mary (Lound) Batte. {CCCR:73; APP 3:166; PGW&D (1713-1728):72-3}

Parham, John m. Mary (N). Their son John b. 26 Sep 1731. {BPR:352}

Parham, Lewis of Prince George Co. gave his cousin (*nephew*?), son of James Parham, a Negro slave. {PGR:73}

Parham, Lewis m. Sarah (N). Their son William b. 22 Apr 1761. {BPR:355}

Parham, Lewis of Sussex Co. m. Rebeccah (N). Their son Henry b. 28 Jan 1792. {BPR:355}

Parham, Simon, a free black man, d. by 1830 leaving widow and children. {PGM:40}

Parram, Thomas (d. ca. 1717) m. Elizabeth (N). Children: Thomas, William, Amy (m. (N) Jones), Elizabeth (m. (N) Tucker), Feebe, Susannah and Jane. {PGW&D (1713-1728):26}

Parham/Parram, Thomas m. Mary (N). Their children: William (b. 22 Sep 1729), Isham (b. 17 Sep 1732) and Thomas (b. 22 Sep 1734). {BPR:351, 353}

Parke, Anne, servant of widow Elizabeth Hacker was presented in 1656 for committing fornication and bearing a child in the time of her service. {CCOB (1655-58):53}

Parker, John d. by 1679, Ann Parker, widow and extx. {CCOB (1677-79):87}

Parker, Richard (b. ca. 1629) consented to allow Mary Perkins, widow of Nicholas Perkins to retain her husband's estate and he would educate her children. [Premarital agreement]. Richard m. Mary Perkins bef. 1 Sep 1656. {CCOB (1655-58): 62, 67; CCOB (1658-61):232}

Parish, Alexander m. by May 1760 Mary (N). {CCCR:143}

Parrish, Charles m. Mary (N). Their dau. Martha b. 10 May 1734. {BPR:353}

Parish, Frederick (b. Sep 1762, Brunswick Co., VA) lived in Prince George and Dinwiddie counties. {RWP}

Parrish, James had a son David, bapt. 4 Jul 1771. {BPR:355}

Parrish, John m. bef. 22 Oct 1663, Margaret (N). {CCOB (1661-64):432}

Parrish, William d. by 1745, Mary Parrish, extx. {CCCR:104}

Parry. See Perry.

Parratt, Nathaniel m. Penelope (N). Their children: Thomas (b. 30 Dec 1724), Nathaniel (b. 12 Feb 1725/6), Mary (b. 21 Nov 1728), James (b. 12 Feb 1730) and Penellope (b. 8 May 1733). {BPR:350, 351, 352}

Parsons, William m. several years bef. 1738, Mary, widow of Samuel Markam and dau. of James Batty. Their children: Mary (m. Edward Smith), Susanna (m. Richard Smith), Jemima (m. John Scott) and William Jr. {PGR:1, 29}

Parsons, Joseph d. by 1656, leaving a dau. Judith under the guardianship of Edward Mosby. Joseph m. 1st (N)(N) and m. 2nd Jane, widow of Thomas Gregory. Jane, m. 3rd Lt. John Stith. {CCOB (1658-61):278; CCOB (1661-64):433}

Parsons, Joseph m. Frances (N). Their son William b. 9 May 1750. {BPR:355}

Parsons, William, son of William and Mary (Batty) Parsons, m. Mary (N). Their children: Edith (b. 7 Aug 1719), Jamime (b. 20 Oct 1722), William (b. 24 May 1726), Batty (b. 22 Aug 1728, d. 11 Oct 1734) and James Markham (b. 31 Mar 1731, d. 26 Oct 1734). {BPR:349, 351, 354, 355}

Parsons, William and his wife of Prince George Co. d. Sep 1792. {BPR:355}

Patrick/Partrick, Luis m. Sarah (N). Their children: Luis (b. 17 Aug 1724) and Littleberry (b. 18 May 1728). {BPR:350, 351}

Patrum, Sara had a son Jeremiah b. 1 Jan 1722. {BPR:349}

Pattison, Benjamin of Prince George Co. m. 1st 6th da., 2nd mo., 1738, Mary Simons of same co. Benjamin m. 2nd 10th da., 12th mo., 1746, Eliza. Jones of the same co., in Prince George Co. {HMM:20, 24, 34}

Pattison, Francis m. bef. 11 Jul 1726, Ann (N). {PGW&D (1713-1728):148}

Paterson, James m. Mary (N). Their son William b. 12 Sep 1768. {BPR:355}

Pattison/Paterson, John m. Jane Smith, dau. of Richard Smith. Their children: Smith (b. 28 Aug 1720), Frances (b. 28 May 1722) and Eady (dau., b. 28 Jul 1724). {BPR:349, 350}

Pattison, John of Bristol Parish, Henrico Co., planter, m. bef. 9 May 1726, Leah, dau. of William Williams. {PGW&D (1713-1728):151}

Patterson, John m. Mary (N). Their son Liewes b. 28 Aug 1728.

{BPR:351}
Patteson, Jonathan m. bef. 5 Jun 1771, Elizabeth (N). {CCCR:35}

Patison, Joseph b. ca. 1657. {CCCR:71}

Patteson, Joseph d. by 1716 leaving a son John. {PGW&D (1713-1728):19}

Patteson/Patterson, Joseph (d. by 1714) m. Jane (N). Son: Tillman. {PGW&D (1713-1728):2, 144}

Patteson, Joseph d. by 1727, son: Francis. {PGW&D (1713-1728):172}

Pattison, Joseph, son of Joseph Pattyson of Prince George Co. m. 10th da., 9th mo., 1741, Elizabeth Simmons, dau. of John Simmons of the same county, in Prince George Co. {HMM:22}

Pattison, William (d. by 1735), son of Joseph Patison of Prince George Co. m. 4th da., 11th mo., 1729, Hanah Peobels, dau of William Peobels. {HMM:16; PGM:13}

Payne, Edward m. Amy (N). Their dau. Mary b. 16 Oct 1741. {BPR:354}

Peachy, Samuel had a dau. Jean, buried 11 Oct 1792. {BPR:355}

Pearce. See also Peirce.

Pearce, Baldwin m. Rebeccah (N). Their dau. Hannah b. 23 Feb 1793. {BPR:356}

Pearcy, Thomas (b. 5 May 1758, Dinwiddie Co.). In 1806 he moved to Sumner Co., TN, then to Wilson Co., then to Rutherford Co. {RWP}

Pearcy, William m. Rebecca (N). Their dau. Martha b. 9 Jan 1721/2. {BPR:349}

Pearman, James d. by 1756, Frances Pearman and William Atkinson, execs. {CCCR:135}

Pearman, Lucy was presented in 1739 for having a bastard child. {CCCR:84}

Pearman, Mary was presented in 1740 for having a bastard child. {CCCR:87}

Pearman, Thomas d. by 1745, Ann Pearman, admx. {CCCR:104}

Pearson, William m. by August 1744, Mary (N). {CCCR:103}

Person, William m. Mary (N). Their son Joseph bapt. 12 Apr 1724. {BPR:350}

Peirce. See also Pearce.

Peirce, Thomas d. by 1738, Martha Green, extx. {CCCR:82}

Peircy, William m. Juliana (N). Their son John b. 30 Sep 1740). {BPR:354}

Peebles, Abner m. by 1788, Dacky (N). {PGR:102, 173}

Peebles, Abram m. Esaia (N). Their son Reuben b. 11 April 1745. {BPR:355}

Peebles, Henry d. by 1738, Agnes Peebles, admx. {PGR:36}

Peebles, James m. Betsy (N). Their dau. Peggie b. 19 Sep 1793. {BPR:355}

Peeples, Joseph d. by 1759, Mary Binford, widow. {PGR:72}

Peebles, Lemuel m. bef. 13 Sep 1791, Rebeckah (N). {PGR:161}

Peebles, Peter of Prince George Co. (b. 5 Jul 1744, d. 1 Jan 1801) m. Mourning Hargrave (b. 29 Apr 1757, d. 28 Oct 1824), dau. of William and Sarah (Hancock) Hargrave. {APP2:331}

Peebles, Richard, son of William and Mary (Carlile) Peebles, m. Mary (N). Children: Abner, Archibald and probably James (m. 29 Sep 1785, Elizabeth Adkins Rives). {APP 3:292}

Peebles, William m. bef. 2 Feb 1662/3, Judith (N). {CCOB (1661-64):354}

Peebles/Peobles, William (d. by 1695, res. of Wynoke Parish) m. bef. 4 Aug 1690, Elizabeth (N). {CCOB (1687-95):85, 209}

Peebles, William m. 1st bef. 7 Nov 1726, Mary Carlile, dau. of Richard and Mary (Tatum) Carlile. They had a son Richard. William m. 2nd Agnes (N). {APP 3:267, 275; PGW&D (1713-1728):152}

Pegram, Daniel m. Frances (N). Their children: Sara (b. 29 Dec 1741),
Mary (b. ca. 1743), Daniel (b. ca. 1745, d. 13 Sep 1827), George (b. ca.
1750, d. 1825), Gideon (b. 1755, d. 1823), Edward (b. ca. 1759), d.
1802), Martha/Patty (b. ca. 1760) and Sarah (b. ca. 1761, d. 1800).
{BPR:354; www.patch.net}

Pegram, Edward m. ca. 1741 Mary Scott Baker. Their children: William
(b. 18 Jun 1742), Mary (b. 6 Mar 1743/4 in Dinwiddie Co.), Edward (b.
13 Jan 1745/6, d. 30 Mar 1816), John (b. 20 Dec 1748), Elizabeth (b. 24
Aug 1750, m. Francis Epes), Sallie W. (b. 12 Jan 1753), Elizabeth (b. 12
Jan 1753), George (b. 29 Aug 1755), Baker (b. 27 Jan 1758, d. 14 Oct
1830), Daniel (b. 25 Apr 1760), Ann /Nancy Baker (b. 4 Jul 1762, d.
after 1806) and Daniel (b. 30 Mar 1767, d. 23 Oct 1832). {BPR:354;
www.patch.net; APP 1:906}

Pegram, William (d. by 1789) m. Elizabeth (N). Children: Daniel (eldest
son), Sally, Elizabeth, Frances, William and Baker (captain in the
militia). {W&M, Vol. 23, No. 3 (Jan., 1915): 215}

Peirce, William m. Juliana (N). Their dau. Sarah b. 17 Aug 1734.
{BPR:354}

Peniston, (N) m. Elizabeth, sister of Abraham Lucas and Anne James.
{PGM:19}

Penticost, George m. Jane (N). Their children: Elizabeth (b. 3 Feb 1732),
William (b. 2 Aug 1734), Lucy (b. 25 Jan 1740) and Anne (b. 8 Sep
1743). {BPR:353, 354}

Perkins, Lewis (LWT dated 2 Jan 1801), brother of John Perkins, m.
(N)(N). Children: Polley (m. (N) Hervey), Williamson Grammar Perkins
and Lewis Green Perkins.It was noted that in 1811 Lewis Perkins had
married since the writing of his will and had a child. {Dinwiddie Co.
GenWeb}

Perkins, Nicholas (d. by 1656) m. Mary (N). Children: Lydia (m. John
Nowell), Elizabeth (b. ca. 1643) and Nicholas (b. ca. 1747). Mary m. 2nd
Richard Parker. {CCOB (1655-58): 62, 67; CCOB (1658-61):232;
CCOB (1664-65):499; GVAT (Genealogies of Virginia Families) II:814}

Perkins, William m. Margaret (N). Their son David b. 11 Oct 1792.
{BPR:355}

Perkinson, John m. Elizabeth (N). Their son Francis b. 5 Aug 1721. {BPR:349}

Perkinson, Syth d. by 1689 leaving a widow Mary. {CCOB (1687-95):46}

Perkinson, Seth m. Mary (N). Their children: Lucy (b. 6 Mar 1725), Alice (b. 15 Jun 1729) and Isham (b. 8 May 1731). {BPR:350, 351, 352}

Perkinson, Seth (d. by 1735) m. Margaret (N). Children: Seth, William, John, Mary, Margaret (m. (N) Belcher) Elizabeth (m. Edward Traler), Sarah (m. (N) Fowler) and Martha (m. (N) Belcher. {HCW 1:201-2; HCW 2:28}

Perkinson/Pirkenson, Seth m. Elisabeth (N). Their dau. Eddith b. 20 Jul 1733. {BPR:353}

Perkinson, William m. Mary (N). Their son Robert b. 13 Sep 1732. {BPR:352}

Perry, Henry, son of William Perry and son-in-law (*step-son*) of George Menefie, m. 1st his step-sister, Elizabeth Menefie, dau. of George Menefie. Their daus.: Elizabeth (m. John Coggs of Rainslop, County Middlesex, England) and Mary (m. Thomas Mercer, stationer of London). Henry m. 2nd Elizabeth Clements and m. 3rd Anna (N). {APP 2:651, 817-8}

Perry, James d. intestate by 1740, William Austin, admin. {CCCR:89}

Perry, John d. by 1762, Elizabeth Perry, extx. {CCCR:158}

Perry, John (b. ca. 1751, d. 3 Oct 1835) m. (N) (N) (b. ca. 1761). He enlisted in the Rev War about 1776 in Charles City Co. By 1821 he was a resident of Pulaski County, KY. They had one dau. who was married and living in VA in 1821. {RWP}

Perry, Nicholas (d. ca. 1770) m. bef. 7 Aug 1671, Elizabeth (N). Children: Pinkethman, Littlebury, Edith, Margaret (m. (N) Christian), Cuzza (m. (N) Cain) and Elizabeth (m. (N) Matthews). {CCCR:28; CCOB (Fragments:534}

Perry, Thomas m. Mary (N). Their son William b. 19 Apr 1742. {BPR:354}

Perry, Thomas was accused in 1738 of abandoning his wife. {PGR:4}

Perry, Thomas d. by 1758. Dau. Mary m. (N) Middleton by whom she had a son James. {CCCR:142}

Perry, Capt. William (d. 6 Aug 1637), res. near Westover. His son, Henry. {W&M Vol. 4, No. 3 (Jan., 1896):144; SWBC:43}

Parry, William m. Phoebe (N). Their dau. Ann b. 7 Sep 1789. {BPR:355}

Peters, Thomas d. by 3 Jun 1662 leaving widow and children. {CCOB (1661-64):326}

Peterson, Israell m. Elizabeth (N). Their dau. Magdaline b. 21 Nov 1740. {BPR:354}

Peterson, John Sr. of Isle of Wight Co. gave his son John Peterson Jr. of Prince George Co. 100 acres in Prince George Co. in 1723. {PGW&D (1713-1728):98}

Peterson, John m. Frances (N). Their children: Nathaniel (b. 12 Nov 1720) and William (b. 25 Oct 1723). {BPR:349, 350}

Peterson, John (d. 1773) m. Martha Thweatt. Their children: Nathaniel (b. 25 Apr 1732) and Frances (b. 3 Sep 1745). {BPR:352, 355; GVAW (Genealogies of Virginia Families) IV:109}

Peterson, Thomas (d. Nov 1788), son of John and Martha (Thweatt) Peterson, m. (bond dated 15 Jun 1775), Elizabeth, dau. of Augustine and Mary (Herbert) Claiborne. Children: John Herbert (b. 30 Mar 1776, d. 26 Dec 1830 in Prince George Co.), Thomas (m. ca. 1809, Sarah Epes, dau. of Peter and Mary (Poythress) Epes), Augustine Claiborne (d. by 1797) and Ann (d. 1794). {PGR:83, 123; PGM:23; APP 1:604-5, 639}

Pettypool/Pool, Seth m. Martha (N). Their children: Elizabeth (b. 8 May 1721), Sarah (b. 7 Nov 1723), John (b. 6 Jan 1725), Peter (b. 17 May 1727) and Anne (b. 25 Sep 1733). {BPR:349, 350, 351, 353}

Pettypoole, William (d. by 1726) m. bef. 11 Jun 1711 Elizabeth (N). Children: William, Seth, Anne (m. Richard Mercy), Mary (m. (N) Broadaway). Grandchildren: William and Martha Mercy. {PGW&D (1710-1713):10; PGW&D (1713-1728):157}

Pettypool/Pool, William m. Frances (N). Their children: Stephen (b. 30

Oct 1721), Tabitha (b. 13 Oct 1726), Phillip (b. 13 Mar 1730), Frances (b. 18 Apr 1733) and Henry (b. 27 Jan 1740/1. {BPR:350, 351, 352, 353, 354}

Phillips, (N) m. (N)(N). Children: Ann (d. testate 21 Mar 1769), James, William, Henry and Henrietta. {CCCR:16}

Phillips, Henry m. (bond dated 26 Oct 1784), Frances Pearman. {MB:194}

Phillips, John m. Ann (N). Their children: Joseph (b. 6 Nov 1726), Mary (b. 11 Apr 1731), John (b. 20 Aug 1740), George (b. 15 Feb 1742) and Elizabeth (b. 5 Feb 1745/6). {BPR:351, 352, 354, 355}

Phillips, John m. bef. 1 Jul 1730, Margery (N). {CCW&D (1725-31):42}

Phillips, John d. by 1740, leaving widow, Mary and dau. Sarah (bound to William Austin). It was ordered that Robert Phillips possess himself of that part of the estate that belongs to his children. {CCCR:88, 92, 95}

Phillips, Samuel d. by 1677, Susannah, widow. His children (unnamed) were ordered to be bound out. Sarah Sproson claimed to be his sister. Mary, orphan dau. of Samuel Phillips was committed to the guardianship of Capt. Daniel Lewellin in 1678. {CCOB (1677-79):24, 38, 52; CCOB (1687-95):29}

Phillips, Thomas m. Isabella (N). Their children: John (b. 8 May 1726), Mason (b. 23 Jul 1728), Mary (b. 9 Mar 1730) and James (b. 12 Sep 1734). {BPR:350, 351, 352, 354}

Phillips, William d. by 1694. Elizabeth, wife of Charles Holdsworth, extx. {CCOB (1687-95):173}

Phipps, James d. by 1769 leaving an orphans John and William. John Dudley was appointed guardian.{CCCR:29, 37}

Pickins, John m. Pricilla (N). Their dau. Obedience b. 26 Oct 1731. {BPR:352}

Pierce, Ann (d. in 1784), sister of Francis and Joseph Pierce. Her sisters Mary Melour and Martha Amous. Her niece Mary Childress. {SWBC:43}

Pierce, Francis (brother of Ann Pierce) m. (N) (N) bef. 1784. Dau.:

Martha. {SWBC:43}

Pierce, Joseph (brother of Ann Pierce) m. (N) (N) bef. 1784. His dau., Ann. {SWBC:43}

Piersey, Capt. Abraham (d. by 1627) was father of Elizabeth (m. 1st Capt. Richard Stephens, m. 2nd Sr. John Harvey) and Mary (m. Capt. Thomas Hill, m. 2nd Thomas Bushrod). {VG&B:146}

Pigeon, Richard (d. 1718), brother of Anne Thomas (wife of Charles Thomas), m. bef. 8 Jul 1712, Elizabeth (N). Children: Richard, Sarah, Mary, Rebecca (m. (N) Barlow), Elizabeth (m. Israel Marks) and Charles. {PGW&D (1710-1713): 20; PGW&D (1713-1728):24, 44}

Pinckard/Pinkard, Thomas m. (marriage agreement dated 8 Apr 1740) m. Frances Anderson, dau. of Rev. Charles Anderson. {CCCR:103; PGR:67; GVAT I:60}

Pistole/Pistol, Charles m. Sarah (N). Their children: Charles (b. 15 Sep 1733), Thomas (b. 2 May 1735) and William (b. 19 Dec 1740). {BPR:353}

Pistole, Charles (b. 1757, Dinwiddie Co., d. 6 Sep 1839), moved to Pittsylvania Co. with his father. He m. Elizabeth (N) (d. 29 Sep 1854). In 1855, their only surviving child was Winney (b. 6 Jul 1806), wife of Thomas Deaton of Independence Co., AR. By Jan 1839, Charles had moved from Nashville, TN to Little Rock, AR. Other children: David (1st son, b. 1785, d. bef. 1849) and Charles (7th child, b. 1799, d. bef. 1855). {RWP}

Pitchford, Samuel m. Amy (N). Their dau. Frances b. 5 Jan 1731. {BPR:352}

Pittillo, James m. Mary (N). Their children: James (b. 23 Dec 1725), Ann (b. 15 Jul 1728), Henry (b. 312 Oct 1730) and Lucy (b. 11 Nov 1733). {BPR:350, 351, 353}

Plaine, Robert d. by 1656) m. Mary (N). They had a son John. Mary m. 2nd Walter Daux and m. 3rd John Flower. {CCOB (1658-61):148}

Plantine/Plentine, Peter m. Frances (N). Their children: Sarah (b. 27 Jun 1726) and William (b. 5 Sep 1729). {BPR:351}

Plat, James m. Mary (N). Their dau. Ann b. 13 Oct 1725. {BPR:350}

Platt, Randle of Westover Parish, son of William Platt of County Lancaster, Great Britain, d. 1719). {PGR (1713-1728):50}

Pleasants, Thomas recorded a deed to his dau. Lidia in Apr 1742. Lidia m. Benjamin Jordan. {CCCR:95, 118} See *Henrico County Marriage References and Family Relationships, 1654-1800* for more on this family and connections.

Pleasants, William Henry of Cedar Creek Monthly Meeting, son of Thomas Pleasants of Goochland Co., m. 8th da., 9th mo., 1795, Mary Ladd, dau. of James Ladd of Charles City Co. {HMM:79, 87}

Pluckrose, Thomas (d. by 1688) m. 1st Ellianore (N). They had a dau. Elizabeth who was placed in the care of Mrs. Sarah Bland until age 18. Thomas m. 2nd Phebe, widow of (N) Parham. Phebe possibly m. 3rd Christopher Hudson. {CCOB (1687-95):10, 23, 36}

Plumer, (N) d. by 1650 leaving a widow, Mary. {CCOB (Fragments):273}

Plumer, Peter m. bef. 10 Sep 1659, (N), widow of William Lawrence. {CCOB (1658-61):203}

Pollock, David (d. by 1726) of Walinford Parish, James City Co., m. Mary (N). Children: John, Hanna, Elizabeth, Judeth and Tabitha. {CCW&D (1725-31):14}

Pool, (N) m. bef. 19 Jul 1711, Elizabeth, dau. of Randolph Birchenhead of Prince George Co. {PGW&D (1710-1713):12}

Poole, Nicholas m. 1656, Elizabeth, widow of Peter Moyle. Elizabeth m. 3rd Thomas Madder and m. 4th Francis Treham. {CCOB (1655-58): 56; CCOB (1661-64):371}

Poole, Ralph was father of Ellinor who was buried 19 Oct 1660. {CCOB 1658-61):270}

Pool, William Jr. had a child b. 15 Feb 1724/5. {BPR:350}

Pope, Ralph was father of Sarah H. Pope who d. 19 Jun 1793. {BPR:356}

Porch, James m. bef. 3 Sep 1694, Jane (N). {CCOB (1687-95):185}

Porter, John m. Elisabeth (N). Their son John b. 20 Feb 1740. {BPR:354}

Porter, Joshua m. Lucy (N). Their dau. Anne b. 7 Oct 1742. {BPR:355}

Pott, Henry d. by 1650 leaving a widow Frances. {CCOB (Fragments):273}

Pott, Peter m. Rebeckah (N). Their children: John (b. 6 Sep 1729) and Jane (b. 10 Feb 1731). {BPR:352}

Pott, Thomas m. Mary (N). Their son John b. 12 Oct 1732. {BPR:353}

Potter, George d. by 1664 leaving a widow, Sara (age 50 in 1665). {CCOB (1661-64):446; CCOB (1664-65):628}

Potter, Robert, age 39 in 1665. {CCOB (1664-65):627}

Potts, Thomas d. by 1719, Mary Potts, admx. {PGW&D (1713-1728):50}

Powell, Edward m. Elizabeth (N). Their children: Thomas (b. 14 Jul 1727), Mary (b. 12 Aug 1733) and Luke (b. 8 May 1746). {BPR:351, 353, 355}

Powell, Hezekiah m. Batiah/Bathia (N). Their children: Ann (b. 16 Jun 1726), Rebeccah (b. 26 Feb 1730, d. 26 Mar 1734). {BPR:351, 352, 353}

Powell, John m. (prenuptial contract dated 25 Jun 1658) Hester Cradock, widow, both of Westover Parish. {CCOB (1655-58):}

Powell, John m. Mary (N). Their children: John (b. 16 Mar 1725), Anna (b. 3 May 1728, m. Thomas Clay) and Robert (b. 17 Nov 1733). {BPR:351, 353; APP 1:651-2}

Powell, Zedekiah m. Bathus (N). Their son William b. 26 Apr 1729. {BPR:351}

Poxon, Oliver had a dau. Anne b. 30 Jul 1725. {BPR:350}

Poynter, Charity was presented in 1758 for having a bastard child. {CCCR:141}

Poynter, Jacob d. by 1758, Mary Poynter, admx. {CCCR:139}

Poynter, Richard of Charles City Co. m. bef. 7 Aug 1771 Elizabeth (N). {HCDB (1750-1774):218}

Poythress, (N) m. Elizabeth who d. by 1739, her son George Poythress, exec. {PGR:63}

Poythress, Charles m. (contract dated 9 Apr 1739), Catherine Crawforth, dau. of Ralph and Elizabeth (Claiborne) Crawforth. Son: John. {APP1:612}

Poythress, David d. by 1740 leaving a son Edmund, admin. {PGR:67}

Poythress, Edward (d. by 1772) m. Mary (LWT dated 21 Jul 1772). Dau.: Tabitha. {Dinwiddie Co. GenWeb; SWBC:58}

Poythress, Capt. Francis (d. by 1661) m. Mary (N). Sons: John and Francis. Mary m. 2nd Robert Wynne. {GVAW IV:173; CCOB (1658-61):272; GVAT (Genealogies of Virginia Families) IV:530-1}

Poythress, Francis (d. by 1688), son of Capt. Francis Poythress, m. Rebecca Wynne. On 4 Jun 1694 Rebecca was summoned to answer information of an "unlawful marriage" to Charles Bartholmew (previously married Frances, sister of Rebecca). Francis and Rebecca were parents of Rebecca, Anne (m. Burrell Green), Francis, John (m. Mary Batte) and Thomas (probably m. Elizabeth Cocke). {CCOB (1687-95):41, 178; GVAW IV (Genealogies of Virginia Families):175, 176, 180; PGW&D (1710-1713):13; PGW&D (1713-1728):77}

Poythress/Poythris, Francis m. Hannah (N). Their dau. Elizabeth b. 1 Feb 1729. {BPR:352}

Poythress, Francis of Prince George Co., son of Francis and Rebecca (Wynne) Poythress, removed to Surry Co., m. (N)(N). They had a son Francis. {GVAW IV (Virginia Genealogies):176}

Poythress, Francis (LWT dated 10 Dec 1796) was father of Mary Peterson Randolph. {Dinwiddie Co. GenWeb; SWBC:58}

Poythress, John (d. ca. 1712) m. bef. 18 Dec 1688, Christian, dau. of Elizabeth Peebles. Their children: Francis, David, Joshua, Robert, William, Elizabeth, Christian, John, Peter and Mary (m. John Woodliffe, son of John Woodliffe). In his LWT John Poythress named his "brothers," Thomas and Joshua Wynne. {CCOB (1687-95):38; APP3:707; PGW&D (1710-1713):26}

Poythress, John Sr., son of Francis and Rebecca (Wynne) Poythress, m. bef. 10 Sep 1720, Mary, dau. of Henry Batte. {PGW&D (1713-1728):72; GVAW IV (Genealogies of Virginia Families):175, 176, 180}

Poythress, John of Martins Brandon Parish (d. ca. 1724), brother of Francis and William Poythress, m. Mary (N). Children: John, Francis, William (bound out in 1738), Rebecca and Elizabeth. {PGW&D (1713-1728):102, 153}

Poythress, Joshua (d. 1739-40) m. (N)(N). Execs.: brother Robert and cousin Thomas Poythress. Brother: William. Children: Joshua, William, Littlebury, Ann, Elizabeth and Mary. {PGR:67; PGR:174}

Poythress, Mary d. by 1760. {PGR:76}

Poythress, Patrick (LWT dated 12 Aug 1818) m. Elizabeth (N). Children mentioned in his LWT but unnamed. {Dinwiddie Co. GenWeb}

Poythress, Peter (d. by 1787), son of Robert (d. 1743) and Elizabeth (Cocke) Poythress, m. Elizabeth Bland (b. 1732/3), dau. of Richard and Ann (Poythress) Bland. Their children: Elizabeth (b. 1759, Prince George Co., d. 1806, m. William Mayo, son of John and Mary (Tabb) Mayo), Ann (m. John Randolph), William (m. 1st Elizabeth Bland, m. 2nd (N) Marrable), Mary (m. John Batte), Susannah (m. Richard Bland), Sally Bland (d. 1828, m. Richard Lee), Agnes (m. Roger Atkinson), Jane (d. 1837, m. 28 Jul 1792 Major Joseph Mayo) and Lucy Bland (m. 23 Jan 1806, Capt. John Eppes). {APP1:156; PGR:82, 139, 161} *See APP1:156 for more details.*

Poythress, Peter (d. by 1782) of Martins Brandon Parish m. Mary (N). In her LWT (dated 9 Feb 1782, recorded 12 Feb 1788) Mary named dau. Wilmuth Harrison and dau. Susanna Poythress. The execs.: Peter Poythress (d. by 1788), Joshua Poythress (d. 1788) and Nicholas Faulcon (ill in 1788, requested to be excused). {PGR:95}

Poythress, Robert (d. 1743) of Prince George Co. m. Elizabeth, dau. of James Cocke (d. 1721). Their children: Robert (d. unm.), Elizabeth (m. John Gilliam (b. 1712, d. 1772 of Prince George Co.), Mary Ann (m. (N) Minge), Agnes (m. 1st Samuel Harwood, m. 2nd Benjamin Cocke), Peter (d. 1785-6, m. Elizabeth Bland), William (d. unm.), Tabitha (m. Henry Randolph), Susannah and Jane. {HMM:91 (Henrico Co. Court records); GVA (Genealogies of Virginia Families II, Cl-Fi:117); APP1:130, 155-6}

Poythress, Thomas, son of Francis and Rebecca (Wynne) Poythress, probably m. Elizabeth Cocke. {GVAW IV (Genealogies of Virginia Families):175, 176, 180}

Poythress, William m. Sarah Epes, dau. of Francis Epes. Their children: Anne Isham (b. 9 Apr 1726, m. Samuel Gordon), William (b. 14 Mar 1727), Sarah (b. 7 Aug 1731) and Elizabeth (b. 21 Sep 1741). {BPR:350, 352; APP 1:868}

Poythress, William (b. 14 Mar 1727/8, d. by 1769 in Prince George Co.), son of William and Sarah (Epes), m. 1st Mary Eppes (b. ca. 1730, d. 4 Oct 1750) and m. 2nd Lucy Edwards, dau. of Benjamin Edwards. William and Lucy were parents of Lucy (m. John Gordon), Ann Isham (m. Col. William Yates), Mary (m. Francis Muir), Benjamin, William and Sally. {APP1:868, 901-2; PGM:12}

Poythress, William (d. 15 Oct 1794), son of Joshua Poythress, m. bef. 2 Oct 1790, Mary (N). Their dau. Mary b. 24 Sep 1793. {PGR:140; BPR:355, 356}

Poythress, William m. bef. 25 Feb 1791, Elizabeth (N). {PGR:169}

Pratt, John d. by 1661 leaving a widow, Elizabeth. {CCOB (1661-64):293}

Prentis, William m. Mary (N). Their son James b. 3 Aug 1793. {BPR:356}

Prescot, Philip m. Rachel (N). Their dau. Rachel b. 3 Mar 1733. {BPR:353}

Presise, Thomas m. Mary (N). Their children: Patty (b. 10 Dec 1740), Thomas (b. 27 Dec 1735) and Mary (b. 29 Mar 1738). {BPR:354}

Preston, Henry m. bef. 3 Dec 1677, (N), widow of George Barefoot. {CCOB (1677-79):34}

Pretlow/Pretlo, Joshua of Blackwater Monthly Meeting m. 2nd da., 6th m. 1753, Ann Crew, dau. of --- of Charles City Co. {HMM:28, 31}

Price, (N) m. bef. 20 Mar 1719/20, Jane (N). Jane m. 2nd John Dewell and m. 3rd Edward Johnson. Jane was mother of James Price, Sarah Price and Mary Dewell. {PGW&D (1713-1728):4, 62, 141}

Price, James m. bef. 8 Apr 1739, Nancy (N). {PGR:40}

Price, John m. Ann (N) who came to VA in 1620. Ann had a dau. Elizabeth who m. (N) Williams. Ann m. 2nd Robert Hallom. {APP 2:849; CCOB (1655-58): 69}

Price, John (d. 1710-11), son of John and Ann (Wall) Price, m. bef. 26 Jan 1693, Jane Pew/Pugh, dau. of Henry and Jane (Womack) Pew of Henrico Co. Their children: Mary, John, Daniel, Pugh and Elizabeth. Ann Wall was the dau. of John Wall. Jane Price m. 2nd Hugh Ligon. {CCCR:76; APP 2:830-1}

Price, John m. Mary (N). Their dau. Elizabeth b. 7 Jun 1722. {BPR:349}

Price, Richard (b. 1627) d. by 1677 leaving orphans and Ann (either widow or dau.). {CCOB (1661-64):399; CCOB 1676-79:8}

Price, Richard, servant of Drury Oliver, d. 29 Jun 1730. {BPR:352}

Pryse, William d. by 1655 leaving widow, Ann, extx. {CCOB (1655-58): 38}

Price, William (d. 1791-3) m. Mary Williamson. Children: Daniel, Samuel, William, Williamson, Nancy (m. Thomas Payne), Mary W. (m. Short Jones), Sarah, Lucy and Elizabeth. {CCCR:73; APP 2:834-5}

Pride, John m. Susanna (N). Their children: William (b. 19 Dec 1721) and Puckett (b. 2 Sep 1729). {BPR:349, 352}

Prince, Jane had a son Thomas, late the servant of Thomas Drew (1658). {CCOB (1658-61):161}

Pritcheat, Arn m. Ann (N). Their son John b. 26 Feb 1740. {BPR:354}

Pritchett, Kaleb m. Frances (N). Their dau. Susannah (b. 24 Aug 1740). {BPR:354}

Pritchett, Joss:/Joshua m. Mary (N). Their children: John (b. 1 May 1716) and William (b. 14 Oct 1719). {BPR:350}

Pritchett, Joshua m. Martha (N). Their dau. Martha b. 15 Apr 1729. {BPR:351}

Pritchett, Joshua m. Catherine (N). Their son Joshua b. 9 May 1732. {BPR:352}

Pritchett, Rice m. bef. 4 Jun 1688, Elizabeth (N). {CCOB (1687-95):21}

Pruitt, Ben[jamin] m. by Nov 1742, Hannah (N). {CCCR:96}

Puckett, John m. Judith (N). Their children: William (b. 15 Sep 1720), Phebe (b. 11 Jan 1720/1), Joel (b. 11 Nov 1723), Sheppyallin (b. 8 Nov 1725), Stephen (b. 17 Oct 1728), Phebe (b. 2 Jan 1728) (*sic*) and Drury (b. 25 Jan 1733). {BPR:349, 350, 351, 353}

Puckett, Richard m. Martha (N). Their son Richard b. 7 Mar 1718/19. {BPR:349}

Puckett, William m. Mary (N). Their children: Lewis (b. 9 Jan 1722/3) and Elizabeth (b. 19 Feb 1725). {BPR:349, 351}

Pucket, William m. Frances (N). Their son Ephraim b. 2 Mar 1729. {BPR:351}

Puckett, Womack m. Mable (N). Their children: Ephraim (b. 24 Jan 1721) and Isham (b. 14 Oct 1724). {BPR:349, 350}

Pully, Ruth ordered on 30 Sep 1677 to complete her indenture of 4 years and 2 additional years for having a bastard child. {CCOB (1677-79):29}

Purreah, Morgan m. Ann (N). Their dau. Ann b. 1 Aug 1741. {BPR:354}

Quigins, James m. bef. 21 Dec 1768, Elizabeth (N). {CCCR:10}

Rably, Thomas m. Jane (N). Both d. by 1688. {CCOB (1687-95):32}

Rabon/Raburn, John m. Rebecca (N). Their son Richard b. 28 May 1723. {PGW&D (1713-1728): 170; BPR:357}

Rachel, Ralph d. by 1679, Elizabeth Rachell, extx. {CCOB 1777-79):118}

Rackly, John m. Mary (N). Their son John b. 14 Jun 1720. {BPR:356}

Ragsdale, Benjamin m. Martha (N). Their children: Daniel (b. 7 May 1724), John (b. 23 Jun 1728), Winfred (b. 17 Feb 1731) and Benjamine (b. 28 Mar 1734). {BPR:357, 358, 359, 360}

Ragsdale/Radgsdale, Godfrey m. Elizabeth, sister of Edward Baxter, Tabitha Calwell and Sarah Royall. Their children: Tabitha (b. 13 Mar

1722), Edward (b. 8 Dec 1723) and Baxter (b. 16 Jun 1739). {BPR:356, 357; HCW2:44}

Ragsdale, Peter m. Alice (N). Their children: Faith (b. 24 Oct 1722), Joseph (b. 17 Jan 1725), Ann (b. 25 May 1727) and Rachel (b. 27 Feb 1732). {BPR:356, 357, 358, 359}

Raine, John probably m. by 1688 the mother of Robert Malone. {CCOB (1687-95):26}

Raines, Ephraim of Bristol Parish, son of Shands and Mary (Lee) Raines and brother of Sarah Raines, m. Elizabeth (N). Children: Charles, Mary (m. (N) Biggins), Rebecca (m. (N) Haddon), Frances (d. by 1787, m. (N) Haddon), Allen, Ephraim, Frederick, Richard, and Archibald. {PGR:71, 105, 165, 170}

Raines, Frederick of Bristol Parish m. bef. 13 Oct 1777 Frances (N). {PGR:154}

Raines, Hartwell, son of Nathaniel Raines, m. bef. 14 Apr 1789 (N)(N). Son: John. {PGR:120}

Raines, John (d. by 1790), probable brother of Phebe Raines (d. 1790), m. (bond dated 5 Oct 1762) Amy, widow of Thomas Mitchell and dau. of John Goodwyn. Children: Thomas, Robert, Cadwallader and Amy. {PGR:129; marriage bond of Sussex Co.; GVAW (Genealogies of Virginia Families) II:728}

Raines, Nathaniel (d. 1789) of Bristol Parish m. Susannah (N). Children: Nathaniel, Sucky Green/Susanna Green, Hartwell, Frances (m. William Lucas) and Ann (m. Thomas Mitchell). Grandchildren: Henry Lucas, Hartwell Mitchell and John Raines. {PGR:120, 160}

Rains, Richard m. Jane (N). Their son Frederick b. 9 Jun 1732. {BPR:359}

Raines, Shands m. bef. 10 Jun 1759, Mary, dau. of Samuel Lee (d. 1759). Their children: son (b. 12 Sep 1731), Ephraim, Sarah and Shands (d. by 1758). {PGW&D (1710-1713):20, 41; PGR:71; APP 3:288-9; BPR:359}

Rhaynes, Thomas m. Elizabeth (N). Their son John b. 5 Jul 1726. {BPR:357}

Rains, William gave his son Richard Rains a piece of farm land in 1714?

and to son Thomas 76 acres in 1715. {PGW&D (1713-1728):9-10}

Rainy, Roger m. Sarah (N). They had a child b. 12 Oct 1733. {BPR:360}

Ramsey, David d. by 1660 leaving a widow, Martha. Children: Elizabeth and Patrick. Elizabeth m. 2nd William Greene. {CCOB 1658-61):271; CCOB (1661-64):309}

Ramsay, Patrick, son of Andrew Ramsay of Scotland, m. 25 Nov 1760, Elizabeth, dau. of William and Sarah (Epes) Poythress and sister of Ann Isham Gordon (d. 1790). Their children: Sophia (b. ca. 1761, m. William Wilson Jr., merchant of Glasgow, Scotland), Elizabeth (b. 19 Mar 1768, d. 18 Jun 1836 at Alexandria, m. Jun 1786, John Potts of Pottstown, PA), Andrew (b. 6 Sep 1772, d. 18 Dec 1818, m. 1795, Catharine Graham), William (b. 6 Sep 1772 and others. {PGR:131; APP 1:868, 902} See APP1 for much more detail.

Randolph, Capt. Henry (d. by 1693) m. 1st 12 Oct 1653, Elizabeth (N). Their children: Henry (b. 2 Sep 1654, d. young) and William (b. James City Co., b. 12 Sep 1658). Henry m. 2nd 12 Dec 1761 Judith Soane. Their children: Henry (b. 12 Jan 1665) and Judith (b. 29 Jul 1671). Judith m. 2nd Peter Field. {CCCR:73; GVAW (Genealogies of Virginia Families IV):229-231}

Randolph, Henry (26 Feb 1693), son of Henry and Judith (Soane) Randolph, m. Sarah Swann. Sarah m. 2nd Giles Webb, son of John and Jane Webb. {GVAW (Genealogies of Virginia Families IV):230}

Randolph, Col. Richard (d. 1747-9) of Curles plantation, m. 1713/14, Jane Bolling (d. by 1767), dau. of John Bolling (d. 1727-9). Their children: Richard (m. Ann Meade), Mary (b. 1727, d. 1781, m. 31 May 1744, Archibald Cary), Jane Bolling (m. Col. Anthony Walke of Princess Anne Co. who m. 2nd Mary Moseley), Brett (b. 1732, d. 1759, m. in London, Mary Scott), Ryland (d. unm. Henrico Co. 1784-5), John (m. Frances Bland), Elizabeth (d. 1774, m. Richard Kidder Meade of Prince George Co., later Clarke Co. who m. 2nd Mary (Grymes) Randolph) {APP3:28-9; HCW 1:171; 2:49, 98, 119-120; HCDB (1750-1774):5; HCWB1:66-7}

Rands, Thomas d. by 1661. Widow, Margaret Moore, extx. Thomas had a son Thomas, age 17 in 1665. Margaret m. twice after the death of Thomas Rands. She d. by 1665. {CCOB (1658-61):273; CCOB (1664-65):586}

Raney, Nathaniel (b. 26 Jul 1764, Sussex Co., VA) lived in Brunswick Co., VA, then moved to Dinwiddie Co. {RWP}

Ranie, Roger m. Sarah (N). Their son Peter b. 20 Mar 1729. {BPR:358}

Ranye, William of Martins Brandon Parish (d. ca. 1722) m. (N)(N). Children: John, Roger, Susannah, William, Elizabeth, Sarah, Rebecca and Richard. {PGW&D (1713-1728):83-4}

Ratlif, John m. Anne (N). Their son Isham b. 10 Oct 1731. {BPR:359}

Ravenscroft, Robert of Petersburg in his LWT (dated 24 Sep 1778) named nephew George Wall, eldest son of Burgess Wall. {Dinwiddie Co. GenWeb}

Rawlinson/Rollinson, William m. 16 Sep 1660, Jane Sparrow (in Martins Brandon Parish church) widow of Charles Sparrow. In 1663 Jane Rollinson confessed to murdering one of her children. However the jury found her not guilty of drowning the child, apparently concluding that Jane was a lunatic. {CCOB (1658-61):254, 270; CCOB (1661-64):417}

Rawlinson, William d. by 1693 leaving a widow Hester. {CCOB (1687-95):155}

Rawthorn, Samuel m. Anne (N). Their son William b. 4 Nov 1741. {BPR:360}

Ray/Raes, Hugh m. Elisabeth (N). Their children: John (b. 14 Jun 1741), Elizabeth (b. 25 Apr 1743) and Neil (b. 19 Feb 1745/6). {BPR:360, 361}

Ray, John of Martins Brandon Parish d. by 1710, Elizabeth Ray, admx. {PGW&D (1710-1713):4}

Rays, Sally, Mulatto slave of Thomas Shore, had a dau. Letty Rays, b. 9 Aug 1791. {BPR:370}

Rayborn, John m. Rebeckah (N). Their children: Thomas (b. 16 Sep 1726) and John (b. 30 Nov 1729). {BPR:358}

Raybon, Richard m. Jean (N). Their dau. Jean b. 28 Apr 1732. {BPR:359}

Rea, Francis (d. by 1718) of Martins Brandon Parish m. Mary Frances (N). Children: Joseph, Francis, Mary (m. (N) Wiggins), Jane (m. (N)

Cooper), Benjamin and Jone (m. (N) Nicholson). {PGW&D (1713-1728):39}

Read. See Reed.

Reading, Joel of Sussex Co. m. Martha (N). Their dau. Susannah b. 4 Jan 1792. {BPR:361}

Reams, Jesse, b. ca. 1752 Dinwiddie Co., moved to Stewart Co., TN. {RWP}

Reames, John m. bef. 13 Oct 1724, Alice (N). {PGW&D (1713-1728):156}

Reams/Reems, Thomas m. Elizabeth (N). Their children: Alse (b. 31 Mar 1732) and Thomas (b. 10 Jan 1733). {BPR:359, 360}

Redish, Edward m. bef. 15 Sep 1677, Brighthood (N). {CCOB (1677-79):20}

Redford, Francis m. bef. 1 Sep 1656, (N), widow of Thomas Moody. CCOB (1655-58): 69}

Read/Reed, Harman m. bef. 11 Mar 1716, Ann (N). {PGW&D (1713-1728):23}

Read, Henry d. by 1688, Ann Read, widow. {CCOB (1687-95):15}

Reed, William m. bef. 13 Mar 1738, Martha (N). {PGR:35}

Reed, William m. Mary (N). Their dau. Jemiah b. 9 Dec 1724. {BPR:358}

Reakes, (N) predeceased his wife Elizabeth who m. 2nd (N) Shipdom and d. by 1679. Her children: Elizabeth Moseby and John Reakes. {CCOB 1676-79):87}

Reekes/Rix John Sr. m. bef. 15 Oct1692, Jane (N). {CCCR:76}

Reiny, Roger m. Sarah (N). Their son William b. 13 Apr 1731. {BPR:359}

Rix, Richard d. by 1662 leaving a son John. {CCOB (1661-64):326}

Renn, Joseph, "brother of James Cureton," m. bef. 29 1715, Elizabeth (N). Their children: James and Susannah. {PGW&D (1713-1728):18}

Reese, (N) m. Mary, dau. of Thomas Anderson (d. by 1711). Son: Thomas. {PGW&D (1710-1713):7-8}

Reese, (N) m. Sarah (N). In her LWT dated 26 Jan 1767 and proved 13 Sep 1768,Sarah Reese named daus.: Ann Wells and Betty Patterson and grandchildren: William Wells, Laban Wells, Patty Wells, and Roody Wells. Exec.: Jeremiah Wells (probable husband of dau. Ann). {PGR:174; SWBC:213}

Riss, Hugh m. Sarah (N). Their children: Prissilla (b. 21 Feb 1729), Isham (b. 8 Aug 1732) and Sarah (b. 10 Oct 1735). {BPR:358, 360}

Reese, Jacob m. Diancy (N). Their son John Fetherstone b. 14 May 1792. {BPR:361}

Reese, John m. Mary (N). Their son Thomas b. 12 Feb 1739. {BPR:360}

Rees(e), Richard d. by 1723, Elizabeth Rees, admx. {PGW&D (1713-1728):98}

Reese, Roger m. Elizabeth (N). Their children: Martha (b. 9 Feb 1730) and Charles (b. 3 Apr 1733). {BPR:359, 360}

Reese, Thomas m. Mary (N). Their children: Francis (b. 5 Dec 1727), Thomas (b. 2 Nov 1729), Mary (b. 8 Oct 1733) and Mason (b. 10 Jul 1740). {BPR:358, 360}

Reese, Thomas was father of John b. 30 Sep 1731. {BPR:359}

Rives, Briggs (b. 1762, d. 1815), son of Timothy and Sarah (Gee) Rives, m. bef. 4 Jan 1791, Anne, dau. of Thomas Cureton. {PGR:144; GVAT (Genealogies of Virginia Families) III:127}

Reives, George of Bristol Parish, Prince George Co. m. bef. 7 Oct 1711, Ursula (N). George Rives was age 59 in 1719. {PGW&D (1710-1713): 15; PGW&D (1713-1728):54}

Rives, Isham d. by 1789 leaving widow Mary Rives and dau. Ann. {PGR:1`25}

Rix. See Reekes and Reakes.

Reeves, James m. (N)(N) who was buried 20 Dec 1794. {BPR:362}

Rives, John d. by 1787, Peter Williams and Amey Rives, execs. {PGR:86}

Reaves, John m. Frances (N). Their children: William (b. 13 Jul 1743), Mary (b. 17 Jul 1745), John (b. 15 Nov 1747), Richard (b. 5 Oct 1750) and Thomas (b. 15 Sep 1753). {BPR:361}

Reeves, Col. John of Sussex Co. buried 15 Mar 1795. {BPR:362}

Reeves/Reaves, Joseph m. Sarah (N). Their children: Daniel (b. 31 Aug 1726), Mary (b. 20 Sep 1730), Joseph (b. 5 Dec 1732) and Isham (b. 25 Jan 1740). {BPR:357, 358, 359, 360}

Reives, Robert m. bef. 5 Aug 1695, Sarah, widow of Morris Caligham. {CCOB (1687-95):209}

Rives, Thomas Rosser (d. 1789), brother of Rebeckah Davenport, m. (N)(N). Children: Tabitha, Judith and Rebeckah. {PGR:112}

Reevs, Timothy d. by 1692, widow Mary admx. {CCOB (1687-95):136}

Reeves, Timothy m. Mary (N). Their dau. Usiller b. 7 Jul 1743. {BPR:360}

Rives, Col. Timothy, son of Timothy Rives, d. by 1804 leaving a widow, Elizabeth. In 1788 he res. adjoining land of George Rives. {PGM:33; PGR:105}

Rives, William m. Elizabeth (N). They resided in Prince George Co. in 1711. {GVAT (Genealogies of Virginia Families) III:127; PGW&D (1713-1728): 169}

Reeves, William m. Priscilla (N). Their dau. Judith b. 10 Aug 1744. {BPR:361}

Renshall, Joseph (d. 1725-6). In his LWT Joseph named sons-in-law (*step-sons?*) John Crew and Arthur Crew and grandchildren: James Renshall and Mary Sooles. {CCW&D (1725-31):10}

Reyner/Rayner, James (b. ca. 1636) gave his son, John, a heifer in 18 Feb 1657/8. {CCOB (1658-61):138; CCOB (1661-64):398}

Reynolds, John m. by Jan 1741, Arabella (N). {CCCR:94}

Richardson, Edward d. by 1711. {PGW&D (1710-1713):5}

Richardson, Robert, son of Elinor (niece of Thomas Quiney of London), m. bef. 19 Aug 1720, Mary (N). {VG&B:149}

Rickman, William (d. by Nov 1783), appointed Director and Chief Physician of the Hospital in Virginia in the service of the Continent in 1776, m. Elizabeth (N). {Legislative Petitions – Library of VA website}

Ridlehurst, John (d. 1772) m. (bond dated 2 May 1764), Judith Miles (spinster). Children: Francis, Valentine, Sarah and Nancy. {CCCR:49; MB:196}}

Ridlehurst, Mary d. by 1761, Jane Cocke, extx. {CCCR:151}

Riddlehurst, Capt. Richard d. by 1728, leaving a son Thomas of Westover Parish. {CCW&D1725-30}

Ridlehurst, Richard (d. 1771), son of Jane Cocke, m. by Sep 1762, Elizabeth (N). Children: William Watson, John, Mary and Samuel. {CCCR:40, 157}

Ridlehurst, William (d. by 1741) m. bef. 28 Apr 1730, Jane (N). Son: Richard. Jane m. 2nd (N) Cocke. {CCW&D (1725-31):40; CCCR:4, 40, 90, 157}

Rigsby, James m. Elizabeth (N). Their children: Mary (b. 10 Oct 1724) and Ann (b. 19 Jan 1726). {BPR:357, 358}

Rivers, John (d. ca. 1720) m. (N)(N). Mary Rivers, extx. Children: John (eldest son), Robert and probably others. {PGW&D (1713-1728):66, 69}

Rivers, Robert m. bef. 29 Apr 1711, Elizabeth (N) (d. by 1759). {PGW&D (1710-1713):7; PGR:69}

Rivers, Robert m. Hannah (N). Their son Thomas b. 28 Jun 1740. {BPR:360}

Rivers, William abandoned his wife Elizabeth ca. 1673. {CCOB (Fragments):543}

Roach, John recorded a deed of gift to his son David Fitz Roach in 1755. {CCCR:130}

Roach, William, son of Elizabeth Roach bound out in 1758. {CCCR:140}

Roberts, John d. by 1739, Judith, widow and extx. Their son Michael b. 7 May 1734. {PGR:50; BPR:360}

Roberts, Thomas (d. by Aug 1737) m. Hannah (N). Their children: John (eldest son), Alexander, Jane, Mary (b. 17 Aug 1726), Thomas, and Francis (b. 29 Jun 1733). His will was recorded in Amelia County. {BPR:357; SWBC:213}

Robins, Peter m. bef. 11 Dec 1739, Mary (N). {PGR:60}

Robinson/Robertson/Robison

Robinson, Christopher m. Sarah (N). Their children: Mary (b. 3 Jun 1720), Nath. (b. 21 Oct 1722) and Martha (b. 27 Feb 1724). {BPR:356, 357}

Robinson, Edward d. by 1689 leaving a widow, Anne. {CCOB (1687-95):74}

Robison, George m. bef. 17 Jul 1726, Mary (N). {BPR:357}

Robinson, Henry m. Ann (N). Their dau. Ann b. 8 May 1734. {BPR:360}

Robertson, Henry of Amelia Co. m. bef. 13 Apr 1757, Ann (N). {PGR:73}

Robinson/Robertson, Henry m. Elizabeth (N). Their children: Liewes (b. 17 Mar 1723) and Deborah (b. 14 Mar 1727). {BPR:357, 358}

Robertson, Henry m. Susanna (N). Their son Peter b. 21 Mar 1742. {BPR:360}

Robinson/Robertson, Israel of Bristol Parish, brother of Edward Robinson, m. Sarah (N). Their children: Matthew (b. 22 Nov 1721), John (b. 8 May 1723), Israel (b. 14 Nov 1725), Nicholas (b. 12 Sep 1731) and Charles (b. 24 Jul 1733). {PGW&D (1713-1728):156; BPR:356, 357, 359}

Robertson, James m. Martha (N). Their children: Elizabeth Archer (b. 27 Nov 1791) and John Alexander (b. 29 May 1793). {BPR:361, 362}

Robyson/Robertson, John m. bef. 6 Feb 1719, Mary (N). Their children: Nathaniel (b. 21 Jun 1723), Abraham (b. 20 Jul 1725), Frances (b. 3 Mar 1726), David (b. 19 Aug 1728), Mark (b. 23 Jun 1729), Edward (b. 22 Dec 1731) and Robert (b. 10 Jun 1734). {PGW&D (1713-1728):59; BPR:357, 358, 359}

Roberson, Martha (*sic*) m. Sarah (N). Their son George b. 6 Dec 1740. {BPR:360}

Robyson, Nicholas m. bef. 10 Jun 1718, Jane (N). {PGW&D (1713-1728):77}

Robison, Temperance d. by 1711, Christopher Robertson, admin. {PGW&D (1710-1713):4}

Robertson, William m. Elizabeth (N). Their dau. Anne b. 25 Nov 1792. {BPR:362}

Rock/Fitz Rock, John d. by 1727. Children: John, William, Henry, Mary (m. (N) Chirn) and Sarah. Heirs: Martha Goodwin, (N) (m. Robert Morgan), Sarah Dispain, William Rock and Henry Rock.{CCW&D (1725-31):25, 29}

Rock, John (d. by 1731), brother of William and Peter, m. Elizabeth (N). Children: Elinor, Mary, Elizabeth, Martha, Daniel and John. Widow Elizabeth m. 2nd (N) ca. 1731 (N) Roach. {CCW&D (1725-31):48}

Rock. Sarah d. by 1740). {CCCR:87}

Rock, William d. by 1737, had a son William. {CCCR:80}

Roe, Robert of Albemarle Parish of Sussex Co. m. Nancy (N). Their son Patrick b. 9 Apr 1792. {BPR:362}

Rogers, Henry d. by 1679, Ellin Rogers, widow and admx. {CCOB (1677-79):101}

Rogers, John (d. by 1730) m. Elizabeth (N). Children: John, Henry, Ann (m. John Whitt), Judith, Sarah, Anna (m. Thomas Coley). Grandson: William Coley. {CCW&D (1725-31):42}

Rodgers, Lucy was presented in 1758 for having a bastard child. {CCCR:141}

Rogers, Philip m. Mary (N). Their son John b. 14 Apr 1745. {BPR:361}

Rogers, Robert of New Kent Co. m. bef. 1 Jun 1725, Susanna (N). {PGW&D (1713-1728):131}

Roland, Christopher m. bef. 7 Oct 1726, Ann (N). Their dau. Agnis b. 7 Jan 1729. {PGW&D (1713-1728):151; BPR:358}

Roland, John m. Elizabeth (N). Their son Benjamin b. 6 Feb 1729. {BPR:358}

Rollings, Thomas m. Ann (N). Their son Nicholas b. 4 Oct 1730. {BPR:358}

Roney, Patrick/Partrick m. Sarah (N). Their children: Elizabeth (b. 5 Mar 1745/6), Thomas (b. 19 Jan 1756) and John (b. 8 Oct 1757). {BPR:361}

Rookins William m. bef. 1 Mar 1726/7 Ellin (N). {CCW&D (1725-31):20}

Roupers, Charles m. Anne (N). Their children: David and Lowerel (twins, b. 29 Jun 1742). {BPR:360}

Roper, David of Orange Co., NC recorded a deed of gift to David Roper of same. {CCCR:158}

Roper, John (d. by 1759), m. by May 1744, Jane/Jean (N). Son: David. Jean Roper, David Roper and Charles Roper, execs. {CCCR:2}

Roper, Thomas (d. ca. 1769) m. bef. 15 Nov 1766, Susannah (N). In his LWT Thomas named brother Joseph Roper and cousin (*niece*?) Jane Edwards. Execs.: wife, Joseph Roper and William Edwards. {CCCR:14}

Roper, William m. by Aug 1748, Mary (N). {CCCR:116}

Rose, Morris/Maurice m. bef. 18 Jun 1658, Feba (N). {CCOB 1658-61):154}

Roshill, Peter m. Sarah (N). Their dau. Sarah b. 1 Mar 1743/4. {BPR:361}

Rosser, David m. bef. 8 Dec 1789, Sarah (N). {PGR:128}

Rosser, John d. by 1791, Sarah, widow, extx. {PGR:157}

Rothwell, Capt. William d. by 1657 leaving children: Milliscent (m. John Huntley), Robert and William. {CCOB (1655-58):130, 131, 156}

Rottenbery, Henry m. 1st Martha (N). Their dau. Martha b. 1 Sep 1720. Henry m. 2nd Margaret (N). Their son Richard b. 30 Jun 1724. {BPR:356, 357}

Rouse, Peter, free man of color (b. c1761), enlisted in the Rev. War in Dinwiddie Co. By 1818, he was living in Bedford Co., PA. By 1830, he was living in Greene Co., PA. {RWP}

Rouse, Robert, innholder, m. Johanna (N). Children: Robert, Jane and Elizabeth, all under the age of 17 in 1665. {CCOB (1664-65):586}

Routon, John d. by 1740, Ann Routon, admx. Son: William chose Col. Benjamin Harrison as his guardian in 1743. Ann m. 2nd William Waddill. {CCCR:88, 98, 99}

Rowland/Rolland, Christopher m. Ann (N). Their children: John (b. 20 May 1727) and Sarah (b. 26 Sep 1732). {BPR:358, 359}

Rowlet, William m. Frances (N). Their son Daniel b. 10 Jun 1721. {BPR:356}

Royall, Henry m. Elizabeth (N). Their children: Francis (b. 10 Jan 1721) and John (b. 23 Oct 1729). {BPR:356, 358}

Royall, Joseph m. 1st Thomasin (N) and m. 2nd by 1637, Ann (N) and m. 3rd ca. 1645, Katherine Banks. Their children: Joseph (had a son Joseph), Katherine (m. Richard Perrin) and Sarah (m. John Wilkinson of Charles City Co.). Katherine, widow of Joseph Royall, m. 2nd Henry Isham (d. ca. 1675). {GVAW I:454; HCW 1:4, 22-3; APP3:44, 861}

Royall, Partrick m. Isabellah (N). Their son James b. 20 Jun 1730. {BPR:358}

Royall, Richard, son of Joseph Royall of Henrico Co., m. by May 1745, Elizabeth (N) (d. by 1779). Their children: Joseph and William. {CCCR:106; APP3:46, 50-1}

Royall, William (d. by 1747), son of Joseph Royal, m. 1712-18, Sarah Baxter (d. by 1747), sister of Edward Baxter (d. by 1727). Their children: William, Joseph of Halifax Co., John and Sarah (m. Nathaniel Terry). {HCW 2:44; APP3:47, 54; CCW&D (1725-31):14, 45}

Royall, William (d. by 1762), son of William Royal (d. by 1747), leaving a widow Sarah. Children: William, John, Elizabeth, Sarah and Richard. In 1770 William's son William was appointed guardian to John. {CCCR:6, 29, 158; APP3:54}

Royall, William m. 7 Feb 1789, Sarah Singleton. Their children: Littleberry (b. 2 Nov 1792), Patcey, Polly and Sally. {BPR:361; APP 3:70}

Royster, Charles d. by 1754, Judith Royster, admx. {CCCR:128}

Royster, David d. intestate by 1738. John Hales Jr. was appointed guardian to David Royster, son of David Royster in 1741. James Royster was appointed guardian of Peter Royster, orphan of David Royster. In 1743 he chose Charles Floyd as his guardian. {CCCR:84, 94, 95, 97}

Royster, George m. Ann (N) bef. Apr 1776. {SWBC:36}

Royster, John was age 25 in 1664. {CCOB (1664-65):559}

Royster, Peter (d. 1766-7) m. Elizabeth, dau. of George Floyd. Children: Charles, Peter, George, William Floyd, John, Susanna and Mary (m. (N) Maynard). {CCCR:3, 8-9}

Ruddock, Alexander d. by 1661, leaving a widow Mary. {CCOB (1661-64):322}

Rudder, Alexander m. by Jun 1750. {CCCR:121}

Ruffin, Edmund (b. 1713, d. ca. 1790, owning land in Brunswick Co., Charlotte Co., Dinwiddie Co. and Prince George Co.), son of Robert Ruffin, m. 1st Anne (Simmons) Edmonds, widow of Southampton Co. Their son Edmond Jr. (b. 2 Jan 1745, d. 1807). Anne d. 1749. Edmund m. 2nd Elizabeth Cocke of Surry Co. Their dau. Elizabeth m. Nathaniel Harrison of Prince George Co. Grandsons: Edmund Harrison and George Ruffin. Great-grandson: Edmund Ruffin Harrison. {PGR:153; GVAW (Genealogies of Virginia Families) IV:336; GVAT (Genealogies of Virginia Families) III:188}

Ruffin, Edmund (b. 1745, d. 1807), son of Edmund Ruffin, m. Jane Skipwith, sister of Sir William Skipwith. Son: George. {GVAW (Genealogies of Virginia Families) IV:336}

Ruffin, George (b. 1765, d. 1810) of Prince George Co., son of Edmund

Ruffin, m. 1st Jane Lucas of Surry Co. Their son: Edward (b. 1794, d. 1865). George m. 2nd Rebecca Cocke of Surry Co. {GVAT (Genealogies of Virginia Families) III:189}

Russell, Charles d. by 1801, Susanna Russell, admx. {PGM:9}

Russel, Robert m. Jenny (N) Their son Robert b. 6 Aug 1792. {BPR:361}

Russell, Thomas m. by Nov 1741 Elizabeth (N). {CCCR:93}

Russell, William m. bef. 1 Mar 1716, Elizabeth (N). Their dau. Martha b. 14 Dec 1722. {PGW&D (1713-1728):24; BPR:356}

Russell, William (d. by 1762) m. by Nov 1755, Elizabeth (N). {CCCR:133, 154}

Russell, William m. Mary (N). Their dau. Mary b. 2 Dec 1719. {BPR:356}

Russell, William m. Rachel (N). Their son Richard b. 10 Sep 1759. {BPR:361}

Rutlidge, James m. Sarah (N). Their son William b. 9 May 1732. {BPR:359}

Ryan, Edmund of the town of Petersburg d. 25 Oct 1792. {BPR:361}

Sampson, Isaac m. by Nov 1749, Sarah (N). {CCCR:119}

Sandburne, William of Martins Brandon, d. by 1711 leaving wife Mary and no children. {PGW&D (1710-1713):7}

Sandon, Thomas m. bef. 6 Jan 1687, Sarah, widow of Paul Williams and admx. of Thomas Stoner. {CCOB (1687-95):4, 22, 162}

Saunders, John of Sussex Co. m. bef. 13 Jun 1789, Sarah Denhart, probable dau. of Drury Denhart. {PGR:81, 111, 128}

Saunders, John m. Mary (N). Their dau. Anne b. 9 Nov 1741. {BPR:367}

Saunders/Sanders, William m. bef. 18 Jun 1658, Jone/Joane. William d. by 1660 leaving a widow Joane who m. 2nd Thomas Douglas. William had a son William Jr. and daus. Susan, Jane and Joane. {CCOB (1658-61):155, 240, 241 (appears to make a distinction between Jane and Joane)}

Saunders, William d. by 1679, Mary Saunders, widow, admx. {CCOB (1677-79):107}

Saunders, William m. Rebecca (N). Their son William b. 7 Mar 1741/2. {BPR:368}

Sandert, James m. Elizabeth (N). Their dau. Elizabeth b. 29 Jul 1722. {BPR:362}

Satterwhite, Thomas m. Mary (N). Their dau. Elizabeth b. 22 Apr 1726. {BPR:364}

Suttawhite, Thomas m. Sarah (N). Their son Thomas b. 15 Feb 1732. {BPR:366}

Sauntie, Mary had a dau. Agge, b. 25 Dec 1731. {BPR:368}

Savage, Thomas (d. 7 Jun 1734) m. Mary (N). Their dau. Ann (b. 28 Dec 1732). {BPR:366}

Savage, William (d. by 1720) of Martins Brandon Parish m. (N)(N). Children: William Hall, John, Sarah, Elizabeth and Francis. {PGW&D (1713-1728):62-3}

Scarbro, Thomas of Martins Brandon Parish (d. ca. 1722) m. Elizabeth (N). Children: Thomas, Mary, Jean, Sarah, Elizabeth and William. Cousin (*nephew?*): Charles Holdsworth. {PGW&D (1713-1728):87}

Scoggin, George m. Elizabeth (N). Their son George b. 28 Jan 1745/6. {BPR:369}

Scoggins, John m. Anne (N). Their son Matthew b. 31 Dec 1741. {BPR:367}

Scoggin/Scoggan, Richard m. Mary (N). Their children: John (b. 22 Jul 1721), Richard (b. 15 Feb 1723), Francis (b. 22 Aug 1725), Martha (b. 11 Jul 1729), Lutia (b. 11 Jul 1729), Mary (b. 1 Jul 1732) and Anne (b. 25 May 1734). {BPR:362, 363, 364, 366}

Scoggin, William of Brunswick Co. m. Rebecca (N). Their children: Rebecca (b. 7 Jan 1721), William (b. 18 Mar 1722/3) and David (b. 27 Nov 1725). {BPR:362, 363; PGW&D (1713-1728): 169}

Scoggin, William m. Selah (N). Their children: James (b. 7 Apr 1790) and Sally (b. 17 Nov 1791). {BPR:370}

Scott, Daniel gave his children, Elizabeth and Daniel, a cow on 17 Dec 1655. {CCOB (1655-58): 29}

Scott, Drew of Wyanoak Parish was brother of John Scott, 1689. {CCCR:66}

Scott, Edward (d. 1786-7) of Martins Brandon Parish m. Elizabeth (N). Children: John, Elizabeth (m. (N) Sykes), Anness (m. (N) Thomas), Lucy and John. {PGR:85}

Scott, John (d. 1724) m. Bethyer (N) (d. by 1725). Children: John (predeceased his father), Bridget (m. Christopher Tatum), Amelia (m. Nathaniel Tatum), Bethyer (m. Philip Burrows Jr.), Elizabeth (m. Samuel Chappell) and Boyce (m. James Gee). In his LWT John also named son-in-law James Gee and grandsons, Thomas and John Scott and their mother Amy Scott. {APP1:356; PGW&D (1713-1728):102-3, 142}

Scott, John Jr. (d. by 1724, predeceasing his father), son of John Scott, m. Amey, dau. of Thomas and Mary Goodwyn. Sons: Thomas and John. Amey m. 2nd Isham Eppes. Amey d. Aug 1777 in Dinwiddie Co. {APP1:356, 870; PGR:178; PGW&D (1713-1728):154}

Scott, John, probable son of John Scott Jr. (d. by 1724), m. bef. 11 Apr 1738, Jemima, dau. of (N) and Mary (Batty) Parsons. Their children: William (b. Sep 1740) and Stephen (b. 31 Aug 1742). {PGR:1, 29; BPR:368}

Scott, Nicholas d. by 1728, Elizabeth Scott, admx. {CCW&D (1725-31):26}

Scott, William (d. by 1771) m. bef. 22 Feb 1769, Frances (N). Sons: William, Robert and Jesse. {CCCR:15}

Sealey, John d. by 1739, Mary Sealey, extx. {CCCR:86}

Sears, John m. bef. 13 Apr 1791, Sarah (N). {PGR:154}

Seares, Lawrence was father of Lawrence who was buried 7 May 1660, Martins Brandon Parish. {CCOB 1658-61):270}

Sental, Ann had a son Henry Fitz, b. 18 Jul 1734. {BPR:366}

Sental(l), Samuel m. Mary (N). Their children: Jonathan (b. 26 May 1729) and Jane (b. 5 Mar 1733). {BPR:364, 366}

Shackleford, Richard m. bef. 5 Sep 1790, Elizabeth, dau. of Thomas Brown. They had a dau. Elizabeth. {PGR:141}

Shand(e)s, Thomas m. bef. 12 Jun 1690, Frances, widow of Thomas Shippey and dau. of Robert Harrison. They had a son William who m. Nazareth Roberts, dau. of John Roberts of Surry Co. and perhaps a dau. Frances who m. Christopher Golightly. {APP3:164-5; HCW 1:32, 66; CCOB (1687-95):82; GVAT (Genealogies of Virginia Families) III:275-6 ; PGR:46; GVAT (Genealogies of Virginia Families) III:276}

Sharp, William m. Winnifred (N). Their dau. Margaret Lang b. 5 Jun 1792. {BPR:370}

Shell, John Sr. (d. 1773) m. Elizabeth (N). Son: Adam. {CCCR:64}

Shell, William d. by 1746, Elizabeth Shell, extx. {CCCR:109}

Shepherd, Baldwin m. by 1790, Susanna probable dau. of Seth Foster. {W&M, Vol. 23, No. 3 (Jan., 1915): 217}

Sheppey/Shippy, Thomas, son of Thomas (d. by 1684) and Martha Sheppey, m. Frances, dau. of Robert Harrison. Their dau. Frances m. Richard Kendall. Frances, widow of Thomas Sheppy, m. 2nd Thomas Shands/Shandes. {APP3:164-5; HCW 1:32, 66; CCOB (1687-95):82; GVAT (Genealogies of Virginia Families) III:275}

Sheppy/Shipey/Shipley, Walter (d. by 1689) of Charles City Co. m. bef. 4 Mar 1684/5, Martha, cousin (niece?) of John Farrar. Martha m. 2nd William Sutton {HCW 1:16; CCOB (1687-95):49}

Sherman, (N) m. Elizabeth (N). Elizabeth d. by 1787 leaving a dau. Suckey wife of (N) Ogbern. {PGR:86}

Sherman, Michael m. bef. 20 Apr 1729, Susanna, dau. of Elizabeth Duke. Their children: Marston Duke Sherman and Elizabeth Sherman. {CCW&D (1725-31):38}

Shern, John m. Mary (N). Their dau. Anne b. 3 Mar 1733. {BPR:366}

Sherwood, William m. bef. 19 Jun 1677, (N), widow of Richard James. {CCOB 1676-79:6}

Shipton, Ann had a dau. Phebe Bast (b. 9 Jul 1721) and a dau. Elizabeth (b. 26 Nov 1722). {BPR:362, 363}

Shore, John m. Anne (N). Their dau. Sarah bapt. 28 Jun 1793. They had a dau. (Sarah?) who d. ca. Nov 1794. {BPR:371}

Shorie, William had a son Thomas William, b. 6 Feb 1726. {BPR:365}

Short(e), Robert (d. 1684-90) m. Alice (N). Children: Thomas, Robert and John. Alice m. 2nd Henry Harman. {CCOB (1687-95):91; CCCR:67}

Short, Thomas m. Mary (N). Their children: Thomas (b. 6 Aug 1741) and Martha (b. 26 Dec 1743). {BPR:367, 368}

Short(e), William of Wyanoak Parish m. bef. 12 Dec 1715, Elizabeth, dau. of Jacob Baily (d. by 1727). {PGW&D (1713-1728):173}

Sildom, Milly, Mulatto dau. of Mary Sildom, was bound out in 1758. {CCCR:140}

Simons, William m. bef. 4 Aug 1679, Elizabeth, widow of Thomas Manfill. {CCOB (1677-79):108}

Simmons, Joel m. bef. 11 May 1790, Mason, granddau. of Rachel Gee. {PGR:130}

Simmons, John d. by 1721, Mary Simmons, admx. {PGW&D (1713-1728):72}

Simmons, John (d. by 1739) m. Lucy, extx. {PGR:62}

Simmons, Joshua d. by 1802, leaving a widow Sally. {PGM:11}

Symonns, Peter, age 31 in 1673. {CCOB (Fragments):527}

Symons, Symon d. by 1659 leaving, widow Amee and children: Symon (bound to Howell Pryse), Samuell, Margarett and Elizabeth. {CCOB (1658-61):201, 212}

Simmons, Thomas gave each of his sons, John, Benjamin and Thomas Jr. 100 acres in 1722. {PGW&D (1713-1728):93}

Simmons, Thomas Jr. m. bef. 7 Apr 1727, Elizabeth (N). {PGW&D (1713-1728):163}

Simmons, Thomas d. by 1739. One of his orphans, Susanna, chose John Bonner as her guardian. {PGM:63}

Simmons, Thomas, son of John Simmons of Prince George Co. m. 7th da., 11th mo., 1738, Ann Fowler, dau. of Godfrey Fowler of Henrico Co. [that part of Henrico Co. that became Chesterfield Co.] {HMM:20; GVAW:III:652}

Simmons, Thomas m. bef. 12 Sep 1787, Lucy (N). {PGR:86}

Simmons, William d. by 1790 leaving widow Huldah Simmons, probable dau. of Robert Hunnicutt. Brothers: Anderson and Joseph Simmons. Sister Ann Hunnicutt's two children: Elizabeth and Thomas Hunnicutt. Sister? Martha Simmons. In 1802, 240 acres of the estate of William Simmons was divided among Dudley Fuqua and wife, William Simmons, Joel Simmns, Daniel and wife (last name not given) and Henry Simmons. {PGM:24, 29, 139; GVAW (Genealogies of Virginia Families):III;99}

Simson/Symson, John d. by 1693 leaving an orphan, John who was bound to John Hill. {CCOB (1687-95):160}

Skelton, Bathurst (b. 1744, d. 1771), son of James and Jane (Meriwether) Skelton, m. Martha (b. 19 Oct 1748, d. 6 Sep 1782), eldest dau. of John and Martha (Eppes) Wayles. Son: John d. young. Martha m. 2nd Thomas Jefferson. {CCCR:37, 39; GVAT Genealogies of Virginia Families) II:436; GVAW (Genealogies of Virginia Families):IV:448-50}

Skipwith, Henry m. (bond dated 7 Jul 1773) Ann Wayles, dau. of John Wayles. {CCCR:37, 39, 53; GVAW (Genealogies of Virginia Families) IV:450; MB:193}

Skipwith, Sir William (d. 25 Feb 1764, age 56), grandson of Sir Gray Skipwith, m. 1st Sarah, dau. of John Peyton of Gloucester Co. William was brother of Dorothy Meams (had a son William Meams Jr. who m. Elizabeth (N)). Their children: Peyton, Robert, Henry, Sarah (m. Robert Kennon), Jane, Mary and possibly Elizabeth who m. William Short. Sons-in-law: Robert Kennon and William Short. *See below (William Skipwith)*. William m. 2nd Elizabeth (N). {PGM:15-16; VG&B (Encyclopedia of Virginia Biography) I:324, II:153, 259; SWBC:213}

Slaid/Slayd, John d. by 1659, leaving an orphan son John and other children. {CCOB (1658-61): 185}

Slaughter, Lawrence m. Susanna (N) bef. Oct 1778. {SWBC: 29}

Sledge, John m. bef. 13 Apr 1693, Mary, widow of John Drinkwater. {CCOB (1687-95):151}

Small, Martha had a dau. Susanna who was bound to Charles Holdsworth in Oct 1737. {CCCR:80}

Smart, James m. Elisabeth (N). Their children: Henry (b. 15 Dec 1740) and dau. Sylvania (b. 12 Jun 1743). {BPR:367, 368}

Smart, Matthew m. Sarah (N). Their son Frederick b. 8 Feb 1740. {BPR:367}

Smelt, Robert m. Sarah (N). Their dau. Maxey b. 30 Dec 1763. {BPR:303}

Smith, (N) d. by 1655, leaving a widow, Temperance Smith. {CCOB (1655-58): 42}

Smith, (N) m. bef. 1725, Mary, dau. of Gibby Gibson. Their children: Tom, Lightfoot, Sarah, Elizabeth, Mary and Rebecca. {CCW&D (1725-31):15}

Smith, (N) m. Jane (N). Jane d. by 1735, leaving sons: Richard and William Smith, execs. {PGR:16}

Smith, Abraham (d.by Feb 1782) of Dinwiddie Co. m. Ann (N). Children: Elizabeth (m. James McFarlane), Richard (unmarried), Nancy (m. Kennon Jones), Martha (m. James French). {SWBC:59}

Smith, Archiball m. Mary (N). Their dau. Mary b. 11 May 1741. {BPR:367}

Smith, Arthur (d. by 1759) m. Elizabeth Bray, dau. of James Bray and widow of Arthur Allen (d. 1725) of Surry Co. Elizabeth m. 3rd (N) Stith. {PGR:75; GVAW (Genealogies of Virginia Families):I:448}

Smith, Benjamin m. Anne (N). Their son John Benjamin, b. 23 Sep 1792. {BPR:370}

Smith, Charity had a dau. Agnis Waller, b. 30 May 1726. {BPR:385}

Smith, David m. Obedience (N). Their children: Clement (b. 27 Nov

1742), David (b. 24 Dec 1744) and Elizabeth (b. 24 Dec 1744). {BPR:368}

Smith, Edward (d. by 1738) of Bristol Parish m. bef. 11 Apr 1738, Mary, dau. of (N) and Mary (Batty) Parsons. {PGR:1, 29, 52}

Smith, George d. by 1690 leaving a widow, Mary. {CCOB (1687-95):77}

Smith, George m. Elizabeth (N). Their children: David (b. 2 Aug 1722), Joss/Joshua (b. 2 Jul 1724) and Jane (b. 1727). {BPR:363, 364}

Smith, George m. Mary (N). Their children: William (b. 4 Aug 1739), Susannah (b. 8 Apr 1741), Joshua (b. 9 Sep 1743) and Millinton (b. 7 Dec 1745). {BPR:367, 368, 369}

Smith, Isaac (d. ca. 1769) m. Martha (N). Children: Mary, William, John and Martha. {CCCR:11}

Smith, James m. by Sep 1748, Elizabeth (N). {CCCR:116}

Smith, John (d. by 3 Mar 1690) m. ca. 1678, Sarah, widow of Nicholas Gattley. John was father of Obediah and Mary. {CCOB (1687-95):85, 91, 103, 130}

Smith, John d. by 1727, Elizabeth Smith, widow. {PGW&D (1713-1728):159}

Smith, John m. Agnis (N). Their children: James (b. 15 Nov 1722) and Sarah (b. 15 Apr 1725). {BPR:363}

Smith, John m. Elizabeth (N). Their son Moses b. 28 Nov 1731. {BPR:365}

Smith, John Jr. m. bef. 12 Feb 1739, Sarah (N). Sarah d. 1759. In her LWT she named dau. Mary Smith and other children(?): all under 16, Mary, John, Sarah, Frances, William and Alexander Smith. Sons Thomas and John, execs. {PGR:63, 74}

Smith, John m. Priscilla (N). Their son David b. 18 Dec 1743. {BPR:368}

Smith, John d. by 1759, Thomas and John Smith, execs. {PGR:72}

Smith, Lewis, free man of color, b. ca. 1752, Prince George Co., VA, d. 20 Aug 1833, Dinwiddie Co. He moved to Dinwiddie Co. just before the Revolutionary War. {RWP}

Smith, Partrick m. Elizabeth (N). Their children: Thomas (b. 23 Oct 1731), Drury (b. 7 Aug 1742) and Lucy (b. 12 Oct 1744). {BPR:366, 368}

Smith, Philip m. bef. Oct 1737, Elizabeth (N). {CCCR:80}

Smith, Richard and his wife, Jane, were convicted ca. Mar 1661/2, of fornication before marriage. Ordered to pay fine to Parish or be whipped. {CCOB (1661-64):377}

Smith, Richard m. bef. 14 Sep 1677, (N), widow of John Crabb. {CCOB (1677-79):19}

Smith, Richard of Bristol Parish (d. ca. 1725) m. (N)(N). Children: Richard, John, William, George, Jane (m. (N) Patteson) and Edward. Grandson: John Smith. {PGW&D (1713-1728):142-3}

Smith, Richard m. Agnes (N). Their children: Agnis (b. 9 Apr 1722) , Sarah (b. 30 Apr 1724) and Benjamine (b. 22 Jun 1741). {PGR:3; BPR:362, 363, 367}

Smith, Richard m. bef. 11 Apr 1738, Susanna, dau. of (N) and Mary (Batty) Parsons. {PGR:1, 29}

Smith, Samuel. In Feb 1664/5 Samuel Smith was presented for fathering a bastard child. {CCOB (1664-65):

Smith, Samuel m. by Oct 1750, Ann (N). CCCR:121}

Smith, Thomas (d. 1718) of Waynoak Parish, brother of Richard Smith, m. Judith (N). Children: John, Thomas, Patrick, William, Richard and John. {PGW&D (1713-1728):39-40}

Smith, William m. bef. 1 Sep 1659, (N), the widow of Thomas Blanks. {CCOB (1658-61):198}

Smith, William. On 5 Aug 1695 William Smith of Swineyards in Westover Parish forbid all persons from having any dealings or commerce with his wife Sarah. {CCOB (1687-95):209}

Smith, William m. bef. 14 May 1717, Susan (N). {PGW&D (1713-1728):26}

Smith, William m. Mary (N). Their children: Phebe (b. 7 May 1722), Catherine (b. 25 Oct 1725) and Jane (b. 28 Nov 1726). {BPR:363, 364}

Smith, William of Petersburg had a son William who d. 8 Apr 1792. {BPR:370}

Snipes, Thomas m. Susannah (N). Their dau. Elizabeth b. 28 Nov 1740. {BPR:367}

Soane, Henry m. bef. 22 May 1726, Sarah, sister of Elizabeth Ballard. {CCW&D (1725-31):16-17}

Soane, Henry d. by 1739. His dau. Elizabeth, m. 1st by 1739, Benskin Marston and m. 2nd 6 Jul 1755, Rev. David Mossom. extx. {CCCR:85; GVAW (Genealogies of Virginia Families) I:725}

Soane, Henry (d. 1750-1) m. Rebecca Hubbard Edloe, dau. of John and Rebecca Huberd Edloe. Their dau. Susanna d. young. Rebecca m. 2nd Littleberry Cocke of Charles City Co. {APP1:847-8, 850-1; GVAW (Genealogies of Virginia Families) I:450}

Soane, John d. by 1744, had a son Henry. {CCCR:103}

Southall, Anne B. d. 8 Oct 1820, in her 74th year. {W&M Vol. 4, No. 3 (Jan., 1896):147}

Southall, Dasey (d. 28 Jun 1767) m. 26 Jul 1720/1, Edith (N) (d. 20 Jan 1782). Their children: Ann (m. Robert Grant), Stephen (b. 17 Nov 1722, d. 1748, unm.), Philip (b. 10 Jul 1724, d. 12 Dec 1759), James Barrett (b. 20 Oct 1726, d. by 1787), William (b. 16 Mar 1732/3) and Turner (b. 25 Jul 1736, d. 1791). Dasey moved from Charles City Co. to Amelia Co. and then to Henrico Co. {GVAW (Genealogies of Virginia Families) IV:529; GVAT (Genealogies of Virginia Families) III:331-2}

Southall, Henry m. (bond dated 27 Dec 1793), Elizabeth Holdsworth. {MB:195}

Southall, Holman of Charles City Co., probable son of John Southall and brother of Furneau Southall, m. in 1760 Elizabeth Dancy in Sussex Co., dau. of William Dancy. {GVAW (Genealogies of Virginia Families) IV:535, 541}

Southall, John m. (contract dated May 1749) Sarah Talbot, widow. Dau. Lucy Talbot chose John Southall as her guardian Nov 1749. Sarah d. ca. 1762; in her LWT Sarah named her children: William Talbott, Sarah (m. (N) Dudley), Frances (m. (N) Bachurst), Mary (m. (N) Johnson) and Lucy (m. (N) Philips). She also named granddau. Sarah Southall, dau. of dec'd. dau. Tabitha Southall. John Southall d. by 1750, John Southall (son?), exec. Furneau Southall may have been a son, also. {CCCR:2, 118, 157}

Southall, John Jr. m. 1st by Apr 1745, Elizabeth (N) and m. 2nd 1754, Mary Talbott. {CCCR:105; GVAW (Genealogies of Virginia Families) IV:531}

Southall, Philip (1724-1759), son of Dasey Southall, m. Betty (N). Execs. of his LWT: James, Dancy and Turner Southall. Children: William, Philip and probably others. {CCCR:157; GVAW (Genealogies of Virginia Families) IV:530}

Southall, Major Stephen (b. 1757, d. 12 Mar 1799), son of Col. Turner (d. 1791) and Martha (VanDewall) Southall, m. 1784, Martha Wood (b. 12 Mar 1768, d. 30 Sep 1834 in Washington, D.C.), dau. of Valentine and Lucy (Henry) Wood of Goochland Co. Their son: Philip Turner (b. in Goochland Co. 1791). Martha m. 2nd George Frederick Stras. {GVAT (Genealogies of Virginia Families) III:332, 333; GVA (Genealogies of Virginia Families II, Cl-Fi:174}

Southall, Col. Turner (b. 1736, d. 27 Apr 1791), son of Dasey and Edith Southall (d. by 1767), m. 3 Feb 1756, Martha VanDewall (d. 3 Mar 1781), dau. of Nathaniell and Martha (Pleasants) VanDewall. Their children: Stephen (b. 16 Jun 1757, d. 12 Mar 1799), William (b. & d. 1759), Anne Barrett (b. 2 Nov 1760, d. 8 Jun 1830, m. 1st John Shelton, m. 2nd Capt. Peter Foster of Hanover Co.), Philip (b. 5 May 1763, d. 27 Oct 1790), William (b. 27 Apr 1765, d. 2 Mar 1796), Pleasants (b. 27 Jul 1767, d. 6 Mar 1798), Paulina/Polina (b. 20 May 1769, m. Calhoun/ Callam Jones), Cynthia (b. 1777, m. ca. 1787, Henry Toler), James Barrett of Isle of Wight Co. (b. 27 Sep 1772, m. 1st Polly Whitfield, m. 2nd Mary Todd), Cynthia (b. 12 Apr 1777), Elizabeth (b. 19 Jun 1779, m. 13 May 1802, Thomas Underwood of Goochland Co.) and John (m. Phoebe, dau. of Dr. John Harris of Herefordshire, England) {HMM:19; GVA (Genealogies of Virginia Families) II, Cl-Fi:136; V, R-Z:339, 342-3); GVAT (Genealogies of Virginia Families):332; APP;1:185-6; HCW2:99}

Southall, Turner (d. by 1821), son of Philip (d. 1759) Southall, m. Mary Christian (d. by 1821), dau. of Charles and Mary (Vaughan) Christian. Children: James Barrett, Mary (m. Samuel Ellis), Rebecca Hunt (m. George Delaware Shell), Sarah (m. Oscar Weisinger) and Elizabeth (m. Thomas Hutton). {GVAW (Genealogies of Virginia Families) IV:530}

Southall, William m. (bond dated 3 Mar 1780), Sarah Dudley. {MB:195}

Southerland, John (d. by Apr 1771 in NC) of Dinwiddie Co. m. Ann (N). Children: Fendall (son), Elizabeth, Sarah, and Mary Ann. {SWBC:59}

Spain, Sarah, dau. of Ann Spain was bound out in 1758. {CCCR:140}

Spain, Thomas m. Martha (N). Their children: Frances (b. 9 Dec 1729), Prisilla (b. 7 Sep 1731) and David (b. 1 Mar 1732). {BPR:365, 366}

Spain, William m. Mary (N). Their children: John (b. 22 Mar 1720/1), William (b. 9 Mar 1723), Joshua (b. 10 Jul 1725), Elizabeth (b. 30 May 1731) and Batt Peter (b. 9 Sep 1733). {BPR:362, 363, 365, 366}

Sparrow, Charles was buried 11 Sep 1660. He d. leaving a widow who m. 2nd William Rawlinson/Rollinson. Son: Selby Sparrow d. by 1664. {CCOB (1658-61):254; CCOB (1661-64):308, 319, 417}

Sparrow, Thomas Wright of Martins Brandon Parish m. bef. 24 Oct 1727, Mary (N). {PGW&D (1713-1728):171}

Spell, John d. by 1711, leaving widow Mary, admx. {PGW&D (1710-1713): 15}

Spell, John of Prince George Co. d. ca, 1712. In his LWT he named wife Anne, son George and grandson Thomas Spell. {PGW&D (1710-1713):27}

Spencer, Richard (d. by 1719), Rebecca Spencer, admx. Rebecca probably m. 1st William Clanthorne and m. 2nd Richard Spencer. {CCOB (1677-79):100, 106; PGW&D (1713-1728):54}

Spencer, Richard m. Elizabeth (N). Their dau. Ann Grant Spencer, b. 15 Feb 1767. {BPR:369}

Spiers, (N) m. Lucy (N). William Speirs, orphan of Lucy Speirs, was bound out in 1761. {CCCR:152}

Spire, Henry m. Catharine (N). Their son Joseph b. 5 Sep 1743.
{BPR:368}

Spier, Robert m. bef. 3 Oct 1695, Elizabeth (N), next of kin of two
orphans of Elias Waad, late dec'd. Mary, their mother-in-law (step-
mother) was accused of neglecting them. {CCOB (1687-95):215}

Spragins, Lt. Thomas of Halifax Co. m. Rebecca B., dau. of Stith and
Charlotte (Edmunds) Bolling. Their children: Stith Bolling Spragins and
Melchijah Spragins, who settled with their mother in AL near
Huntsville). {VBR:246-7}

Spragins, William (d. 1772-3) m. (N)(N). Children: Thomas, William
and Jane Richardson. Grandchildren: William Spragins and Amey
Griffin. {CCCR:51-2}

Spruce, Polly, a free Mulatto, had a dau. Elizabeth, b. 1 May 1791.
{BPR:370}

Stagg, Charles d. by 1761, Mary Stagg, his widow and admx.
{CCCR:152}

Stainup, John Price d. by 1756, leaving an orphan, Ann Stainup.
{CCCR:136}

Stainback – heirs of (N): William, Robert, Nicholas and George
Stainback. {PGM:31}

Stainback, Francis d. by 1805. Heirs: Littlebury E., Mary, L. E. and Mary
Stainback. {PGM:34}

Stainback, George d. by 1788. {PGR:101}

Stainback, John d. by 1756 leaving land to his son John. {PGR:79}

Standback, William Sr. of Prince George Co. gave to his son William Jr.
100 acres in 1713. William Sr. d. by 1739. Sons, John and William
Stainback, execs. {PGW&D (1710-1713):38; PGR:44}

Stainback, William m. Ann Lamboth (N). Their children: Elizabeth (b.
20 Nov 1766), Ann (b. 20 Feb 1769) and Rebecka (b. 4 Feb 1770).
{BPR:369}
Stanfield, Robert m. Frances (N). Their children: Mary (b. 6 Jan 1724)
and Robert (b. 11 Mar 1729). {BPR:363, 364}

Stanford, John m. by Mar 1754, Elizabeth (N). John and Richard
Stanford sold some property to Silvanus Gregory in 1754. {+CCCR:127}

Stanley, Archilaus, son of Joseph and Mary Stanley of Hanover Co. m.
4th da., 6th mo., 1758, Elizabeth Ladd, dau. of John and Mary Ladd of
Charles City Co. {HMM:34}

Stanly, Christopher m. bef. 6 Jun 1791, Betty Anne (N). They res. in
Goochland Co. in 1794. {HCDB 3:47; HCDB 5:87}

Stanly, Dancy m. by Jun 1750, Elizabeth (N). {CCCR:120}

Stanley/Stenly, Edward (d. 1726) m. 1st Hannah, widow of Charles Clay
and dau. of John Wilson. Edward m. 2nd Martha (N). Dau.: Hannah (m.
(N) Thweat). {HCW 1:151, 161}

Stanley, Jacob of Cedar Creek took a wife not a Quaker, sometime bef.
7/7/1723. {HMM:12}

Stanley, James (d. by 1765), son of James Stanly of Hanover Co. m. 23rd
da., 10th mo., 1754, Elizabeth Elison, dau. of William Ellyson of New
Kent Co. Elizabeth m. 2nd bef. Mar 1765, (N)(N) who was not of the
Society of Friends and disowned. In 1774 Elizabeth Martin, late Stanley,
condemned her outgoing in marriage. {HMM:29, 30-1, 41, 52}

Stanley, James, son of Thomas Stanley of Hanover Co. m. 5th da., 3rd
mo., 1728, Catherine Hutchins, dau. of Nicholas Hutchins of Henrico Co.
{HMM:16}

Stanley, Madox, son of Thomas Stanley of Hanover Co. m. 2nd da., 12th
mo., 1745/6, Huldah Macgahea/McGee, dau. of Samuel
Macgahea/McGee of the same co., at the Swamp Meeting House.
{HMM:24}

Stanley, Pleasants, son of Thomas Stanley of Hanover Co. m. 4th da., 12th
mo., 1757, Sarah McGee, dau. of Samuel McGee of afsd. county, dec'd.,
at a meeting house at Wainoak in Charles City Co. {HMM:31, 33}

Stanley, Richard m. Ann (N). Their dau. Elizabeth b. 26 Jun 1727.
{BPR:364}

Stanley, Shadrack of Caroline Monthly Meeting, son of John Stanley of
Hanover Co., m. 2nd da., 12th mo., 1764, Agness Ladd, dau. of James
Ladd of Charles City Co., in Waynoak Parish in Charles City Co.

{HMM:41}

Stanley, Thomas having brought before the meeting a woman, not being a Friend (Quaker), declared his intentions of taking to wife on 1/6/1724. Thomas Stanley took a wife not of the Society and has been publickly drunk. Reported on 1/8/1726. {HMM:13, 15}

Stenley, Thomas Jr., of Hanover Co. m. 8th da., 9th mo., 1726, Elizabeth Crew, dau. of John Crew of Charles City Co. {HMM:15}

Stanly, Waddy, son of Thomas and Sarah Stanly of Hanover Co., m. 4th da., 11th mo., 1794, Rebeckah Ladd, dau. of James and Sarah Ladd, dec'd., of Charles City Co., married with consent of parents. {HMM:78, 87}

Stanley/Standley, William m. Elizabeth (N). Their children: Priscilla (b. 10 Aug 1728), William (b. 11 Jan 1729), James (b. 16 Oct 1734) and James (b. 11 Nov 1740). {BPR:364, 367}

Stanley, Zachariah from Cedar Monthly Meeting, m. 6th da., 3rd mo., 1775, Sarah Crew at the meeting house in Charles City Co. {HMM:53, 55}

Staples, Thompson m. Ruth (N). Their children: Thompson (b. 12 Nov 1720), and Frances (b. 14 May 1724). {BPR:362, 363, 372}

Stark, Bellfield, son of Bolling Stark, m. bef. May 1790, Elizabeth (N). She received a gift from Lewis Burwell of Mecklenburg Co. in 1790. {W&M, Vol. 23, No. 3 (Jan., 1915): 217}

Stark William m. Mary (N). Their son Bolling b. 21 Sep 1733. On 11 May 1760 Mary Stark of Prince George Co. gave her son Bolling Stark of Dinwiddie Co., 3 Negroes. Bolling Stark m. Ann (N). Their son Belfield m. Elizabeth (N). {PGR:79; BPR:366; GVAW (Genealogies of Virginia Families) IV:564}

Stark, William (b. c1757) entered the Rev. War in Dinwiddie Co. He d. 1 Aug 1844, Norfolk, VA, leaving no widow, nor children. {RWP}

Stegge, Thomas (d. 1652, prob. in England) m. Elizabeth, sister of Emelion Read. His son, Thomas. Dau. Grace Byrd (had dau., Elizabeth Byrd). Thomas' sister, Alice Stegge; brother, Christopher Stegge. {SWBC:45}

Stell, George m. Ann (N). Their children: Angelica (b. 18 Dec 1718) and James (b. 17 Apr 1720). {BPR:362}

Stevens, John (d. 1720) of Martins Brandon Parish m. (N)(N). Children: John, Thomas, Richard, Ann and Joseph. {PGW&D (1713-1728):61}

Stephens, Mary had a dau. Patie Tadlock, b. 25 Aug 1741. {BPR:367}

Stephens, Capt. Richard m. Elizabeth, dau. of Capt. Abraham Piersey. Elizabeth m. 2nd Sir John Harvey. {VG&B:146}

Stevens, Thomas d. by 1679. Dau.: Sarah. {CCOB (1677-79):111}

Stevenson, Thomas of Martins Brandon Parish was father of Sara (bapt. 29 Sep 1660). {CCOB 1658-61):270}

Steward, Ann had a dau. Fanney b. 1 Aug 1740. {BPR:367}

Stuard, Elizabeth had children: Edward (b. 19 Aug 1721), Matthew (b. 6 Jan 1726) and Martha (b. 3 Oct 1741). {BPR:362}

Stuart, John m. Mary (N). Their son John b. 16 Oct 1734. {BPR:367}

Stewart, Matt and Mary Toney were parents of Charles, b. 22 Dec 1750. {BPR:369}

Stewart, Richard Sr. (d. ca. 1791, owning land in Dinwiddie Co.) of Bristol Parish m. Edith (N). Children: Ann (m. William Lyell), Jane and Richard. {PGR:152-3}

Stewart, Susanna had a son John b. 30 Aug 1741. {BPR:367}

Stiff, Jacob m. by Nov 1760, Ruth (N). {CCCR:145}

Still, John m. Mary (N). Their son James b. 28 Feb 1740/1. {BPR:367}

Still, Richard Cross m. Frances (N). Their son William b. 13 Apr 1740. {BPR:367}

Stillman, George m. Goodith (N). Their dau. Mary b. 8 Oct 1743. {BPR:368}

Stimpson, Charles m. Ellen (N). Their dau. Sally Hall, b. 24 Jan 1792. {BPR:370}

Stith, Anderson, son of John and Elizabeth (Anderson) Stith, m. Joanna, dau. of William and Elizabeth (Churchill) Bassett. {APP 3:309-310; GVAW (Genealogies of Virginia Families) IV:571}

Stith, Drury, son of John and Jane Stith, m. ca. 1693, Susanna Bathurst, dau. of Lancelot Bathurst of New Kent Co. Lt. Col. Drury Stith d. by 1741, Susanna and William Stith, execs. Their children: Drury, William and John. {CCCR:77, 94; GVAW IV:123, 567}

Stith, Drury, Jr. m. Elizabeth, probable dau. of William Buckner of York Co. Their children: Griffin (b. 28 Nov 1721), John (b. 20 Mar 1723/4), Barthurst (b. 19 Sep 1729) and Thomas (b. 29 Dec 1731). {BPR:362, 363, 364, 365; PGW&D (1713-1728):168; GVAW (Genealogies of Virginia Families) I:794}

Stith, Major John, Sr. of Westover Parish, d. 3 Oct 1693-3 Apr 1694, m. 1656 Jane Parsons, widow of (1) Thomas Gregory and (2) Joseph Parsons. Their children: John (oldest son, m. Mary Randolph), Jane (m. Capt. Daniel Llewellyn/Luellin), Ann (m. Robert Bolling), Agnes (m. Thomas Wynn) and Drury. {CCOB (1655-58): 81CCOB (1677-79):22; CCOB (1687-95):136, 174; CCCR:77; GVAW IV:565-6}

Stith, John (d. 1762) m. Elizabeth, dau. of Rev. Charles and Frances Anderson. Children: Anderson, William, Frances, Jane, Anne and Charlotte. Anderson Stith and Booth Armistead were two of the execs. of the LWT of John Stith. {CCCR:1, 86, 156}

Stith, John, son of John and Jane (Parsons), m. Mary Randolph, dau. of Col. William and Mary (Isham) Randolph. Their children: Rev. William (b. 1707, d. 19 Sep 1755, m. Judith Randolph) and Mary (m. William Dawson). {GVAW (Genealogies of Virginia Families) IV:566}

Stith, William d. intestate 1749, son of Drury and Jane Stith, owning land in Charles City Co. and Prince George Co. {CCCR:120}

Stoker/Stoaker, Robert m. Elizabeth (N). Their children: Elizabeth (b. 14 Oct 1723), Matthew (b. 21 Aug 1729), Ann (b. 30 Jan 1731) and Margaret (b. 26 Aug 1734). {BPR:363, 364, 367}

Stokes, Henry, probable son of Silvanus Stokes and probable brother of Young Stokes, m. bef. 6 Nov 1728, Ann (N). {CCW&D (1725-31):33}
Stokes, Jones of Surry Co. m. bef. 1 Mar 1725, Ann (N). {CCW&D (1725-31):9}

Stokes, Samuel of Westover Parish m. bef. 5 Oct 1725, Sarah (N). {CCW&D (1725-31):6}

Stokes, Sylvanus (b. ca. 1636) apparently m. bef. 23 Sep 1658 Mary, dau. of Capt. John Bishopp. Probable sons: John and Sylvanus. {CCOB (1658-61):169; CCOB (1664-65):489; GVAT (Genealogies of Virginia Families) III:369}

Stone, Launcelot m. Elizabeth (N). Their dau. Sarah Howlet, b. 30 Jan 1793. {BPR:370}

Stone, Thomas d. by 1741, leaving a widow Minerva. Minerva d. by 1745, James Jackson, admin. The orphans, John, Ann, Joanna, William and Elizabeth were bound out to James Jackson. {CCCR:91-2, 105}

Stone, William m. bef. 6 Mar 1791, Mary, sister of Lessenbury Williams. Their son: James W. Stone. {PGR:151}

Stonebank, Thomas m. Mary (N). Their dau. Mary b. 10 Oct 1722. {BPR:362}

Stott, Ebenezer m. Elizabeth (N). Their dau. Helen b. 15 Aug 1796, d. 5 Sep 1797. {BPR:371}

Stow, William m. Margaret (N). Their children: Hannah (bapt. 24 May 1724) and Abraham (b. 6 Oct 1726). {BPR:363}

Strachan, Dr. Alexander Glass (d. by 1806) m. 1st (bond dated 18 Oct 1777), Lucy, dau. of Halcott and Mary (Briggs) Pride. Children: R. G., A. J., J.F. and Mary. Alexander m. 2nd Sarah (N). Their dau. Sarah Field b. 22 Jan 1792, d. 17 May 1792. {BPR:370; PGM:35; APP 2:217}

Stradford, Clemond had a son Hardship b. 2 Dec 1740. {BPR:367}

Stratton, Edward Jr. (d. 1698), son of Edward Stratton Sr. and his 1st wife, m. ca. 1678, Martha Sheppey, dau. of Thomas and Martha Sheppey. Their children: Edward (the third), Martha (m. George Cox), Prudence (m. Henry Anderson of Prince George and Henrico cos.), Mary (m. William Batte), Anna (m. Joseph Watson), Sarah (m. Col. Richard Jones) and Elizabeth (m. 1st Thomas Chamberlayne, m. 2nd Gilbert Fyfe/Style). Martha, widow of Edward Stratton Jr., m. 2nd 12 Oct 1703, John Brown. {APP3:165; GVAW V:766; HCW 1:33, 58}

Stratton, Edward the third (d. intestate by 1731), son of Edward Jr. and

Martha (Sheppey) Stratton, m. Anne Batte, dau. of Capt. Henry and Mary (Loud) Batte of Charles City and Prince George cos. Children: Thomas, William and probably Henry. {APP3:166}

Stringer, Elizabeth, servant to Edmund Irby was convicted of having a bastard by a Negro. Fined 1000 lbs. of tobacco and to serve her master two additional years. {CCOB (1687-95):96}

Strong, Thomas apprenticed his dau. Joan in 1677 to Col. Edward Hill for 8 years until 21. {CCOB (1677-79):16\9}

Stroud, John m. Jane/Jean (N). Their children: Olive (b. 17 Feb 1726) and Mary (b. 29 Apr 1730). {BPR:364, 365}

Stroud, John d. by 1739, Hannah Stroud, extx. {PGM:56}

Stroud, Joseph m. bef. 8 Nov 1724, Sarah (N). {PGW&D (1713-1728):126}

Stroud, Joseph m. Mary (N). Their children: William (b. 22 Feb 1729) and David (b. 19 Mar 1731). {BPR:364, 365}

Stroud, Joshua abandoned his wife, leaving the county (Prince George Co.). {PGR:45}

Stroud, William m. Margaret (N). Their son John b. 29 Nov 1726. {BPR:364}

Stubblefield, John d. by 1754. Probable heirs: Simon, John and Edward Stubblefield. {CCCR:129}

Stubblefield, Seth m. (bond dated 15 Jan 1784), Lucy Timberlake Southall. {MB:195}

Stunks, Thomas m. Ann (N). Their children: Mary (b. 12 Aug 1726), Elizabeth (b. 25 Apr 1728) and Prissilla (b. 25 Aug 1731). {BPR:364, 365}

Sturdivant, Biggen (d. ca. 1783), possible son of Llewellyn Sturdivant, m. Sarah (N). Their dau. Elizabeth b. 28 Apr 1732, m. (N) Marder by whom she had a son John). {BPR:365; APP 2:237, 246}
Sturdivant, Chichester of Bristol Parish m. 1st Elizabeth (N) and m. 2nd Katherine (N). Chichester gave to each his sons, John and Thomas, 100 acres in 1728. {PGW&D (1713-1728):179; APP 2:234-5}

Sturdivant, Daniel (b. bef. 1670), son of John and Sarah (Hallom) Sturdivant, m. (N)(N). Children: James, Daniel and probably John. {APP 2:232-4}

Sturdivant, Daniel, son of Daniel Sturdivant, m. Sarah (N). Children: James (b. 18 Jun 1735), Martha (b. 22 Mar 1740), Molly (b. 5 Aug 1744) and Daniel (b. 29 Mar 1746). {APP 2:236; BPR:367, 369}

Sturdivant, Daniel, son of Daniel Sturdivant, d. 21 Jan 1798, had a son William and a son who d. May 1795. {BPR:371; APP 2:238}

Sturdivant, Francis, had a dau. Susanna, b. 13 Mar 1741/2. {BPR:368}

Sturdivant, James, son of Daniel Sturdivant, m. Mary (N). Their children: Frances D. (b. 25 Aug 1724), Mary (b. 18 Aug 1729, m. Daniel Jones), Rebeckah (b. 22 Apr 1733, m. Richard Hayes) and James (b. 28 Mar 1735, m. Elizabeth (N)). Their 3rd son John b. 22 Sep 1766. {BPR:363, 364, 366, 367, 369; APP 2:235}

Sturdivant, James m. Patsy (N). Their children: Nathaniel Birchett (b. 7 Mar 1790) and Robert (b. 9 Jan 1792). {BPR:370}

Sturdivant, Joel (d. by 1777), son of John Sturdivant, mariner, m. Anne (N). In his LWT he named Joel, son of brother John; dec'd brother William and his children, John and Sarah; and Mary Leath, John Leath and Peter Leath, children of sister Catharine Leath. In Anne's LWT (recorded 1787) she named Susanna and Mary Birch, Elizabeth and Martha Holden, Michael Burke, Thomas Butler, Instance Hall and John Cook. {PGM:20; APP2:240; PGR:94; SWBC:215}

Sturdivant, Joel (b. 6 Jun 1763, Dinwiddie Co.), probable son of John and Elizabeth Sturdivant, m. Frances W. (N). Their dau. Mary Anne Thompson, b. 9 Jul 1789. {BPR:370; APP 2:241-2; RWP}

Sturdivant, John m. bef. 14 Sep 1660, Sarah, widow of Samuel Woodward and dau. of Robert Hallom. Sarah d. by 1690. Sons: Daniell, Matthew, Chichester, perhaps John and perhaps Llewellyn. {CCOB (1687-95):96; APP2:234}

Sturdivant, John, son of Chichester Sturdivant, m. Elizabeth (N). Their son William b. 12 Nov 1723. {BPR:363}

Sturdivant, John (d. 18 Feb 1795) m. Mary (N). Their children: Catherine

(b. 23 Oct 1721), John, William, Matthew (b. 29 Apr 1726), Mary (b. 21 Nov 1728) and Joell (b. 18 May 1732). {APP 2:236; BPR:362, 364, 365, 371}

Sturdivant, John Sr. of Bristol Parish (d. 25 Aug 1793), possible son of Daniel, owning land in Prince George Co., Chesterfield Co. and the town of Blandford, m. Ann Thompson. Children: Mary Epes (b. 18 Jan 1750, m. Christopher Manlove, had dau. Mary), Thompson (b. 11 Sep 1752, d. 25 Aug 1793), Ann Isham (b. 10 Oct 1754, d. 11 Sep 1787), John (b. 20 May 1756, d. 18 Feb 1795), Sally (b. 20 Jul 1758), Joel (b. 15 Jan 1764, d. 7 Aug 1801, m. Frances W. Burnett) and William (d. by 1769). {PGM:19; APP2:239; PGR:92, 177; BPR:369, 371; SWBC:215}

Sturdivant, John gave his son James Sturdivant Jr. 30 acres in 1792. {PGR:167}

Sturdivant, Lewellin, possible son of Llewellyn Sturdivant, m. Mary (N). Their children: Elizabeth (b. 19 Nov 1729), Mary (b. 20 Nov 1731) and Isaac (b. 8 Jun 1734). {BPR:364, 366; APP 2:237}

Sturdivant, Matthew, son of John and Sarah (Hallom) Sturdivant, moved to Chowan Precinct, NC with wife Sarah Jul 1716. Their children: Hallom, Henry, Matthew, John Anderson and Abner. {APP 2:234}

Sturdivant, Thomas (d. Nov 1763 in Dinwiddie Co.) m. Mary (N). Their dau. Elizabeth b. 18 Nov 1727. {BPR:364; APP 1:237}

Sturdivant, William (d. by Jan 1769) of Dinwiddie Co. m. Frances (N). Children: James (under 21 in 1769), Robert (under 21 in 1769), William (under 21 in 1769), John (under 21 in 1769), Joel (under 21 in 1769), Mary, Martha, Sarah (under 21 in 1769), Elizabeth (under 21). Brothers: John and Joel. {SWBC:60}

Summerell, Jacob m. Mary (N). Their children: Mary (b. 11 Mar 1730), a son (b. 25 Jun 1727) and William (b. 29 May 1733). {BPR:365, 366}

Suttawhite. See Satterwhite.

Sutton, William (d. by 1693) m. bef. 3 Apr 1689, Martha, widow of Walter Shippey/Shipley and dau. of Col. William Farrar. {CCOB (1687-95):49, 169; GVA (Genealogies of Virginia Families II, Cl-Fi:749); APP1:929-30; HCW 1:1}

Swann, Col. Thomas (d. 16 Sep 1680), son of William Swann (d. 1738), patented land in 1668 which he devised to his son Major Samuel Swann. Thomas may have married 5 times. Possible marriages, m. 1st (N)(N) had a dau. Susanna; m. 2nd (N) Codd by whom he had Samuel, m. 3rd (N)(N), m. 4th? 1662, Anne Browne, widow of Henry Browne, m. 5th Mary who m. 2nd Col. Robert Randall. {CCW&D (1725-31):30; GVAW (Genealogies of Virginia Families) II:41; V:862-3}

Sykes, Bernard d. by 1718, Bernard Sykes, admin. {PGW&D (1713-1728):37}

Sykes, Bernard d. by 1739, Frances Hall and her husband, William Hall, execs. {PGR:65}

Sykes, Bernard (d. ca. 1791) m. (N)(N). Son: Hubbard Sykes. In his LWT Bernard also named Hubbard Williams, son of Drury Williams. {PGR:146}

Sykes, John m. bef. 10 Feb 1722, Frances, sister of John Wyatt and granddau. of Nicholas Wyatt. {PGW&D (1713-1728):87-8}

Symon. See Simon.

Tackett, Bennony d. bef. 1777 in the service of the Rev. War, leaving widow, Lydia, and three small children (unnamed). {Legislative Petitions – Library of VA website}

Talbot, Mary appeared at July Court 1745 to answer complaint of Edward Bryan for having a bastard child. Bryan was ordered to give security to indemnify the parish from maintenance of said child. {CCCR:107}

Tolbert/Tolbot, Matthew m. Mary (N). Their children: Matthew (b. 27 Nov 1729) and James (b. 7 Nov 1732). {BPR:374, 376}

Talbott, Michael m. bef. 3 Jun 1679, (N), widow of John Niblett. Michal Talbott d. by 1717, Michal and Peter Talbott, admins. {CCOB (1677-79):101; PGW&D (1713-1728):32}

Talbott, Michael of Martins Brandon Parish d. by 1718. Heirs: Edward, Elizabeth and Francis Wyatt, children of Capt. Edward Wyatt, exec. {PGW&D (1713-1728):42}

Talbott, Peter m. bef. 22 Oct 1719, Sarah, dau. of James Haley. Children: William, Jane and Sarah. {PGW&D (1713-1728):56}

Talbot, Peter m. Sarah (N). They both d. by 1750 leaving an orphan dau.,. Lucy who chose John Dudley as her guardian. {CCCR:124}

Talley, Henry of Bristol Parish m. bef. 10 Oct 1715, Mary (N). {PGW&D (1713-1728):11}

Tally, Henry m. Judith (N). Their children: Littlepage (b. 13 Jan 1731) and Martha (b. 31 Jan 1733). {BPR:375, 376}

Tally/Talley, John m. Ann (N). Their children: Abraham (b. 2 Sep 1721), Ruth (b. 28 Jan 1723/4) and John (b. 9 Sep 1724). {PGR:179, 373}

Tally, John (d. by Nov 1740, Amelia Co.) of Prince George Co., Bristol Parish, m. Anna (N). Children: John, Henry, Lodowick, William, Allen, Abrams, Sibbella, Ruth and Mary (m. (N) Powell). Grandsons: John Tucker and John Powell. {SWBC:215}

Tally, John m. Judith (N). Their dau. Kezia b. 23 Sep 1730. {BPR:374}

Tally, Richard m. Mary (N). Their son Martin b. 15 Jul 1727. {PGR:179; BPR:373}

Talman, Capt. Henry (d. in London in 1775) of New Kent Co., son of William Talman, the architect, m. bef. 22 May 1726, Anna Eliza Ballard, dau. of Thomas and Elizabeth Ballard. Their children: William (m. Elizabeth Hewlett), Martha (b. 16 Mar 1733), Rebecca (m. 2 Apr 1737 and Henry (b. 26 Dec 1739, d. young). One dau. m. (N) Hewlett and the other dau. m. John Bacon. {CCW&D (1725-31):16-17; GVAW:I:221; IV:774}

Talman, William, son of Capt. Henry and Anna (Ballard) Talman, m. Elizabeth (N). Their children: John (b. 27 Feb 1756), Elizabeth (b. 15 Jan 1758), Anna/Hannah (b. 6 Apr 1760) and James (b. 17 Jun 1767). GVAW IV:774}

Tame, Henry m. (d. 21 Feb 1671/2-73) m. Ann (N). Son: Francis (under the age of 21 in 1673). {CCOB (Fragments):538}

Tapley/Tapler, Adam of Westover Parish, son of Adam Tapley, m. bef. 5 Aug 1714, Elizabeth (N). {PGW&D (1713-1728):4, 27}

Tate, William m. Sarah (N). Their children: Lucia (b. 19 Feb 1733), Nathan (b. 23 Apr 1736), William (b. 26 Aug 1738) and Samuel (b. 29 Oct 1741). {BPR:376, 376, 377}

Tatum family. See APP 3 for much more detail.

Tatum, Epes of Sussex Co. (d. 1789), son of Peter and Mary (Epes) Tatum, m. Lucy (b. 16 Oct 1748), dau. of Richard Carter. Children: Littlebery Epes, (b. 1768), Joel Carter, Peter, Epes and Jane (m. (N) Daniel). {PGR:127-8; APP 3:268, 276-7}

Tatum, Henry m. Mary, probable dau. of Thomas Branch. Their children: Henry (b. 28 May 1721), Frances (b. 6 Jun 1724) and Agnis (b. 14 Oct 1727). {BPR:371, 372, 374; APP 1:368-9}

Tatum/Tatem/Taytem, John (d. by 1688) m. bef. 15 Sep 1673, Elizabeth. Dau.: Elizabeth. Elizabeth, widow of John Tatem m. John Good. {CCOB (Fragments):544; CCOB (1687-95):24, 81}

Tatum, Nathaniel (d. by 1719), son of Nathaniel Tatum and Ellen (Kirk) Tatum, m. (N)(N). Children: Henry, Christopher, Peter and Edward. {PGW&D (1713-1728):57; APP 3:260-1 (*See for more detail.*)}

Tatum, Nathaniel Sr. m. bef. 10 Jan 1718, Elizabeth (N). Their children: Nathaniel, Samuel, Peter and possibly Edward. Nathaniel Tatum Sr. of Bristol Parish gave his sons, Nathaniel, Samuel and Peter, several hundred acres in 1727. {PGW&D (1713-1728):43, 162-3; APP 3:266}

Tatum, Nathaniel, son of Edward Tatum, m. Emilia Elelea Scott, dau. of John and Bethia Scott. Their son Robert b. 30 Jan 1725. {BPR:373; APP 3:268}

Tatem/Tatum, Peter, son of Edward Tatem, m. Mary Eppes, dau. of Littlebury Eppes. Their children: Littleberry (b. 10 Apr 1731), Epes and Peter (b. 27 Jan 1742/3). {APP 1:862-3; APP 3:268; CCCR:78; BPR:375, 377}

Tatum, Robert (b. 30 Jan 1725/6, d. 1759) of Prince George Co., son of Nathaniel and Emilia (Scott) Tatum, m. Cozier/Keziah, dau. of Robert Dobie. Children: Nathaniel (b. 30 Mar 1745), Robert (d. by 1810, m. Amy Gee), Betty/Elizabeth (d. young) and David. {PGR:73; APP 3:276; BPR:378}

Tatum, Samuel Sr. (d. by 1715) m. Mary (N) (d. ca. 1716). In her LWT Mary named sons: Samuel Tatum and Nathaniel Tatum; daus.: Ann Lee and Rebecca Temple. Their children: Samuel, Nathaniel, Ann (m. Hugh Lee), Rebecca (m. William Temple), Mary (m. Richard Carlile) and Barbara (m. Thomas Mitchell). {PGW&D (1713-1728):13, 37; APP

3:261-2, 266-7}

Tatum, Samuel, son of Samuel and Mary Tatum, m. 1st Phoebe (N). Their son John b. 7 Jun 1710. Samuel m. 2nd Elizabeth (N). Their children: William (b. 26 Jun 1717) and Elizabeth (b. 29 Nov 1718). Samuel m. 3rd Mary (N). Their son Francis b. 17 Apr 1721. {BPR:372}

Taylor, Alice d. 17 Aug 1750. {BPR:378}

Taylor, Henry m. (prenuptial contract in 1743), Charlotte, dau. of Rev. Charles Anderson. Henry d. by 1749, owning land in Charles City Co. and Brunswick Co. - Etheldred Taylor and William Taylor, execs. {CCCR:100, 119; GV AT (Generalogies of Virginia Families), I:60}

Taylor, Hubert d. by 1694, Agnes West, wife of Thomas West, admx. {CCOB (1687-95):200}

Taylor, Capt. John (d. 1707-9, Prince George Co., son of Richard and Sarah (Barker) Taylor, m. by 1673, Henrietta Maria/Mary (N). Children: Elizabeth (m. Henry Duke), Frances (m. (N) Greenhill), Henrietta Maria (m. John Hardyman) and Sarah (m. Francis Hardyman, brother of her sister's husband). {CCOB (1687-95):93, 118; VG&B:151}

Taylor, Richard (d. by 1684) m. Sarah, dau. of William and Frances (Ward) Barker. Their children: John, Elizabeth (m. John Hamblin), Frances (m. Richard Bradford) and Richard (d. without issue). Sarah, widow of Richard Taylor, m. 2nd Robert Lucy and m. 3rd Capt. James Bisse. Sarah and Robert Lucy gave their son John Lucy land in 1677/8. {CCOB (1677-79):48; CCOB (1687-95):26-7, 38; VG&B:149-51}

Taylor, Richard res. St. Michaels Parish, Island of Barbadoes, predeceased his wife Elizabeth, who res. on Barbadoes in 1725. {PGW&D (1713-1728):160}

Taylor, Capt. Richard m. (N), dau. of George and Ann (Keith) Walker. Richard gave his son George Keith Taylor land purchased of Instance Hall, in 1790. {PGR:129; GVAW (Genealogies of Virginia Families) V:337}

Taylor, Richard m. Sarah (N). Their children: Elizabeth (b. 29 Jun 1736), George (b. 23 Jun 1738), Richard (b. 26 Dec 1739) Anna Nanney (b. 1 May 1742). {BPR:378}

Taylor, Richard (d. by Jun 1801) of Prince George Co. m. Mary (N).

Children: Richard Field Taylor, Nanny Birchett, Elizabeth Taylor, and Sally Taylor. Granddaus: Martha Douglas Holloway and Mary Taylor Holloway, daus. of Mary Holloway (dec'd. dau.). {SWBC:216}

Taylor, Richard m. (bond dated 13 Oct 1773) Lucy Gregory (widow). {MB:193}

Taylor, Robert m. Mary (N). Their son William b. 22 Aug 1730. {BPR:374}

Tayler, Roger m. Elizabeth (N). Their children: John (b. 12 Nov 1731) and William (b. 16 May 1734). {BPR:375, 376}

Taylor, Thomas of Southwark Parish, Surry Co., planter, gave his daus., Elizabeth (m. John Chamless) and Katherine (m. Edward Holloway Jr.), each a slave in 1728. PGW&D (1713-1728):180}

Taylor, William of the town of Petersburg d. 30 Dec 1792. {BPR:379}

Temple, Eppes m. Elizabeth (N). Their son William Eppes b. 16 Dec 1792. {BPR:379}

Temple, Jacob m. bef. 3 Apr 1786 Mary, widow of Samuel Lee. They res. in SC in 1786. {PGR:84}

Temple, John was brother of Sela Temple (d. by 1788). {PGR:102}

Temple, Peter m. Nanny (N). Their dau. Candace b. 18 Jul 1792. {BPR:379}

Temple, Samuel m. Elizabeth Jr. (N). Their children: Samuel (b. 7 Jan 1720) and Mary (b. 20 Sep 1722). {BPR:372}

Temple, Samuel m. Mary (N). Their children: David (b. 23 Oct 1741) and Jacob (b. 24 Sep 1744). {BPR:377}

Temple, Samuel m. Frances (N). Their children: Elizabeth (b. 1 Apr 1744) and Mary (b. 26 Mar 1745). {BPR:377, 378}

Temple, Thomas had a child b. 4 June 1724, d. 7 Jun 1724. {BPR:372}

Temple, Thomas, son of William and Rebecca (Tatum) Temple, m. Frances (N). Their dau. Rebeckah b. 18 Nov 1732. {BPR:375}

Temple, William Sr. of Bristol Parish m. bef. 7 Sep 1724, Rebecca, dau. of Samuel and Mary Tatum. Children: Thomas, Samuel, William and John. {PGW&D (1713-1728):107; APP 3:266-7}

Temple, William, son of William and Rebecca (Tatum) Temple, m. Elizabeth Chambliss, dau. of Henry and Mary Chambliss. Their children: Elizabeth (b. 7 Mar 1725), Amy (b. 3 Jun 1731) and Lucretia (b. 16 Sep 1744). {BPR:373, 375, 377; APP 3:275}

Tench, Henry m. Nancy (N). Their dau. Mary Tench or Mary Henry Tench, b. 12 Mar 1792. {BPR:378}

Tench, Henry m. bef. 11 Oct 1791 Sarah, widow of William Gary of Martins Brandon Parish. {PGR:161}

Tenheart, James m. Mary (N). Their dau. Lucy b. 10 May 1723. {BPR:372}

Terrell, Jessee, son of Pleasants Terrell of Caroline Co. m. 6th da., 3rd mo., 1787, Mary Ladd, dau. of Amos Ladd of Charles City Co. with consent of parents, at a meeting house in Charles City Co. {HMM:71}

Terrel, William m. 1st (N)(N) and m. 2nd (marriage contract dated Aug 1749) Mary Collier, widow of William Collier. William and Mary Collier were parents of Charles (m. Milly (N)), Mildred, William and Elizabeth (m. William Christian). William Terrrell was father of Richmond, Rebecca, Martha and William Terrell. {CCCR:117, 118, 152, 157}

Thacker, John m. Phelis (N). Their son William b. 10 Nov 1730. {BPR:374}

Thomas, Charles d. by 1712 leaving a widow Anne Thomas of Waynoak Parish, sister of Richard Pigeon. {PGW&D (1710-1713): 19}

Thomas, Elizabeth was presented in 1739 for having a bastard child. {CCCR:86}

Thomas, Isham (d. 1789) of Martins Brandon Parish, brother of Hubbard and David Thomas and Sally Howell (had a dau. Ann). {PGR:126}

Thomas, Martha was presented in 1741 for having a bastard child. Charges dismissed. {CCCR:93, 96}

Thomas, Peter m. Elizabeth (N). Their children: Peter (b. 2 Dec 1734) and David (b. 24 Dec 1740). {BPR:376, 377}

Thomas, Philip m. bef. 3 Dec 1688 Anne, widow of Thomas Booth. {CCOB (1687-95):35}

Thomas, Richard m. Mary (N). Their children: Mary (b. 12 Mar 1739/40) and Catharine (b. 3 May 1742). {BPR:377}

Thomas, Susanna, dau. of Elizabeth Thomas was presented for having a bastard child. Her mother paid the bond. {CCCR:90}

Thompson/Thomson, Charles m. Frances (N). Their son John b. 28 Aug 1740. {CCCR:90; BPR:377}

Thompson, Ellianore, servant to Edward Braine, was convicted in 1688 of having a bastard child. {CCOB (1687-95):25}

Thompson, Henry (d. ca. 1720) m. Sarah (N). Sons: Humphrey, John and Richard. {PGW&D (1713-1728):62}

Thompson/Tomson, Henry d. by 1769 leaving an orphan, Flanders Thompson/Tomson. {CCCR:18, 29}

Thompson, Dr. James (d. 1746-7) of Henrico Co. m. bef. 12 Sep 1726, Mary, widow of William Randolph and dau. of Col. Francis and Ann (Isham) Epes. Dau.: Anne (b. 3 Feb 1726). Son-in-law (*step-son*) Isham Randolph. {PGW&D (1713-1728):149; APP1:868; HCW 2:37; BPR:373}

Thompson, James d. by 1756, m. Sarah (N). Son: James. {CCCR:137}

Thompson, James gave his dau. Sarah Thompson a 4 year old Negro girl, Nancy, in 1769. {CCCR:20}

Thompson, James m. Mary (N). Their dau. Ann b. 3 Feb 1726. {BPR:374}

Thompson, James (d. 1773) m. (N)(N). Children: Sarah, Herman, James, Mary, Elizabeth, Martha, Thomas, Ruth and George. Son-in-law: William Emory. {CCCR:52}
Thomson, Mary was presented in 1741 for having a bastard child. {CCCR:90}

Thompson, Perkins m. bef. 12 Jun 1739, Ann (N). {CCCR:150; PGR:46}

Thompson, William, son of (N) and Mary Thompson, m. by 1761 Anne (N). Dau.: Eleanor. His mother, Mary, m. 2ⁿᵈ (N) Drinkard. In 1761 Anne Thompson made a complaint against her husband, William Thompson. William Thompson d. by 1802, Eleanor Everidge, admx. (probably the dau.) {CCCR:38, 152; PGM:11}

Thomson, William d. by 1750, Ling Thomson, exec. {CCCR:120}

Thorn, Richard m. Elizabeth (N). Their dau. Willmoth b. 10 Jun 1734. {BPR:376}

Thweatt, Burrell, son of Miles and Sarah (Green) Thweatt, m. Jane Manson, dau. of John and Martha Manson. They res. Dinwiddie Co. Their children: Priscilla, Elizabeth, Rebecca, Ann, Susanna (m. Thomas Rives, moved to Chatham Co., NC), Mary, Burwell Green and John Manson. {APP 1:260}

Thweat, Drury m. Elizabeth (N). Their children: David (b. 27 Oct 1741), Elizabeth (b. 10 Feb 1742/3), Edith (b. 25 Apr 1745) and Frankee (bapt. 17 Feb 1750). {BPR:377, 378}

Thweat, Edward m. Mary (N). Their children: Mary (b. 17 Sep 1745) and possibly William* (b. 12 Aug 1742). {BPR:378, 391} * BPR shows Willim Wheat, son of Edward and Mary – perhaps miscopied.

Thweat, Henry m. Hannah (N). Their children: George (b. 7 Mar 1719/20), John (b. 12 Apr 1722), Obedience (b. 15 Sep 1724) and Elizabeth (b. 20 Aug 1727). {BPR:371, 372, 373, 374}

Thweatt, James m. bef. 3 Jun 1693, Mary (N). Mary Thweatt of Prince George Co. d. by 1712. In her LWT she named children: James, Henry, Elizabeth, Archer (dau.), John, Judith and Mary; grandsons: James Thweatt, James Studevant, Edward Thweet, James Parram, Miles Thweet and Matthew Parram. {CCCR:73; PGW&D (1710-1713):27-8}

Thweat, James (d. 1717) m. 24 Nov 1701, Mrs. Judith Soane, sister of Samuel Soane and Martha Buzby of Prince George Co. {HMM:92 (Henrico Co. Court records); GVAW IV:231; HCW 1:179; PGW&D (1713-1728):30}
Thweat, James m. Mary (N). Their dau. Mary b. 28 Feb 1724. {BPR:372}

Thweat, James m. Ann (N). Their children: Frances (b. 25 Dec 1724), Christian (dau., b. 9 Feb 1729/30), Martha (b. 29 Sep 1731) and Elizabeth (b. 5 Aug 1734). {BPR:373, 375, 376}

Thweat, James m. Sarah (N). Their children: John (b. 12 Jun 1745), Tabitha (b. 27 May 1749) and James (b. 3 Apr 1752). {BPR:378}

Thweatt, John (d. by 1759) m. Judith (N). Children: John (b. 11 Jan 1720, d. 10 Jun 1722), James (b. 20 May 1722, predeceased his father, left sons John, James, Thomas, and Peterson), William (b. 11 Sep 1728), Elizabeth (b. 11 Mar 1724, m. (N) Burchett), John (b. 22 Aug 1726), Martha (m. Thomas Goodwyn, had dau. Amy), Mary and Judith (b. 19 Jun 1743). Grandchildren: John, James and Peterson Thweatt, sons of James. {PGR:69; BPR:371, 372, 373, 374, 377; GVAW (Genealogies of Virginia Families) II:727; SWBC:216}

Thweat/Thwet, Miles m. Sarah Green. Their children: Burrell (b. 4 Jul 1732), William (b. 14 Sep 1734) and Alick (b. 29 Jan 1741/2). {BPR:375, 376, 377; APP 1:260}

Thweatt, Miles (d. 1766-7), brother of William Thweatt, m. (N). Children: Martha (m. (N) Wilkins), James and Ellick. {PGR:174}

Thweatt, Thomas d. by 1786. His widow Betty, m. 2nd ca. 1786 Nathaniel Dunn of Sussex Co. {PGR:88, 121}

Tillman, (N) m. Susannah (N). In her LWT dated 1716) Susannah named sons: Thomas Parram, George Tillman and John Tillman; and daus.: Jane Robinson, Christian Abernathy; and grandchildren: Mary Bethell and Robert Abernathy. {PGW&D (1713-1728):23}

Tillman, George m. bef. 10 Jan 1711, Mary, dau. of William Avery. Their children: Tabitha (b. 14 Sep 1720), William (b. 21 May 1723) and Sarah (b. 8 Oct 1731). {PGW&D (1710-1713): 15; PGM:56; BPR:371, 372, 375}

Tillman, John m. Margret (N). Their son John b. 20 Apr 1734. {BPR:376}

Tillman, Robert – His children were bound out in 1738. {PGR:18}

Tillman, Roger d. by 1717, son: George. {PGW&D (1713-1728):34}

Tillman/Tilmon, Roger m. Mary (N). Their children: George (b. 21 Jan

1725) and Elizabeth (b. 15 Nov 1726). {BPR:373, 374}

Timberlake, Francis d. by 1760 leaving orphans, James and Elizabeth, who chose Francis Timberlake [*their brother*?] as their guardian. Francis and Catherine Timberlake were execs. of the will of Francis Timberlake. {CCCR:143, 149}

Timberlake, John m. (bond dated 20 May 1788) Susanna Christian, dau. of Gideon Christian. {MB:193}

Timberlake, Richard m. by Jun 1748, Susanna (N). {CCCR:116}

Tidmarsh, James (d. 1718), brother of Richard Tidmarsh, m. Elizabeth (N). Son: Richard. {PGW&D (1713-1728):40}

Titmarsh, Jeremiah d. by 1804 leaving a widow, Mary and son Richard. {PGM:33}

Titmarsh, John d. by 1718, Elizabeth Tidmarsh, extx. {PGW&D (1713-1728):41}

Tidmarsh, John d. by 1803, leaving a widow Jemima who m. Henry Timmons. {PGM:24}

Tidmarsh/Tidmust, Richard of Bristol Parish (d. ca. 1725) m. Elizabeth (N). Children: John (b. 28 Dec 1721), Sarah, Mary and Elizabeth. Cousins: Richard Tidmarsh, William Stainback and John Burge. {PGW&D (1713-1728):129-30}

Tidmarsh, Richard d. by 1738. Elizabeth Tidmarsh, one of the orphans chose Thomas Poythress as her guardian. {PGR:11}

Tippett, John m. bef. 29 Jan 1660/1, Winifred Rosser (still in her minority). {CCOB (1658-61):258}

Tomlinson, John m. Elizabeth (N). Their dau. Jane b. 16 Jul 1732. {BPR:375}

Tomlinson, Richard m. bef. 9 Jan 1721, Elinor, widow of Richard Walpole. {PGW&D (1710-1713):32; PGW&D (1713-1728):1, 21, 98; GVAT (Genealogies of Virginia Families) IV:25}

Toney, Betty was mother of Margaret and Elizabeth, to be bound out in 1738. {PGR:35}

Torborn, Dr. William m. bef. 1 Apr 1768, Mary Ann, dau. of Richard (?) and Mary (Cocke) Eppes. Their son Andrew m. Elizabeth Gilliam Arthur. {APP1:872, 917-8; CCCR:8}

Totty, Thomas m. Elizabeth (N). Their son Thomas b. 5 Apr 1730. {BPR:374}

Totty, William m. Mary (N). Their children: William (b. 5 Dec 1725), William (b. 15 Mar 1727) and Margret (b. 30 Feb 1732). {BPR:373, 374, 376}

Toudress, Henry m. Elizabeth (N). Their dau. Anne b. 15 Aug 1741. {BPR:377}

Towler, Benjamin (b. c1752, Charles City Co.) moved to Dinwiddie Co. where he was drafted into the Rev. War. In 1832 he was living in Rutherford Co., TN. {RWP}

Traylor, Edmond m. Elisabeth (N). Their children: Phebe (b. 2 Sep 1725) and Blanch (b. 17 Sep 1732). {BPR:373, 375}

Traylor, Edward m. Mary (N). Their son William b. 12 Jun 1733. {BPR:376}

Traylor, George m. Elizabeth (N). Their dau. Judith b. 8 Mar 1733. {BPR:376}

Traylor, John m. Martha (N). Their dau. Judith (b. 6 Mar 1727. {BPR:374}

Traylor, John (d. 7 Jun 1729) m. Mary (N). Their children: Archer (b. 20 Apr 1729), Wilmut (b. 19 Aug 1731) and Lucretia (b. 16 Aug 1734). {BPR:374, 375, 376}

Traylor, William d. by 1678. His widow m. 2nd Emanuel Alberry. {CCOB 1676-79):61}

Traylor, William m. Sarah (N). Their children: Ann (b. 23 Aug 1734) and Martha (b. 18 Oct 1741). {BPR:376, 377}

Tree, George (d. by 1742) m. bef. Aug 1741, Elizabeth, widow of John

Wright. {CCCR:92}///

Treham/Trehan, Francis m. bef. 28 Feb 1659/60, Elizabeth, widow of (1) Peter Moyles, (2) Nicholas Polle and (3) Thomas Madder. {CCOB (1655-58): 56; CCOB (1661-64):371, 391}

Trower, Samuel m. (bond dated 19 Jun 1787), Alice, dau. of Gideon Christian. {MB:194}

Tucker, Abram m. Helenour (N). Their son Miles b. 16 Feb 1741/2. {BPR:377}

Tucker, Daniel (d. by 1739) m. Elizabeth (N). Their son Nevil b. 25 Apr 1730. {PGR:63; BPR:374}

Tucker, David m. (contract dated 1789) Frances Jackson, proved by the oathes of Nathaniel Epes, Ralph Jackson & Daniel Tucker {W&M, Vol. 23, No. 3 (Jan., 1915): 216}

Tucker, Francis had a son John (b. by 1712). {PGM:2}

Tucker, Francis m. Anne (N). Their children: Amy (b. 12 May 1721), Francis (b. 1 Nov 1723), John (b. 25 Jun 1726), Ann (b. 19 Feb 1729 and Martha (b. 21 Feb 1732). {BPR:371, 372, 373, 374, 375}

Tucker, Francis, the Elder, of Bristol Parish (d. ca. 1723) m. bef. 10 Jun 1718, Mary (N). Children: Francis, John, Henry, Abram and Mathew. {PGW&D (1713-1728):35, 96-7}

Tucker, George m. Frances (N). Their children: Hanna (b. 30 Mar 1731) and Robert (b. 3 Dec 1733). {BPR:375, 376}

Tucker, Henry m. Elisabeth (N). Their children: Elizabeth (b. 2 Sep 1729) and a dau. b. 8 May 1731. {BPR:374, 375}

Tucker, Henry m. Amy (N). Their dau. Frances (b. 25 Apr 1733). {BPR: 299, 376}

Tucker, James m. Mary (N). Their children: Micael (b. 11 Jul 1721), Amy (b. 23 Aug 1726), Lucretia (b. 5 Jun 1729) and Warner (b. 15 Apr 1732). {BPR:371, 374, 375}

Tucker, John m. Catharine (N). Their son Drury b. 24 Sep 1719. {BPR:371}

Tucker, John Jr. m. bef. 13 Jan 1723, Ann (N). Their children: Sara (b. 12 Jan 1722) and Francis (b. 3 Jan 1726). {PGW&D (1713-1728):97; BPR:371, 373}

Tucker, John m. Mary (N). Their children: David (b. 25 Sep 1730), Isham (b. 1 Feb 1732), Joseph (b. 14 Nov 1732) and probably Abraham (b. 22 Jan 1734). {BPR:374, 375, 376}

Tucker, Joseph of Prince George and Dinwiddie cos. m. Lucretia, dau. of Robert and Martha (Jefferson) Wynne of Surry Co. They sold land in Prince George Co. in 1718. Their children: Lucretia (b. 15 Aug 1731), Martha (m. Benjamin Bell), Robert (m. Mary Green), Joel (d. by 1772, m. Judith (N)) and Mary (b. 26 May 1745). {APP 1:379-80, 421-2; BPR:375, 377}

Tucker, Joseph m. Martha (N). Their son David b. 24 Dec 1729. {BPR:374}

Tucker, Joseph d. by 1789. {W&M, Vol. 23, No. 3 (Jan., 1915): 216}

Tucker, Joss:/Joshua m. Martha (N). Their son Robert b. 3 Oct 1720. {BPR:371}

Tucker, Nathaniel m. Katheren (N). Their son Nathaniel b. 20 Feb 1723. {BPR:372}

Tucker, Robert m. bef. 4 Feb 1694, Elizabeth (N). {CCOB (1687-95):199}

Tucker, Robert m. Martha (N). Their children: Anne (b. 29 Aug 1720), Joseph (b. 22 Jun 1723) and Daniel (b. 31 Jan 1725). {BPR:371, 372, 373}

Tucker, Robert m. Frances (N). Their children: Martha (b. 10 Jul 1727), Frances (b. 11 Mar 1730) and William (b. 15 Apr 1733). {BPR:374, 375, 376}

Tucker, Robert of Sussex Co. m. bef. 6 Nov 1788, Sarah (N). {PGR:132}

Tucker, Robert of the town of Petersburg d. by 1790, Ann Tucker, extx. {PGR:145}

Tucker, Thomas m. Elizabeth (N). Their son Thomas b. 30 Mar 1728. {BPR:374}

Tucker, William m. Elizabeth (N). Their children: Susanna (b. 19 Apr 1721), George (b. 4 Sep 1723) and Daniel (b. 29 Jan 1725). {PGW&D (1713-1728):107; BPR:372, 373}

Tunks, Thomas m. Anne (N). Their son Thomas b. 29 Oct 1741. {BPR:377}

Turberville, John b. ca. 1649. {CCOB (Fragments):529}

Turbevill/Turbifeild, John (d. by 1688) m. Susan, probable dau. of Walter Vaux (d. by 1678). Susan m. 2nd John Andrews. Mary, orphan of John Turbevill chose William Gardner as her guardian in 1694. {CCOB (1687-95):19}

Turbyfield, Richard [or Robert?] of Bristol Parish m. bef. 10 Jun 1714, Ann (N). {PGW&D (1713-1728):2, 3}

Turnbull, Robert, nephew of Charles Turnbull of Dinwiddie, m. 1st 16 Sep 1770, his step-sister, Mary Cole, dau. of Roscow and Rachel (Robinson) Cole and sister of William Cole. Mary d. spring of 1789 leaving him with a large family of young children. Children: Charles (b. 8 Dec 1772, d. by 1811, m. Nancy Marshall), Anne (b. 20 Jan 1775, m. Benjamn Harrison), Thomas Craefurd (b. 20 Sep 1776), Robert (b. 21 Dec 1778, d. 17 Dec 1839 in Brunswick Co., m. 24 Dec 1801, Elizabeth Jones Stith), William Cole (b. 31 Oct 1780, d. 11 Nov 1780), Mary Cole (b. 14 May 1782, d. 1860, m. Armistead Burwell of Dinwiddie Co.), Margaret (b. 11 Dec 1783, d. 6 May 1836, m. 13 Nov 1803, Edward Randolph) and William (b. 12 Apr 1786, d. by 1803). Robert Turnbull m. 2nd in 1790, Mrs. Sarah Buchanan, relict of a Gentleman of Maryland. In Oct 1791, Robert petitioned for a divorce from Sarah, his 2nd wife. Robert d. 1804. {Legislative Petitions – Library of VA website; APP 1:720-1}

Turner, Arthur and Tabitha Turner d. by 1762. {CCCR:155}

Turner, Edward d. by 1737 leaving an orphan son William to whom was appointed a guardian, Thomas Jackson. {CCCR:81}

Turner, John d. by 1694, Jone Turner, widow and extx. {CCOB (1687-95):206}

Turner, Joseph m. Elizabeth (N). Their children: John (b. 11 Dec 1725), Holenberry (son, 14 Jun 1728), Ann (b. 8 Nov 1730), Joseph (b. 2 Apr

1733) and Elizabeth (b. 6 Oct 1735). {BPR:373, 374, 376}

Turner, Mathew d. by 1690 leaving widow, Mary. {CCOB (1687-95):86}

Turner, William m. Anne (N). Their dau. Elizabeth b. 3 Sep 1745. {BPR:378}

Tuttle, William d. by 1688 leaving widow, Jane. {CCOB (1687-95):29}

Twitty, Thomas m. bef. 14 Mar 1738, Mary (N), admx. of Henry Wyatt. Thomas and Mary were parents of Rebeckah (b. 5 Sep 1740). {PGR:38, 55; BPR:377}

Tyas, (N) m. bef. 22 Jul 1776, Rebecca, dau. of William and Silvia Bonner. Probable children: Pamela and Edwin. {PGR:112}

Tye, Allen m. bef. 1 Feb 1727, Mary (N). Their children: Frances (b. 16 Mar 1724), William (b. 10 May 1730), Agnis (b. 9 Mar 1732), Solomon (b. 20 Mar 1734) and Anderson (b. 11 Mar 1741/2). {PGW&D (1713-1728):176; BPR:373, 374, 376, 377}

Tye, Lambert (d. 1728) m. Mary (N). Children: Jeane (m. (N) Overbee), Allen and Elizabeth (m. (N) Blackburn). {CCW&D (1725-31):28}

Tye, Richard m. Joyce, widow of Chainey Boyce and d. by 1659 leaving children, Elizabeth and others. {CCOB (1658-61):203; CCOB (1661-64):355}

Tyree, Catharine was presented in 1762 for having a bastard child. {CCCR:158}

Tyree, Francis (d. by 1754) m. bef. Jul 1740, Mary (N). Mary Tyree, extx. Their son Francis d. testate 1769. {CCCR:19, 88, 127}

Tyree, William d. by 1740, Francis Tyree, exec. {CCCR:87}

Underhill, Howel of Sussex Co. m. Nancy (N). Their son John b. 3 Mar 1792. {BPR:382}

Unckle, Lewis had a dau. Anne who d. Sep 1792. {BPR:382}

Urvin, Nathaniel m. bef. 13 Feb 1715, Elizabeth (N). {PGW&D (1713-1728):14}

Vaden. See also Vodin.

Vaden/Vauden/Voden, Henry m. Martha (N). Their children: Anne (b. 19 Jan 1722), Henry (b. 6 Feb 1724/5), Susannah (b. 19 Nov 1728) and Burrell (b. 2 Sep 1733). {BPR:379, 380}

Vaiden, Isaac of New Kent Co. m. bef. 29 Dec 1771, Elizabeth (N). {CCCR:36}

Valentine, Charles, a Mulatto, son of Martha Harris was bound to Lewellin Eppes in 1748. {CCCR:111}

Valentine, Edward, son of Mary Valentine, was bound to Thomas Coley in 1748. {CCCR:118}

Valentine, Elizabeth had a son James, b. 27 Aug 1733. {BPR:381}

Vodin, Henry m. Elizabeth (N). Their son Henry b. 12 Sep 1694. {BPR:380}

Vodin, William m. Frances (N). Their dau. Frances b. 18 Sep 1728. {BPR:380}

Vandivan, John of Bristol Parish (d. by 1728) m. Mary (N). Children: Elizabeth (m. (N) Rosser), Frances (m. [John] Leadbetter), Margaret (m. [Howard] Owen) and Mary. {PGW&D (1713-1728):154}

Vaughan, (N) (d. by 1768, leaving widow Elizabeth and son Thomas. {HCDB (1750-1774):174}

Vaughan, Abraham/Abram (b. Jan 1764, Amelia Co., d. 31 Jul 1836) entered the Rev. War from Dinwiddie Co. He m. 30 Apr 1832, Margaret S. Gold, Wilson Co., TN, where Abraham moved in 1807. {RWP}

Vaughan, Absalom (d. 15 Apr 1839, Dinwiddie Co.) m. ca. 1 Oct 1788, Martha Vaughan, spinster (d. 18 Sep 1843) by Pastor Harrison in the Episcopal Church, Dinwiddie Co. Henry Vaughan was a surety on the marriage bond. Their eldest child was born ca. 1790. Children: Rebecca (m. Hartwell Ivy), Mary (m. Josiah Farlow), and Hartwell Vaughan (went west), only living children at the time of Martha's death. {RWP}

Vaughan, Benjamin, son of William S. Vaughan, late of Charles City Co., m. 6th da., 5th mo., 1794, Margaret Ladd, dau. of John Ladd of the same co. Relations at wedding: Polley Ladd, Martha Charles, Elizabeth

Hargrave, Meriam Crew, Elizabeth Crew, John Ladd, Shadrick Vaughan, Benjamin Ladd, William Ladd, Elizabeth Ladd. {HMM:87}

Vaughan, Daniel m. Elizabeth (N). Their children: Joss/Joshua (b. 14 Dec 1722/3), William (b. 14 Aug 1724), Isham (b. 4 Feb 1725), Ann (b. 15 Dec 1727) and Peter (b. 28 Sep 1730). {BPR:379, 380}

Vaughan, Daniel m. Ann (N). Their children: Ann (b. 10 Oct 1732), Mary (b. 1 Jan 1734/5) and Phebe (b. 12 Nov 1743). {BPR:380, 381}

Vaughan, Elizabeth married by a priest to a man not of the Society of Friends ca. May 1780. {HMM:59}

Vaughan, Ephraim b. ca. 1768, Dinwiddie Co. {RWP}

Vaughan, Drury m. Susannah (N). Their dau. Mary Ann Elizabeth, b. 21 Apr 1793. {BPR:382}

Vaughan, Enoch m. Mary (N). Their son Robert Winn, b. 3 Apr 1793. {BPR:382}

Vaughan, Henry m. Elizabeth (N). Their son Ezekiel b. 29 Dec 1750. {BPR:381}

Vaughan, Isham m. Temperance (N). Their dau. Wilmot b. 3 Mar 1732. {BPR:380}

Vaughan, James of Bristol Parish, m. bef. 14 Apr 1719, Ann (N). James owned land adjoining Richard Vaughan, Daniel Vaughan, John Vaughan and William Vaughan. {PGW&D (1713-1728):47}

Vaughan, James d. by 1738. {HCW 2:4}

Vaughan, Jesse (b. c1759, d. 1836-8 in Brunswick Co.) m. Sarah (N) (b. ca. 1768). Their dau., Patience b. ca. 1803. Jesse d. leaving two children, unnamed. {RWP}

Vaughan, John m. Elinor (N). Their dau. Abigaell d. 23 Feb 1720/1, in her 6th year. {BPR:379}

Vaughan, Joshua m. Sarah (N). Their children: James (b. 22 Jan 1745/6) and Jessee (bapt. 28 Apr 1751). {BPR:381}

Vaughan, Morris/Maurice m. Rebecca (N). Their children: Henry (b. 14

Dec 1734), David (b. 1 Jan 1741/2), Martha (b. 10 Mar 1743/4) and Jemina (bapt. 21 Jun 1752). {BPR:380, 381, 382}

Vaughan, Nathanael m. Amith (N). Their dau. Ruth b. 28 Dec 1741. {BPR:381}

Vaughan, Nicholas (d. by 1739) m. bef. 13 Jul 1719, Ann (N). Their children: Luis (b. 20 Feb 1719), Abraham (b. 16 Mar 1721/2), Elizabeth (b. 18 Apr 1727) and Nicolas (b. 20 Feb 1728). Ann m. 2nd Henry Fitz. {BPR:379, 380; PGR:51; PGW&D (1713-1728):52}

Vaughan, Peter m. Anne (N). Their son Abram b. 11 Mar 1741/2. {BPR:381}

Vaughan, Rabley (d. 1770-2) m. bef. 22 Sep 1726, Mary, dau. of Edward and Mary Cocke. Children: William, Sarah (m. Brothers Finch), Martha (m. (N) Hill), Hannah (m. (N) Willcox) and Nance (m. John Nance). {CCW&D 1725-31:14, 18, 33; CCCR:12, 44}

Vaughan, Richard m. Alice/Alce (N). Their children: James (b. 23 Jan 1721/2), Martha (b. 18 Nov 1724) and Richard (b. 16 Oct 1726). {BPR:379, 380}

Vaughan, Robert m. Martha (N). Their children: Pheboe (b. 18 May 1732) and Nicholas (b. 21 Nov 1734). {BPR:380, 381}

Vaughan, Salathiel m. Anne (N). Their children: Phebe (b. 23 Nov 1743), William (b. 16 Feb 1744/5) and David (bapt. 4 Mar 1749/50). {BPR:381}

Vaughan, Samuel d. by 1718, Sarah Vaughn, admx. {PGW&D (1713-1728):39}

Vaughan, Samuel m. Margrett (N). Their children: Sarah (b. 29 Jul 1735), Sylvana (b. 1 Aug 1742) and Silvester (b. 14 Mar 1744/5). {BPR:381}

Vaughan, Samuel m. bef. 13 Dec 1789, Ann, dau. of William Williams. {PGR:128, 155}

Vaughan, Samuel d. by 1805 leaving a widow (N). Children: Samuel, Nancy, Martha (m. John Blackwell), Thomas, Epes and Williamson. {PGM:33}

Vaughan, Sarah had a son James Thompson b. 24 Sep 1726. {BPR:380}

Vaughan, Susanna had a son Littlebury, bound out in 1760. {HCW 2:103}

Vaughan, Thomas of James City Co. m. bef. 3 Sep 1729, Martha, dau. of Mary Cocke. {CCW&D1725-35}

Vaughan, Thomas m. Elizabeth (N). Their son Thomas b. 12 Jul 1742. {BPR:381}

Vaughan, William, age 48 in 1673 and Sarah Vaughan, age 39 in 1674. {CCOB (Fragments):518}

Vaughan, William m. Ann (N). Their dau. Elizabeth b. 14 Sep 1721. {BPR:379}

Vaughan, William m. Prissilla (N). Their children: Peare (b. 15 Mar 1722), William (5 Aug 1724), James (b. 6 Mar 1725), Susannah (b. 25 Dec 1727) and Mary (b. 12 Nov 1732). {BPR:379, 380}

Vaughan, William m. Mable (N). Their children: Abigal (b. 15 Jan 1729), Caleb (b. 25 Jan 1731), Abner (b. 25 Feb 1733) and Mabel (b. 12 Jan 1740). {BPR:380, 381}

Vaughan, William m. bef. 14 Feb 1734, Julia (N). {BPR:380}

Vaughan, William m. Mary (N). Their children: Anne (b. 7 Jan 1735) and Anne (b. 20 Jan 1741/2). {BPR:381}

Vaughan, William m. Ellinor (N0. Their dau. Mary b. 26 Jul 1752. {BPR:382}

Vaughan, William m. (bond dated 13 Sep 1768), Ann Dancy, dau. of John Dancy. {CCCR:12; MB:195}

Vaughan, William Shields (d. by 1797) of Charles City Co. m. (N)(N). Children: Frances Ann (m. ca. 1779, outside the Society of Friends), Shields Jr. (m. ca. 1779 outside the Society of Friends) and Hannah (had a bastard child ca. 1797). {HMM:58, 81}

Vaughan, William Shields, son of William Vaughan of New Kent Co., m. 4th da., 9th mo., 1750, Hannah Crew, dau. of Andrew Crew of Charles City Co. Children of Wm. Shields and Hannah Vaughan: James

Vaughan, b. 27/8/1751, d. 12/3/--; Shields (b. 30/9/1753, m. ca. 1779 outside the Society of Friends), Elizabeth (b. 18/9/1755), Francis Ann (b. 9/8/1757, m. ca. 1779 outside the Society of Friends); William (b. 10/5/1759), Molly (b. 9/10/1761), Benjamin (b. 29/9/1763), Sarah (b. 30/10/1765), Hannah (b. 6/12/1767, had a bastard chil ca. 1797), Shadrack (b. 5/6/1770), James (the second of that name. b. 20/3/1773) and Ann (b. 28/4/1775). Hannah Vaughan, mother to the above children d. 1778. {HMM:26, 58, 64, 81}

Vaughan, Willis (LWT dated 7 Jul 1819) m. Francis (N). Children: Jerdin J., Rebecca and Robert. {Dinwiddie Co. GenWeb}

Vernon, Walter d. by 1740, Robert Brooks, admin. {CCCR:90}

Verell, John Jr. m. Martha (N). Their dau. Sally Newsum b. 15 Apr 1792. {BPR:382}

Vincent/Vinson, John (d. by 1727) of Brunswick Co. m. Mary (N). Children: Thomas, John, Mary and the child "wife is big with." Mary m. 2nd Walter Long. {PGR:3; PGW&D (1713-1728):174}

Vincent, Sarah and her son Thomas Vincent leased 100 acres in Bristol Parish in 1713. {PGW&D (1710-1713):34}

Waddill, Jacob d. by 1750, Ann Waddill, extx. {CCCR:120}

Waddill, Pridgin m. bef. Dec 1737, Martha, widow of Thomas Hales and dau. of Richard and Mary Dennis. {APP3:48, 56-7; CCW&D 1725-31:2; HCW 1:22-3, 154, 156; CCCR:81}

Waddill, William m. by Jun 1743, Ann Routon, widow of John Routon. {CCCR:99}

Wade/Waid, Benjamin of Martins Brandon Parish m. Naomie (N). Naomi d. 1660, buried 22 Oct 1660. Benjamin was father of Elias (bapt. 12 Aug 1660). {CCOB 1658-61):270}

Wade, Elias m. bef. 3 Oct 1693, Mary. Elias and Mary were execs. of the estate of Margaret Roome (d. by 1693). {CCOB (1687-95):159}

Wade, Joseph m. bef. Oct 1738, Sarah (N). {CCCR:83}

Wade, Mary d. by 1762, Joab Mountcastle, exec. {CCCR:158}

Waid. See Wade.

Walker, Alexander, son of David and Mary Walker m. Rebecca, dau. of Edward Broadnax. They had a son, Edward Broadnax Walker. Rebecca, widow of Alexander m. 2nd Henry Dolony of Mecklenburg Co. {GVAT (Genealogies of Virginia Families) II: 745-8; GVAW (Genealogies of Virginia Families) I:466}

Walker, Alexander, son of [James] and Locke Walker, m. by 1773, (N)(N). Daus.: Elizabeth and Lockey. {CCCR:63}

Walker, Anthony m. Anne (N). Their children: Sarah (b. 16 Feb 1744/5) and Robert (b. 16 Aug 1747). Anthony d. Sep 1747 (a son or the father?). {BPR:392, 393}

Walker, Benjamin, son of [James] and Locke Walker, m. (N)(N). Dau. Elizabeth. {CCCR:63}

Walker, David of Dinwiddie Co., probable son of David Walker, m. bef. 24 Sep 1765, Mary, dau. of Robert Munford. Children: Alexander (b. 3 Oct 1727), Robert (b. 10 Oct 1729), David and Mary (twins, b. 6 Mar 1731) and Freeman (b. 3 Sep 1734). {GVAT (Genealogies of Virginia Families II): 733, 748; BPR:386, 388, 390}

Walker, Edward (d. by Nov 1781) of Dinwiddie Co. m. Priscilla (N). Children: Nathaniel and John. Brother: Robert Walker. {SWBC:61}

Walker, Edward m. (bond dated 28 Dec 1795) Nancy Lored. {MB:193}

Walker, Freeman, son of David and Mary (Munford) Walker, m. Frances Belfield. Their children: Alexander, Thomas Belfield and Frances (b. 1764, m. 1786, Francis Webb). {GVAT (Genealogies of Virginia Families II): 733-4}

Walker, Freeman, son of [James] and Locke Walker, m. by Jun 1761, Sarah Minge, dau. of George Minge. Freeman removed to Richmond Co., GA. Their children: Lockey (m. William B. Clayton of New Kent Co.), Jane, Wyatt (b. 1762, d. Dec 1832), George, Robert, Valentine and Freeman. {CCCR:63, 149; GVAW I:469-70}

Walker, Henry (d. by 1772), son of [James] and Locke Walker, m. (N)(N). Dau.: Sarah. {CCCR:63}

Walker, James d. by 1745, owning land in Charles City Co. and

Brunswick Co., Henry Walker and Capt. Edward Brodnax, execs. Orphans of James Walker: Richardson and Alexander Walker, chose Edward Brodnax as their guardian. In 1747 Henry Walker was appointed guardian to Jane and Mary Walker, orphans of James Walker. In 1754 Jane Walker chose Philip Southall as her guardian. {CCCR:108, 113, 127}

Walker, [James], son of David and Mary Walker, m. Locke (d. 1772-3), dau. of George Minge. Children: Freeman, Alexander, Benjamin, William, David, Henry (d. by 1772) and Jane. Granddaus.: Elizabeth, Mary, Lockey, Elizabeth, Sarah and Lockey Walker. {GVAW I:469-70; CCCR:63, 128}

Walker, John m. Catherine (N). Their son Daniel b. 14 Feb 1712/13. {BPR:383}

Walker, Joseph m. Penelope (N). Their children: Gollorthun (b. 10 Sep 1745), Reubin (b. 20 Mar 1751), Penelope (b. 3 Aug 1753), Pattey (b. 19 Nov 1755), Lettisha (b. 9 Feb 1758) and Martin (b. 16 Nov 1759). {BPR:393}

Walker, Robert (d. c1780) m. Susanna (N). Children: Sarah, Robert, Benjamin, and Thomas (last three underage). Susanna m. 2nd Hugh Lyle in Dec 1785. {SWBC:46}

Walker, Robert C., son of Wyatt and Elizabeth (Christian) Walker, m. Mary A. Clayton. Their children: Elizabeth W., Valentine, Robert C., Mary A., Wyatt Beverly, Clayton, Udorah and Jones Oliver Christian. {GVAT III:106; GVAW I:469}

Walker, Thomas m. Frances (N). Their children: Joel (b. 14 Jun 1727), Peter (b. 19 Jul 1733) and David (b. 23 Sep 1734). {BPR:386, 389, 390}

Walker, Wyatt (d. Dec 1832), son of Freeman and Sarah Walker, m. Elizabeth Christian. Their children: William F., Robert C. (b. 2 Jun 1800), George Minge and Thomas. {GVAW I:469; GVAT (Genealgoies of Virginia Families):III:106}

Wall, Daniel m. Anne (N). Their children: Richard (b. 19 Apr 1724). {BPR:384}

Wall, Daniel m. Amy (N). Their children: John (b. 10 Dec 1733), Daniel (b. 25 Mar 1726), Martha (b. 23 Jun 1`729), Mary (b. 23 Aug 1731) and John (b. 10 Dec 1733). {BPR:286, 385, 386, 389}

Wall, Henry d. by 1712, leaving a widow, Elizabeth. {PGW&D (1710-1713): 21}

Wall, Capt. John (d. by 1665) m. Elizabeth, widow of John Clay. On 3 Oct 1660 John Wall gave his son-in-law (*step-son*), Charles Clay, 2 ewes {CCOB (1655-58): 24; CCOB (1658-61):245; CCOB (1664-65):531}

Wall, John (d. 1717) of Westover Parish m. 3 Oct 1692, Sarah (N). Children: John and Michael. {PGW&D (1713-1728):29, 31; CCOB (1687-95):137}

Wall, John m. Ann (N). Their children: Burgess (b. 22 May 1723), David (b. 12 Jun 1725), Mary (b. 13 Dec 1726) and Zachariah (b. 25 Jul 1731). {BPR:383, 385, 387}

Wall, John (b. ca. 1758, d. 24 Dec 1832, New Hanover Co., NC) m. Zelpha (N). He entered the Rev. War while residing in Dinwiddie Co. {RWP}

Wall, Joseph d. by 1665 leaving widow Elizabeth and son Joseph. {CCOB (1664-65):596}

Wall, Joseph (d. ca. 1693) m. bef. 3 Oct 1692, Elizabeth (N). {CCOB (1687-95):137}

Wall, Joss:/Joshua m. Martha (N). Their children: Joss: (b. 21 Feb 1722/3), Isham (b. 25 Nov 1724), Henry (b. 3 Jan 1726), Winiford (b. 20 Jan 1728), Frances (b. 11 Oct 1733) and Martha (b. 23 Aug 1741). {BPR:383, 385, 386, 389, 391}

Wall, William of Brunswick Co. m. bef. 12 Jun 1727, Ann (N). Their children: Elizabeth (b. 6 Sep 1723), Drury (b. 31 Jul 1725) and (N) (b. 15 Dec 1726). {PGW&D (1713-1728):163; BPR:384, 385}

Wallace, Amey was presented in 1755 for having a bastard child. {CCCR:133}

Wallace, James m. bef. 3 May 1661, (N), widow of John Banister. {CCOB (1658-61):271; CCOB (1677-79):58}

Wallace, James of *Merchants Hope*, m. bef. 19 May 1664, Joane (N), widow of Thomas Wheeler. {CCOB 1661-64):476; CCOB (1664-65):562}

Wallis/Wallace, James m. Elizabeth, widow of Caesar Walpole and dau. of (N) Nance. Both James and Elizabeth Wallis d. by 1691. Their dau.

Sarah m. William Epes. {CCOB (1687-95):122; APP1:860}

Wallis, John d. by 1689 leaving a widow Sarah, admx. They had a son Mihell (b. 15 Feb 1681) who was bound to Mihell Jennings in 1690 and a son William who was bound to Randall Mattux. {CCOB (1687-95):69, 84, 85}

Wallace, Martha was mother of Philip and Lucy who were bound out in 1745. On her petition Martha was discharged from service of Thomas Ballard. Lucy was set at liberty in 1761. {CCCR:108, 150}

Wallace, Michael (LWT dated 1753) of Martins Brandon Parish m. Jane (N). Children: Benjamin, Elizabeth (m. [Abraham] Wammack) and Susanna. Granddau.: Susanna Acock, dau. of John Acock. Seven children mentioned in the will, but unnamed. {PGR:175; SWBC:216}

Walmsley, John, mariner, was accused in 1689 of open fornication with Sarah Way, an idle, vagrant, lewd woman, "living in a loose wandering condition." {CCOB (1687-95):59}

Wamsley, Roger (d. by 1678). His widow m. 2nd James Mason. {CCOB 1676-79):76}

Walpole, Cesar (d. by 1688) m. Elizabeth Nance, dau. of John Nance. Their children: Sarah (m. 1st William Jones, m. 2nd William Epes) and Richard. {CCOB (1687-95):18, 122; APP1:860; GVAT (Genealogies of Virginia Families) IV:24; PGW&D (1713-1728):14}

Walpole/Walpool/Warpole, Richard (d. by 1718), son of Cesar Walpole, m. bef. 6 Mar 1712, Ellenor/Elin, probable dau. of John Nance. Ellenor m. 2nd Richard Tomlinson. {PGW&D (1710-1713):32; PGW&D (1713-1728):1, 21, 98; GVAT (Genealogies of Virginia Families) IV:25}

Walter, William m. Elizabeth (N). Their son Thomas b. 16 Jan 1727. {BPR:386}

Walthal(l), Francis m. Martha (N). Their children: Benjamin (b. 9 Feb 1730) and Daniel (b. 8 Mar 1732). {BPR:388, 390}

Walthal, Gerrat/Jerrott m. Elizabeth (N). Their children: Gerrat (b. 25 Feb 1729) and Edward (b. 17 Mar 1731). {BPR:387, 388}

Walthall, Henry m. Mary (N). Their children: Jeremiah (b. 28 Apr 1721) and John (b. 5 Nov 1723). {BPR:382, 384}

Walthall, Henry m. Phebe, dau. of Thomas Ligon (d. 1705). Their children: Elizabeth (b. 10 Jan 1723), Maball (dau., b. 10 May 1725), Henry (b. 25 Jun 1728), Richard (b. 15 Jun 1731) and Ann (b. 10 Mar 1733). {BPR:383, 384, 386 (miscopies Walthall as Walton), 388, 389; GVAW (Genealogies of Virginia Families) III:503}

Walthall, Richard m. Mary (N). Their children: Ann (b. 25 Oct 1721/2), Christopher (b. 28 Jan 1724/5), Mary (b. 7 Sep 1730) and Henry (b. 16 May 1733). {BPR:383, 384, 387, 390}

Walthall, Thomas m. Frances (N). Their dau. Amy b. 19 Feb 1729.

Walthall, William m. bef. 12 Feb 1739, Martha (N). {PGR:63}

Wamack. See Womack.

Warburton, Thomas d. by 1760, Mary Warburton, admx. {CCCR:143}

Warren, Elizabeth was presented in 1744 for having a bastard child. Elizabeth d. by 1745. {CCCR:104}

Warren, John was father of Matthew and Charles (bapt. 1750). Churchwardens bound out Matthew in 1760 as his father was not able to bring him up and educate him. {CCCR:145; GVAT (Genealogies of Virginia Families) III:143}

Warren, John (b. ca. 1759) entered the Rev. War while a resident of Dinwiddie Co. He moved to Rutherford Co., TN. where he d. 26 Sep 1836, leaving children, unnamed. {RWP}

Warradine, James d. by 1655, leaving a widow, Elizabeth and three children: James, Sara and a dau. who m. Thomas Holford. Elizabeth m. 2nd bef. 20 Aug 1656, James Barker. {CCOB (1655-58): 23, 59, 65}

Warthen, (N) m. Elizabeth (N) who d. by 1788, grandmother of Rebecca, Elizabeth and Hubbard Sledge; and grandmother of Edward, Sarah, Littlebury and James Eppes. {PGR:108}

Warthen, (N) m. Elizabeth (N) who d. 1791. In her LWT Elizabeth Warthen of Martins Brandon Parish named children: John, Walter, Jemimah and Worpah. {PGR:145}

Warthen, John of Martins Brandon Parish m. bef. 10 Jun 1788, Martha (N). {PGR:101}

Washington, Langsdown m. Elizabeth (N). Their son Edward b. 18 Oct 1734. {BPR:390}

Watkins, Henry of Martins Brandon Parish m. bef. 3 Jan 1791, Elizabeth (N), widow of John Clay. {PGR:161; HCDB 3:38}

Watkins, James d. by 1694, Judith Watkins, admx. {CCOB (1687-95):191}

Watson, Joseph (d. 1751-2) m. Anna Stratton (d. by 1756), dau. of Edward Jr. and Martha (Sheppey) Stratton. Their children: John, Martha (m. James Bell of Charles City Co.), Lucy (m. Thomas Jones, son of Abraham and Sarah (Batte) Jones) and perhaps Joseph. {APP3:167, 176; HCW 2:57, 70}

Watkins, Joseph m. by 1789, Mary, dau. of James Boisseau (d. by 1789). {W&M Vol. 23, No. 3 (Jan., 1915):214}

Watts, Arthur m. Alice (N). Their children: Sarah (b. 24 Jan 1748) and Edward (b. 20 Apr 1753). {BPR:393}

Watts, John m. Elizabeth (N). Their son John b. 10 Oct 1726. {BPR:385}

Wayles, John (d. by 1770) m. 23 Jul 1760, Elizabeth, widow of Reuben Skelton. Children: Martha (m. Bathurst Skelton), Elizabeth (m. Francis Eppes), Tabitha and Ann (m. Henry Skipwith). Son-in-law: Thomas Jefferson. Grandchildren: Richard Eppes, John Wayles Eppes and Patty Jefferson. {CCCR:37, 39, 53; GVAW (Genealogies of Virginia Families) IV:450; MB:193}

Weathers, Edmund of Sussex Co. m. Mary (N). Their dau. Martha b. 18 Mar 1792. {BPR:394}

Weatherspoon, John d. by 1726, m. Sarah (N) who was extx. of his LWT. {CCW&D (1725-31):10, 13}

Wetherspoon, William d. by 1746, Peter Perry, admin. Peter Perry and his wife, Agnes and Bernard Major and his wife Christian were co-heirs of William Wetherspoon, dec'd. In 1747 they conveyed land to Dancy Stanly.{CCCR:109, 112}

Webster, Jonathan m. Elisabeth (N). Their son Jonathan b. 11 Nov 1740. {BPR:390}

Webster, Thomas m. Mary (N). Their son Thomas b. 20 Jun 1720. {BPR:382}

Weed, Robert m. Sarah (N). Their son John b. 10 Dec 1741. {BPR:391}

Weisiger, Joseph d. by 1801, Ann Weisiger, admx. Daniel Weisiger was surviving admin. in 1803. {PGM:10, 11}

Weldon, Samuel d. by 1694, Sarah Weldon, admx. {CCOB (1687-95):190}

Wells, Abraham m. Sarah (N). Their children: Ruben (b. 28 Jul 1731) and Abram (b. 7 Sep 1733). {BPR:388, 389}

Wells, Abraham m. Amy (N). Their dau. Jane b. 23 Sep 1735. {BPR:390}

Wells, Adam m. Elener/Helenor (N). Their children: Mary (b. 18 Jun 1734), Anne (b. 6 Oct 1735), Deury (b. 4 May 1741), Sarah (b. 18 Feb 1742/3, Henry (b. 5 Feb 1744/5), Pattie (b. 6 Apr 1746) and Randolph (b. 15 Feb 1749). {BPR:390, 391, 392, 393}

Wells, Barnabas m. Joyce (N). Their dau. Margerett b. 1 Dec 1734. {BPR:390}

Wells, Bolling (b. 1760, Dinwiddie Co., d. 4 Dec 1843) m. 27 Oct 1796, Betsey Moody in the Methodist Episcopal Church. {RWP}

Wells, David m. Sarah (N). Their son Jeremiah b. 16 Dec 1735. {BPR:390}

Wells, Jeremiah probably m. Ann, dau. of Sarah Reese who d. 1767-8. Son: William. {PGR:174}

Wells, Richard m. Hannah (N). Their son Richard b. 17 Feb 1747/8. {BPR:393}

Wells, Sloman b. 15 Jun 1764, Dinwiddie Co. {RWP}

Wells, William m. Sarah (N). Their dau. Anne b. 8 Mar 1723/4. {BPR:384}

Wells, William m. Frances (N). Their children: William (b. 20 Oct 1728), David (b. 23 Nov 1730), Phebe (b. 31 Dec 1732), Frances (b. 4 Apr 1741) and Isham (b. 4 Aug 1743). {BPR:386, 387, 389, 391, 392}

Wells, William gave his dau. Martha and son-in-law, William Gibbs a Mulatto woman slave in 1760. {PGR:80}

West, (N) m. bef. 21 May 1658, Mary, widow of John Butler. {CCOB (1658-61):151}

West, Francis m. Elizabeth (N). Their children: Ephraim (b. 2 Feb 1723/4), Francis (b. 9 Feb 1726), John (b. 2 Mar 1729) and Amy (b. 2 Jun 1733). {BPR:384, 385, 387, 389}

West, John m. bef. 8 Aug 1721, Mary, sister of Elizabeth (m. George Woodliffe) and dau. of James Wallace. Their children: William (b. 12 Sep 1721) and Abraham (b. 2 Feb 1723/4). {BPR:383, 384; PGW&D (1713-1728):74; APP 3:707-8}

West, John m. Elizabeth (N). Their dau. Anne b. 5 Nov 1742. {BPR:391}

West, John (d. by 1764), m. bef. 13 Jun 1720, Elizabeth, dau. of John Gilliam (d. by 1720). John and Elizabeth were parents of Anne (b. 5 Nov 1742) and probably parents of John, Joice, Stephen and Sarah who m. John Fuglar. {BPR; CCCR:1, 40-1, 99; PGW&D (1713-1728):74}

West, John m. (bond dated 5 Apr 1786) Rebecca Willcox. {MB:194}

West, Robert m. Mary (N). Their children: Elizabeth (b. 21 Mar 1721/22), Susannah (b. 2 Mar 1725), Frances (b. 2 Mar 1725), Martha (b. 17 May 1728), Lusie (b. 4 Feb 1729) and Christian (dau., b. 8 Apr 1732). {BPR:383, 385, 386, 387, 388}

West, Robert m. Temporance (N). Their children: John (b. 10 May 1729), Mary (b. 7 Sep 1730), Amy (b. 24 Sep 1732), Ephraim (b. 4 Sep 1734) and Robert (b. 17 Sep 1740). {BPR:387, 389, 390, 391}

West, Robert d. by 1744, probable servant of Thomas Jacobs, widow Margaret, admx. {CCCR:104; PGR:65}

West, Thomas m. bef. 4 Feb 1694, Agnes, widow of Hubert Taylor. {CCOB (1687-95):200, 202}

Westbrooke, James (d. 1711) of Bristol Parish m. Elizabeth (N).

Children: Samuel, William, John, James, Margaret, Frances and Elizabeth. {PGW&D (1710-1713): 14-15}

Westbrook(e), William m. Sarah (N). Their children: John (b. 4 May 1733) and Mary (b. 3 Jan 1734/5). {BPR:390}

Westmore, Joseph m. Elizabeth (N). Their son William Baird b. 10 Nov 1791. {BPR:394}

Westmoreland, Joseph m. Isabella/Sybilla/Sib (N). Their children: Susannah (b. 30 Apr 1729) and Abigall (b. 30 Apr 1729); James (b. 28 Sep 1731), Christian (dau., b. 26 Feb 1732) and Robert Hicks (b. 16 Sep 1740). {BPR:387, 389, 391}

Westmoreland, Richard m. Ann (N). Their dau. Ann b. 2 Apr 1722. {BPR:385}

Westmoreland, Thomas m. Mary (N). Their dau. Ann b. 12 Apr 1726. {BPR:385}

Westmoreland, Thomas m. Margret (N). Their children: Marthew (son, b. 18 Mar 1727), Elisabeth (b. 31 Oct 1733) and Joseph (b. 16 Sep 1740). {BPR:386, 389, 391}

Wheeler, John m. bef. 14 Feb 1677/8, (N), dau. of Walter Vaux. {CCOB (1677-79):42}

Wheeler, Nevett d. by 1678, Mrs. Elizabeth Tatum, admx. {CCOB 1676-79):73}

Wheeler, Nevet m. bef. 15 Apr 1778, Hannah (N). Both d. by 15 Apr 1778? {CCOB (1677-79):50}

Wheeler, Robert d. by 1687 leaving an orphan, Elizabeth. {CCOB (1687-95):8}

Wheeler, William drowned in Wards Creek ca. Jun 1658. {CCOB 1658-61):154}

White, John of Martins Brandon Parish m. bef. 9 Sep 1718, Elizabeth (N). {PGW&D (1713-1728):38}

White, Richard m. Rebecca (N). Their son Richard b. 13 Nov 1721. {BPR:383}

Whitehall, Robert m. Anne (N). Their children: Thomas (b. 17 Dec 1738) and Amy (b. 7 Jun 1742). {BPR:391}

Whitmore, John m. Elizabeth (N). Their son Thomas b. 4 Apr 1734. {BPR:390}

Whitmore, John Y. (b. ca. 1757) lived all his life in Dinwiddie Co. {RWP}

Whitmore, Nicholas m. bef. 13 Mar 1661/2, Mary, widow of Richard Pace, one of the execs. of Hugh Kerkerland's LWT. {CCOB (1687-95):131}

Whittmore, Nicholas Jr. d. by 1718, Elizabeth Whittmore, admx. {PGW&D (1713-1728):36}

Whittmore, Richard d. by 1738, Honour Whittmore, admx. {PGR:39}

Whitamore, William m. Sarah (N). Their son Abraham b. 14 Feb 1721. {BPR:383}

Whitmell, Thomas (d. by 1693) m. Mary (N) who m. 2nd Arthur Cavenaugh. {CCOB (1687-95):163, 209}

Whitt, Edward m. Mary (N). Their children: Anne (b. 11 Dec 1730) and John (b. 10 Jul 1734). {BPR:388, 390}

Whitt, John m. bef. 8 Aug 1730, Ann, dau. of John Rogers (d. by 1730). {CCW&D (1725-31):42}

Wicket, John of Westover Parish, m. bef. 8 May 1711, Elizabeth, widow of John Jane. {PGW&D (1710-1713):6}

Wilburn, John of Waynoak Parish d. 1712. Son: John. {PGW&D (1710-1713):26}

Wilkerson, Frederick m. bef. 9 Jun 1789, Sarah (N). {PGR:116}

Wilkerson, Henry m. bef. 20 Feb 1802, Mason, widow of William Edwards. On 4 Dec 1802 Henry Wilkerson was married to Lillason [*probably Mason misread*]. {PGM:10}

Wilkerson, Jesse of Prince George Co. m. bef. 10 Jun 1788 Mary (N). {PGR:101}

Wilkins, (N) m. Mary (N). Their children: Francis and John. {PGW&D (1710-1713):13}

Wilkins, Charles of NC, brother of Francis Wilkins of Prince George Co., m. bef. 13 Nov 1710, Elizabeth (N). {PGW&D (1710-1713):1}

Wilkins, Francis, son of (N) and Mary Wilkins, m. by 1708 (N)(N). Children: Mary and Elizabeth. {PGW&D (1710-1713):13}

Wilkins, John, son of (N) and Mary Wilkins, m. by 1708 (N)(N). Children: William and Frances. {PGW&D (1710-1713):13}

Wilkins, John m. bef. 8 Sep 1713, Hester (N). In 1713, John, Francis and Robert Wilkins sold 2 acres on Ward Run with a mill. {PGW&D (1710-1713):35}

Wilkins, Robert (d. by 1738) m. Mary Limbrey, dau. of John Limbrey. In his LWT Robert named wife Mary and son John Limbrey (d. by 1760). Robert probably had a dau. Rebecca. In her will Rebecca Limbrey named cousens John Limbrey Wilkins and Rebecca Wilkins. {PGR:28, 75; PGW&D (1713-1728):62-3}

Wilkins, Thomas m. bef. 3 Aug 1693 Martha, sister of Bradford Wynd/Winde and Elizabeth Wynd. {CCOB (1687-95):156}

Wilkins, William Sr. gave his son John 150 acres in 1693 which he acquired in 1684. {CCCR:75}

Wilkinson, Edward, son of Joseph and Priscilla (Branch) Wilkinson, m. Ann, dau. of Lewellin Epes of Charles City Co. Their children: Joseph (m. Elizabeth Bass) and Angelica (m. Peter Field Trent. {GVAW I:426-7; APP 1:406}

Wilkinson, Frederick d. by 1803. Widow m. 2nd Hamilton Burge. Heirs: Patsy Wilkinson, Wyatt Wilkinson, Adain Heath and Richard Moore. {PGM:31}

Wilkinson, Jesse d. by 1804 leaving a widow Mary. {PGM:32}

Wilkinson/Wilkason/Wilkison, Henry m. Mary (N). Their children: Henry (b. 26 Feb 1742/3) and Agnes (b. 8 Sep 1745). {BPR:290, 392}

Wilkinson, James (b. Jul 1763, Dinwiddie Co., d. 4 Apr 1846, Catawba Co., NC) moved to Warren Co., NC, then to TN, and ca. 1793 to Lincoln

Co., NC. He m. 27 Aug 1818, Nancy Stiles, Lincoln Co., NC. Nancy was living in Pickens Co., AL with her son [*name not given*] in 1869. James mentioned a sister, not named. {RWP}

Wilkinson, John m. Sarah. They d. by 1689, leaving orphans: Ruth and John (age 14 in 1690). {CCOB (1687-95):61, 69, 97}

Wilkinson, Joseph m. Priscilla, widow of Edward Skerme and dau. of John Branch. Their children: Joseph Jr. (m. Mary (N)), Edward (m. Ann Epes, dau. of Lewellin Epes of Charles City Co.) and Martha (b. by 1710, m. Thomas Howlett). {GVAW I:426-7; APP1:377-8; APP3:156; HCW 1:91}

Wilkinson/Wilkison, Martin/Marth, son of John Wilkinson, m. Anne (N). Their children: John, Mary (b. 28 Oct 1741, m. (N) Hall), Prudence (m. (N) Standley) and William. {BPR:391; APP 3:59}

Wilkinson, Thomas m. Elizabeth (N). Their son John b. 25 Nov 1723. {BPR:384}

Wilkerson/Wilkinson, Thomas (b. ca. 1758) m. Martha (N) (b. ca. 1770). Their children: Thomas (b. ca. 1802), Francis (b. ca. 1805), Joll (b. ca. 1811), and Martha (b. ca. 1815). {RWP}

Willabe, William d. 7 Jun 1723, in his 30th year. {W&M Vol. 4, No. 3 (Jan., 1896):143}

Willcox, William, living in 1753, was the son of William Willcox. {CCCR:1}

Williams, (N) m. (N). Their children, Thomas Harris Williams and Lucy Williams were ordered to be bound to John Roper in 1745. {CCCR:105}

Williams, (N) m. Rachel (N). In her LWT (dated 13 Sep 1793) Rachel named dau.: Elizabeth Orders; son: Edward/Edmond Williams and his daus.: Mary Williams and Anne Lewis; and son-in-law William Lewis and his dau. Mary. {Dinwiddie Co. GenWeb; SWBC:61}

Williams, Allen d. by 1758. His son Allen was bound out. {CCCR:141}

Williams, Anthony gave his son Isham 133 acres in 1790. {PGR:140}

Williams, Brazure m. (bond dated 16 Jun 1762), Agathy Johnson, widow of Squire Johnson. {CCCR:158; HMM:22, 38; MB:194}
Williams, Charles d. by 1691. Sons: Charles and William. {CCOB

(1687-95):126}

Williams, Charles, son of John Williams (d. by 1721) m. bef. 12 Feb 1721, Anne (N). Their children: Charles (b. 26 May 1722), Sarah (b. 20 Sep 1725), Lucy (b. 6 May 1727), John (b. 2 Sep 1729), Mary (b. 5 Aug 1731) and John (b. 14 May 1734). {PGW&D (1713-1728):78; BPR:383, 385, 387, 388, 390}

Williams, Charles m. bef. 23 Feb 1724, Elizabeth (N). Their children: Martha (b. 18 Oct 1720), Elizabeth (b. 24 Apr 1722), Margaret (b. 19 Nov 1723), Charles (b. 11 Jun 1725), Mary (b. 19 Apr 1727), Helen (b. 3 Jun 1728), John (b. 11 Mar 1729), Edward (b. 11 Jun 1732) and Joseph (b. 2 Jan 1733). {PGW&D (1713-1728):99; BPR:382, 383, 384, 385, 386, 387, 388, 389}

Williams, Charles of Brunswick Co. m. bef. 8 Mar 1760, Elizabeth, dau. of Peter Leath (d. by 1760). {PGR:77}

Williams, David d. by 1689 leaving a widow who m. 2nd Henry King. {CCOB (1687-95):46}

Williams, David of Bristol Parish m. bef. 26 Apr 1712, Sarah, dau. of John Williams. {PGW&D (1710-1713):22; PGW&D (1713-1728):139}

Williams, David m. Sarah (N). Their children: Sarah (b. 15 Mar 1721), Mary (b. 29 Aug 1723), John (b. 23 Jan 1725/6), Jones (b. 23 Apr 1731) and Martha (b. 22 Mar 1734). {BPR:384, 385, 388, 390}

Williams, David d. by 1738, William Jones and Miles Williams, execs. {PGR:32}

Williams, David d. by 1791. {PGR:160}

Williams, Drury was father of Hubbard Williams (named in the will of Bernard Sykes). {PGR:146}

Williams, Frances d. by 1758 leaving an orphan dau. Frances Williams who chose John Hopkins as her guardian. {CCCR:139}

Williams, George m. Sibil/Sibbilla (N). Their children: David (b. 22 Apr 1721), Sibilla (b. 18 Aug 1723), Henry (b. 4 Nov 1725), Mary (b. 15 Oct 1727) and (N) (b. 12 Oct 1728). {BPR:382, 384, 385, 386}

Williams, Hubbard m. bef. Apr 1803, Sally Jordan, widow of Josiah

Jordan and dau. of Glaister and Jane (Pleasants) Hunnicutt. {PGM:9; APP2:385}

Williams, Hubbard Bates, admin. of James Williams (d. by 1749) and admin. of Isaac Williams, d. by 1756. His widow Frances m. 2nd John Hopkins of James City Co. Dau. Frances chose John Hopkins as her guardian. {CCCR:119, 136, 139}

Williams, Isaac m. by 1687, (N), widow of Charles Hamlin. {CCOB (1687-95):3}

Williams, Isaac d. by 1744, leaving widow Agnes, admx. Allen Williams, orphan of Isaac Williams, chose Benjamin Buck as his guardian in 1754. John Williams, orphan of Isaac Williams chose William Hopkins as his guardian in 1757. Anthany Williams, orphan of Isaac Williams Jr. chose George Ming, Gent., as his guardian in 1761. Agnes m. 2nd Francis Dancy. {CCCR:103, 149, 153}

Williams, James m. Olive (N). Their children: Charles (b. 23 Feb 1721), Obedience (b. 10 May 1724) and Miles (b. 15 Jan 1729). {BPR:383, 384, 387}

Williams, James of Bristol Parish sold 325 acres to his brother, Charles Williams, in 1726. {PGW&D (1713-1728):145, 146}

Williams, James m. Ann (N). Their son Peter b. 7 Dec 1728. {BPR:385}

Williams, James m. Jane (N). Children: Millison (b. 3 Dec 1745), Elizabeth (b. 21 Apr 1752), Frederick (b. 24 Oct 1749) and Joshua. {BPR:392, 393}

Williams, James d. by 1749, Hubbard Bates Williams, exec. {CCCR:119}

Williams, John (d. by 1710) m. Mary (N). Children: Charles, Sarah (m. David Williams) and Elizabeth (m. Benjamin Blicke). Mary, widow of John Williams, m. 2nd Richard Dearden. {PGW&D (1710-1713):3, 13, 22; PGW&D (1713-1728):172}

William (*sic*), John of the town and Parish of St. Michaels of Barbadoes m. bef. 15 Jun 1713, Rebeckah, widow of Robert Minnett. {PGW&D (1710-1713):39}

Williams, John m. Elizabeth (N). Their children: Richard (b. 14 Sep

1724), Joseph (b. 15 Jul 1726), Ann (b. 25 Oct 1728) and Frances (b. 21 Feb 1732). {BPR:384, 385, 386, 389}

Williams, John d. 16 Jan 1725. {BPR:385}

Williams, Joseph (d. ca. 1789), brother of William Williams, m. Edith (N) who m. 2nd Joseph Heath. {PGM:23; PGR:117}

Williams, Lessenbury (d. 1791). Sisters: Ann, Sarah and Mary (m. William Stone). {PGR:151}

Williams, Lewellen (b. 19 Jun 1763, Dinwiddie Co., d. 28 Nov 1838, Bedford Co., TN) m. (bond dated 17 Nov 1803), Winifred Lovell, Franklin Co., VA. Markham Lovell was a surety on the marriage bond. Son: James E. Williams. {RWP}

Williams, Ludwell of Sussex Co. m. Johannah (N). Their son John b. 25 Mar 1792. {BPR:393}

Williams, Miles m. Martha (N). Their dau. Hannah b. 7 Jun 1752. {BPR:393}

Williams, Robert m. bef. 5 Jan 1690, Elizabeth, widow of John Frost and dau. of Christopher Batty. {CCOB (1687-95):63, 95}

Williams, Robert m. Elizabeth (N). Their children: Robert (b. 17 Jun 1732) and John (b. 27 Jul 1734). {BPR:388, 390}

Williams, Thomas m. Jane (N). Their children: Roland (b. 19 Jul 1739), Jane (b. 12 Jun 1741), Thomas (b. 24 Oct 1743) and Lucy (b. 2 Jan 1745/6). {BPR:391, 392}

Williams, William d. by 1717, Charles Williams, admin. {PGW&D (1713-1728):30}

Williams, William m. Mary (N). Their children: William (b. 30 Aug 1743) and Thomas (b. 27 Dec 1744). {BPR:392}

Williams, William was father of Leah (m. by 1726 John Pattison) and Rachel. {PGW&D (1713-1728):151}

Williams, William (d. by 1789) was father of William, Thomas, Sarah and Ann (m. Samuel Vaughan). {PGR:128}

Williams, William (d. by 1789 without issue), son of William Williams (d. by 1789) m. Martha (N). {PGR:128}

Williams, William m. bef. 6 Nov 1771, Mary (N), possible widow of Robert Craddock. {CCCR:38-9}

Williamson, Charles m. Prissilla (N). Their children: Susan (b. 1 Mar 1727), John (b. 1730), Elisabeth (b. Jan 1733) and Drusilla (b. 12 Nov 1741). {BPR:386, 389, 391}

Williamson, George d. by 1769. His son George apprenticed himself to Jesse Bradley. {CCCR:20}

Williard, Benjamin, mariner, m. bef. 14 Sep 1725, Elizabeth (N). {PGW&D (1713-1728):138}

Willingham, John m. Mary (N). Their dau. Jane b. 2 May 1727. {BPR:385}

Willis, Francis m. 1st Anne Rich, dau. of Edward Rich of Middlesex Co. Francis m. 2nd bef. 9 May 1738, Elizabeth, widow of Henry Harrison (d. 1732) and dau. of John Smith of *Purton*. Francis and Elizabeth Willis and Benjamin Harrison were execs of Henry Harrison, Esq. (d. 1732). {PGR:5, 32; GVAW (Genealogies of Virginia Families) V:494}

Willsheir, (N) m. Elizabeth (N) and after being condemned for fornication, he ran away bef. 1687 {CCOB (1687-95):8}

Wills, Amey. In her LWT (dated 23 Apr 1791) Amey Wills named daus.: Katty and Nancy Burrow Wills; granddaus.: Jinsy Wills and Amy Vaughan; son-in-law: Adam Wells. {Dinwiddie Co. GenWeb}

Wills, John (d. c1791) m. Jane (N). Their dau., Betsey Fuqua. {SWBC:47}

Wilson, Edward m. Martha (N). Their son Joseph b. 1 Feb 1727. {BPR:385}

Wilson, Francis m. 1st bef. 7 Aug 1771, Elizabeth (N). {CCCR:41-2}

Wilson, George m. Elizabeth (N). Their son Gardner b. 15 Feb 1721. {BPR:382}

Wilson, Henry (d. by 1721) m. Mary (N). Their son Stevens b. 15 Sep 1721. {BPR:383}

Wilson/Willson, Henry m. Martha (N). Their children: Sarah (b. 9 Dec 1726), Mary (b. 24 Nov 1728), Elizabeth (b. 28 Sep 1730), Martha (b. 7 Sep 1731), Judith (b. 24 Feb 1732), James (b. 19 Dec 1734), Anne (b. 10 Feb 1740) and Katharine (b. 24 Oct 1745). {BPR:385, 386, 387, 388, 389, 390, 392}

Wilson, John m. Catherine (N). Their son Joel b. 6 Nov 1727. {BPR:385}

Wilson, John m. Ann (N). Their children: Micael (b. 18 Apr 1728), Samuel (b. 31 Oct 1730), Mark (b. 20 Nov 1732) and Elimelech (b. 18 Apr 1742). {BPR:386, 388, 389, 391}

Willson/Willson, John m. Mary (N). Their children: Phebe, Mary (b. 16 Jun 1730) and John (b. 11 Sep 1732). {BPR:387, 388}

Wilson, Joseph m. Margaret (N). Their dau. Margarit b. 27 Oct 1726). {BPR:385}

Wilson, Richard m. Judith (N). Their children: Sarah (b. 23 Dec 1721) and Richard (b. 18 May 1724). {BPR:383, 384}

Wilson, Thomas m. Amy (N). Their son Thomas b. 21 Jun 1721. {BPR:382}

Wilson, Thomas m. Frances (N). Their children: John (b. 5 Dec 1741) and Thomas (b. 30 Mar 1746). {BPR:391}

Window, William m. by 1688, Joane, widow of William Coleby. {CCOB (1687-95):22, 27}

Wines, Robert m. Frances (N). Their dau. Margret b. 25 Oct 1741. {BPR:391}

Winfield, Edward m. Mary (N). Their children: Joell (b. 30 Dec 1731), Edward (b. 2 Jul 1742) and Hannah (b. 12 Dec 1744). {BPR:388, 391, 392}

Winfield, John m. Ann (N). Their dau. Hannah b. 12 Feb 1733. {BPR:390}

Winingham, Isack m. Sarah (N). Their son Henry b. 16 Jun 1731. {BPR:388}

Winingham, John m. bef. 18 Sep 1695, (N)(N). {CCOB (1687-95):212}

Winingham, John m. Mary (N). Their children: Christian (b. 20 Mar 1731) and Gerrald (b. 1 Aug 1734). {BPR:388, 390}

Winingham, Thomas m. Elizabeth (N). Their children: Edward (b. 3 May 1729) and Precillah (b. 30 Jun 1730). Thomas m. 2nd Mary (N). Their dau. Amy b. 11 Aug 1733. {BPR:387, 389}

Winingham, William m. Sarah (N). Their son William b. 16 Dec 1731. {BPR:388}

Winkles, William of Martins Brandon Parish, son of Richard Winkles, m. bef. 5 Feb 1723, Esther (N). {PGW&D (1713-1728):100}

Winston, William m. bef. Oct 1740, Elizabeth (N). {CCCR:89}

Winston, William m. by 1721, Rebecca, dau. of Thomas Bobby. {SWBC: 29}

Winters. See Wynters.

Womack, Elizabeth had a dau. Laurana, b. 20 Mar 1728. {BPR:386}

Wamack, James d. by 1806. Children: William, Patsy and Jane. {PGM:38}

Womack, John Sr. m. bef. 14 Aug 1714 Mary (N). Probable sons: John Jr. and Richard. {PGW&D (1713-1728):3, 24}

Womack, John of Martins Brandon Parish (d. ca. 1725) m. Mary (N). Children: Abraham (youngest son), William and John (eldest son). {PGW&D (1713-1728):141}

Wamack, John (d. 1787) of Martns Brandon Parish m. Hannah (N). Children: Travis, Nathaniel and others. Nathaniel Marks, Edward Marks and James Womack, execs. {PGR:91, 103}

Wamock, Peyton A. d. by 1796 when his land was divided among John P. Wamock, Peyton Wamock Jr., William Wamock and John Tatum and wife. {PGM:22}

Womack, Richard gave his brother John Womack 100 acres in Charles City Co. sometime prior to 5 Jun 1693. {CCCR:72}

Womack, William m. Martha (N). Their son William b. 10 Sep 1723. {BPR:384}

Wood, Abraham (d. by 1682) m. (N) (N). Dau., Mary Chamberlaine. Grandchildren in law: Abraham, Richard, Peter, and William Jones. {SWBC:48}

Wood, Aron m. Mary (N). Their children: Elizabeth (b. 5 Jun 1727) and Richard (b. 15 Sep 1729). {BPR:386, 387}

Wood, Bowry d. by 1756, Betty Wood, admx. {CCCR:135}

Wood, Henry d. by Jun 1756. His orphan Ann, chose Lewellin Eppes as her guardian. {CCCR:134}

Wood, James m. Katharine (N). They had a child b. 31 Oct 1723. {BPR:384}

Whood, William m. Margret (N). Their dau. Ann b. 24 Mar 1729). {BPR:387}

Woodard, Ann was presented in 1746 for having a bastard child. Francis Hardyman promised to pay 50 shillings (fine). {CCCR:110}

Woodcock, Robert d. by 1761, Thomas Woodcock, admin. {CCCR:147}

Wooddrop, John (d. by Aug 1779) m. Mary (N). Children: John and Mary Ann. Brother in law, Samuel Harwood. {SWBC:47}

Wodrop, John m. (bond dated 12 Jan 1769), Mary Clarke. {MB:194}

Woodhall, Jeremy d. by 1677 leaving a widow who m. James Gunne. {CCOB (1677-79):3, 20}

Woodham, Edward m. bef. 3 Oct 1689, (N), widow of William Crosse. {CCOB (1687-95):62}

Woodhouse, Hammon d. by 1677 leaving widow, Rachell. {CCOB 1676-79:8}

Woodhouse, James (d. by 1692) m. Ann/Annis (N). Ann d. ca. 1728. In her LWT she named dau. Mary Gunn, grandson John Phillips, grandson Robert Phillips. {CCW&D (1725-31):28}

Woodland, John m. bef. 1 Mar 1713, Sara, dau. of John Eaton of York Co. {PGW&D (1713-1728):1}

Woodliffe,/Woodleigh, Edward (d. 1718), probable son of John and Mary (Poythress) Woodliffe, m. bef. 12 Jun 1690, Sarah (N). Their children: John, Joseph, Edward (d. testate without issue, 1759), James, Sarah (m. (N) Pace), Ann (m. (N) Ledbetter), Susannah and Mary (m. William Lovesay/Loffsy) {CCOB (1687-95):81; APP3:709; PGR:70; PGW&D (1713-1728):43}

Woodlief, Edward (d. by 1787) m. Elizabeth. Their children, Ann, Pattey, John and Polley were under the guardianship of Burwell Rosser in 1787. {PGR105}

Woodliefe, George (age 19 in 1665), son of John Woodliffe, m. Norah, dau. of Col. Robert Wynne. Their children: George and John. {CCOB (1664-65):567; APP3:706-7; PGW&D (1713-1728):84}

Woodliffe, George (d. by 1701), son of George Woodliffe, m. Elizabeth, dau. of James Wallace. Their dau. Mary m. (N) Carter. {APP3:707-8; PGW&D (1713-1728):154}

Woodliffe, Capt. John (age 51 in 1665), son of John Woodliffe, m. (N)(N). Sons: George and John. In 1664 Capt. John Woodleife was presented for getting his servant, Ann Berrey, with child. {APP 3:706; CCOB (1664-65):521, 634}

Woodliffe, John, son of Capt. John Woodliff, m. Mary Poythress, dau. of John and Christian (Peebles) Poythress. Children: George (m. Norah Wynne), probably Edward and possibly Joshua. {APP 3:707; PGW&D (1713-1728):84}

Woodlief, John (d. by 1738), son of George Woodliffe, m. Rebecca Harrison, dau. of William Harrison. Children: John, Peter, possibly Robert, and possibly a dau. {PGR:11; APP 3:708}

Woodleif, John d. by 1788, brother of Thomas Woodleif and Peter Woodleif, devised 800 acres to brother Thomas which Thomas sold to Noel Quesnell of Blandford. Edmund Ruffin and Edmund Ruffin Jr. relinquished their right to the land in 1788. {PGR:104}

Woodlief, Peter, son of John Woodliffe (d. by 1738), m. (N)(N). Children: John, Peter, Thomas and Hannah (m. John Cox). {APP 3:709}

Woodleif, Peter (d. 30 Aug 1816), son of Peter Woodlief (son of John Woodlief), m. 1st bef. 4 Feb 1801, Anne Poythress (Bland) Morrison, widow of John Morrison. Peter m. 2nd 6 Jul 1813, Rebecca (Cocke) Ruffin. {PGM:8; APP 3:709}

Woodlith, Thomas m. Elizabeth (N). Their son Edward b. 9 Nov 1742. {BPR:391}

Woodlief, Thomas of Martins Brandon Parish, son of Peter Woodlief, m. 1st (approved by her guardian, John Banister, 8 Jul 1777) Elizabeth Hill Eppes (d. 1778-85), dau. of Francis Eppes, and m. 2nd bef. 6 Jul 1787, Martha Taylor. {PGR:107; APP 1:909; APP 3:709; Southside Virginian Vol.VI, No. 1, p. 6}

Woodson, Dr. John (1586-1644), son of (N) Woodson of Bristol, England, m. Sara Winston. Lived at Fleur de Hundred on south side of James River in what became Prince George Co., about 30 miles north of Jamestown. Sons: John (b. 1632) and Robert (b. 1634). {GVA (Genealogies of Virginia Families II, Cl-Fi:175)}

Woodson, John (b. 1632, d. 1684), son of Dr. John Woodson, m. 1st (N)(N). Their sons: John and Robert. John m. 2nd bef. 1 Oct 1677, Sarah Brown, widow of John Brown. {APP3:713; GVAW IIIi:805; HCW 1:15}

Woodson, Robert (b. 1634, d. after 1 Oct 1707), son of John Woodson, m. ca. 1656 Elizabeth Ferris, dau. of Richard Ferris of Curles, descendant of Henri de Ferniers of Normandy. Children: John, Sarah (m. Edward Moseby), Elizabeth (m. William Lewis), Judith (m. William Kennon/ Cannon), Mary (m. George Payne), Robert, Richard, Joseph and Benjamin. {APP3:713-4; GVAW V:770-1}

Woodward, Lancelot of Blissland Parish, James City Co. m. bef. 19 Feb 1705, Elizabeth (N). {CCW&D (1725-31):28-9}

Woodward, Nathaniel of Boston, Suffolk Co., MA, blockmaker, was son of Samuel and Elizabeth Woodward of Boston, MA (d. by 1722) who was heir at law to Christopher Woodward of VA (d. in New England and his wife Priscilla. Samuel Woodward m. a dau. of Francis Hudson of New England. {PGW&D (1713-1728):89, 90}

Woodward, Samuel m. bef. 10 Aug 1654, Sara, dau. of Robert Hallam (d. by 1654). Children: Samuel and another child. {APP 2:231-2; CCOB (1655-58):56; CCOB (1658-61):275; APP 3:844-5}

Woolfolk, Francis of Sussex Co. m. Jean (N). Jean d. 21 Mar 1792. {BPR:393}

Wootten, Miles m. Elisabeth (N). Their son William b. 14 Feb 1740. {BPR:391}

Worsham, Essex m. Ann (N). Their children: Henry (b. 5 Aug 1727) and Essex (b. 11 Jun 1732). {BPR:386, 388}

Worsham, Joseph m. Martha (N). Their son John b. 3 Oct 1740. {BPR:391}

Worsham, Joshua m. Martha (N). Their children: Daniel (b. 29 Apr 1742) and Mary (b. 4 Nov 1745). {BPR:391, 392}

Worsham, William, son of William Worsham, had a cut on his ear by a fall by 1655. [*Recorded to prevent wrongful assumption that he had received it as legal punishment.*]{CCOB (1655-58): 37}

Worsham, William, age 18 in 1664. {CCOB (1664-65):560}

Worsham, William m. Elizabeth (N). Their daus.: Elizabeth (m. Richard Kennon (d. 1696)) and Mary (m. Richard Lygon). Elizabeth, widow of William Worsham, m. 2nd Francis Eppes. {GVAT (Genealogies of Virginia Families I:648; GVAW (Genealogies of Virginia Families): III:504}

Worsham, William m. Rosamund/Rose/Roson (N). Their children: Daniel (b. Nov 1721), William (b. 27 Sep 1722) Frances (b. 8 Feb 1727). {BPR:382, 383, 386}

Worsham, William m. Dorcas (N). Their children: Martha (b. 18 Nov 1720) and Martha (b. 26 Mar 1720/1. {BPR:382, 383}

Worsham, William m. Clarissa (N). Their son Henry b. 17 Aug 1792. {BPR:394}

Wortham, James m. Elizabeth (N). Their dau. Mary b. 13 Dec 1744. {BPR:392}

Wright, John (d. by 1741) m. Elizabeth (N). They had a son George. Elizabeth m. 2nd George Tree. {CCCR:92}

Wright/Write, John m. Susannah (N). Their children: Sarah (b. 2 Aug

1730), Susanah (b. 26 Dec 1732) and Joseph (b. 3 Feb 1734). {BPR:387, 389, 390}

Wright, William m. (bond dated 23 Dec 1781) Martha Jackson (spinster). {MB:193}

Wyatt, Anthony (age 25 in 1673) of Martins Brandon m. bef. 12 Jun 1690 Elizabeth, granddau. of Elizabeth Tatem Good (widow of John Tatem) and nearest of kin to John Wheeler. Anthony had a son Nicholas who m. Frances (Rookins?). {CCOB (1687-95):81, 155; GVAW (Genealogies of Virginia Families) V:576}

Wyatt, Arthur m. Alice (N). Their dau. Mary b. 24 Jan 1745/6. {BPR:393}

Wyatt, Capt. Edward (d. ca. 1726) m. bef. 1 Feb 1718, (N)(N). Children: Edward (minor in 1727), Elizabeth, Sarah and Francis. {PGW&D (1713-1728):42, 145, 177}

Wyatt, Edward, son of Edward Wyatt, dec'd. of Prince George Co. bound himself in 1760 as apprentice to Theodorick Bland to be taught the business of County Clerk, until age 21. {PGR:80}

Wyatt, Francis m. Elizabeth (N). Their children: Elisabeth (b. 22 dec 1732) and Susanna (b. 15 Jun 1742). {BPR:389, 391}

Wyatt, Henry (d. by 1739), probable son of Anthony Wyatt (son of Nicholas Wyatt) m. bef. 71 Mar 1725/6 Mary (N). Their son Francis b. 29 Mar 1731. Mary m. 2nd Thomas Twitty. {CCW&D (1725-31):9; PGM:55; BPR:387; GVAW (Genealogies of Virginia Families) V:577}

Wyatt, Hubbard m. (bond dated 23 Jul 1767), Tabitha Minge, dau. of George Minge. {MB:195}

Wyatt, Nicholas (d. ca. 1720) m. (N)(N). Sons: Anthony, Edward and Nicholas (d. an infant) and dau.: Susan (m. (N) Reeks). Grandchildren: Elizabeth (m. Edward Bettes), Frances (m. John Sykes), Sarah and John Wyatt (d. without issue). {PGW&D (1713-1728):46-7, 66-7, 87-8, 95-6}

Wynd, Anthony (d. by 1687) m. (N)(N). Dau. Martha m. George Hunt. Anthony's widow m. 2nd Thomas Hamlin. {CCOB (1687-95):2}

Winn, John of Sussex Co. m. Katy (N). Their dau. Sally Allen b. 8 Jan 1792. {BPR:393}

Wyn, Joseph m. Mary (N). Their son Thomas b. 6 Apr 1726. {BPR:385}

Wynne, Major Joshua (d. by 1712), son of Robert Wynne, m. Mary (N)..
{PGW&D (1713-1728):12}

Wynne, Joshua (d. 1725-6) of Prince George Co. m. (prenuptial contract
dated 10 Feb 1711) Frances Cocke, widow of Thomas Cocke. {PGW&D
(1710-1713):14; APP1:123}

Wynne, Joshua/Joss:, son of Col. Robert Wynne, m. Mary, dau. of Peter
and Margaret (Wood) Jones. Their children: Martha (b. 1 May 1720),
Joss:/Joshua (b. 24 Jan 1721/22, Margaret (b. 31 Dec 1723), Margaret (b.
25 Nov 1724 and Tabitha (b. 23 May 1731). Mary m. 2nd Thomas Cocke.
{BPR:382, 383, 384, 385, 388; GVAT (Virginia Genealogies) IV:532}

Wynne, Joshua m. Lucretia (N). Their son Sloman (b. 13 Oct 1745).
{BPR:393)

Wynne, Peter (predeceased his wife), son of Major Joshua Wynne, m.
Frances Anderson, dau. of John Anderson of Prince George Co. and
widow of John Herbert (d. 1704). Frances d. ca. 1726. In her LWT she
named dau. Martha Cocke, sons: Richard and Buller Herbert and dau.-in-
law: Mary Herbert. {GVAT (Virginia Genealogies) IV:532-3; PGW&D
(1713-1728):158}

Wynne, Peter d. by 1739. His son Harry was bound to William Cryer.
{PGR:45}

Wynne, Robert (came from Kent, England, d. 1675-8) of Jordans Parish,
Charles City Co. (that part that became Prince George Co.), m. Mary,
widow of Capt. Francis Poythress. They were parents of Robert
(predeceased his father), Thomas, Joshua (d. by 1712), Wodlief (dau.),
and Norah (m. George Woodleif, had son George). {GVAT
{Genealogies of Virginia Families) IV:180, 530-1; PGW&D (1710-
1713):29; PGW&D (1713-1728):84; SWBC:48}

Wynne, Robert of Surry Co. m. bef. 8 1718, Martha (N). {PGW&D
(1713-1728):28}

Wynn, Robert m. Mary (N). Their children: Mary (b. 26 Nov 1722) and
Joss:/Joshua (b. 3 Aug 1722). {BPR:383}

Wynne, Robert m. Frances (N). Their dau. Mason b. 29 May 1745.
{BPR:392}

Wynne, Capt. Thomas (d. ca. 1718), son of Col. Robert and Mary
Wynne, res. Prince George Co. in 1704, m. Agnes (N). Children:
Thomas, Lucy, Robert and Mary (m. (N) Melone in Surry Co.). {GVAT
(Genealogies of Virginia Families) IV:532}

Wynters, Thomas d. by 1679, Mrs. Elizabeth Tatum, admx. {CCOB
1777-79):119}

Yarbrough, William m. Dianer (N). Their children: James Smith (b. 2
Sep 1745), Richard (b. 18 Mar 1747/8), Elizabeth (b. 23 Oct 1750),
William (b. 7 Apr 1753), Ozwell (b. 24 Apr 1756) and Joseph (b. 4 Nov
1758. Dianer d. 18 May 1767, aged 42 years. {BPR:394, 395}

Yates, Col. William d. by 1790. Sons: William Yates (eldest son) and
Benjamin Poythress Yates. {PGR:131}

Yeans/Yanes, Edward m. Mary (N). Their children: Edward (b. 5 Jan
1722/3), John (b. 2 Jul 1725), Elizabeth (b. 6 May 1727), Thomas (b. 7
Feb 1728) and Josiah (b. 17 Jun 1733). {BPR:394}

Yeargan, Thomas (b. 25 May 1762, Dinwiddie Co., d. Dec 1838) was
raised in Brunswick Co., VA. He m. 1st (N) (N) who died leaving several
children. He m. 2nd Mar 1814, (N) (N). {RWP}

York, John m. Sarah (N). Their children: Jane (b. 7 Sep 1729), Martha
(b. 3 Jun 1732), Sarah (b. 17 Feb 1734) and Martha (b. 3 Jun 1732).
{BPR:359; BPR:381, 394}

Youille/Yuille, John of Charles City Co. d. by 1747, Thomas Youille,
admin. {HCW2:38; CCCR:112}

Young, Dorrill, son of Thomas and Ann Young and brother of John
Young, m. bef. 3 Aug 1671, Ann (N). Dorrill res. in Surry Co. in 1724.
{CCOB (Fragments):524; PGW&D (1713-1728):128}

Young, Henry/Harry of Bath Parish, Dinwiddie Co., son of Edward and
Kerrenhappush Young, m. Winney Tucker Goodwyn (b. ca. 1770), dau.
of James Goodwyn. Their children: James Goodwin (b. 30 Mar 1790, m.
1st Elizabeth Ann Dean, m. 2nd Catherine Brewer, m. 3rd Elizabeth
Clements Young), Major Henry (b. 3 May 1792, m. Frances Vaughan),
Judith (b. 1794, m. Jacob Mitchell). {BPR:395; GVAW (Genealogies of
Virginia Families) II:712, 714, 715}

Young, Micael Cadet m. Temperance (N). Their son Francis Cadet b. 25

Oct 1731. {BPR:394}

Young, Samuel m. Judith (N). Their son John b. 10 Sep 1733.
{BPR:394}

Young, Tabitha d. by 1745, Thomas Young, admin. {CCCR:107}

Young, Thomas d. by 1750. Son Henry was appointed a guardian, John
Fuglar. {CCCR:120, 137}

Young, Thomas (predeceased his wife, m. Anne who d. by 1694 leaving
an orphan dau., Joan, who chose at age 15 in 1694, her guardian, Henry
Harman. In 1677 Ann Young gave to her 3 sons, Dorrill, John and
Thomas, a heifer, a mare and a gun each. {CCOB (1677-79):25; CCOB
(1687-95):188; CCOB (Fragments, 1696):89}

INDEX

Walter, 49
Chirn
  Mary, 222
Chisnall
  Alexander, 49
Chiswell
  Bersheba, 38
Chrecher
  Agnis, 49
  Hannah, 49
  Millesin, 49
  Mourning, 49
  Titus, 49
Christian
  Alice, 50, 258
  Anne, 50
  Augustus, 50
  Benjamin, 51
  Charles, 11, 50, 134,
    237
  Eaton, 50
  Edmund, 50, 175
  Edmund Oliver, 50
  Elizabeth, 50, 51,
    53, 60, 134, 252,
    268
  Fanny, 50
  Francis, 50
  Gideon, 50, 256,
    258
  Isham, 51
  James, 50
  Joel, 50
  John, 50, 173
  Judith Bray, 175
  Lucy, 50, 51, 107
  Lucy Grice, 50
  Margaret, 203
  Martha S., 50
  Mary, 50, 51, 173,
    237
  Mary Lightfoot, 50
  Mildred, 50

  Patrick, 50
  Philip, 50
  Rebecca, 50
  Richard, 50, 51, 107
  Robert Walker, 50
  Samuel, 51
  Sarah, 50
  Susan, 50
  Susanna, 50, 256
  Thomas, 50, 51
  Turner, 50
  Turner Hunt, 51
  Virginia, 50
  William, 50, 51, 60,
    252
  William Allen, 50
  William Brown, 50
Church
  Ann, 51
Churchill
  Elizabeth, 242
Claiborne
  Anne Carter, 117
  Augustine, 51, 117,
    204
  Burnell, 51
  Daniel, 51, 117
  Elizabeth, 4, 204,
    209
  Elizabeth Randolph,
    117
  Hannah, 51
  Henry, 182
  Martha, 51
  Mary, 51, 117, 182,
    204
  Mary Cole, 105
  Matthew Maury,
    117
  Sallie, 51
  Thomas, 51
  Thomas B., 51
  William, 4

Clanthorne
  Rebecca, 237
  William, 51, 237
Clark(e)
  Ann, 53
  Bolling, 51
  Charles, 94
  Daniel, 51, 52, 56
  Edward, 52
  Elisabeth, 52
  Elizabeth, 31, 52
  Frances, 52
  Henrietta Maria, 52
  Henry, 52, 54
  James, 52, 114, 189
  John, 52, 53, 54
  Joice, 52
  Joseph, 51, 52
  Joseph S., 52
  Lewis, 52
  Lucy, 53
  Margret, 52
  Maria, 114
  Martha, 52
  Mary, 52, 53, 56,
    80, 285
  Nathaniel Hamlin,
    51
  Phebe, 51
  Rebecca, 52, 53
  Rebeckah, 51
  Richard, 130
  Sally, 52
  Sarah, 52
  Thomas, 51, 53, 80
  William, 51, 52, 53,
    54
Clay
  Amy, 53
  Ann, 53
  Anna, 208
  Charles, 53, 239,
    269

John, 270
Mihell, 270
Sarah, 270
William, 270
Walmsley
John, 270
Walpole. See also
  Warpole.
Caesar, 85, 87, 270
Cesar, 145, 270
Elin, 270
Elinor, 256
Elizabeth, 87, 270
Ellenor, 270
Richard, 256, 270
Sarah, 85, 87, 145,
  270
Walter
Elizabeth, 270
Thomas, 270
William, 270
Walthal(l)
Amy, 271
Ann, 271
Benjamin, 270
Christopher, 271
Daniel, 270
Edward, 270
Elizabeth, 160, 270,
  271
Frances, 271
Francis, 270
Gerrat, 270
Henry, 160, 271
Jeremiah, 271
Jerrott, 270
John, 271
Maball, 271
Martha, 270, 271
Mary, 271
Phebe, 160, 271
Richard, 271
Thomas, 271

William, 271
Wam(m)ack/Wamock.
  See also Womack.
Abraham, 270
Elizabeth, 270
Hannah, 284
James, 284
Jane, 284
John P., 284
Nathaniel, 284
Patsy, 284
Peyton A., 284
Travis, 284
William, 284
Wamsley
Mary, 99, 170
Roger, 99, 170, 270
Warburton/Warberton
Benjamin, 25
Mary, 271
Nancy, 25
Susan, 25
Thomas, 271
Ward
Ann, 4
Benjamin, 4
Frances, 11, 193,
  250
James, 11, 193
Mary, 105
Warpole
Cesar, 185
Elin, 185
Warradine
Elizabeth, 11, 271
James, 11, 271
Sara, 271
Warren
Charles, 271
Elizabeth, 271
John, 271
Matthew, 271
William, 193

Warriner
Priscilla, 21
Warthen
Elizabeth, 271
Jemimah, 271
John, 271, 272
Martha, 272
Walter, 271
Worpah, 271
Washington
Edward, 272
Elizabeth, 152, 153,
  272
Langsdown, 272
Lucy, 53
Pricilla, 152, 153
Richard, 53, 152,
  153
Thomas, 53, 54, 153
Watkins
Elizabeth, 272
Henry, 182, 272
James, 272
Joseph, 26, 272
Judith, 272
Mary, 26, 182, 272
Molley Holt, 26
Watson
Ann, 272
Anna, 141, 144, 243
John, 28, 272
Joseph, 141, 144,
  243, 272
Lucy, 141, 144, 272
Martha, 28, 272
Susannah, 28
Watts
Alice, 272
Arthur, 272
Edward, 272
Elizabeth, 272
John, 272
Sarah, 272

Francis, 282
Gardner, 282
George, 282
Hannah, 239
Henry, 110, 282,
283
James, 283
Joel, 283
John, 162, 239, 283
Joseph, 282, 283
Judith, 283
Katharine, 283
Margaret, 283
Margarit, 283
Mark, 283
Martha, 282, 283
Mary, 282, 283
Micael, 283
Phebe, 283
Richard, 283
Samuel, 283
Sarah, 283
Sophia, 215
Stevens, 282
Thomas, 283
William, 215
Window
Joane, 58, 283
William, 58, 283
Wines
Frances, 283
Margret, 283
Robert, 283
Winfield
Ann, 283
Edward, 283
Hannah, 283
Joell, 283
John, 283
Mary, 283
Winingham
Amy, 284
Christian, 284

Edward, 284
Elizabeth, 284
Gerrald, 284
Henry, 283
Isack, 283
John, 284
Mary, 284
Precillah, 284
Sarah, 283, 284
Thomas, 284
William, 284
Winkfield
Jarvis, 76
Robert, 76
Winkles
Esther, 284
Richard, 284
William, 284
Winn. See also
Wynne.
John, 289
Katy, 289
Sally Allen, 289
Winson
Cuthbert, 32
Winston
Elizabeth, 13, 284
Geddes, 26
Peter, 92
Rebecca, 26, 284
Samuel, 13
Sara, 287
William, 9, 26, 284
Winter
Thomas, 89
Wod(d)rop. See also
Wooddrop.
John, 285
Margaret, 184
Mary, 285
Womack. See also
Wamack.
Abraham, 284

Elizabeth, 284
James, 284
Jane, 160, 212
John, 284
Laurana, 284
Martha, 285
Mary, 284
Richard, 284
William, 284, 285
Wood
Abraham, 46, 57,
285
Ann, 285
Aron, 285
Betty, 285
Bowry, 285
Elizabeth, 285
Henry, 285
James, 285
Katharine, 285
Lucy, 236
Margaret, 290
Martha, 236
Mary, 46, 285
Mary Chamberlaine,
285
Richard, 285
Valentine, 236
Woodard
Ann, 285
Woodcock
Robert, 285
Thomas, 285
Wooddrop
John, 285
Mary, 285
Mary Ann, 285
Wooddy
Cisilia, 82
Micajah, 82
Sarah, 82
Woodhall
Jeramyah, 25

www.ingramcontent.com/pod-product-compliance
Lightning Source LLC
Chambersburg PA
CBHW071830270326
41929CB00013B/1943